BANKS MILLER
JENNIFER S. HOLMES
*The University of Texas
at Dallas*

READINGS IN
AMERICAN NATIONAL GOVERNMENT

Kendall Hunt
publishing company

Kendall Hunt
publishing company

www.kendallhunt.com
Send all inquiries to:
4050 Westmark Drive
Dubuque, IA 52004-1840

Copyright © 2017 by Kendall Hunt Publishing Company

ISBN 978-1-5249-4304-2

Published in the United States of America

CONTENTS

CHAPTER 1
FUNDAMENTALS

GROUP SIZE AND GROUP BEHAVIOR

MANCUR OLSON

The Coherence and Effectiveness of Small Groups

The greater effectiveness of relatively small groups—the "privileged" and "intermediate" groups—is evident from observation and experience as well as from theory. Consider, for example, meetings that involve too many people, and accordingly cannot make decisions promptly or carefully. Everyone would like to have the meeting end quickly, but few if any will be willing to let their pet concern be dropped to make this possible. And though all of those participating presumably have an interest in reaching sound decisions, this all too often fails to happen. When the number of participants is large, the typical participant will know that his own efforts will probably not make much difference to the outcome, and that he will be affected by the meeting's decision in much the same way no matter how much or how little effort he puts into studying the issues. Accordingly, the typical participant may not take the trouble to study the issues as carefully as he would have if he had been able to make the decision by himself. The decisions of the meeting are thus public goods to the participants (and perhaps others), and the contribution that each participant will make toward achieving or improving these public goods will become smaller as the meeting becomes larger. It is for these reasons, among others, that organizations so often turn to the small group; committees, subcommittees, and small leadership groups are created, and once created they tend to play a crucial role.

This observation is corroborated by some interesting research results. John James, among others, has done empirical work on this subject, with results that support the theory offered in this study, though his work was not done to prove any such theory. Professor James found that in a variety of institutions, public and private, national and local, "action taking" groups and subgroups tended to be much smaller than "non-action taking" groups and subgroups. In one sample he studied, the average size of the "action taking" subgroups was 6.5 members, whereas the average size of the "non-action taking" subgroups was 14 members. These subgroups were in a large banking concern, whose secretary spontaneously offered the following opinion: "We have found," he wrote, "that committees should be small when you expect action and relatively large when you are looking for points of view, reactions, etc."[1] This is apparently not a situation restricted to banking. It is widely known that in the United States Congress and in the state legislatures, power resides to a remarkable, and what is to many an alarming degree, in the committees and subcommittees.[2] James found that U.S. Senate subcommittees at the time of his investigation had 5.4 members on the average, House subcommittees had 7.8, the Oregon state government, 4.7, and the Eugene, Oregon, municipal government, 5.3.[3] In short, the groups that actually do the work are quite small. A different study corroborates James's findings; Professor A. Paul Hare, in controlled experiments with groups of five and twelve boys, found that the performance of the groups of five was generally superior.[4] The sociologist Georg Simmel explicitly stated that smaller groups could act more decisively and use their resources more effectively than large groups: "Small, centripetally organized groups usually call on and use all their energies, while in large groups, forces remain much oftener potential."[5]

The fact that the partnership can be a workable institutional form when the number of partners is quite small, but is generally unsuccessful when the number of partners is very large, may provide another illustration of the advantages of smaller groups. When a partnership has many members, the individual partner observes that his own effort or contribution will not greatly affect the performance of the enterprise, and expects that he will get his prearranged share of the earnings whether or not he contributes as much as he could have done. The earnings of a partnership, in which each partner gets a prearranged percentage of the return, are a collective good to the partners, and when the number of partners increases, the incentive for each partner to work for the welfare of the enterprise lessens. This is to be sure only one of a number of reasons why partnerships tend to persist only when the number of partners is fairly small, but it is one that could be decisive in a really large partnership.[6]

The autonomy of management in the large modern corporation, with thousands of stockholders, and the subordination of management in the corporation owned by a small number of stockholders, may also illustrate the special difficulties of the large group. The fact that management tends to control the large corporation and is able, on occasion, to further its own interest at the expense of the stockholders, is surprising, since the common stockholders have the legal power to discharge the management at their pleasure, and since they have, as a group, also an incentive to do so, if the management is running the corporation partly or wholly in the interest of the managers. Why, then, do not the stockholders exercise their power? They do not because, in a large corporation, with thousands of stockholders, any effort the typical stockholder makes to oust the management will probably be unsuccessful; and even if the stockholder should be successful, most of the returns in the form of higher dividends and stock prices will go to the rest of the stockholders, since the typical stockholder owns only a trifling percentage of the outstanding stock. The income of the corporation is a collective good to the stockholders, and the stockholder who holds only a minute percentage of the total stock, like any member of a latent group, has no incentive to work in the group interest. Specifically, he has no incentive to challenge the management of the company, however inept or corrupt it might be. (This argument does not, however, entirely apply to the stockholder who wants the manager's position and pelf for himself, for he is not working for a collective good; it is significant that most attempts to overthrow corporate management are started by those who want to take over the management themselves.) Corporations with a small number of stockholders, by contrast, are not only *de jure*, but also *de facto*, controlled by the stockholders, for in such cases the concepts of privileged or intermediate groups apply.[7]

There is also historical evidence for the theory presented here. George C. Homans, in one of the best-known books in American social science,[8] has pointed out that the small group has shown much more durability throughout history than the large group:

At the level of . . . the small group, at the level, that is, of a social unit (no matter by what name we call it) each of whose members can have some firsthand knowledge of each of the others, human society, for many millennia longer than written history, has been able to cohere . . . They have tended to produce a surplus of the goods that make organization successful.

. . . ancient Egypt and Mesopotamia were civilizations. So were classical India and China; so was Greco-Roman civilization, and so is our own Western civilization that grew out of medieval Christendom . . .

The appalling fact is that, after flourishing for a span of time, every civilization but one has collapsed . . . formal organizations that articulated the whole have fallen to pieces . . . much of the technology has even been forgotten for lack of the large scale cooperation that could put it in effect . . . the civilization has slowly sunk to a Dark Age, a situation, much like the one from which it started on its upward path, in which the mutual hostility of small groups is the condition of the internal cohesion of each one . . . Society can fall thus far, but apparently no farther . . . One can read the dismal story, eloquently told, in the historians of civilization from Spengler to Toynbee. The one civilization that has not entirely gone to pieces is our Western Civilization, and we are desperately anxious about it.

[But] At the level of the tribe or group, society has always found itself able to cohere.[9]

Homans' claim that the smallest groups are the most durable is quite persuasive and certainly supports the theory offered here. But his deduction from these historical facts is not wholly consistent with the approach in this study. His book focuses on the following idea: "Let us put our case for the last time: At the level of the small group, society has always been able to cohere. We infer, therefore, that if civilization is to stand, it must retain . . . some of the features of the small group itself."[10] Homans' conclusion depends on the assumption that the techniques or methods of the small group are more effective. But this is not necessarily true; the small, or "privileged," group is in a more advantageous position from the beginning, for some or all of its members will have an incentive to see that it does not fail. This is not true of the large group; the large group does not automatically find that the incentives that face the group also face the individuals in the group. Therefore, it does not follow that, because the small group has historically been more effective, the very large group can prevent failure by copying its methods. The "privileged" group, and for that matter the "intermediate" group, are simply in a more advantageous position.[11]

Problems of the Traditional Theories

Homans' belief that the lessons of the small group should be applied to large groups has much in common with the assumption upon which much small-group research is based. There has been a vast amount of research into the small group in recent years, much of it based on the idea that the results of (experimentally convenient) research on small groups can be made directly applicable to larger groups merely by multiplying these results by a scale factor.[12] Some social psychologists, sociologists, and political scientists assume that the small group is so much like the large group, in matters other than size, that it must behave according to somewhat similar laws. But if the distinctions drawn here among the "privileged" group, the "intermediate" group, and the "latent" group have any meaning, this assumption is unwarranted, at least so long as the groups have a common, collective interest. For the small, privileged group can expect that its collective needs will probably be met one way or another, and the fairly small (or intermediate) group has a fair chance that voluntary action will solve its collective problems, but the large, latent group cannot act in accordance with its common interests so long as the members of the group are free to further their individual interests.

The distinctions developed in this study also suggest that the traditional explanation of voluntary associations explained in Chapter I needs amendment. The traditional theory emphasizes the (alleged) universality of participation in voluntary associations in modern societies and explains small groups and large organizations in terms of the same causes. In its most sophisticated form, the traditional theory argues that the prevalence of participation in the modern voluntary association is due to the "structural differentiation" of developing societies; that is, to the fact that as the small, primary groups of primitive society have declined or become more specialized, the functions that multitudes of these small groups used to perform are being taken over by large voluntary associations. But, if the meaningless notion of a universal "joiner instinct" is to be rejected, how is the membership in these new, large voluntary associations recruited? There are admittedly functions for large associations to perform, as small, primary groups become more specialized and decline. And the performance of these functions no doubt would bring benefits to large numbers of people. But will these benefits provide an incentive for any of the individuals affected to join, much less create, a large voluntary association to perform the function in question? The answer is that, however beneficial the functions large voluntary associations are expected to perform, there is no incentive for any individual in a latent group to join such an association.[13] However important a function may be, there is no presumption that a latent group will be able to organize and act to perform this function. Small primary groups by contrast presumably can act to perform functions that are beneficial to them. The traditional theory of voluntary associations is therefore mistaken to the extent that it implicitly assumes that latent groups will act to perform functional purposes the same way small groups will. The existence of such large organizations as do exist must moreover be explained by different factors from those that explain the existence of smaller groups. This suggests that the traditional theory is incomplete, and needs to be modified in the light of the logical relationships explained in this study. This contention is strengthened by the fact that the traditional theory of voluntary associations is not at all in harmony with the empirical evidence, which indicates that participation in large voluntary organizations is very much less than that theory would suggest.[14]

There is still another respect in which the analysis developed here can be used to modify the traditional analysis. This involves the question of group consensus. It is often assumed (though usually implicitly) in discussions of organizational or group cohesion that the crucial matter is the degree of consensus; if there are many serious disagreements, there will be no coordinated, voluntary effort, but if there is a high degree of agreement on what is wanted and how to get it there will almost certainly be effective group action.[15] The degree of consensus is sometimes discussed as though it were the *only* important determinant of group action or group cohesion. There is, of course, no question that a lack of consensus is inimical to the prospects for group action and group cohesion. But it does not follow that perfect consensus, both about the desire for the collective good and the most efficient means of getting it, will always bring about the achievement of the group goal. In a large, latent group there will be no tendency for the group to organize to achieve its goals through the voluntary, rational action of the members of the group, even if there is perfect consensus. Indeed, *the assumption made in this work is that there is perfect consensus.* This is, to be sure, an unrealistic assumption, for perfection of consensus, as of other things, is at best very rare. But the results obtained under this assumption are, for that reason, all the stronger, for if voluntary, rational action cannot enable a large, latent group to organize for action to achieve its collective goals, even with perfect consensus, then *a fortiori* this conclusion should hold in the real world, where consensus is usually incomplete and often altogether absent. It is thus very important to distingiush between the obstacles to group-oriented action that are due to a lack of group consensus and those that are due to a lack of individual incentives.

Social Incentives and Rational Behavior

Economic incentives are not, to be sure, the only incentives; people are sometimes also motivated by a desire to win prestige, respect, friendship, and other social and psychological objectives. Though the phrase "socio-economic status" often used in discussions of status suggests that there may be a correlation between economic position and social position, there is no doubt that the two are sometimes different. The possibility that, in a case where there was no economic incentive for an individual to contribute to the achievement of a group interest, there might nonetheless be a social incentive for him to make such a contribution, must therefore be considered. And it is obvious that this is a possibility. If a small group of people who had an interest in a collective good happened also to be personal friends, or belonged to the same social club, and some of the group left the burden of providing that collective good on others, they might, even if they gained economically by this course of action, lose socially by it, and the social loss might outweigh the economic gain. Their friends might use "social pressure" to encourage them to do their part toward achieving the group goal, or the social club might exclude them, and such steps might be effective, for everyday observation reveals that most people value the fellowship of their friends and associates, and value social status, personal prestige, and self-esteem.

The existence of these social incentives to group-oriented action does not, however, contradict or weaken the analysis of this study. If anything, it strengthens it, *for social status and social acceptance are individual, noncollective goods*. Social sanctions and social rewards are "selective incentives"; that is, they are among the kinds of incentives that may be used to mobilize a latent group. It is in the nature of social incentives that they can distinguish among individuals: the recalcitrant individual can be ostracized, and the cooperative individual can be invited into the center of the charmed circle. Some students of organizational theory have rightly emphasized that social incentives must be analyzed in much the same way as monetary incentives.[16] Still other types of incentives can be analyzed in much the same way.[17]

In general, social pressure and social incentives operate only in groups of smaller size, in the groups so small that the members can have face-to-face contact with one another. Though in an oligopolistic industry with only a handful of firms there may be strong resentment against the "chiseler" who cuts prices to increase his own sales at the expense of the group, in a perfectly competitive industry there is usually no such resentment; indeed, the man who succeeds in increasing his sales and output in a perfectly competitive industry is usually admired and set up as a good example by his competitors. Anyone who has observed a farming community, for instance, knows that the most productive farmer, who sells the most and thus does the most to lower the price, is usually the one with the highest status. There are perhaps two reasons for this difference in the attitudes of large and small groups. First, in the large, latent group, each member, by definition, is so small in relation to the total that his actions will not matter much one way or another; so it would seem pointless for one perfect competitor, or a member of some other latent group, to snub or abuse another for a selfish, antigroup action, because the recalcitrant's action would not be decisive in any event. Second, in any large group everyone cannot possibly know everyone else, and the group will *ipso facto* not be a friendship group; so a person will ordinarily not be affected socially if he fails to make sacrifices on behalf of his group's goals. To return to the case of the farmer, it is clear that one farmer cannot possibly know all the other farmers who sell the same commodity; he would not feel that the social group within which he measured his status had much to do with the group with which he shared the interest in the collective good. Accordingly, there is no presumption that social incentives will lead individuals in the latent group to obtain a collective good.

There is, however, one case in which social incentives may well be able to bring about group-oriented action in a latent group. This is the case of a "federal" group—a group divided into a number of small groups, each of which has a reason to join with the others to form a federation representing the large group as a whole. If the central or federated organization provides some service to the small constituent organizations, they may be induced to use their social incentives to get the individuals belonging to each small group to contribute toward the achievement of the collective goals of the whole group. Thus, organizations that use selective *social* incentives to mobilize a latent group interested in a collective good must be federations of smaller groups. The more important point, however, is that social incentives are important mainly only in the small group, and play a role in the large group only when the large group is a federation of smaller groups.

The groups small enough to be classified here as "privileged" and "intermediate" groups are thus twice blessed in that they have not only economic incentives, but also perhaps social incentives, that lead their members to work toward the achievement of the collective goods. The large, "latent" group, on the other hand, always contains more people than could possibly know each other, and is not likely (except when composed of federated small groups) to develop social pressures that would help it satisfy its interest in a collective good. There is, of course, much evidence for this skepticism about social pressures in a large group in the history of perfectly competitive industries in the United States. Now, if the conclusion that the strength of social pressures varies greatly between small and large groups has validity, it further weakens the traditional theory of voluntary organizations.[18]

Some critics may protest that even if social pressure does not exist in the large or latent group, it does not follow that the completely selfish or profit-maximizing behavior, which the concept of latent groups apparently assumes, is necessarily significant either; people might even in the absence of social pressure act in a selfless way. But this criticism of the concept of the latent group is not relevant, for that concept does *not* necessarily assume the selfish, profit-maximizing behavior that economists usually find in the marketplace. The concept of the large or latent group offered here holds true whether behavior is selfish or unselfish, so long as it is strictly speaking "rational." Even if the member of a large group were to neglect his own interests entirely, he still would not rationally contribute toward the provision of any collective or public good, since his own contribution would not be perceptible. A farmer who placed the interests of other farmers above his own would not necessarily restrict his production to raise farm prices, since he would know that his sacrifice would not bring a noticeable benefit to anyone. Such a rational farmer, however unselfish, would not make such a futile and pointless sacrifice, but he would allocate his philanthropy in order to have a perceptible effect on someone. Selfless behavior that has no perceptible effect is sometimes not even considered praiseworthy. A man who tried to hold back a flood with a pail would probably be considered more of a crank than a saint, even by those he was trying to help. It is no doubt possible infinitesimally to lower the level of a river in flood with a pail, just as it is possible for a single farmer infinitesimally to raise prices by limiting his production, but in both cases the effect is imperceptible, and those who sacrifice themselves in the interest of imperceptible improvements may not even receive the praise normally due selfless behavior.

The argument about large, latent groups, then, does not necessarily imply self-interested behavior, though such behavior would be completely consistent with it.[19] The only requirement is that the behavior of individuals in large groups or organizations of the kind considered should generally be rational, in the sense that their objectives, whether selfish or unselfish, should be pursued by means that are efficient and effective for achieving these objectives.

The foregoing arguments, theoretical and factual, in this and the previous chapter should at the least justify the separate treatment that large and small groups are given in this study. These arguments are not meant as attacks on any previous interpretations of group behavior, though it seems that some of the usual explanations of large voluntary associations may need elaboration because of the theories offered here. All that need be granted, to accept the main argument of this study, is that large or latent groups will *not* organize for co-ordinated action merely because, as a group, they have a reason for doing so, though this could be true of smaller groups.

Most of the rest of this study will deal with large organizations and will attempt to prove that most of the large economic organizations in the United States have had to develop special institutions to solve the membership problem posed by the large scale of their objectives.

End Notes

1. John James, "A Preliminary Study of the Size Determinant in Small Group Interaction," *American Sociological Review*, XVI (August 1951), 474–477.
2. Bertram M. Gross, *The Legislative Struggle* (New York: McGraw-Hill, 1953), pp. 265–337; see also Ernest S. Griffith, *Congress* (New York: New York University Press, 1951).
3. For a light-hearted and humorous, but nonetheless helpful, argument that the ideal committee or cabinet has only five members, see C. Northcote Parkinson, *Parkinson's Law* (Boston: Houghton Mifflin, 1957), pp. 33–34.
4. A. Paul Hare, "A Study of Interaction and Consensus in Different Sized Groups," *American Sociological Review*, XVII (June 1952), 261–268.
5. Georg Simmel, *The Sociology of George Simmel*, trans. Kurt H. Wolff (Glencoe, Ill.: Free Press [1950]), p. 92. In another place Simmel says that socialist societies, by which he appears to mean voluntary groups that share their incomes according to some principle of equity, must necessarily be small. "Up to this day, at least, socialistic or nearly socialistic societies have been possible only in very small groups and have always failed in larger ones" (p. 88).
6. The foregoing argument need not apply to partners that are *supposed* to be "sleeping partners," i.e., provide only capital. Nor does it take account of the fact that in many cases each partner is liable for the losses of the whole partnership.
7. See Adolph A. Berle, Jr., and Gardiner C. Means, *The Modern Corporation and Private Property* (New York: Macmillan, 1932); J. A. Livingston, *The American Stockholder*, rev. ed. (New York: Collier Books, 1963); P. Sargent Florence, *Ownership, Control and Success of Large Companies* (London: Sweet & Maxwell, 1961); William Mennell, *Takeover* (London: Lawrence & Wishart, 1962).
8. George C. Homans, *The Human Group* (New York: Harcourt, Brace, 1950).
9. *Ibid.*, pp. 454–456. See also Neil W. Chamberlain, *General Theory of Economic Process* (New York: Harper, 1955), esp. pp. 347–348, and Sherman Krupp, *Pattern in Organization Analysis* (Philadelphia: Chilton, 1961), pp. 118–139 and 171–176.
10. Homans, p. 468.
11. The difference between latent groups and privileged or intermediate groups is only one of several factors accounting for the instability of many ancient empires and civilizations. I have pointed to another such factor myself in a forthcoming book.
12. Kurt Lewin, *Field Theory in Social Change* (New York: Harper, 1951), pp. 163–164; Harold H. Kelley and John W. Thibaut, *The Social Psychology of Groups* (New York: John Wiley, 1959), pp. 6, 191–192; Hare, "Study of Interaction and Consensus," pp. 261–268; Sidney Verba, *Small Groups*

and Political Behavior (Princeton, N.J.: Princeton University Press, 1961), pp. 4, 14, 99–109, 245–248.

13. There is no suggestion here, of course, that all groups are necessarily explained in terms of monetary or material interests. The argument does not require that individuals have only monetary or material wants. See note 17 below.

14. Mirra Komaravsky, "The Voluntary Associations of Urban Dwellers," *American Sociological Review*, XI (December 1946), 686–698; Floyd Dotson, "Patterns of Voluntary Membership among Working Class Families," *American Sociological Review*, XVI (October 1951), 687; John C. Scott, Jr., "Membership and Participation in Voluntary Associations," *American Sociological Review*, XXII (June 1957), 315; and Murray Hausknecht, *The Joiners—A Sociological Description of Voluntary Association Membership in the United States* (New York: Bedminster Press, 1962).

15. See Hare, "Study of Interaction and Consensus"; Raymond Cattell, "Concepts and Methods in the Measurement of Group Syntality," in *Small Groups*, ed. A. Paul Hare, Edward F. Borgatta, and Robert F. Bales (New York: Alfred A. Knopf, 1955); Leon Festinger, *A Theory of Cognitive Dissonance* (Evanston, Ill.: Row, Peterson, 1957); Leon Festinger, Stanley Schachter, and Kurt Back, "The Operation of Group Standards," in *Group Dynamics*, ed. Dorwin Cartwright and Alvin Zander (Evanston, Ill.: Row, Peterson, 1953); David B. Truman, *The Governmental Process* (New York: Alfred A. Knopf, 1958).

16. See especially Chester I. Barnard, *The Functions of the Executive* (Cambridge, Mass.: Harvard University Press, 1938), chap xi, "The Economy of Incentives," pp. 139–160, and the same author's *Organization and Management* (Cambridge, Mass.: Harvard University Press, 1948), chap. ix, "Functions and Pathology of Status Systems in Formal Organizations," pp. 207–244; Peter B. Clark and James Q. Wilson, "Incentive Systems: A Theory of Organizations," *Administrative Science Quarterly*, VI (September 1961), 129–166; and Herbert A. Simon, *Administrative Behavior* (New York: Macmillan, 1957), esp. pp. 115–117. I am indebted to Edward C. Banfield for helpful suggestions on social incentives and organization theory.

17. In addition to monetary and social incentives, there are also erotic incentives, psychological incentives, moral incentives, and so on. To the extent that any of these types of incentives leads a latent group to obtain a collective good, it could again only be because they are or can be used as "selective incentives," i.e., because they distinguish between those individuals who support action in the common interest and those who do not. Even in the case where moral attitudes determine whether or not a person will act in a group-oriented way, the crucial factor is that the moral reaction serves as a "selective incentive." If the sense of guilt, or the destruction of self-esteem, that occurs when a person feels he has forsaken his moral code, affected those who had contributed toward the achievement of a group good, as well as those who had not, the moral code could not help to mobilize a latent group. To repeat: the point is that moral attitudes could mobilize a latent group only to the extent they provided selective incentives. The adherence to a moral code that demands the sacrifices needed to obtain a collective good therefore need *not* contradict any of the analysis in this study; indeed, this analysis shows the need for such a moral code or for some other selective incentive.

At no point in this study, however, will any such moral force or incentive be used to explain any of the examples of group action that will be studied. There are three reasons for this. First, it is not possible to get empirical proof of the motivation behind any person's action; it is not possible definitely to say whether a given individual acted for moral reasons or for other reasons in some particular case. A reliance on moral explanations could thus make the theory untestable. Second, no such explanation is needed, since there will be sufficient explanations on other grounds for all the group action that will be considered. Third, most organized pressure groups are explicitly working for gains for themselves, not gains for other groups, and in such cases it is hardly plausible to ascribe group action to any moral code. Moral motives or incentives for group action have therefore been discussed, not to explain any given example of group action, but rather to show that their existence need not contradict the theory offered here, and could if anything tend to support it.

The erotic and psychological incentives that must be important in family and friendship groups could logically be analyzed within the framework of the theory. On the other hand, "affective" groups such as family and friendship groups could normally be studied much more usefully with entirely different sorts of theories, since the analysis used in this study does not shed much light on these groups. On the special features of "affective" groups, see Verba (note 12, above), p. 6 and pp. 142–184.

18. There is, however, another kind of social pressure that may occasionally be operative. That is the social pressure that is generated, not primarily through person-to-person friendships, but through mass media. If the members of a latent group are somehow continuously bombarded with propaganda about the worthiness of the attempt to satisfy the common interest in question, they may perhaps in time develop social pressures not entirely unlike those that can be generated in a face-to-face group, and these social pressures may help the latent group to obtain the collective good. A group cannot finance such propaganda unless it is already organized, and it may not be able to organize until it has already been subjected to the propaganda; so this form of social pressure is probably not ordinarily sufficient by itself to enable a group to achieve its collective goals. It would, for example, seem unlikely that there would be much prospect of success in a program to persuade farmers through propaganda to further their interests by voluntarily restricting output, unless there were some captive source of funds to finance the effort. So this form of social pressure generated by mass media does not seem likely to be an important independent source of coordinated effort to bring about the satisfaction of a common interest. Moreover, as was emphasized earlier, the nation-state, with all the emotional loyalty it commands, cannot support itself without compulsion. Therefore it does not seem likely that many large private groups could support themselves solely through social pressure.

19. Organizations with primarily economic purposes, like labor unions, farm organizations, and other types of pressure groups, normally claim that they are serving the interests of the groups they represent, and do not contend that they are mainly philanthropic organizations out to help other groups. Thus it would be surprising if most of the members of these "interest groups" should always neglect their own, individual interests. An essentially selfish group interest would not normally attract members who were completely selfless. Thus self-interested behavior may in fact be common in organizations of the kind under study. For intelligent arguments contending that self-interested behavior is general in politics, see James M. Buchanan and Gordon Tullock, *The Calculus of Consent* (Ann Arbor: University of Michigan Press, 1962), pp. 3–39. See also the interesting book by Anthony Downs, *An Economic Theory of Democracy* (New York: Harper, 1957), pp. 3–35.

THE TRAGEDY OF THE COMMONS[1]

The population problem has no technical solution;
it requires a fundamental extension in morality

GARRETT HARDIN[2]

At the end of a thoughtful article on the future of nuclear war, Wiesner and York[3] concluded that: "Both sides in the arms race are . . . confronted by the dilemma of steadily increasing military power and steadily decreasing national security. It is our considered professional judgment that this dilemma has no technical solution. If the great powers continue to look for solutions in the area of science and technology only, the result will be to worsen the situation." I would like to focus your attention not on the subject of the article (national security in a nuclear world) but on the kind of conclusion they reached, namely that there is no technical solution to the problem. An implicit and almost universal assumption of discussions published in professional and semi-popular scientific journals is that the problem under discussion has a technical solution. A technical solution may be defined as one that requires a change only in. the techniques of the natural sciences, demanding little or nothing in the way of change in human values or ideas of morality. [. . .]

The class of "No technical solution problems" has members. My thesis is that the "population problem," as conventionally conceived, is a member of this class. How it is conventionally conceived needs some comment. It is fair to say that most people who' anguish over the population problem are trying to find a way to avoid the evils of overpopulation without relinquishing any of the privileges they now enjoy. They think that farming the seas or developing new strains of wheat will solve the problem-technologically. I try to show here that the solution they seek cannot be found. The population problem cannot be solved in a technical way, any more than can the problem of winning the game of tick-tack-toe.

What Shall We Maximize?

Population, as Malthus said, naturally tends to grow "geometrically," or, as we would now say, exponentially. In a finite world, this means that the per capita share of the world's goods must steadily decrease. Is ours a finite world? [. . .] A finite world can support only a finite population; therefore, population growth must eventually equal zero. [. . .] When this condition is met, what will be the situation of mankind? Specifically, can Bentham's goal of "the greatest good for the greatest number" be realized? No-for two reasons, each sufficient by itself. The first is a theoretical one. It is not mathematically possible to maximize for two (or more) variables at the same time. [. . .] The second reason springs directly from biological facts. To live, any organism must have a source of energy (for example, food). This energy is utilized for two purposes: mere maintenance and work. For man,

From *The Tragedy of the Commons* by Garrett Hardin, Science, 13 Dec 1968: 1243-1248. Reprinted with permission from AAAS.

maintenance of life requires about 1600 kilocalories a day ("maintenance calories"). [**Beyond just staying alive, anything that a person does is work. And it is supported by work calories taken in by him. This is needed for every type of activity, and in order to maximize population the per person work calorie must approach zero**]. [. . .] I think that everyone will grant, without argument or proof, that maximizing population does not maximize goods. Bentham's goal is impossible. [**The conclusion is that the acquisition of energy that is the problem**]. [. . .] Given an infinite source of energy, population growth still produces an inescapable problem. [. . .]

The optimum population is, then, less than the maximum. The difficulty of defining the optimum is enormous; so far as I know, no one has seriously tackled this problem. Reaching an acceptable and stable solution will surely require more than one generation of hard analytical work-and much persuasion. [**What is good remains the question, and goods cannot be compared as they are incommensurable**]. Theoretically this may be true; but in real life incommensurables *are* commensurable. [. . .] Natural selection commensurate the incommensurables. The compromise achieved depends on a natural weighting of the values of the variables.

[. . .]

Tragedy of Freedom in a Commons

[. . .] The tragedy of the commons develops in this way. Picture a pasture open to all. It is to be expected that each herdsman will try to keep as many cattle as possible on the commons. Such an arrangement may work reasonably satisfactorily for centuries because tribal wars, poaching, and disease keep the numbers of both man and beast well below the carrying capacity of the land. Finally, however, comes the day of reckoning, that is, the day when the long-desired goal of social stability becomes a reality. At this point, the inherent logic of the commons remorselessly generates tragedy.

This utility has one negative and one positive component. 1) The positive component is a function of the increment of one animal. Since the herdsman receives all the proceeds from the sale of the additional animal, the positive utility is nearly +1. 2) The negative component is a function of the additional overgrazing created by one more animal. Since, however, the effects of overgrazing are shared by all the herdsmen, the negative utility for any decision-making herdsman is only a fraction of −1.

Adding together the component partial utilities, the rational herdsman concludes that the only sensible course for him to pursue is to add another animal to his herd. And another; and another. . . . But this is the conclusion reached by each and every rational herdsman sharing a common. [. . .] Some would say that this is a platitude. Would that it were! In a sense, it was learned thousands of years ago, but natural selection favors the forces of psychological denial.[4] The individual benefits as an individual from his ability to deny the truth even though society as a whole, of which he is a part, suffers. Education can counteract the natural tendency to do the wrong thing, but the inexorable succession of generations requires that the basis for this knowledge be constantly refreshed. [. . .]

The logic of the commons has been understood for a long time, perhaps since the discovery of agriculture or the invention of private property in real estate. But it is understood mostly only in special cases which are not sufficiently generalized. Even at this late date, cattlemen leasing national land on the western ranges demonstrate no more than an ambivalent understanding, in constantly pressuring federal authorities to increase the head count to the point where overgrazing produces erosion and weed dominance. Likewise, the oceans of the world continue to suffer from the survival of the philosophy of the commons. Maritime nations still respond automatically to the shibboleth of the "freedom of the seas." Professing to believe in the "inexhaustible resources of the oceans," they bring species after species of fish and whales closer to extinction.[5] [...]

Pollution

In a reverse way, the tragedy of the commons reappears in problems of pollution. Here it is not a question of taking something out of the commons, but of putting something in-sewage, or chemical, radioactive, and heat wastes into water; noxious and dangerous fumes into the air; and distracting and unpleasant advertising signs into the line of sight. The calculations of utility are much the same as before. The rational man finds that his share of the cost of the wastes he discharges into the commons is less than the cost of purifying his wastes before releasing them. Since this is true for everyone, we are locked into a system of "fouling our own nest," so long as we behave only as independent, rational, free-enterprisers. [...]

The pollution problem is a consequence of population. It did not much matter how a lonely American frontiersman disposed of his waste. "Flowing water purifies itself every 10 miles," my grandfather used to say, and the myth was near enough to the truth when he was a boy, for there were not too many people. But as population became denser, the natural chemical and biological recycling processes became overloaded, calling for a redefinition of property rights.

How to Legislate Temperance?

Analysis of the pollution problem as a function of population density uncovers a not generally recognized principle of morality, namely: the morality of an act is a function of the state of the system at the time it is performed.[6] [...]

In passing, it is worth noting that the morality of an act cannot be determined from a photograph. One does not know whether a man killing an elephant or setting fire to the grassland is harming others until one knows the total system in which his act appears. "One picture is worth a thousand words," said an ancient Chinese; but it may take 10,000 words to validate it. It is as tempting to ecologists as it is to reformers in general to try to persuade others by way of the photographic shortcut. But the essence of an argument cannot be photographed: it must be presented rationally-in words.

That morality is system-sensitive escaped the attention of most codifiers of ethics in the past. "Thou shalt not . . ." is the form of traditional ethical directives which make no allowance for particular circumstances. The laws of our society follow the pattern of ancient ethics, and therefore are poorly suited to governing a complex, crowded, changeable world. Our epicyclic solution is to augment statutory law with administrative law. Since it is practically impossible to spell out all the conditions under which it is safe to burn trash in the back yard or to run an automobile without smog-control, by law we delegate the details to bureaus.

[...]

Freedom to Breed is Intolerable

In a welfare state, how shall we deal with the family, the religion, the race, or the class (or indeed any distinguishable and cohesive group) that adopts overbreeding as a policy to secure its own aggrandizement/[7] To couple the concept of freedom to breed with the belief that everyone born has an equal right to the commons is to lock the world into a tragic course of action. Unfortunately, this is just the course of action that is being pursued by the United Nations. In late 1967, some 30 nations agreed to the following.[8]

> The Universal Declaration of Human Rights describes the family as the natural and fundamental unit of society. It follows that any choice and decision with regard to the size of the family must irrevocably rest with the family itself, and cannot be made by anyone else.

It is painful to have to deny categorically the validity of this right; denying it, one feels as uncomfortable as a resident of Salem, Massachusetts, who denied the reality of witches in the 17th century. At the present time, in liberal quarters, something like a taboo acts to inhibit criticism of the United Nations. There is a feeling that the United Nations is "our last and best hope," that we shouldn't find fault with it; we shouldn't play into the hands of the archconservatives. However, let us not forget what Robert Louis Stevenson said: "The truth that is suppressed by friends is the readiest weapon of the enemy." If we love the truth we must openly deny the validity of the Universal Declaration of Human Rights, even though it is promoted by the United Nations. We should also join with Kingsley Davis[9] in attempting to get Planned Parenthood-World Population to see the error of its ways in embracing the same tragic ideal.

Conscience is Self-Eliminating

[. . .] In C. G. Darwin's words: "It may well be that it would take hundreds of generations for the progenitive instinct to develop in this way, but if it should do so, nature would have taken her revenge, and the variety *Homo contracipiens* would become extinct and would be replaced by the variety Homo progenitivus"[10]. [. . .]

Pathogenic Effects of Conscience

[. . .] To conjure up a conscience in others is tempting to anyone who wishes to extend his control beyond the legal limits. Leaders at the highest level succumb to this temptation. Has any President during the past generation failed to call on labor unions to moderate voluntarily their demands for higher wages, or to steel companies to honor voluntary guidelines on prices? I can recall none. The rhetoric used on such occasions is designed to produce feelings of guilt in noncooperators. [. . .] Paul Goodman speaks from the modern point of view when he says: "No good has ever come from feeling guilty, neither intelligence, policy, nor compassion. The guilty do not pay attention to the object but only to themselves, and not even to their own interests, which might make sense, but to their anxieties"[11]. If the word responsibility is to be used at all, I suggest that it be in the sense Charles Frankel uses it[12]. "Responsibility," says this philosopher, "is the product of definite social arrangements." Notice that Frankel calls for social arrangements-not propaganda.

Mutual Coercion

Mutually Agreed upon

The social arrangements that produce responsibility are arrangements that create coercion, of some sort. Consider bank-robbing. The man who takes money from a bank acts as if the bank were a commons. How do we prevent such action? Certainly not by trying to control his behavior solely by a verbal appeal to his sense of responsibility. Rather than rely on propaganda we follow Frankel's lead and insist that a bank is not a common; we seek the definite social arrangements that will keep it from becoming a common. That we thereby infringe on the freedom of would-be robbers we neither deny nor regret. [...]

Taxing is a good coercive device. To keep downtown shoppers temperate in their use of parking space we introduce parking meters for short periods, and traffic fines for longer ones. We need not actually forbid a citizen to park as long as he wants to; we need merely make it increasingly expensive for him to do so. Not prohibition, but carefully biased options are what we offer him. A Madison Avenue man might call this persuasion; I prefer the greater candor of the word coercion. [...]

An alternative to the commons need not be perfectly just to be preferable. With real estate and other material goods, the alternative we have chosen is the institution of private property coupled with legal inheritance. Is this system perfectly just? As a genetically trained biologist I deny that it is. It seems to me that, if there are to be differences in individual inheritance, legal possession should be perfectly correlated with biological inheritance-that those who are biologically more fit to be the custodians of property and power should legally inherit more. But genetic recombination continually makes a mockery of the doctrine of "like father, like son" implicit in our laws of legal inheritance. [...]

But we can never do nothing. That which we have done for thousands of years is also action. It also produces evils. Once we are aware that the status quo is action, we can then compare its discoverable advantages and disadvantages with the predicted advantages and disadvantages of the proposed reform, discounting as best we can for our lack of experience. On the basis of such a comparison, we can make a rational decision which will not involve the unworkable assumption that only perfect systems are tolerable.

Recognition of Necessity

Perhaps the simplest summary of this analysis of man's population problems is this: the commons, if justifiable at all, is justifiable only under conditions of low-population density. As the human population has increased, the commons has had to be abandoned in one aspect after another. First, we abandoned the commons in food gathering, enclosing farm land and restricting pastures and hunting and fishing areas. These restrictions are still not complete throughout the world. Somewhat later we saw that the commons as a place for waste disposal would also have to be abandoned. Restrictions on the disposal of domestic sewage are widely accepted in the Western world; we are still struggling to close the commons to pollution by automobiles, factories, insecticide sprayers, fertilizing operations, and atomic energy installations. [...]

The most important aspect of necessity that we must now recognize, is the necessity of abandoning the commons in breeding. No technical solution can rescue us from the misery of overpopulation.

Freedom to breed will bring ruin to all. At the moment, to avoid hard decisions many of us are tempted to propagandize for conscience and responsible parenthood. The temptation must be resisted, because an appeal to independently acting consciences selects for the disappearance of all conscience in the long run, and an increase in anxiety in the short. The only way we can preserve and nurture other and more precious freedoms is by relinquishing the freedom to breed, and that very soon. "Freedom is the recognition of necessity"-and it is the role of education to reveal to all the necessity of abandoning the freedom to breed. Only so, can we put an end to this aspect of the tragedy of the commons.

End Notes

1. *Science* 162 (3859), 1243–1248. [doi: 10.1126/science.162.3859.1243]
2. The author is professor of biology, University of California, Santa Barbara. This article is based on a presidential address presented before the meeting of the Pacific Division of the American Association for the Advancement of Science at Utah State University, Logan, 25 June 1968.
3. J. B. Wiesner and H. F. York, *Sci. Amer.* 11 (No. 4), 27 (1964).
4. G. Hardin, Ed. *Population, Evolution, and Birth Control* (Freeman, San Francisco, 1964), p. 56.
5. S. McVay, *Sci. Amer.* 216 (No. 8>, 13 (1966).
6. J. Fletcher, *Situation Ethics* (Westminster, Philadelphia, 1966).
7. G. Hardin, *Perspec. Biol. Med.* 6, 366 (1963).
8. U. Thant, *Int. Planned Parenthood News,* No. 168 (February 1968>, p. 3.
9. K. Davis, *Science* 158, 730 (1967).
10. S. Tax, Ed., *Evolution after Darwin* (Univ. of Chicago Press, Chicago, 1960), vol. 2, p. 469.
11. P. Goodman, *New York Rev. Books* 10(8), 22 (23 May 1968).
12. C. Frankel, *The Case for Modern Man* (Harper, New York, 1955), p. 203.

POLITICS AS A VOCATION

MAX WEBER

[. . .] What do we understand by politics? The concept is extremely broad and comprises any kind of independent leadership in action. One speaks of the currency policy of the banks, of the discounting policy of the Reichsbank, of the strike policy of a trade union; one may speak of the educational policy of a municipality or a township, of the policy of the president of a voluntary association, and, finally, even of the policy of a prudent wife who seeks to guide her husband. Tonight, our reflections are, of course, not based upon such a broad concept. We wish to understand by politics only the leadership, or the influencing of the leadership, of a political association, hence today, of a state. [. . .]

But what is a 'political' association from the sociological point of view? What is a 'state'? Sociologically, the state cannot be defined in terms of its ends. There is scarcely any task that some political association has not taken in hand, and there is no task that one could say has always been exclusive and peculiar to those associations which are designated as political ones: today the state, or historically, those associations which have been the predecessors of the modern state. Ultimately, one can define the modern state sociologically only in terms of the specific means peculiar to it, as to every political association, namely, the use of physical force.

'Every state is founded on force,' said Trotsky at Brest-Litovsk. That is indeed right. If no social institutions existed which knew the use of violence, then the concept of 'state' would be eliminated, and a condition would emerge that could be designated as 'anarchy,' in the specific sense of this word. Of course, force is certainly not the normal or the only means of the state—nobody says that—but force is a means specific to the state. Today the relation between the state and violence is an especially intimate one. In the past, the most varied institutions—beginning with the sib—have known the use of physical force as quite normal. Today, however, we have to say that a state is a human community that (successfully) claims the monopoly of the legitimate use of physical force within a given territory. Note that 'territory' is one of the characteristics of the state. Specifically, at the present time, the right to use physical force is ascribed to other institutions or to individuals only to the extent to which the state permits it. The state is considered the sole source of the 'right' to use violence. Hence, 'politics' for us means striving to share power or striving to influence the distribution of power, either among states or among groups within a state.

This corresponds essentially to ordinary usage. When a question is said to be a 'political' question, when a cabinet minister or an official is said to be a 'political' official, or when a decision is said to be 'politically' determined, what is always meant is that interests in the distribution, maintenance, or transfer of power are decisive for answering the questions and determining the decision or the official's sphere of activity. He who is active in politics strives for power either as a means in serving other aims, ideal or egoistic, or as 'power for power's sake,' that is, in order to enjoy the prestige-feeling that power gives. [. . .]

There are three inner justifications [. . .]-

First, the authority of the 'eternal yesterday,' i.e. of the mores sanctified through the unimaginably ancient recognition and habitual orientation to conform. This is 'traditional' domination exercised by the patriarch and the patrimonial prince of yore.

There is the authority of the extraordinary and personal gift of grace (charisma), the absolutely personal devotion and personal confidence in revelation, heroism, or other qualities of individual leadership. This is 'charismatic' domination, as exercised by the prophet or—in the field of politics—by the elected war lord, the plebiscitarian ruler, the great demagogue, or the political party leader.

Finally, there is domination by virtue of 'legality,' by virtue of the belief in the validity of legal statute and functional 'competence' based on rationally created rules. In this case, obedience is expected in discharging statutory obligations. This is domination as exercised by the modern 'servant of the state' and by all those bearers of power who in this respect resemble him.

It is understood that, in reality, obedience is determined by highly robust motives of fear and hope—fear of the vengeance of magical powers or of the power-holder, hope for reward in this world or in the beyond-and besides all this, by interests of the most varied sort. Of this we shall speak presently. However, in asking for the 'legitimations' of this obedience, one meets with these three 'pure' types: 'traditional,' 'charismatic,' and 'legal.' [. . .]

Charismatic leadership has emerged in all places and in all historical epochs. Most importantly in the past, it has emerged in the two figures of the magician and the prophet on the one hand, and in the elected war lord, the gang leader and *condotierre* on the other hand. Political leadership in the form of the free 'demagogue' who grew from the soil of the city state is of greater concern to us; like the city state, the demagogue is peculiar to the Occident and especially to Mediterranean culture. Furthermore, political leadership in the form of the parliamentary 'party leader' has grown on the soil of the constitutional state, which is also indigenous only to the Occident.

These politicians by virtue of a 'calling,' in the most genuine sense of the word, are of course nowhere the only decisive figures in the cross-currents of the political struggle for power. The sort of auxiliary means that are at their disposal is also highly decisive. How do the politically dominant powers manage to maintain their domination? The question pertains to any kind of domination, hence also to political domination in all its forms, traditional as well as legal and charismatic.

Organized domination, which calls for continuous administration, requires that human conduct be conditioned to obedience towards those masters who claim to be the bearers of legitimate power. On the other hand, by virtue of this obedience, organized domination requires the control of those material goods which in a given case are necessary for the use of physical violence. Thus, organized domination requires control of the personal executive staff and the material implements of administration.

The administrative staff, which externally represents the organization of political domination, is, of course, like any other organization, bound by obedience to the power-holder and not alone by the concept of legitimacy, of which we have just spoken. There are two other means, both of which appeal to personal interests: material reward and social honor. [...]

To maintain a dominion by force, certain material goods are required, just as with an economic organization. All states may be classified according to whether they rest on the principle that the staff of men themselves own the administrative means, or whether the staff is 'separated' from these means of administration. This distinction holds in the same sense in which today we say that the salaried employee and the proletarian in the capitalistic enterprise are 'separated' from the material means of production. The power-holder must be able to count on the obedience of the staff members, officials, or whoever else they may be. The administrative means may consist of money, building, war material, vehicles, horses, or whatnot. The question is whether or not the power-holder himself directs and organizes the administration while delegating executive power to personal servants, hired officials, or personal favorites and confidants, who are non-owners, i.e. who do not use the material means of administration in their own right but are directed by the lord. The distinction runs through all administrative organizations of the past. [...]

However, everywhere, reaching back to the earliest political formations, we also find the lord himself directing the administration. He seeks to take the administration into his own hands by having men personally dependent upon him: slaves, household officials, attendants, personal 'favorites,' and prebendaries enfeoffed in kind or in money from his magazines. He seeks to defray the expenses from his own pocket, from the revenues of his patrimonium; and he seeks to create an army which is dependent upon him personally because it is equipped and provisioned out of his granaries, magazines, and armories. In the association of 'estates,' the lord rules with the aid of an autonomous 'aristocracy' and hence shares his domination with it; the lord who personally administers is supported either by members of his household or by plebeians. These are propertyless strata having no social honor of their own; materially, they are completely chained to him and are not backed up by any competing power of their own. All forms of patriarchal and patrimonial domination, Sultanist despotism, and bureaucratic states belong to this latter type. The bureaucratic state order is especially important; m its most rational development, it is precisely characteristic of the modern state.

Everywhere the development of the modern state is initiated through the action of the prince. He paves the way for the expropriation of the autonomous and 'private' bearers of executive power who stand beside him, of those who in their own right possess the means of administration, warfare, and financial organization, as well as politically usable goods of all sorts. The whole process is a complete parallel to the development of the capitalist enterprise through gradual expropriation of the independent producers. In the end, the modern state controls the total means of political organization, which actually come together under a single head. No single official personally owns the money he pays out, or the buildings, stores, tools, and war machines he controls. In the contemporary 'state'—and this is essential for the concept of state—the 'separation' of the administrative staff, of the administrative officials, and of the workers from the material means of administrative organization is completed. Here the most modern development begins, and we see with our own eyes the attempt to inaugurate the expropriation of this expropriator of the political means, and therewith of political power. [...]

[...] Politics, just as economic pursuits, may be a man's avocation or his vocation. One may engage in politics, and hence seek to influence the distribution of power within and between political structures, as an 'occasional' politician. We are all 'occasional' politicians when we cast our ballot or consummate a similar expression of intention, such as applauding or protesting in a 'political' meeting, or delivering a 'political' speech, etc. The whole relation of many people to politics is restricted to this. Politics as an avocation is today practiced by all those party agents and heads of voluntary political associations who, as a rule, are politically active only in case of need and for whom politics is, neither materially nor ideally, 'their life' in the first place. The same holds for those members of state counsels and similar deliberative bodies that function only when summoned. It also holds for rather broad strata of our members of parliament who are politically active only during sessions. [...]

There are two ways of making politics one's vocation: Either one lives 'for' politics or one lives 'off' politics. By no means is this contrast an exclusive one. The rule is, rather, that man does both, at least in thought, and certainly he also does both in practice. He who lives 'for' politics makes politics his life, in an internal sense. Either he enjoys the naked possession of the power he exerts, or he nourishes his inner balance and self-feeling by the consciousness that his life has meaning in the service of a 'cause.' In this internal sense, every sincere man who lives for a cause also lives off this cause. The distinction hence refers to a much more substantial aspect of the matter, namely, to the economic. He who strives to make politics a permanent source of income lives 'off' politics as a vocation, whereas he who does not do this lives 'for' politics. Under the dominance of the private property order, some—if you wish—very trivial preconditions must exist in order for a person to be able to live 'for' politics in this economic sense. Under normal conditions, the politician must be economically independent of the income politics can bring him. This means, quite simply, that the politician must be wealthy or must have a personal position in life which yields a sufficient income.

This is the case, at least in normal circumstances. The war lord's following is just as little concerned about the conditions of a normal economy as is the street crowd following of the revolutionary hero. Both live off booty, plunder, confiscations, contributions, and the imposition of worthless and compulsory means of tender, which in essence amounts to the same thing. But necessarily, these are extraordinary phenomena. In everyday economic life, only some wealth serves the purpose of making a man economically independent. Yet this alone does not suffice. The professional politician must also be economically 'dispensable,' that is, his income must not depend upon the fact that he constantly and personally places his ability and thinking entirely, or at least by far predominantly, in the service of economic acquisition. In the most unconditional way, the rentier is dispensable in this sense. [...]

[...] The leadership of a state or of a party by men who (in the economic sense of the word) live exclusively for politics and not off politics means necessarily a 'plutocratic' recruitment of the leading political strata. To be sure, this does not mean that such plutocratic leadership signifies at the same time that the politically dominant strata will not also seek to live 'off' politics, and hence that the dominant stratum will not usually exploit their political domination in their own economic interest. All that is unquestionable, of course. There has never been such a stratum that has not somehow lived 'off' politics. Only this is meant: that the professional politician need not seek remuneration directly for his political work, whereas every politician without means must absolutely claim this. On the other hand, we do not mean to say that the property less politician will pursue private economic advantages through politics, exclusively, or even predominantly. Nor do we mean that he will not think, in the first place, of 'the subject matter.' Nothing would be more incorrect. According to all experience, a care for the economic 'security' of his existence is consciously or unconsciously a cardinal point in the whole life orientation of the wealthy man. A quite reckless and unreserved political idealism is found if not exclusively at least predominantly among those strata who by virtue of their propertylessness stand entirely outside of the strata who are interested in maintaining the economic order of a given society. This holds especially for extraordinary and hence revolutionary epochs. A non-plutocratic recruitment of interested politicians, of leadership and following, is geared to the selfunderstood precondition that regular and reliable income will accrue to those who manage politics.

Either politics can be conducted 'honorifically' and then, as one usually says, by 'independent,' that is, by wealthy, men, and especially by rentiers. Or, political leadership is made accessible to propertyless men who must then be rewarded. The professional politician who lives 'off' politics may be a pure 'prebendary' or a salaried 'official.' [. . .]

The development of modern officialdom into a highly qualified, professional labor force, specialized in expertness through long years of preparatory training, stands opposed to all these arrangements. Modern bureaucracy in the interest of integrity has developed a high sense of status honor; without this sense the danger of an awful corruption and a vulgar Philistinism threatens fatally. And without such integrity, even the purely technical functions of the state apparatus would be endangered. The significance of the state apparatus for the economy has been steadily rising, especially with increasing socialization, and its significance will be further augmented.

In the United States, amateur administration through booty politicians in accordance with the outcome of presidential elections resulted in the exchange of hundreds of thousands of officials, even down to the mail carrier. The administration knew nothing of the professional civil-servant-for-life, but this amateur administration has long since been punctured by the Civil Service Reform. Purely technical, irrefrageable needs of the administration have determined this development. [. . .]

The development of the 'leading politicians' was realized along with the ascendancy of the specially trained officialdom, even if in far less noticeable transitions. Of course, such really decisive advisers of the princes have existed at all times and all over the world. In the Orient, the need for relieving the Sultan as far as possible from personal responsibility for the success of the government has created the typical figure of the 'Grand Vizier.' In the Occident, influenced above all by the reports of the Venetian legates, diplomacy first became a consciously cultivated art in the age of Charles V, in Machiavelli's time. The reports of the Venetian legates were read with passionate zeal in expert diplomatic circles. The adepts of this art, who were in the main educated humanistically, treated one another as trained initiates, similar to the humanist Chinese statesmen in the last period of the 'warring states. The necessity of a formally unified guidance of the whole policy, including that of home affairs, by a leading statesman finally and compellingly arose only through constitutional development. Of course, individual personalities, such as advisers of the princes, or rather, in fact, leaders, had again and again existed before then. But the organization of administrative agencies even in the most advanced states first proceeded along other avenues. Top collegial administrative agencies had emerged. In theory, and to a gradually decreasing extent in fact, they met under the personal chairmanship of the prince who rendered the decision. This collegial system led to memoranda, counter-memoranda, and reasoned votes of the majority and the minority. In addition to the official and highest authorities, the prince surrounded himself with purely personal confidants—the 'cabinet'—and through them rendered his decisions, after considering the resolutions of the state counsel, or whatever else the highest state agency was called. The prince, coming more and more into the position of a dilettante, sought to extricate himself from the unavoidably increasing weight of the expertly trained officials through the collegial system and the cabinet. He sought to retain the highest leadership in his own hands. This latent struggle between expert officialdom and autocratic rule existed everywhere. Only in the face of parliaments and the power aspirations of party leaders did the situation change. Very different conditions led to the externally identical result, though to be sure with certain differences. Wherever the dynasties retained actual power in their hands—as was especially the case in Germany—the interests of the prince were joined with those of officialdom against parliament and its claims for power. The officials were also interested in having leading position, that is, ministerial positions, occupied by their own ranks, thus making these positions an object of the official career. The monarch, on his part, was interested in being able to appoint the ministers from the ranks of devoted officials according to his own discretion. Both parties, however, were interested in seeing the political leadership confront parliament in a unified and solidary fashion, and hence in seeing the collegial system replaced by a single cabinet head. Furthermore, in order to be removed in a purely formal way from the struggle of parties and from party attacks, the monarch needed a single personality to cover him and to assume responsibility, that is, to answer to parliament and to negotiate with the parties. All these interests worked together and in the same direction: a minister emerged to direct the officialdom in a unified way.

Where parliament gained supremacy over the monarch—as in England—the development of parliamentary power worked even more strongly in the direction of a unification of the state apparatus. In England, the 'cabinet,' with the single head of Parliament as its 'leader,' developed as a committee of the party which at the time controlled the majority. This party power was ignored by official law but, in fact, it alone was politically decisive. The official collegial bodies as such were not organs of the actual ruling power, the party, and hence could not be the bearers of real government. The ruling party required an ever-ready organization composed only of its actually leading men, who would confidentially discuss matters in order to maintain power within and be capable of engaging in grand politics outside. The cabinet is simply this organization. However, in relation to the public, especially the parliamentary public, the party needed a leader responsible for all decisions—the cabinet head. The English system has been taken over on the Continent in the form of parliamentary ministries. In America alone, and in the democracies influenced by America, a quite heterogeneous system was placed into opposition with this system. The American system placed the directly and popularly elected leader of the victorious party at the head of the apparatus of officials appointed by him and bound him to the consent of 'parliament' only in budgetary and legislative matters. [...]

After all, things in a private economic enterprise are quite similar: the real 'sovereign,' the assembled shareholders, is just as little influential in the business management as is a 'people' ruled by expert officials. And the personages who decide the policy of the enterprise, the bank-controlled 'directorate,' give only directive economic orders and select persons for the management without themselves being capable of technically directing the enterprise. Thus the present structure of the revolutionary state signifies nothing new in principle. It places power over the administration into the hands of absolute dilettantes, who, by virtue of their control of the machine-guns, would like to use expert officials only as executive heads and hands.

We have seen that in the past 'professional politicians' developed through the struggle of the princes with the estates and that they served the princes. Let us briefly review the major types of these professional politicians.

Confronting the estates, the prince found support in politically exploitable strata outside of the order of the estates. Among the latter, there was, first, the clergy in Western and Eastern India, in Buddhist China and Japan, and in Lamaist Mongolia, just as in the Christian territories of the Middle Ages. The clergy were technically useful because they were literate. The importation of Brahmins, Buddhist priests, Lamas, and the employment of bishops and priests as political counselors, occurred with an eye to obtaining administrative forces who could read and write and who could be used in the struggle of the emperor, prince, or Khan against the aristocracy. [...]

The humanistically educated literati comprised a second such stratum. There was a time when one learned to produce Latin speeches and Greek verses in order to become a political adviser to a prince and, above all things, to become a memorialist. This was the time of the first flowering of the humanist schools and of the princely foundations of professorships for 'poetics.' This was for us a transitory epoch, which has had a quite persistent influence upon our educational system, yet no deeper results politically. In East Asia, it has been different.

The third stratum was the court nobility. After the princes had succeeded in expropriating political power from the nobility as an estate, they drew the nobles to the court and used them in their political and diplomatic service. The transformation of our educational system in the seventeenth century was partly determined by the fact that court nobles as professional politicians displaced the humanist literati and entered the service of the princes.

The fourth category was a specifically English institution. A patrician stratum developed there which was comprised of the petty nobility and the urban rentiers; technically they are called the 'gentry.' The English gentry represents a stratum that the prince originally attracted in order to counter the barons. [...]

A fifth stratum, the university-trained jurist, is peculiar to the Occident, especially to the European continent, and has been of decisive significance for the Continent's whole political structure. [...]

[...] The significance of the lawyer in Occidental politics since the rise of parties is not accidental. The management of politics through parties simply means management through interest groups. We shall soon see what that means. The craft of the trained lawyer is to plead effectively the cause of interested clients. In this, the lawyer is superior to any 'official,' as the superiority of enemy propaganda [Allied propaganda 1914–18] could teach us. Certainly he can advocate and win a cause supported by logically weak arguments and one which, in this sense, is a 'weak' cause. Yet he wins it because technically he makes a 'strong case' for it. But only the lawyer successfully pleads a cause that can be supported by logically strong arguments, thus handling a 'good' cause 'well.' All too often the civil servant as a politician turns a cause that is good in every sense into a 'weak' cause, through technically 'weak' pleading. This is what we have had to experience. To an outstanding degree, politics today is in fact conducted in public by means of the spoken or written word. To weigh the effect of the word properly falls within the range of the lawyer's tasks; but not at all into that of the civil servant. The latter is no demagogue, nor is it his purpose to be one. If he nevertheless tries to become a demagogue, he usually becomes a very poor one.

According to his proper vocation, the genuine official—and this is decisive for the evaluation of our former regime—will not engage in politics. Rather, he should engage in impartial 'administration.' This also holds for the so-called 'political' administrator, at least officially, in so far as the *raison d'etat,* that is, the vital interests of the ruling order, are not in question. *Sine ira et studio,* 'without scorn and bias,' he shall administer his office. Hence, he shall not do precisely what the politician, the leader as well as his following, must always and necessarily do, namely, *fight.*

To take a stand, to be passionate—ira et studium—is the politician's element, and above all the element of the political leader. His conduct is subject to quite a different, indeed, exactly the opposite, principle of responsibility from that of the civil servant. The honor of the civil servant is vested in his ability to execute conscientiously the order of the superior authorities, exactly as if the order agreed with his own conviction. This holds even if the order appears wrong to him and if, despite the civil servant's remonstrances, the authority insists on the order. Without this moral discipline and self-denial, in the highest sense, the whole apparatus would fall to pieces.

[...]

This analogy is still more striking when one considers that, on the one hand, the military organization of the medieval party constituted a pure army of knights organized on the basis of the registered feudal estates and that nobles occupied almost all leading positions, and, on the other hand, that the Soviets have preserved, or rather reintroduced, the highly paid enterpriser, the group wage, the Taylor system, military and workshop discipline, and a search for foreign capital. Hence, in a word, the Soviets have had to accept again absolutely all the things that Bolshevism had been fighting as bourgeois class institutions. They have had to do this in order to keep the state and the economy going at all. Moreover, the Soviets have reinstituted the agents of the former Ochrana [Tsarist Secret Police] as the main instrument of their state power. But here we do not have to deal with such organizations for violence, but rather with professional politicians who strive for power through sober and 'peaceful' party campaigns in the market of election votes.

Parties, in the sense usual with us, were at first, for instance in England, pure followings of the aristocracy. If, for any reason whatever, a peer changed his party, everybody dependent upon him likewise changed. Up to the Reform Bill [of 1832], the great noble families and, last but not least, the king controlled the patronage of an immense number of election boroughs. Close to these aristocratic parties were the parties of notables, which develop everywhere with the rising power of the bourgeois. Under the spiritual leadership of the typical intellectual strata of the Occident, the propertied and cultured circles differentiated themselves into parties and followed them. These parties were formed partly according to class interest, partly according to family traditions, and partly for ideological reasons. Clergymen, teachers, professors, lawyers, doctors, apothecaries, prosperous farmers, manufacturers—in England the whole stratum that considered itself as belonging to the class of gentlemen—formed, at first, occasional associations at most local political clubs. In times of unrest the petty bourgeoisie raised its voice, and once in a while the proletariat, if leaders arose who, however, as a rule did not stem from their midst. In this phase, parties organized as permanent associations between localities do not yet exist in the open country. Only the parliamentary delegates create the cohesion; and the local notables are decisive for the selection of candidates. The election programs originate partly in the election appeals of the candidates and partly in the meetings of the notables; or, they originate as resolutions of the parliamentary party. Leadership of the clubs is an avocation and an honorific pursuit, as demanded by the occasion. [...]

The members of parliament are interested in the possibility of inter-local electoral compromises, in vigorous and unified programs endorsed by broad circles and in a unified agitation throughout the country. In general these interests form the driving force of a party organization which becomes more and more strict. In principle, however, the nature of a party apparatus as an association of notables remains unchanged. This is so, even though a network of local party affiliations and agents is spread over the whole country, including middle-sized cities. [. . .]

Now then, the most modern forms of party organizations stand in sharp contrast to this idyllic state in which circles of notables and, above all, members of parliament rule. These modern forms are the children of democracy, of mass franchise, of the necessity to woo and organize the masses, and develop the utmost unity of direction and the strictest discipline. The rule of notables and guidance by members of parliament ceases. 'Professional' politicians outside the parliaments take the organization in hand. They do so either as 'entrepreneurs'—the American boss and the English election agent are, in fact, such entrepreneurs—or as officials with a fixed salary. Formally, a fargoing democratization takes place. The parliamentary party no longer creates the authoritative programs, and the local notables no longer decide the selection of candidates. Rather assemblies of the organized party members select the candidates and delegate members to the assemblies of a higher order. Possibly there are several such conventions leading up to the national convention of the party. Naturally power actually rests in the hands of those who, within the organization, handle the work continuously. Otherwise, power rests in the hands of those on whom the organization in its processes depends financially or personally—for instance, on the Maecenases or the directors of powerful political clubs of interested persons (Tammany Hall). It is decisive that this whole apparatus of people-characteristically called a 'machine' in Anglo-Saxon countries—or rather those who direct the machine, keep the members of the parliament in check. They are in a position to impose their will to a rather far-reaching extent, and that is of special significance for the selection of the party leader. The man whom the machine follows now becomes the leader, even over the head of the parliamentary party. In other words, the creation of such machines signifies the advent of *plebiscitarian* democracy.

The party following, above all the party official and party entrepreneur, naturally expect personal compensation from the victory of their leader—that is, offices or other advantages. It is decisive that they expect such advantages from their leader and not merely from the individual member of parliament. They expect that the demagogic effect of the leader's personality during the election fight of the party will increase votes and mandates and thereby power, and, thereby, as far as possible, will extend opportunities to their followers to find the compensation for which they hope. Ideally, one of their mainsprings is the satisfaction of working with loyal personal devotion for a man, and not merely for an abstract program of a party consisting of mediocrities. In this respect, the 'charismatic' element of all leadership is at work in the party system. [. . .]

According to Washington's idea, America was to be a commonwealth administered by 'gentlemen.' In his time, in America, a gentleman was also a landlord, or a man with a college education—this was the case at first. In the beginning, when parties began to organize, the members of the House of Representatives claimed to be leaders, just as in England at the time when notables ruled. The party organization was quite loose and continued to be until 1824. In some communities, where modern development first took place, the party machine was in the making even before the eighteen-twenties. But when Andrew Jackson was first elected President—the election of the western farmers' candidate— the old traditions were overthrown. Formal party leadership by leading members of Congress came to an end soon after 1840, when the great parliamentarians, Calhoun and Webster, retired from political life because Congress had lost almost all of its power to the party machine in the open country. That the plebiscitarian 'machine' has developed so early in America is due to the fact that there, and there alone, the executive—this is what mattered—the chief of office-patronage, was a President elected by plebiscite. By virtue of the 'separation of powers' he was almost independent of parliament in his conduct of office. Hence, as the price of victory, the true booty object of the office-prebend was held out precisely at the presidential election. Through Andrew Jackson the 'spoils system' was quite systematically raised to a principle and the conclusions were drawn. [. . .]

In America, the spoils system, supported in this fashion, has been technically possible because American culture with its youth could afford purely dilettante management. With 300,000 to 400,000 such party men who have no qualifications to their credit other than the fact of having performed good services for their party, this state of affairs of course could not exist without enormous evils. A corruption and wastefulness second to none could be tolerated only by a country with as yet unlimited economic opportunities.

Now then, the boss is the figure who appears in the picture of this system of the plebiscitarian party machine. Who is the boss? He is a political capitalist entrepreneur who on his own account and at his own risk provides votes. He may have established his first relations as a lawyer or a saloon-keeper or as a proprietor of similar establishments, or perhaps as a creditor. From here he spins his threads out until he is able to 'control' a certain number of votes. When he has come this far he establishes contact with the neighboring bosses, and through zeal, skill, and above all discretion, he attracts the attention of those who have already further advanced in the career, and then he climbs. The boss is indispensable to the organization of the party and the organization is centralized in his hands. He substantially provides the financial means. [. . .] The boss has no firm political 'principles'; he is completely unprincipled in attitude and asks merely: What will capture votes? Frequently he is a rather poorly educated man. But as a rule he leads an inoffensive and correct private life. In his political morals, however, he naturally adjusts to the average ethical standards of political conduct, as a great many of us also may have done during the hoarding period in the field of economic ethics. That as a 'professional' politician the boss is socially despised does not worry him. That he personally does not attain high federal offices, and does not wish to do so, has the frequent advantage that extra-party intellects, thus notables, may come into candidacy when the bosses believe they will have great appeal value at the polls.

Thus, there exists a strong capitalist party machine, strictly and thoroughly organized from top to bottom, and supported by clubs of extraordinary stability. These clubs, such as Tammany Hall, are like Knight orders. They seek profits solely through political control, especially of the municipal government, which is the most important object of booty. This structure of party life was made possible by the high degree of democracy in the United States—a 'New Country.' This connection, in turn, is the basis for the fact that the system is gradually dying out. America can no longer be governed only by dilettantes. Scarcely fifteen years ago, when American workers were asked why they allowed themselves to be governed by politicians whom they admitted they despised, the answer was: 'We prefer having people in office whom we can spit upon, rather than a caste of officials who spit upon us, as is the case with you.' This was the old point of view of American 'democracy.' [. . .]

[. . .] Therefore, today, one cannot yet see in any way how the management of politics as a 'vocation' will shape itself. Even less can one see along what avenue opportunities are opening to which political talents can be put for satisfactory political tasks. He who by his material circumstances is compelled to live 'of politics will almost always have to consider the alternative positions of the journalist or the party official as the typical direct avenues. Or, he must consider a position as representative of interest groups—such as a trade union, a chamber of commerce, a farm bureau, a craft association, a labor board, an employer's association, et cetera, or else a suitable municipal position. Nothing more than this can be said about this external aspect: in common with the journalist, the party official bears the odium of being declasse. 'Wage writer' or 'wage speaker' will unfortunately always resound in his ears, even though the words remain unexpressed. He who is inwardly defenseless and unable to find the proper answer for himself had better stay away from this career. For in any case, besides grave temptations, it is an avenue that may constantly lead to disappointments. Now then, what inner enjoyments can this career offer and what personal conditions are presupposed for one who enters this avenue?

Well, first of all the career of politics grants a feeling of power. The knowledge of influencing men, of participating in power over them, and above all, the feeling of holding in one's hands a nerve fiber of historically important events can elevate the professional politician above everyday routine even when he is placed in formally modest positions. But now the question for him is: Through what qualities can I hope to do justice to this power (however narrowly circumscribed it may be in the individual case)? How can he hope to do justice to the responsibility that power imposes upon him? With this we enter the field of ethical questions, for that is where the problem belongs: What kind of a man must one be if he is to be allowed to put his hand on the wheel of history?

One can say that three pre-eminent qualities are decisive for the politician: passion, a feeling of responsibility, and a sense of proportion. This means passion in the sense of matter-of-factness, of passionate devotion to a 'cause,' to the god or demon who is its overlord. It is not passion in the sense of that inner bearing which my late friend, Georg Simmel, used to designate as 'sterile excitation,' and which was peculiar especially to a certain type of Russian intellectual (by no means all of them!). It is an excitation that plays so great a part with our intellectuals in this carnival we decorate with the proud name of 'revolution.' It is a 'romanticism of the intellectually interesting,' running into emptiness devoid of all feeling of objective responsibility.

[. . .]

Therefore, daily and hourly, the politician inwardly has to overcome a quite trivial and all-too-human enemy: a quite vulgar vanity, the deadly enemy of all matter-of-fact devotion to a cause, and of all distance, in this case, of distance towards one's self.

Vanity is a very widespread quality and perhaps nobody is entirely free from it. In academic and scholarly circles, vanity is a sort of occupational disease, but precisely with the scholar, vanity—however disagreeably it may express itself—is relatively harmless; in the sense that as a rule it does not disturb scientific enterprise. With the politician the case is quite different. He works with the striving for power as an unavoidable means. Therefore, 'power instinct,' as is usually said, belongs indeed to his normal qualities. The sin against the lofty spirit of his vocation, however, begins where this striving for power ceases to be objective and becomes purely personal self-intoxication, instead of exclusively entering the service of 'the cause.' For ultimately there are only two kinds of deadly sins in the field of politics: lack of objectivity and-often but not always identical with it—irresponsibility. Vanity, the need personally to stand in the foreground as clearly as possible, strongly tempts the politician to commit one or both of these sins. This is more truly the case as the demagogue is compelled to count upon 'effect.' He therefore is constantly in danger of becoming an actor as well as taking lightly the responsibility for the outcome of his actions and of being concerned merely with the 'impression' he makes. His lack of objectivity tempts him to strive for the glamorous semblance of power rather than for actual power. His irresponsibility, however, suggests that he enjoy power merely for power's sake without a substantive purpose. Although, or rather just because, power is the unavoidable means, and striving for power is one of the driving forces of all politics, there is no more harmful distortion of political force than the parvenu-like braggart with power, and the vain selfreflection in the feeling of power, and in general every worship of power per se. The mere 'power politician' may get strong effects, but actually his work leads nowhere and is senseless. (Among us, too, an ardently promoted cult seeks to glorify him.) In this, the critics of 'power politics' are absolutely right. From the sudden inner collapse of typical representatives of this mentality, we can see what inner weakness and impotence hides behind this boastful but entirely empty gesture. It is a product of a shoddy and superficially blase attitude towards the meaning of human conduct; and it has no relation whatsoever to the knowledge of tragedy with which all action, but especially political action, is truly interwoven.

The final result of political action often, no, even regularly, stands in completely inadequate and often even paradoxical relation to its original meaning. This is fundamental to all history, a point not to be proved in detail here. But because of this fact, the serving of a cause must not be absent if action is to have inner strength. Exactly what the cause, in the service of which the politician strives for power and uses power, looks like is a matter of faith. The politician may serve national, humanitarian, social, ethical, cultural, worldly, or religious ends. The politician may be sustained by a strong belief in 'progress'—no matter in which sense—or he may coolly reject this kind of belief. He may claim to stand in the service of an 'idea' or, rejecting this in principle, he may want to serve external ends of everyday life. However, some kind of faith must always exist. Otherwise, it is absolutely true that the curse of the creature's worthlessness overshadows even the externally strongest political successes. [. . .]

But even herewith the problem is not yet exhausted. No ethics in the world can dodge the fact that in numerous instances the attainment of 'good' ends is bound to the fact that one must be willing to pay the price of using morally dubious means or at least dangerous ones—and facing the possibility or even the probability of evil ramifications. From no ethics in the world can it be concluded when and to what extent the ethically good purpose 'justifies' the ethically dangerous means and ramifications.

The decisive means for politics is violence. You may see the extent of the tension between means and ends, when viewed ethically, from the following: as is generally known, even during the war the revolutionary socialists Zimmerwald faction) professed a principle that one might strikingly formulate: 'If we face the choice either of some more years of war and then revolution, or peace now and no revolution, we choose-some more years of war!' Upon the further question: 'What can this revolution bring about?' Every scientifically trained socialist would have had the answer: One cannot speak of a transition to an economy that in our sense could be called socialist; a bourgeois economy will re-emerge, merely stripped of the feudal elements and the dynastic vestiges. For this very modest result, they are willing to face 'some more years of war.' One may well say that even with a very robust socialist conviction one might reject a purpose that demands such means. With Bolshevism and Spartanism, and, in general, with any kind of revolutionary socialism, it is precisely the same thing. It is of course utterly ridiculous if the power politicians of the old regime are morally denounced for their use of the same means, however justified the rejection of their aims may be.

The ethic of ultimate ends apparently must go to pieces on the problem of the justification of means by ends. As a matter of fact, logically it has only the possibility of rejecting all action that employs morally dangerous means—in theory! In the world of realities, as a rule, we encounter the ever-renewed experience that the adherent of an ethic of ultimate ends suddenly turns into a chiliastic prophet. Those, for example, who have just preached 'love against violence' now call for the use of force for the last violent deed, which would then lead to a state of affairs in which an violence is annihilated. In the same manner, our officers told the soldiers before every offensive: 'This will be the last one; this one will bring victory and therewith peace.' The proponent of an ethic of absolute ends cannot stand up under the ethical irrationality of the world. He is a cosmic-ethical 'rationalist.' Those of you who know Dostoievski will remember the scene of the 'Grand Inquisitor,' where the problem is poignantly unfolded. If one makes any concessions at all to the principle that the end justifies the means, it is not possible to bring an ethic of ultimate ends and an ethic of responsibility under one roof or to decree ethically which end should justify which means. [. . .]

Surely, politics is made with the head, but it is certainly not made with the head alone. In this the proponents of an ethic of ultimate ends are right. One cannot prescribe to anyone whether he should follow an ethic of absolute ends or an ethic of responsibility, or when the one and when the other. One can say only this much: If in these times, which, in your opinion, are not times of 'sterile' excitation—excitation is not, after all, genuine passion—if now suddenly the Weltanschauungs politicians crop up en masse and pass the watchword, 'The world is stupid and base, not I,' 'The responsibility for the consequences does not fall upon me but upon the others whom I serve and whose stupidity or baseness I shall eradicate,' then I declarefrankly that I would first inquire into the degree of inner poise backing this ethic of ultimate ends. I am under the impression that in nine out of ten cases I deal with windbags who do not fully realize what they take upon themselves but who intoxicate themselves with romantic sensations. From a human point of view this is not very interesting to me, nor does it move me profoundly. However, it is immensely moving when a mature man—no matter whether old or young in years—is aware of a responsibility for the consequences of his conduct and really feels such responsibility with heart and soul. He then acts by following an ethic of responsibility and somewhere he reaches the point where he says: 'Here I stand; I can do no other.' That is something genuinely human and moving. And every one of us who is not spiritually dead must realize the possibility of finding himself at some time in that position. In so far as this is true, an ethic of ultimate ends and an ethic of responsibility are not absolute contrasts but rather supplements) which only in unison constitute a genuine man—a man who can have the 'calling for politics.' [. . .]

Politics is a strong and slow boring of hard boards. It takes both passion and perspective. Certainly, all historical experience confirms the truth—that man would not have attained the possible unless time and again he had reached out for the impossible. But to do that a man must be a leader, and not only a leader but a hero as well, in a very sober sense of the word. And even those who are neither leaders nor heroes must arm themselves with that steadfastness of heart which can brave even the crumbling of all hopes. This is necessary right now, or else men will not be able to attain even that which is possible today. Only he has the calling for politics who is sure that he shall not crumble when the world from his point of view is too stupid or too base for what he wants to offer. Only he who in the face of all this can say 'In spite of all!' has the calling for politics.

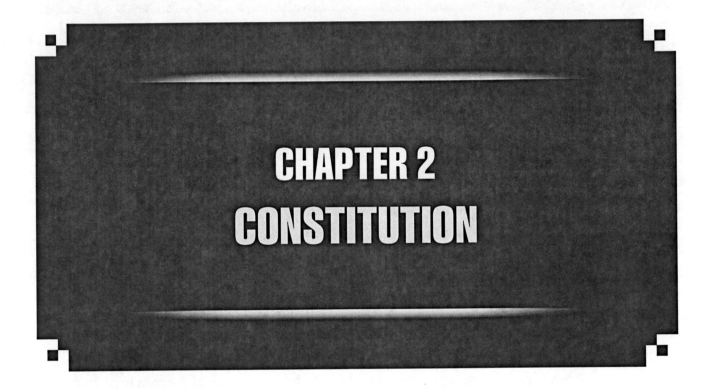

CHAPTER 2
CONSTITUTION

FEDERALIST NO. 10

The Same Subject Continued
(The Union as a Safeguard Against Domestic Faction and Insurrection)

FROM THE DAILY ADVERTISER
Thursday, November 22, 1787

PUBLIUS (MADISON)

To the People of the State of New York:

AMONG the numerous advantages promised by a well constructed Union, none deserves to be more accurately developed than its tendency to break and control the violence of faction. The friend of popular governments never finds himself so much alarmed for their character and fate, as when he contemplates their propensity to this dangerous vice. He will not fail, therefore, to set a due value on any plan which, without violating the principles to which he is attached, provides a proper cure for it. The instability, injustice, and confusion introduced into the public councils, have, in truth, been the mortal diseases under which popular governments have everywhere perished; as they continue to be the favorite and fruitful topics from which the adversaries to liberty derive their most specious declamations. The valuable improvements made by the American constitutions on the popular models, both ancient and modern, cannot certainly be too much admired; but it would be an unwarrantable partiality, to contend that they have as effectually obviated the danger on this side, as was wished and expected. Complaints are everywhere heard from our most considerate and virtuous citizens, equally the friends of public and private faith, and of public and personal liberty, that our governments are too unstable, that the public good is disregarded in the conflicts of rival parties, and that measures are too often decided, not according to the rules of justice and the rights of the minor party, but by the superior force of an interested and overbearing majority. However anxiously we may wish that these complaints had no foundation, the evidence, of known facts will not permit us to deny that they are in some degree true. It will be found, indeed, on a candid review of our situation, that some of the distresses under which we labor have been erroneously charged on the operation of our governments; but it will be found, at the same time, that other causes will not alone account for many of our heaviest misfortunes; and, particularly, for that prevailing and increasing distrust of public engagements, and alarm for private rights, which are echoed from one end of the continent to the other. These must be chiefly, if not wholly, effects of the unsteadiness and injustice with which a factious spirit has tainted our public administrations.

By a faction, I understand a number of citizens, whether amounting to a majority or a minority of the whole, who are united and actuated by some common impulse of passion, or of interest, adversed to the rights of other citizens, or to the permanent and aggregate interests of the community.

SOURCE: Alexander Hamilton, John Jay, and James Madison, *The Federalist Papers,* 1787

There are two methods of curing the mischiefs of faction: the one, by removing its causes; the other, by controlling its effects.

There are again two methods of removing the causes of faction: the one, by destroying the liberty which is essential to its existence; the other, by giving to every citizen the same opinions, the same passions, and the same interests.

It could never be more truly said than of the first remedy, that it was worse than the disease. Liberty is to faction what air is to fire, an aliment without which it instantly expires. But it could not be less folly to abolish liberty, which is essential to political life, because it nourishes faction, than it would be to wish the annihilation of air, which is essential to animal life, because it imparts to fire its destructive agency.

The second expedient is as impracticable as the first would be unwise. As long as the reason of man continues fallible, and he is at liberty to exercise it, different opinions will be formed. As long as the connection subsists between his reason and his self-love, his opinions and his passions will have a reciprocal influence on each other; and the former will be objects to which the latter will attach themselves. The diversity in the faculties of men, from which the rights of property originate, is not less an insuperable obstacle to a uniformity of interests. The protection of these faculties is the first object of government. From the protection of different and unequal faculties of acquiring property, the possession of different degrees and kinds of property immediately results; and from the influence of these on the sentiments and views of the respective proprietors, ensues a division of the society into different interests and parties.

The latent causes of faction are thus sown in the nature of man; and we see them everywhere brought into different degrees of activity, according to the different circumstances of civil society. A zeal for different opinions concerning religion, concerning government, and many other points, as well of speculation as of practice; an attachment to different leaders ambitiously contending for pre-eminence and power; or to persons of other descriptions whose fortunes have been interesting to the human passions, have, in turn, divided mankind into parties, inflamed them with mutual animosity, and rendered them much more disposed to vex and oppress each other than to co-operate for their common good. So strong is this propensity of mankind to fall into mutual animosities, that where no substantial occasion presents itself, the most frivolous and fanciful distinctions have been sufficient to kindle their unfriendly passions and excite their most violent conflicts. But the most common and durable source of factions has been the various and unequal distribution of property. Those who hold and those who are without property have ever formed distinct interests in society. Those who are creditors, and those who are debtors, fall under a like discrimination. A landed interest, a manufacturing interest, a mercantile interest, a moneyed interest, with many lesser interests, grow up of necessity in civilized nations, and divide them into different classes, actuated by different sentiments and views. The regulation of these various and interfering interests forms the principal task of modern legislation, and involves the spirit of party and faction in the necessary and ordinary operations of the government.

No man is allowed to be a judge in his own cause, because his interest would certainly bias his judgment, and, not improbably, corrupt his integrity. With equal, nay with greater reason, a body of men are unfit to be both judges and parties at the same time; yet what are many of the most important acts of legislation, but so many judicial determinations, not indeed concerning the rights of single persons, but concerning the rights of large bodies of citizens? And what are the different classes of legislators but advocates and parties to the causes which they determine? Is a law proposed concerning private debts? It is a question to which the creditors are parties on one side and the debtors on the other. Justice ought to hold the balance between them. Yet the parties are, and must be, themselves the judges; and the most numerous party, or, in other words, the most powerful faction must be expected to prevail. Shall domestic manufactures be encouraged, and in what degree, by restrictions on foreign manufactures? are questions which would be differently decided by the landed and the manufacturing classes, and probably by neither with a sole regard to justice and the public good. The apportionment of taxes on the various descriptions of property is an act which seems to require the most exact impartiality; yet there is, perhaps, no legislative act in which greater opportunity and temptation are given to a predominant party to trample on the rules of justice. Every shilling with which they overburden the inferior number, is a shilling saved to their own pockets.

It is in vain to say that enlightened statesmen will be able to adjust these clashing interests, and render them all subservient to the public good. Enlightened statesmen will not always be at the helm. Nor, in many cases, can such an adjustment be made at all without taking into view indirect and remote considerations, which will rarely prevail over the immediate interest which one party may find in disregarding the rights of another or the good of the whole.

The inference to which we are brought is, that the CAUSES of faction cannot be removed, and that relief is only to be sought in the means of controlling its EFFECTS.

If a faction consists of less than a majority, relief is supplied by the republican principle, which enables the majority to defeat its sinister views by regular vote. It may clog the administration, it may convulse the society; but it will be unable to execute and mask its violence under the forms of the Constitution. When a majority is included in a faction, the form of popular government, on the other hand, enables it to sacrifice to its ruling passion or interest both the public good and the rights of other citizens. To secure the public good and private rights against the danger of such a faction, and at the same time to preserve the spirit and the form of popular government, is then the great object to which our inquiries are directed. Let me add that it is the great desideratum by which this form of government can be rescued from the opprobrium under which it has so long labored, and be recommended to the esteem and adoption of mankind.

By what means is this object attainable? Evidently by one of two only. Either the existence of the same passion or interest in a majority at the same time must be prevented, or the majority, having such coexistent passion or interest, must be rendered, by their number and local situation, unable to concert and carry into effect schemes of oppression. If the impulse and the opportunity be suffered to coincide, we well know that neither moral nor religious motives can be relied on as an adequate control. They are not found to be such on the injustice and violence of individuals, and lose their efficacy in proportion to the number combined together, that is, in proportion as their efficacy becomes needful.

From this view of the subject it may be concluded that a pure democracy, by which I mean a society consisting of a small number of citizens, who assemble and administer the government in person, can admit of no cure for the mischiefs of faction. A common passion or interest will, in almost every case, be felt by a majority of the whole; a communication and concert result from the form of government itself; and there is nothing to check the inducements to sacrifice the weaker party or an obnoxious individual. Hence it is that such democracies have ever been spectacles of turbulence and contention; have ever been found incompatible with personal security or the rights of property; and have in general been as short in their lives as they have been violent in their deaths. Theoretic politicians, who have patronized this species of government, have erroneously supposed that by reducing mankind to a perfect equality in their political rights, they would, at the same time, be perfectly equalized and assimilated in their possessions, their opinions, and their passions.

A republic, by which I mean a government in which the scheme of representation takes place, opens a different prospect, and promises the cure for which we are seeking. Let us examine the points in which it varies from pure democracy, and we shall comprehend both the nature of the cure and the efficacy which it must derive from the Union.

The two great points of difference between a democracy and a republic are: first, the delegation of the government, in the latter, to a small number of citizens elected by the rest; secondly, the greater number of citizens, and greater sphere of country, over which the latter may be extended.

The effect of the first difference is, on the one hand, to refine and enlarge the public views, by passing them through the medium of a chosen body of citizens, whose wisdom may best discern the true interest of their country, and whose patriotism and love of justice will be least likely to sacrifice it to temporary or partial considerations. Under such a regulation, it may well happen that the public voice, pronounced by the representatives of the people, will be more consonant to the public good than if pronounced by the people themselves, convened for the purpose. On the other hand, the effect may be inverted. Men of factious tempers, of local prejudices, or of sinister designs, may, by intrigue, by corruption, or by other means, first obtain the suffrages, and then betray the interests, of the people. The question resulting is, whether small or extensive republics are more favorable to the election of proper guardians of the public weal; and it is clearly decided in favor of the latter by two obvious considerations:

In the first place, it is to be remarked that, however small the republic may be, the representatives must be raised to a certain number, in order to guard against the cabals of a few; and that, however large it may be, they must be limited to a certain number, in order to guard against the confusion of a multitude. Hence, the number of representatives in the two cases not being in proportion to that of the two constituents, and being proportionally greater in the small republic, it follows that, if the proportion of fit characters be not less in the large than in the small republic, the former will present a greater option, and consequently a greater probability of a fit choice.

In the next place, as each representative will be chosen by a greater number of citizens in the large than in the small republic, it will be more difficult for unworthy candidates to practice with success the vicious arts by which elections are too often carried; and the suffrages of the people being more free, will be more likely to centre in men who possess the most attractive merit and the most diffusive and established characters.

It must be confessed that in this, as in most other cases, there is a mean, on both sides of which inconveniences will be found to lie. By enlarging too much the number of electors, you render the representatives too little acquainted with all their local circumstances and lesser interests; as by reducing it too much, you render him unduly attached to these, and too little fit to comprehend and pursue great and national objects. The federal Constitution forms a happy combination in this respect; the great and aggregate interests being referred to the national, the local and particular to the State legislatures.

The other point of difference is, the greater number of citizens and extent of territory which may be brought within the compass of republican than of democratic government; and it is this circumstance principally which renders factious combinations less to be dreaded in the former than in the latter. The smaller the society, the fewer probably will be the distinct parties and interests composing it; the fewer the distinct parties and interests, the more frequently will a majority be found of the same party; and the smaller the number of individuals composing a majority, and the smaller the compass within which they are placed, the more easily will they concert and execute their plans of oppression. Extend the sphere, and you take in a greater variety of parties and interests; you make it less probable that a majority of the whole will have a common motive to invade the rights of other citizens; or if such a common motive exists, it will be more difficult for all who feel it to discover their own strength, and to act in unison with each other. Besides other impediments, it may be remarked that, where there is a consciousness of unjust or dishonorable purposes, communication is always checked by distrust in proportion to the number whose concurrence is necessary.

Hence, it clearly appears, that the same advantage which a republic has over a democracy, in controlling the effects of faction, is enjoyed by a large over a small republic,—is enjoyed by the Union over the States composing it. Does the advantage consist in the substitution of representatives whose enlightened views and virtuous sentiments render them superior to local prejudices and schemes of injustice? It will not be denied that the representation of the Union will be most likely to possess these requisite endowments. Does it consist in the greater security afforded by a greater variety of parties, against the event of any one party being able to outnumber and oppress the rest? In an equal degree does the increased variety of parties comprised within the Union, increase this security. Does it, in fine, consist in the greater obstacles opposed to the concert and accomplishment of the secret wishes of an unjust and interested majority? Here, again, the extent of the Union gives it the most palpable advantage.

The influence of factious leaders may kindle a flame within their particular States, but will be unable to spread a general conflagration through the other States. A religious sect may degenerate into a political faction in a part of the Confederacy; but the variety of sects dispersed over the entire face of it must secure the national councils against any danger from that source. A rage for paper money, for an abolition of debts, for an equal division of property, or for any other improper or wicked project, will be less apt to pervade the whole body of the Union than a particular member of it; in the same proportion as such a malady is more likely to taint a particular county or district, than an entire State.

In the extent and proper structure of the Union, therefore, we behold a republican remedy for the diseases most incident to republican government. And according to the degree of pleasure and pride we feel in being republicans, ought to be our zeal in cherishing the spirit and supporting the character of Federalists.

PUBLIUS

FEDERALIST NO. 51

The Structure of the Government Must Furnish the Proper Checks and Balances Between the Different Departments.

FOR THE INDEPENDENT JOURNAL.
Wednesday, February 6, 1788.

PUBLIUS (MADISON)

To the People of the State of New York:

TO WHAT expedient, then, shall we finally resort, for maintaining in practice the necessary partition of power among the several departments, as laid down in the Constitution? The only answer that can be given is, that as all these exterior provisions are found to be inadequate, the defect must be supplied, by so contriving the interior structure of the government as that its several constituent parts may, by their mutual relations, be the means of keeping each other in their proper places. Without presuming to undertake a full development of this important idea, I will hazard a few general observations, which may perhaps place it in a clearer light, and enable us to form a more correct judgment of the principles and structure of the government planned by the convention.

In order to lay a due foundation for that separate and distinct exercise of the different powers of government, which to a certain extent is admitted on all hands to be essential to the preservation of liberty, it is evident that each department should have a will of its own; and consequently should be so constituted that the members of each should have as little agency as possible in the appointment of the members of the others. Were this principle rigorously adhered to, it would require that all the appointments for the supreme executive, legislative, and judiciary magistracies should be drawn from the same fountain of authority, the people, through channels having no communication whatever with one another. Perhaps such a plan of constructing the several departments would be less difficult in practice than it may in contemplation appear. Some difficulties, however, and some additional expense would attend the execution of it. Some deviations, therefore, from the principle must be admitted. In the constitution of the judiciary department in particular, it might be inexpedient to insist rigorously on the principle: first, because peculiar qualifications being essential in the members, the primary consideration ought to be to select that mode of choice which best secures these qualifications; secondly, because the permanent tenure by which the appointments are held in that department, must soon destroy all sense of dependence on the authority conferring them.

It is equally evident, that the members of each department should be as little dependent as possible on those of the others, for the emoluments annexed to their offices. Were the executive magistrate, or the

SOURCE: Alexander Hamilton, John Jay, and James Madison, *The Federalist Papers,* 1788

judges, not independent of the legislature in this particular, their independence in every other would be merely nominal.

But the great security against a gradual concentration of the several powers in the same department, consists in giving to those who administer each department the necessary constitutional means and personal motives to resist encroachments of the others. The provision for defense must in this, as in all other cases, be made commensurate to the danger of attack. Ambition must be made to counteract ambition. The interest of the man must be connected with the constitutional rights of the place. It may be a reflection on human nature, that such devices should be necessary to control the abuses of government. But what is government itself, but the greatest of all reflections on human nature? If men were angels, no government would be necessary. If angels were to govern men, neither external nor internal controls on government would be necessary. In framing a government which is to be administered by men over men, the great difficulty lies in this: you must first enable the government to control the governed; and in the next place oblige it to control itself. A dependence on the people is, no doubt, the primary control on the government; but experience has taught mankind the necessity of auxiliary precautions.

This policy of supplying, by opposite and rival interests, the defect of better motives, might be traced through the whole system of human affairs, private as well as public. We see it particularly displayed in all the subordinate distributions of power, where the constant aim is to divide and arrange the several offices in such a manner as that each may be a check on the other—that the private interest of every individual may be a sentinel over the public rights. These inventions of prudence cannot be less requisite in the distribution of the supreme powers of the State.

But it is not possible to give to each department an equal power of self-defense. In republican government, the legislative authority necessarily predominates. The remedy for this inconveniency is to divide the legislature into different branches; and to render them, by different modes of election and different principles of action, as little connected with each other as the nature of their common functions and their common dependence on the society will admit. It may even be necessary to guard against dangerous encroachments by still further precautions. As the weight of the legislative authority requires that it should be thus divided, the weakness of the executive may require, on the other hand, that it should be fortified. An absolute negative on the legislature appears, at first view, to be the natural defense with which the executive magistrate should be armed. But perhaps it would be neither altogether safe nor alone sufficient. On ordinary occasions it might not be exerted with the requisite firmness, and on extraordinary occasions it might be perfidiously abused. May not this defect of an absolute negative be supplied by some qualified connection between this weaker department and the weaker branch of the stronger department, by which the latter may be led to support the constitutional rights of the former, without being too much detached from the rights of its own department?

If the principles on which these observations are founded be just, as I persuade myself they are, and they be applied as a criterion to the several State constitutions, and to the federal Constitution it will be found that if the latter does not perfectly correspond with them, the former are infinitely less able to bear such a test.

There are, moreover, two considerations particularly applicable to the federal system of America, which place that system in a very interesting point of view.

First. In a single republic, all the power surrendered by the people is submitted to the administration of a single government; and the usurpations are guarded against by a division of the government into distinct and separate departments. In the compound republic of America, the power surrendered by the people is first divided between two distinct governments, and then the portion allotted to each subdivided among distinct and separate departments. Hence a double security arises to the rights of the people. The different governments will control each other, at the same time that each will be controlled by itself.

Second. It is of great importance in a republic not only to guard the society against the oppression of its rulers, but to guard one part of the society against the injustice of the other part. Different interests necessarily exist in different classes of citizens. If a majority be united by a common interest, the rights of the minority will be insecure. There are but two methods of providing against this evil: the one by creating a will in the community independent of the majority—that is, of the society itself; the other, by comprehending in the society so many separate descriptions of citizens as will render an unjust combination of a majority of the whole very improbable, if not impracticable. The first method prevails in all governments possessing an hereditary or self-appointed authority. This, at best, is but a precarious security; because a power independent of the society may as well espouse the unjust views of the major, as the rightful interests of the minor party, and may possibly be turned against both parties. The second method will be exemplified in the federal republic of the United States. Whilst all authority in it will be derived from and dependent on the society, the society itself will be broken into so many parts, interests, and classes of citizens, that the rights of individuals, or of the minority, will be in little danger from interested combinations of the majority. In a free government the security for civil rights must be the same as that for religious rights. It consists in the one case in the multiplicity of interests, and in the other in the multiplicity of sects. The degree of security in both cases will depend on the number of interests and sects; and this may be presumed to depend on the extent of country and number of people comprehended under the same government. This view of the subject must particularly recommend a proper federal system to all the sincere and considerate friends of republican government, since it shows that in exact proportion as the territory of the Union may be formed into more circumscribed Confederacies, or States oppressive combinations of a majority will be facilitated: the best security, under the republican forms, for the rights of every class of citizens, will be diminished: and consequently the stability and independence of some member of the government, the only other security, must be proportionately increased. Justice is the end of government. It is the end of civil society. It ever has been and ever will be pursued until it be obtained, or until liberty be lost in the pursuit. In a society under the forms of which the stronger faction can readily unite and oppress the weaker, anarchy may as truly be said to reign as in a state of nature, where the weaker individual is not secured against the violence of the stronger; and as, in the latter state, even the stronger individuals are prompted, by the uncertainty of their condition, to submit to a government which may protect the weak as well as themselves; so, in the former state, will the more powerful factions or parties be gradually induced, by a like motive, to wish for a government which will protect all parties, the weaker as well as the more powerful. It can be little doubted that if the State of Rhode Island was separated from the Confederacy and left to itself, the insecurity of rights under the popular form of government within such narrow limits would be displayed by such reiterated oppressions of factious majorities that some power altogether independent of the people would soon be called for by the voice of the very factions whose misrule had proved the necessity of it. In the extended republic of the United States, and among the great variety of interests, parties, and sects which it embraces, a coalition of a majority of the whole society could seldom take place on any other principles than those of justice and the general good; whilst there being thus less danger to a minor from the will of a major party, there must be less pretext, also, to provide for the security of the former, by introducing into the government a will not dependent on the latter, or, in other words, a will independent of the society itself. It is no less certain than it is important, notwithstanding the contrary opinions which have been entertained, that the larger the society, provided it lie within a practical sphere, the more duly capable it will be of self-government. And happily for the REPUBLICAN CAUSE, the practicable sphere may be carried to a very great extent, by a judicious modification and mixture of the FEDERAL PRINCIPLE.

PUBLIUS

MCCULLOCH V. MARYLAND

SUPREME COURT OF THE UNITED STATES
17 U.S. 316 (1819)

[Congress charted a bank that Maryland subsequently decided to tax. There are two major questions arising in this case: (1) does Congress have the power to create a federal bank?, and (2) does Maryland have the authority to tax a federal bank if Congress has the power to create one?]

MARSHALL, Chief Justice, delivered the opinion of the Court.

In the case now to be determined, the defendant, a sovereign State, denies the obligation of a law enacted by the legislature of the Union, and the plaintiff, on his part, contests the validity of an act which has been passed by the legislature of that State. The Constitution of our country, in its most interesting and vital parts, is to be considered, the conflicting powers of the Government of the Union and of its members, as marked in that Constitution, are to be discussed, and an opinion given which may essentially influence the great operations of the Government. No tribunal can approach such a question without a deep sense of its importance, and of the awful responsibility involved in its decision. But it must be decided peacefully, or remain a source of hostile legislation, perhaps, of hostility of a still more serious nature; and if it is to be so decided, by this tribunal alone can the decision be made. On the Supreme Court of the United States has the Constitution of our country devolved this important duty.

The first question made in the cause is—has Congress power to incorporate a bank?

It has been truly said that this can scarcely be considered as an open question entirely unprejudiced by the former proceedings of the Nation respecting it. The principle now contested was introduced at a very early period of our history, has been recognised by many successive legislatures, and has been acted upon by the Judicial Department, in cases of peculiar delicacy, as a law of undoubted obligation.

It will not be denied that a bold and daring usurpation might be resisted after an acquiescence still longer and more complete than this. But it is conceived that a doubtful question, one on which human reason may pause and the human judgment be suspended, in the decision of which the great principles of liberty are not concerned, but the respective powers of those who are equally the representatives of the people, are to be adjusted, if not put at rest by the practice of the Government, ought to receive a considerable impression from that practice. An exposition of the Constitution, deliberately established by legislative acts, on the faith of which an immense property has been advanced, ought not to be lightly disregarded.

The power now contested was exercised by the first Congress elected under the present Constitution.

The bill for incorporating the Bank of the United States did not steal upon an unsuspecting legislature and pass unobserved. Its principle was completely understood, and was opposed with equal zeal and ability. After being resisted first in the fair and open field of debate, and afterwards in the executive cabinet, with as much persevering talent as any measure has ever experienced, and being supported by arguments which convinced minds as pure and as intelligent as this country can boast, it became a law. The original act was permitted to expire, but a short experience of the embarrassments to which the refusal to revive it exposed the Government convinced those who were most prejudiced against the measure of its necessity, and induced the passage of the present law. It would require no ordinary share of intrepidity to assert that a measure adopted under these circumstances was a bold and plain usurpation to which the Constitution gave no countenance. These observations belong to the cause; but they are not made under the impression that, were the question entirely new, the law would be found irreconcilable with the Constitution.

In discussing this question, the counsel for the State of Maryland have deemed it of some importance, in the construction of the Constitution, to consider that instrument not as emanating from the people, but as the act of sovereign and independent States. The powers of the General Government, it has been said, are delegated by the States, who alone are truly sovereign, and must be exercised in subordination to the States, who alone possess supreme dominion.

It would be difficult to sustain this proposition. The convention which framed the Constitution was indeed elected by the State legislatures. But the instrument, when it came from their hands, was a mere proposal, without obligation or pretensions to it. It was reported to the then existing Congress of the United States with a request that it might "be submitted to a convention of delegates, chosen in each State by the people thereof, under the recommendation of its legislature, for their assent and ratification."

This mode of proceeding was adopted, and by the convention, by Congress, and by the State legislatures, the instrument was submitted to the people. They acted upon it in the only manner in which they can act safely, effectively and wisely, on such a subject—by assembling in convention. It is true, they assembled in their several States—and where else should they have assembled? No political dreamer was ever wild enough to think of breaking down the lines which separate the States, and of compounding the American people into one common mass. Of consequence, when they act, they act in their States. But the measures they adopt do not, on that account, cease to be the measures of the people themselves, or become the measures of the State governments.

From these conventions the Constitution derives its whole authority. The government proceeds directly from the people; is "ordained and established" in the name of the people, and is declared to be ordained, "in order to form a more perfect union, establish justice, insure domestic tranquillity, and secure the blessings of liberty to themselves and to their posterity."

The assent of the States in their sovereign capacity is implied in calling a convention, and thus submitting that instrument to the people. But the people were at perfect liberty to accept or reject it, and their act was final. It required not the affirmance, and could not be negatived, by the State Governments. The Constitution, when thus adopted, was of complete obligation, and bound the State sovereignties.

It has been said that the people had already surrendered all their powers to the State sovereignties, and had nothing more to give. But surely the question whether they may resume and modify the powers granted to Government does not remain to be settled in this country. Much more might the legitimacy of the General Government be doubted had it been created by the States. The powers delegated to the State sovereignties were to be exercised by themselves, not by a distinct and independent sovereignty created by themselves. To the formation of a league such as was the Confederation, the State sovereignties were certainly competent. But when, "in order to form a more perfect union," it was deemed necessary to change this alliance into an effective Government, possessing great and sovereign powers and acting directly on the people, the necessity of referring it to the people, and of deriving its powers directly from them, was felt and acknowledged by all. The Government of the Union then (whatever may be the influence of this fact on the case) is, emphatically and truly, a Government of the people. In form and in substance, it emanates from them. Its powers are granted by them, and are to be exercised directly on them, and for their benefit.

This Government is acknowledged by all to be one of enumerated powers. The principle that it can exercise only the powers granted to it would seem too apparent to have required to be enforced by all those arguments which its enlightened friends, while it was depending before the people, found it necessary to urge; that principle is now universally admitted. But the question respecting the extent of the powers actually granted is perpetually arising, and will probably continue to arise so long as our system shall exist. In discussing these questions, the conflicting powers of the General and State Governments must be brought into view, and the supremacy of their respective laws, when they are in opposition, must be settled.

If any one proposition could command the universal assent of mankind, we might expect it would be this—that the Government of the Union, though limited in its powers, is supreme within its sphere of action. This would seem to result necessarily from its nature. It is the Government of all; its powers are delegated by all; it represents all, and acts for all. Though any one State may be willing to control its operations, no State is willing to allow others to control them. The nation, on those subjects on which it can act, must necessarily bind its component parts. But this question is not left to mere reason; the people have, in express terms, decided it by saying, "this Constitution, and the laws of the United States, which shall be made in pursuance thereof," "shall be the supreme law of the land," and by requiring that the members of the State legislatures and the officers of the executive and judicial departments of the States shall take the oath of fidelity to it. The Government of the United States, then, though limited in its powers, is supreme, and its laws, when made in pursuance of the Constitution, form the supreme law of the land, "anything in the Constitution or laws of any State to the contrary notwithstanding."

[. . .]

Although, among the enumerated powers of Government, we do not find the word "bank" or "incorporation," we find the great powers, to lay and collect taxes; to borrow money; to regulate commerce; to declare and conduct a war; and to raise and support armies and navies. The sword and the purse, all the external relations, and no inconsiderable portion of the industry of the nation are intrusted to its Government. It can never be pretended that these vast powers draw after them others of inferior importance merely because they are inferior. Such an idea can never be advanced. But it may with great reason be contended that a Government intrusted with such ample powers, on the due execution of which the happiness and prosperity of the Nation so vitally depends, must also be intrusted with ample means for their execution. The power being given, it is the interest of the Nation to facilitate its execution. It can never be their interest, and cannot be presumed to have been their intention, to clog and embarrass its execution by withholding the most appropriate means.

[...]

It is not denied that the powers given to the Government imply the ordinary means of execution. That, for example, of raising revenue and applying it to national purposes is admitted to imply the power of conveying money from place to place as the exigencies of the Nation may require, and of employing the usual means of conveyance. But it is denied that the Government has its choice of means, or that it may employ the most convenient means if, to employ them, it be necessary to erect a corporation. On what foundation does this argument rest? On this alone: the power of creating a corporation is one appertaining to sovereignty, and is not expressly conferred on Congress. This is true. But all legislative powers appertain to sovereignty. The original power of giving the law on any subject whatever is a sovereign power, and if the Government of the Union is restrained from creating a corporation as a means for performing its functions, on the single reason that the creation of a corporation is an act of sovereignty, if the sufficiency of this reason be acknowledged, there would be some difficulty in sustaining the authority of Congress to pass other laws for the accomplishment of the same objects. The Government which has a right to do an act and has imposed on it the duty of performing that act must, according to the dictates of reason, be allowed to select the means, and those who contend that it may not select any appropriate means that one particular mode of effecting the object is excepted take upon themselves the burden of establishing that exception.

[...]

[T]he Constitution of the United States has not left the right of Congress to employ the necessary means for the execution of the powers conferred on the Government to general reasoning. To its enumeration of powers is added that of making "all laws which shall be necessary and proper for carrying into execution the foregoing powers, and all other powers vested by this Constitution in the Government of the United States or in any department thereof."

The counsel for the State of Maryland have urged various arguments to prove that this clause, . . . the argument on which most reliance is placed is drawn from that peculiar language of this clause. Congress is not empowered by it to make all laws which may have relation to the powers conferred on the Government, but such only as may be "necessary and proper" for carrying them into execution. The word "necessary" is considered as controlling the whole sentence, and as limiting the right to pass laws for the execution of the granted powers to such as are indispensable, and without which the power would be nugatory. That it excludes the choice of means, and leaves to Congress in each case that only which is most direct and simple.

Is it true that this is the sense in which the word "necessary" is always used? Does it always import an absolute physical necessity so strong that one thing to which another may be termed necessary cannot exist without that other? We think it does not. If reference be had to its use in the common affairs of the world or in approved authors, we find that it frequently imports no more than that one thing is convenient, or useful, or essential to another. To employ the means necessary to an end is generally understood as employing any means calculated to produce the end, and not as being confined to those single means without which the end would be entirely unattainable. Such is the character of human language that no word conveys to the mind in all situations one single definite idea, and nothing is more common than to use words in a figurative sense. Almost all compositions contain words which, taken in a rigorous sense, would convey a meaning different from that which is obviously intended. It is essential to just construction that many words which import something excessive should be understood in a more mitigated sense—in that sense which common usage justifies. The word "necessary" is of this description. It has not a fixed character peculiar to itself. It admits of all degrees of comparison, and is often connected with other words which increase or diminish the impression the mind receives of the urgency it imports. A thing may be necessary, very necessary, absolutely or indispensably necessary. To no mind would the same idea be conveyed by these several phrases. The comment on the word is well illustrated by the passage cited at the bar from the 10th section of the 1st article of the Constitution. It is, we think, impossible to compare the sentence which prohibits a State from laying "imposts, or duties on imports or exports, except what may be absolutely necessary for executing its inspection laws," with that which authorizes Congress "to make all laws which shall be necessary and proper for carrying into execution" the powers of the General Government without feeling a conviction that the convention understood itself to change materially the meaning of the word "necessary," by prefixing the word "absolutely." This word, then, like others, is used in various senses, and, in its construction, the subject, the context, the intention of the person using them are all to be taken into view.

Let this be done in the case under consideration. The subject is the execution of those great powers on which the welfare of a Nation essentially depends. It must have been the intention of those who gave these powers to insure, so far as human prudence could insure, their beneficial execution. This could not be done by confiding the choice of means to such narrow limits as not to leave it in the power of Congress to adopt any which might be appropriate, and which were conducive to the end. This provision is made in a Constitution intended to endure for ages to come, and consequently to be adapted to the various crises of human affairs. To have prescribed the means by which Government should, in all future time, execute its powers would have been to change entirely the character of the instrument and give it the properties of a legal code. It would have been an unwise attempt to provide by immutable rules for exigencies which, if foreseen at all, must have been seen dimly, and which can be best provided for as they occur. To have declared that the best means shall not be used, but those alone without which the power given would be nugatory, would have been to deprive the legislature of the capacity to avail itself of experience, to exercise its reason, and to accommodate its legislation to circumstances.

[. . .]

In ascertaining the sense in which the word "necessary" is used in this clause of the Constitution, we may derive some aid from that with which it is associated. Congress shall have power "to make all laws which shall be necessary and proper to carry into execution" the powers of the Government. If the word "necessary" was used in that strict and rigorous sense for which the counsel for the State of Maryland contend, it would be an extraordinary departure from the usual course of the human mind, as exhibited in composition, to add a word the only possible effect of which is to qualify that strict and rigorous meaning, to present to the mind the idea of some choice of means of legislation not strained and compressed within the narrow limits for which gentlemen contend.

But the argument which most conclusively demonstrates the error of the construction contended for by the counsel for the State of Maryland is founded on the intention of the convention as manifested in the whole clause. To waste time and argument in proving that, without it, Congress might carry its powers into execution would be not much less idle than to hold a lighted taper to the sun. As little can it be required to prove that, in the absence of this clause, Congress would have some choice of means. That it might employ those which, in its judgment, would most advantageously effect the object to be accomplished. That any means adapted to the end, any means which tended directly to the execution of the Constitutional powers of the Government, were in themselves Constitutional. This clause, as construed by the State of Maryland, would abridge, and almost annihilate, this useful and necessary right of the legislature to select its means. That this could not be intended is, we should think, had it not been already controverted, too apparent for controversy.

[. . .]

The result of the most careful and attentive consideration bestowed upon this clause is that, if it does not enlarge, it cannot be construed to restrain, the powers of Congress, or to impair the right of the legislature to exercise its best judgment in the selection of measures to carry into execution the Constitutional powers of the Government. If no other motive for its insertion can be suggested, a sufficient one is found in the desire to remove all doubts respecting the right to legislate on that vast mass of incidental powers which must be involved in the Constitution if that instrument be not a splendid bauble.

We admit, as all must admit, that the powers of the Government are limited, and that its limits are not to be transcended. But we think the sound construction of the Constitution must allow to the national legislature that discretion with respect to the means by which the powers it confers are to be carried into execution which will enable that body to perform the high duties assigned to it in the manner most beneficial to the people. Let the end be legitimate, let it be within the scope of the Constitution, and all means which are appropriate, which are plainly adapted to that end, which are not prohibited, but consist with the letter and spirit of the Constitution, are Constitutional.

[. . .]

After the most deliberate consideration, it is the unanimous and decided opinion of this Court that the act to incorporate the Bank of the United States is a law made in pursuance of the Constitution, and is a part of the supreme law of the land.

[. . .]

It being the opinion of the Court that the act incorporating the bank is constitutional, and that the power of establishing a branch in the State of Maryland might be properly exercised by the bank itself, we proceed to inquire:

2. Whether the State of Maryland may, without violating the Constitution, tax that branch?

That the power of taxation is one of vital importance; that it is retained by the States; that it is not abridged by the grant of a similar power to the Government of the Union; that it is to be concurrently exercised by the two Governments—are truths which have never been denied. But such is the paramount character of the Constitution that its capacity to withdraw any subject from the action of even this power is admitted.

[. . .]

This great principle is that the Constitution and the laws made in pursuance thereof are supreme; that they control the Constitution and laws of the respective States, and cannot be controlled by them.

[. . .]

That the power of taxing it by the States may be exercised so as to destroy it is too obvious to be denied. But taxation is said to be an absolute power which acknowledges no other limits than those expressly prescribed in the Constitution, and, like sovereign power of every other description, is intrusted to the discretion of those who use it. But the very terms of this argument admit that the sovereignty of the State, in the article of taxation itself, is subordinate to, and may be controlled by, the Constitution of the United States. How far it has been controlled by that instrument must be a question of construction. In making this construction, no principle, not declared, can be admissible which would defeat the legitimate operations of a supreme Government. It is of the very essence of supremacy to remove all obstacles to its action within its own sphere, and so to modify every power vested in subordinate governments as to exempt its own operations from their own influence.

[. . .]

The argument on the part of the State of Maryland is not that the States may directly resist a law of Congress, but that they may exercise their acknowledged powers upon it, and that the Constitution leaves them this right, in the confidence that they will not abuse it.

[. . .]

The sovereignty of a State extends to everything which exists by its own authority or is introduced by its permission, but does it extend to those means which are employed by Congress to carry into execution powers conferred on that body by the people of the United States? We think it demonstrable that it does not. Those powers are not given by the people of a single State. They are given by the people of the United States, to a Government whose laws, made in pursuance of the Constitution, are declared to be supreme. Consequently, the people of a single State cannot confer a sovereignty which will extend over them.

[. . .]

That the power to tax involves the power to destroy; that the power to destroy may defeat and render useless the power to create; that there is a plain repugnance in conferring on one Government a power to control the constitutional measures of another, which other, with respect to those very measures, is declared to be supreme over that which exerts the control, are propositions not to be denied.

[. . .]

If the States may tax one instrument, employed by the Government in the execution of its powers, they may tax any and every other instrument. They may tax the mail; they may tax the mint; they may tax patent rights; they may tax the papers of the custom house; they may tax judicial process; they may tax all the means employed by the Government to an excess which would defeat all the ends of Government. This was not intended by the American people. They did not design to make their Government dependent on the States.

[...]

We are unanimously of opinion that the law passed by the Legislature of Maryland, imposing a tax on the Bank of the United States is unconstitutional and void.

This opinion does not deprive the States of any resources which they originally possessed. It does not extend to a tax paid by the real property of the bank, in common with the other real property within the State, nor to a tax imposed on the interest which the citizens of Maryland may hold in this institution, in common with other property of the same description throughout the State. But this is a tax on the operations of the bank, and is, consequently, a tax on the operation of an instrument employed by the Government of the Union to carry its powers into execution. Such a tax must be unconstitutional.

ARTICLES OF CONFEDERATION

TO ALL TO WHOM these Presents shall come, we the undersigned Delegates of the States affixed to our Names send greeting.

Whereas the Delegates of the United States of America in Congress assembled did on the fifteenth day of November in the Year of our Lord One Thousand Seven Hundred and Seventyseven, and in the Second Year of the Independence of America agree to certain articles of Confederation and perpetual Union between the States of New hampshire, Massachusetts-bay, Rhode Island and Providence Plantations, Connecticut, New York, New Jersey, Pennsylvania, Deleware, Maryland, Virginia, North-Carolina, South-Carolina and Georgia in the Words following, viz.

"Articles of Confederation and perpetual Union between the States of New hampshire, Massachusetts-bay, Rhode Island and Providence Plantations, connecticut, New-York, New-Jersey, Pennsylvania, Deleware, Maryland, Virginia, North-Carolina, South-Carolina and Georgia.

ARTICLE I. The stile of this confederacy shall be "The United States of America."

ARTICLE II. Each State retains its sovereignty, freedom and independence, and every power, jurisdiction and right, which is not by this confederation expressly delegated to the United States, in Congress assembled.

ARTICLE III. The said States hereby severally enter into a firm league of friendship with each other, for their common defense, the security of their liberties, and their mutual and general welfare, binding themselves to assist each other, against all force offered to, or attacks made upon them, or any of them, on account of religion, sovereignty, trade or any other pretence whatever.

ARTICLE IV. The better to secure and perpetuate mutual friendship and intercourse among the people of the different States in this Union, the free inhabitants of each of these States, paupers, vagabonds and fugitives from justice excepted, shall be entitled to all privileges and immunities of free citizens in the several States; and the people of each State shall have free ingress and regress to and from any other State, and shall enjoy therein all the privileges of trade and commerce, subject to the same duties, impositions and restrictions as the inhabitants thereof respectively, provided that such restrictions shall not extend so far as to prevent the removal of property imported into any State, to any other State of which the owner is an inhabitant; provided also that no imposition, duties or restriction shall be laid by any State, on the property of the United States, or either of them.

SOURCE: The Articles of Confederation, 1777

If any person guilty of, or charged with treason, felony, or other high mesdemeanor in any State, shall flee from justice, and be found in any of the United States, he shall upon demand of the Governor or Executive power, of the State from which he fled, be delivered up and removed to the State having jurisdiction of his offence.

Full faith and credit shall be given in each of these States to the records, acts and judicial proceedings of the courts and magistrates of every other State.

ARTICLE V. For the more convenient management of the general interests of the United States, delegates shall be annually appointed in such manner as the legislature of each State shall direct, to meet in Congress on the first Monday in November, in every year, with a power reserved to each State, to recall its delegates, or any of them, at any time within the year, and to send others in their stead, for the remainder of the year.

No State shall be represented in Congress by less than two, nor by more than seven members; and no person shall be capable of being a delegate for more than three years in any term of six years; nor shall any person, being a delegate, be capable of holding any office under the United States, for which he, or another for his benefit receives any salary, fees or emolument of any kind.

Each State shall maintain its own delegates in a meeting of the States, and while they act as members of the committee of the States.

In determining questions in the United States, in Congress assembled, each State shall have one vote.

Freedom of speech and debate in Congress shall not be impeached or questioned in any court, or place out of Congress, and the members of Congress shall be protected in their persons from arrests and imprisonments, during the time of their going to and from, and attendance on Congress, except for treason, felony, or breach of the peace.

ARTICLE VI. No State without the consent of the United States in Congress assembled, shall send any embassy to, or receive any embassy from, or enter into any conference, agreement, alliance or treaty with any king, prince or state; nor shall any person holding any office of profit or trust under the United States, or any of them, accept of any present, emolument, office or title of any kind whatever from any king, prince or foreign state; nor shall the United States in Congress assembled, or any of them, grant any title of nobility.

No two or more States shall enter into any treaty, confederation or alliance whatever between them, without the consent of the United States in Congress assembled, specifying accurately the purposes for which the same is to be entered into, and how long it shall continue.

No State shall lay any imposts or duties, which may interfere with any stipulations in treaties, entered into by the United States in Congress assembled, with any king, prince or state, in pursuance of any treaties already proposed by Congress, to the courts of France and Spain.

No vessels of war shall be kept up in time of peace by any State, except such number only, as shall be deemed necessary by the United States in Congress assembled, for the defence of such State, or its trade; nor shall any body of forces be kept up by any State, in time of peace, except such number only, as in the judgment of the United States, in Congress assembled, shall be deemed requisite to garrison the forts necessary for the defense of such State; but every State shall always keep up a well regulated and disciplined militia, sufficiently armed and accoutred, and shall provide and constantly have ready for use, in public stores, a due number of field pieces and tents, and a proper quantity of arms, ammunition and camp equipage.

No State shall engage in any war without the consent of the United States in Congress assembled, unless such State be actually invaded by enemies, or shall have received certain advice of a resolution being for med by some nation of Indians to invade such State, and the danger is so imminent as not to admit of a delay, till the United State in Congress assembled can be consulted; nor shall any State grant commissions to any ships or vessels of war, nor letters of marque or reprisal, except it be after a declaration of war by the United States in Congress assembled, and then only against the kingdom or state and the subjects thereof, against which war has been so declared, and under such regulations as shall be established by the United States in Congress assembled, unless such State be infested by pirates, in which case vessels of war may be fitted out for the occasion, and kept so long as the danger shall continue, or until the United States in Congress assembled shall determine otherwise.

ARTICLE VII. When land-forces are raised by any State of the common defence, all officers of or under the rank of colonel, shall be appointed by the Legislature of each State respectively by whom such forces shall be raised, or in such manner as such State shall direct, and all vacancies shall be filled up by the State which first made the appointment.

ARTICLE VIII. All charges of war, and all other expenses that shall be incurred for the common defense or general welfare, and allowed by the United States in Congress assembled, shall be defrayed out of a common treasury, which shall be supplied by the several States, in proportion to the value of all land within each State, granted to or surveyed for any person, as such land and the buildings and improvements thereon shall be estimated according to such mode as the United States in Congress assembled, shall from time to time direct and appoint.

The taxes for paying that proportion shall be laid and levied by the authority and direction of the Legislatures of the several States within the time agreed upon by the United States in Congress assembled.

ARTICLE IX. The United States in Congress assembled, shall have the sole and exclusive right and power of determining on peace and war, except in the cases mentioned in the sixth article—of sending and receiving ambassadors—entering into treaties and alliances, provided that no treaty of commerce shall be made whereby the legislative power of the respective States shall be restrained from imposing such imposts and duties on foreigners, as their own people are subjected to, or from prohibiting the exportation or importation of and species of goods or commodities whatsoever—of establishing rules for deciding in all cases, what captures on land or water shall be legal, and in what manner prizes taken by land or naval forces in the service of the United States shall be divided or appropriated—of granting letters of marque and reprisal in times of peace—appointing courts for the trial of piracies and felonies committed on the high seas and establishing courts for receiving and determining finally appeals in all cases of captures, provided that no member of Congress shall be appointed a judge of any of the said courts.

The United States in Congress assembled shall also be the last resort on appeal in all disputes and differences now subsisting or that hereafter may arise between two or more States concerning boundary, jurisdiction or any other cause whatever; which authority shall always be exercised in the manner following. Whenever the legislative or executive authority or lawful agent of any State in controversy with another shall present a petition to Congress, stating the matter in question and praying for a hearing, notice thereof shall be given by order of Congress to the legislative or executive authority of the other State in controversy, and a day assigned for the appearance of the parties by their lawful agents, who shall then be directed to appoint by joint consent, commissioners or judges to constitute a court for hearing and determining the matter in question: but if they cannot agree, Congress shall name three persons out of each of the United States, and from the list of such persons each party shall alternately strike out one, the petitioners beginning, until the number shall be reduced to thirteen; and from that number not less than seven, nor more than nine names as Congress shall direct, shall in the presence of Congress be drawn out by lot, and the persons whose names shall be so drawn or any five of them, shall be commissioners or judges, to hear and finally determine the controversy, so always as a major part of the judges who shall hear the cause shall agree in the determination: and if either party shall neglect to attend at the day appointed, without reasons, which Congress shall judge sufficient, or being present shall refuse to strike, the Congress shall proceed to nominate three persons out of each State, and the Secretary of Congress shall strike in behalf of such party absent or refusing; and the judgment and sentence of the court to be appointed, in the manner before prescribed, shall be final and conclusive; and if any of the parties shall refuse to submit to the authority of such court, or to appear or defend their claim or cause, the court shall nevertheless proceed to pronounce sentence, or judgment, which shall in like manner be final and decisive, the judgment or sentence and other procedings being in either case transmitted to Congress, and lodged among the acts of Congress for the security of the parties concerned: provided that every commissioner, before he sits in judgment, shall take an oath to be administered by one of the judges of the supreme or superior court of the State where the cause shall be tried, "well and truly to hear and determine the matter in question, according to the best of his judgment, without favour, affection or hope of reward:" provided also that no State shall be deprived of territory for the benefit of the United States.

All controversies concerning the private right of soil claimed under different grants of two or more States, whose jurisdiction as they may respect such lands, and the states which passed such grants are adjusted, the said grants or either of them being at the same time claimed to have originated antecedent to such settlement of jurisdiction, shall on the petition of either party to the Congress of the United States, be finally determined as near as may be in the same manner as is before prescribed for deciding disputes respecting territorial jurisdiction between different States.

The United States in Congress assembled shall also have the sole and exclusive right and power of regulating the alloy and value of coin struck by their own authority, or by that of the respective State—fixing the standard of weights and measures throughout the United States—regulating the trade and managing all affairs with the Indians, not members of any of the States, provided that the legislative right of any State within its own limits be not infringed or violated—establishing and regulating post-offices from one State to another, throughout all of the United States, and exacting such postage on the papers passing thro' the same as may be requisite to defray the expenses of the said office—appointing all officers of the land forces, in the service of the United States, excepting regimental officers—appointing all the officers of the naval forces, and commissioning all officers whatever in the service of the United States—making rules for the government and regulation of the said land and naval forces, and directing their operations.

The United Sates in Congress assembled shall have authority to appoint a committee, to sit in the recess of Congress, to be denominated "a Committee of the States," and to consist of one delegate from each State; and to appoint such other committees and civil officers as may be necessary for managing the general affairs of the United States under their direction—to appoint one of their number to preside, provided that no person be allowed to serve in the office of president more than one year in any term of three years; to ascertain the necessary sums of money to be raised for the service of the United States, and to appropriate and apply the same for defraying the public expenses—to borrow money, or emit bills on the credit of the United States, transmitting every half year to the respective States an account of the sums of money so borrowed or emitted,—to build and equip a navy—to agree upon the number of land forces, and to make requisitions from each State for its quota, in proportion to the number of white inhabitants in such State; which requisition shall be binding, and thereupon the Legislature of each State shall appoint the regimental officers, raise the men and cloath, arm and equip them in a soldier like manner, at the expense of the United States; and the officers and men so cloathed, armed and equipped shall march to the place appointed, and within the time agreed on by the United States in Congress assembled: but if the United States in Congress assembled shall, on consideration of circumstances judge proper that any State should not raise men, or should raise a smaller number of men than the quota thereof, such extra number shall be raised, officered, cloathed, armed and equipped in the same manner as the quota of such State, unless the legislature of such State shall judge that such extra number cannot be safely spared out of the time, in which case they shall raise officer, cloath, arm and equip as many of such extra number as they judge can be safely spared. And the officers and men so cloathed, armed and equipped, shall march to the place appointed, and within the time agreed on by the United States in Congress assembled.

The United States in Congress assembled shall never engage in a war, nor grant letters of marque and reprisal in time of peace, nor enter into any treaties or alliances, nor coin money, nor regulate the value thereof, nor ascertain the sums and expenses necessary for the defence and welfare of the United States, or any of them, nor emit bills, nor borrow money on the credit of the United States, nor appropriate money, nor agree upon the number of vessels to be built or purchased, or the number of land or sea forces to be raised, nor appoint a commander in chief of the army or navy, unless nine States assent to the same: nor shall a question on any other point, except for adjourning from day to day be determined, unless by the votes of a majority of the United States in Congress assembled.

The Congress of the United States shall have power to adjourn to any time within the year, and to any place within the United States, so that no period of adjournment be for a longer duration than the space of six months, and shall publish the journal of their proceedings monthly, except such parts thereof relating to treaties, alliances or military operations, as in their judgment require secrecy; and the yeas and nays of the delegates of each State on any question shall be entered on the Journal, when it is desired by any delegate; and the delegates of a State, or any of them, at his or their request shall be furnished with a transcript of the said journal, except such parts as are above excepted, to lay before the Legislatures of the several States.

ARTICLE X. The committee of the States, or any nine of them, shall be authorized to execute, in the recess of Congress, such of the powers of Congress as the United States in Congress assembled, by the consent of nine States, shall from time to time think expedient to vest them with; provided that no power be delegated to the said committee, for the exercise of which, by the articles of confederation, the voice of nine States in the Congress of the United States assembled is requisite.

ARTICLE XI. Canada acceding to this confederation, and joining in the measures of the United States, shall be admitted into, and entitled to all the advantages of this Union: but no other colony shall be admitted into the same, unless such admission be agreed to by nine States.

ARTICLE XII. All bills of credit emitted, monies borrowed and debts contracted by, or under the authority of Congress, before the assembling of the United States, in pursuance of the present confederation, shall be deemed and considered as a charge against the United States, for payment and satisfaction whereof the said United States, and the public faith are hereby solemnly pledged.

ARTICLE XIII. Every State shall abide by the determinations of the United States in Congress assembled, on all questions which by this confederation are submitted to them. And the articles of this confederation shall be inviolably observed by every State, and the Union shall be perpetual; nor shall any alteration at any time hereafter be made in any of them; unless such alteration be agreed to in a Congress of the United States, and be after wards confirmed by the Legislatures of every State.

And whereas it has pleased the Great Governor of the world to incline the hearts of the Legislatures we respectively represent in Congress, to approve of, and to authorize us to ratify the said articles of confederation and perpetual union. Know ye that we the undersigned delegates, by virtue of the power and authority to us given for that purpose, do by these presents, in the name and in behalf of our respective constituents, fully and entirely ratify and confirm each and every of the said articles of confederation and perpetual union, and all and singular the matters and things therein contained: and we do further solemnly plight and engage the faith of our respective constituents, that they shall abide by the determinations of the United States in Congress assembled, on all questions, which by the said confederation are submitted to them. And that the articles thereof shall be inviolably observed by the States we respectively represent, and that the Union shall be perpetual.

In witness thereof we have hereunto set our hands in Congress. Done at Philadelphia in the State of Pennsylvania the ninth day of July in the year of our Lord one thousand seven hundred and seventy-eight, and in the third year of the independence of America.

US Government Record

CHAPTER 3
FEDERALISM

FEDERALIST NO. 39

The Conformity of the Plan to Republican Principles

FOR THE INDEPENDENT JOURNAL
Wednesday, January 16, 1788

PUBLIUS (MADISON)

To the People of the State of New York:

THE last paper having concluded the observations which were meant to introduce a candid survey of the plan of government reported by the convention, we now proceed to the execution of that part of our undertaking.

The first question that offers itself is, whether the general form and aspect of the government be strictly republican. It is evident that no other form would be reconcilable with the genius of the people of America; with the fundamental principles of the Revolution; or with that honorable determination which animates every votary of freedom, to rest all our political experiments on the capacity of mankind for self-government. If the plan of the convention, therefore, be found to depart from the republican character, its advocates must abandon it as no longer defensible.

What, then, are the distinctive characters of the republican form? Were an answer to this question to be sought, not by recurring to principles, but in the application of the term by political writers, to the constitution of different States, no satisfactory one would ever be found. Holland, in which no particle of the supreme authority is derived from the people, has passed almost universally under the denomination of a republic. The same title has been bestowed on Venice, where absolute power over the great body of the people is exercised, in the most absolute manner, by a small body of hereditary nobles. Poland, which is a mixture of aristocracy and of monarchy in their worst forms, has been dignified with the same appellation. The government of England, which has one republican branch only, combined with an hereditary aristocracy and monarchy, has, with equal impropriety, been frequently placed on the list of republics. These examples, which are nearly as dissimilar to each other as to a genuine republic, show the extreme inaccuracy with which the term has been used in political disquisitions.

If we resort for a criterion to the different principles on which different forms of government are established, we may define a republic to be, or at least may bestow that name on, a government which derives all its powers directly or indirectly from the great body of the people, and is administered by persons holding their offices during pleasure, for a limited period, or during good behavior. It is ESSENTIAL to such a government that it be derived from the great body of the society, not from an inconsiderable proportion, or a favored class of it; otherwise a handful of tyrannical nobles, exercising their oppressions by a delegation of their powers, might aspire to the rank of republicans, and

SOURCE: Alexander Hamilton, John Jay, and James Madison, *The Federalist Papers,* 1788

claim for their government the honorable title of republic. It is SUFFICIENT for such a government that the persons administering it be appointed, either directly or indirectly, by the people; and that they hold their appointments by either of the tenures just specified; otherwise every government in the United States, as well as every other popular government that has been or can be well organized or well executed, would be degraded from the republican character. According to the constitution of every State in the Union, some or other of the officers of government are appointed indirectly only by the people. According to most of them, the chief magistrate himself is so appointed. And according to one, this mode of appointment is extended to one of the co-ordinate branches of the legislature. According to all the constitutions, also, the tenure of the highest offices is extended to a definite period, and in many instances, both within the legislative and executive departments, to a period of years. According to the provisions of most of the constitutions, again, as well as according to the most respectable and received opinions on the subject, the members of the judiciary department are to retain their offices by the firm tenure of good behavior.

On comparing the Constitution planned by the convention with the standard here fixed, we perceive at once that it is, in the most rigid sense, conformable to it. The House of Representatives, like that of one branch at least of all the State legislatures, is elected immediately by the great body of the people. The Senate, like the present Congress, and the Senate of Maryland, derives its appointment indirectly from the people. The President is indirectly derived from the choice of the people, according to the example in most of the States. Even the judges, with all other officers of the Union, will, as in the several States, be the choice, though a remote choice, of the people themselves, the duration of the appointments is equally conformable to the republican standard, and to the model of State constitutions The House of Representatives is periodically elective, as in all the States; and for the period of two years, as in the State of South Carolina. The Senate is elective, for the period of six years; which is but one year more than the period of the Senate of Maryland, and but two more than that of the Senates of New York and Virginia. The President is to continue in office for the period of four years; as in New York and Delaware, the chief magistrate is elected for three years, and in South Carolina for two years. In the other States the election is annual. In several of the States, however, no constitutional provision is made for the impeachment of the chief magistrate. And in Delaware and Virginia he is not impeachable till out of office. The President of the United States is impeachable at any time during his continuance in office. The tenure by which the judges are to hold their places, is, as it unquestionably ought to be, that of good behavior. The tenure of the ministerial offices generally, will be a subject of legal regulation, conformably to the reason of the case and the example of the State constitutions.

Could any further proof be required of the republican complexion of this system, the most decisive one might be found in its absolute prohibition of titles of nobility, both under the federal and the State governments; and in its express guaranty of the republican form to each of the latter.

"But it was not sufficient," say the adversaries of the proposed Constitution, "for the convention to adhere to the republican form. They ought, with equal care, to have preserved the FEDERAL form, which regards the Union as a CONFEDERACY of sovereign states; instead of which, they have framed a NATIONAL government, which regards the Union as a CONSOLIDATION of the States." And it is asked by what authority this bold and radical innovation was undertaken? The handle which has been made of this objection requires that it should be examined with some precision.

Without inquiring into the accuracy of the distinction on which the objection is founded, it will be necessary to a just estimate of its force, first, to ascertain the real character of the government in question; secondly, to inquire how far the convention were authorized to propose such a government; and thirdly, how far the duty they owed to their country could supply any defect of regular authority.

First. In order to ascertain the real character of the government, it may be considered in relation to the foundation on which it is to be established; to the sources from which its ordinary powers are to be drawn; to the operation of those powers; to the extent of them; and to the authority by which future changes in the government are to be introduced.

On examining the first relation, it appears, on one hand, that the Constitution is to be founded on the assent and ratification of the people of America, given by deputies elected for the special purpose; but, on the other, that this assent and ratification is to be given by the people, not as individuals composing one entire nation, but as composing the distinct and independent States to which they respectively belong. It is to be the assent and ratification of the several States, derived from the supreme authority in each State, the authority of the people themselves. The act, therefore, establishing the Constitution, will not be a NATIONAL, but a FEDERAL act.

That it will be a federal and not a national act, as these terms are understood by the objectors; the act of the people, as forming so many independent States, not as forming one aggregate nation, is obvious from this single consideration, that it is to result neither from the decision of a MAJORITY of the people of the Union, nor from that of a MAJORITY of the States. It must result from the UNANIMOUS assent of the several States that are parties to it, differing no otherwise from their ordinary assent than in its being expressed, not by the legislative authority, but by that of the people themselves. Were the people regarded in this transaction as forming one nation, the will of the majority of the whole people of the United States would bind the minority, in the same manner as the majority in each State must bind the minority; and the will of the majority must be determined either by a comparison of the individual votes, or by considering the will of the majority of the States as evidence of the will of a majority of the people of the United States. Neither of these rules have been adopted. Each State, in ratifying the Constitution, is considered as a sovereign body, independent of all others, and only to be bound by its own voluntary act. In this relation, then, the new Constitution will, if established, be a FEDERAL, and not a NATIONAL constitution.

The next relation is, to the sources from which the ordinary powers of government are to be derived. The House of Representatives will derive its powers from the people of America; and the people will be represented in the same proportion, and on the same principle, as they are in the legislature of a particular State. So far the government is NATIONAL, not FEDERAL. The Senate, on the other hand, will derive its powers from the States, as political and coequal societies; and these will be represented on the principle of equality in the Senate, as they now are in the existing Congress. So far the government is FEDERAL, not NATIONAL. The executive power will be derived from a very compound source. The immediate election of the President is to be made by the States in their political characters. The votes allotted to them are in a compound ratio, which considers them partly as distinct and coequal societies, partly as unequal members of the same society. The eventual election, again, is to be made by that branch of the legislature which consists of the national representatives; but in this particular act they are to be thrown into the form of individual delegations, from so many distinct and coequal bodies politic. From this aspect of the government it appears to be of a mixed character, presenting at least as many FEDERAL as NATIONAL features.

The difference between a federal and national government, as it relates to the OPERATION OF THE GOVERNMENT, is supposed to consist in this, that in the former the powers operate on the political bodies composing the Confederacy, in their political capacities; in the latter, on the individual citizens composing the nation, in their individual capacities. On trying the Constitution by this criterion, it falls under the NATIONAL, not the FEDERAL character; though perhaps not so completely as has been understood. In several cases, and particularly in the trial of controversies to which States may be parties, they must be viewed and proceeded against in their collective and political capacities only. So far the national countenance of the government on this side seems to be disfigured by a few federal features. But this blemish is perhaps unavoidable in any plan; and the operation of the government on the people, in their individual capacities, in its ordinary and most essential proceedings, may, on the whole, designate it, in this relation, a NATIONAL government.

But if the government be national with regard to the OPERATION of its powers, it changes its aspect again when we contemplate it in relation to the EXTENT of its powers. The idea of a national government involves in it, not only an authority over the individual citizens, but an indefinite supremacy over all persons and things, so far as they are objects of lawful government. Among a people consolidated into one nation, this supremacy is completely vested in the national legislature. Among communities united for particular purposes, it is vested partly in the general and partly in the municipal legislatures. In the former case, all local authorities are subordinate to the supreme; and may be controlled, directed, or abolished by it at pleasure. In the latter, the local or municipal authorities form distinct and independent portions of the supremacy, no more subject, within their respective spheres, to the general authority, than the general authority is subject to them, within its own sphere. In this relation, then, the proposed government cannot be deemed a NATIONAL one; since its jurisdiction extends to certain enumerated objects only, and leaves to the several States a residuary and inviolable sovereignty over all other objects. It is true that in controversies relating to the boundary between the two jurisdictions, the tribunal which is ultimately to decide, is to be established under the general government. But this does not change the principle of the case. The decision is to be impartially made, according to the rules of the Constitution; and all the usual and most effectual precautions are taken to secure this impartiality. Some such tribunal is clearly essential to prevent an appeal to the sword and a dissolution of the compact; and that it ought to be established under the general rather than under the local governments, or, to speak more properly, that it could be safely established under the first alone, is a position not likely to be combated.

If we try the Constitution by its last relation to the authority by which amendments are to be made, we find it neither wholly NATIONAL nor wholly FEDERAL. Were it wholly national, the supreme and ultimate authority would reside in the MAJORITY of the people of the Union; and this authority would be competent at all times, like that of a majority of every national society, to alter or abolish its established government. Were it wholly federal, on the other hand, the concurrence of each State in the Union would be essential to every alteration that would be binding on all. The mode provided by the plan of the convention is not founded on either of these principles. In requiring more than a majority, and principles. In requiring more than a majority, and particularly in computing the proportion by STATES, not by CITIZENS, it departs from the NATIONAL and advances towards the FEDERAL character; in rendering the concurrence of less than the whole number of States sufficient, it loses again the FEDERAL and partakes of the NATIONAL character.

The proposed Constitution, therefore, is, in strictness, neither a national nor a federal Constitution, but a composition of both. In its foundation it is federal, not national; in the sources from which the ordinary powers of the government are drawn, it is partly federal and partly national; in the operation of these powers, it is national, not federal; in the extent of them, again, it is federal, not national; and, finally, in the authoritative mode of introducing amendments, it is neither wholly federal nor wholly national.

PUBLIUS

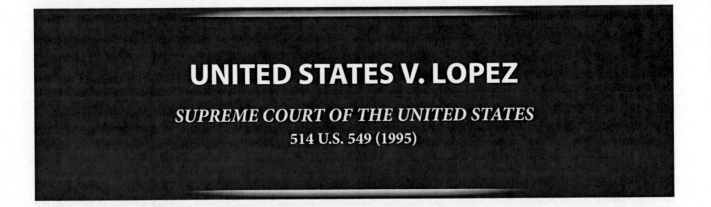

UNITED STATES V. LOPEZ

SUPREME COURT OF THE UNITED STATES
514 U.S. 549 (1995)

CHIEF JUSTICE **REHNQUIST** delivered the opinion of the Court.

In the Gun-Free School Zones Act of 1990, Congress made it a federal offense "for any individual knowingly to possess a firearm at a place that the individual knows, or has reasonable cause to believe, is a school zone." 18 U.S.C. § 922 (q)(1)(A). The Act neither regulates a commercial activity nor contains a requirement that the possession be connected in any way to interstate commerce. We hold that the Act exceeds the authority of Congress "to regulate Commerce . . . among the several States . . . ." U.S. Const., Art. I, § 8, cl. 3.

On March 10, 1992, respondent, who was then a 12th-grade student, arrived at Edison High School in San Antonio, Texas, carrying a concealed .38 caliber handgun and five bullets. Acting upon an anonymous tip, school authorities confronted respondent, who admitted that he was carrying the . . . The next day, the state charges were dismissed after federal agents charged respondent by complaint with violating the Gun-Free School Zones Act of 1990. 18 U.S.C. § 922(q)(1)(A) .

[. . .]

The District Court conducted a bench trial, found him guilty of violating § 922(q), and sentenced him to six months' imprisonment and two years' supervised release.

On appeal, respondent challenged his conviction based on his claim that § 922(q) exceeded Congress' power to legislate under the Commerce Clause. The Court of Appeals for the Fifth Circuit agreed and reversed respondent's conviction.

[. . .]

We start with first principles. The Constitution creates a Federal Government of enumerated powers. See Art. I, § 8. As James Madison wrote, "the powers delegated by the proposed Constitution to the federal government are few and defined. Those which are to remain in the State governments are numerous and indefinite." The Federalist No. 45, pp. 292–293 (C. Rossiter ed. 1961). This constitutionally mandated division of authority "was adopted by the Framers to ensure protection of our fundamental liberties." *Gregory* v. *Ashcroft*, 501 U.S. 452, 458. "Just as the separation and independence of the coordinate branches of the Federal Government serve to prevent the accumulation of excessive power in any one branch, a healthy balance of power between the States and the Federal Government will reduce the risk of tyranny and abuse from either front." *Ibid.*

The Constitution delegates to Congress the power "to regulate Commerce with foreign Nations, and among the several States, and with the Indian Tribes." Art. I, § 8, cl. 3. The Court, through Chief Justice Marshall, first defined the nature of Congress' commerce power in *Gibbons* v. *Ogden*, 22 U.S. 1:

> "Commerce, undoubtedly, is traffic, but it is something more: it is intercourse. It describes the commercial intercourse between nations, and parts of nations, in all its branches, and is regulated by prescribing rules for carrying on that intercourse."

The commerce power "is the power to regulate; that is, to prescribe the rule by which commerce is to be governed. This power, like all others vested in congress, is complete in itself, may be exercised to its utmost extent, and acknowledges no limitations, other than are prescribed in the constitution." *Id.*, at 196. The *Gibbons* Court, however, acknowledged that limitations on the commerce power are inherent in the very language of the Commerce Clause.

> "It is not intended to say that these words comprehend that commerce, which is completely internal, which is carried on between man and man in a State, or between different parts of the same State, and which does not extend to or affect other States. Such a power would be inconvenient, and is certainly unnecessary.

> "Comprehensive as the word 'among' is, it may very properly be restricted to that commerce which concerns more States than one. . . . The enumeration presupposes something not enumerated; and that something, if we regard the language, or the subject of the sentence, must be the exclusively internal commerce of a State." *Id.*, at 194–195.

[. . .]

In *Wickard* v. *Filburn*, the Court upheld the application of amendments to the Agricultural Adjustment Act of 1938 to the production and consumption of homegrown wheat. 317 U.S. at 128–129. The *Wickard* Court explicitly rejected earlier distinctions between direct and indirect effects on interstate commerce, stating:

> "Even if appellee's activity be local and though it may not be regarded as commerce, it may still, whatever its nature, be reached by Congress if it exerts a substantial economic effect on interstate commerce, and this irrespective of whether such effect is what might at some earlier time have been defined as 'direct' or 'indirect.'" *Id.*, at 125.

The *Wickard* Court emphasized that although Filburn's own contribution to the demand for wheat may have been trivial by itself, that was not "enough to remove him from the scope of federal regulation where, as here, his contribution, taken together with that of many others similarly situated, is far from trivial." *Id.*, at 127–128.

[. . .]

Consistent with this structure, we have identified three broad categories of activity that Congress may regulate under its commerce power. . . . First, Congress may regulate the use of the channels of interstate commerce. . . Second, Congress is empowered to regulate and protect the instrumentalities of interstate commerce, or persons or things in interstate commerce, even though the threat may come only from intrastate activities. . . . Finally, Congress' commerce authority includes the power to regulate those activities having a substantial relation to interstate commerce. . . .

[. . .]

We now turn to consider the power of Congress, in the light of this framework, to enact § 922(q). The first two categories of authority may be quickly disposed of: § 922(q) is not a regulation of the use of the channels of interstate commerce, nor is it an attempt to prohibit the interstate transportation of a commodity through the channels of commerce; nor can § 922(q) be justified as a regulation by which Congress has sought to protect an instrumentality of interstate commerce or a thing in interstate commerce. Thus, if § 922(q) is to be sustained, it must be under the third category as a regulation of an activity that substantially affects interstate commerce.

First, we have upheld a wide variety of congressional Acts regulating intrastate economic activity where we have concluded that the activity substantially affected interstate commerce. . . . Where economic activity substantially affects interstate commerce, legislation regulating that activity will be sustained.

Even *Wickard*, which is perhaps the most far reaching example of Commerce Clause authority over intrastate activity, involved economic activity in a way that the possession of a gun in a school zone does not. Roscoe Filburn operated a small farm in Ohio, on which, in the year involved, he raised 23 acres of wheat. It was his practice to sow winter wheat in the fall, and after harvesting it in July to sell a portion of the crop, to feed part of it to poultry and livestock on the farm, to use some in making flour for home consumption, and to keep the remainder for seeding future crops. The Secretary of Agriculture assessed a penalty against him under the Agricultural Adjustment Act of 1938 because he harvested about 12 acres more wheat than his allotment under the Act permitted. The Act was designed to regulate the volume of wheat moving in interstate and foreign commerce in order to avoid surpluses and shortages, and concomitant fluctuation in wheat prices, which had previously obtained.

[. . .]

Section 922(q) is a criminal statute that by its terms has nothing to do with "commerce" or any sort of economic enterprise, however broadly one might define those terms.[3] Section 922(q) is not an essential part of a larger regulation of economic activity, in which the regulatory scheme could be undercut unless the intrastate activity were regulated. It cannot, therefore, be sustained under our cases upholding regulations of activities that arise out of or are connected with a commercial transaction, which viewed in the aggregate, substantially affects interstate commerce.

[. . .]

The Government's essential contention, *in fine*, is that we may determine here that § 922(q) is valid because possession of a firearm in a local school zone does indeed substantially affect interstate commerce. . . . The Government argues that possession of a firearm in a school zone may result in violent crime and that violent crime can be expected to affect the functioning of the national economy in two ways. First, the costs of violent crime are substantial, and, through the mechanism of insurance, those costs are spread throughout the population. . . . Second, violent crime reduces the willingness of individuals to travel to areas within the country that are perceived to be unsafe. . . . The Government also argues that the presence of guns in schools poses a substantial threat to the educational process by threatening the learning environment. A handicapped educational process, in turn, will result in a less productive citizenry. That, in turn, would have an adverse effect on the Nation's economic well-being. As a result, the Government argues that Congress could rationally have concluded that § 922(q) substantially affects interstate commerce.

We pause to consider the implications of the Government's arguments. The Government admits, under its "costs of crime" reasoning, that Congress could regulate not only all violent crime, but all activities that might lead to violent crime, regardless of how tenuously they relate to interstate commerce. . . . Similarly, under the Government's "national productivity" reasoning, Congress could regulate any activity that it found was related to the economic productivity of individual citizens: family law (including marriage, divorce, and child custody), for example. Under the theories that the Government presents in support of § 922(q), it is difficult to perceive any limitation on federal power, even in areas such as criminal law enforcement or education where States historically have been sovereign. Thus, if we were to accept the Government's arguments, we are hard pressed to posit any activity by an individual that Congress is without power to regulate.

[. . .]

JUSTICE BREYER focuses, for the most part, on the threat that firearm possession in and near schools poses to the educational process and the potential economic consequences flowing from that threat. . . . This analysis would be equally applicable, if not more so, to subjects such as family law and direct regulation of education.

For instance, if Congress can, pursuant to its Commerce Clause power, regulate activities that adversely affect the learning environment, then, *a fortiori*, it also can regulate the educational process directly. Congress could determine that a school's curriculum has a "significant" effect on the extent of classroom learning. As a result, Congress could mandate a federal curriculum for local elementary and secondary schools because what is taught in local schools has a significant "effect on classroom learning," and that, in turn, has a substantial effect on interstate commerce.

[. . .]

Admittedly, a determination whether an intrastate activity is commercial or noncommercial may in some cases result in legal uncertainty. But, so long as Congress' authority is limited to those powers enumerated in the Constitution, and so long as those enumerated powers are interpreted as having judicially enforceable outer limits, congressional legislation under the Commerce Clause always will engender "legal uncertainty."

[. . .]

These are not precise formulations, and in the nature of things they cannot be. But we think they point the way to a correct decision of this case. The possession of a gun in a local school zone is in no sense an economic activity that might, through repetition elsewhere, substantially affect any sort of interstate commerce. Respondent was a local student at a local school; there is no indication that he had recently moved in interstate commerce, and there is no requirement that his possession of the firearm have any concrete tie to interstate commerce.

[. . .]

JUSTICE BREYER, with whom JUSTICE STEVENS, JUSTICE SOUTER, and JUSTICE GINSBURG join, dissenting.

The issue in this case is whether the Commerce Clause authorizes Congress to enact a statute that makes it a crime to possess a gun in, or near, a school. 18 U.S.C. § 922(q)(1)(A). . . . In my view, the statute falls well within the scope of the commerce power as this Court has understood that power over the last half century.

[. . .]

[I]n determining whether a local activity will likely have a significant effect upon interstate commerce, a court must consider, not the effect of an individual act (a single instance of gun possession), but rather the cumulative effect of all similar instances (*i. e.*, the effect of all guns possessed in or near schools). . . .

[T]he Constitution requires us to judge the connection between a regulated activity and interstate commerce, not directly, but at one remove. Courts must give Congress a degree of leeway in determining the existence of a significant factual connection between the regulated activity and interstate commerce—both because the Constitution delegates the commerce power directly to Congress and because the determination requires an empirical judgment of a kind that a legislature is more likely than a court to make with accuracy. . . . Thus, the specific question before us, as the Court recognizes, is not whether the "regulated activity sufficiently affected interstate commerce," but, rather, whether Congress could have had "*a rational basis*" for so concluding.

[. . .]

Applying these principles to the case at hand, we must ask whether Congress could have had a *rational basis* for finding a significant (or substantial) connection between gun-related school violence and interstate commerce. Or, to put the question in the language of the *explicit* finding that Congress made when it amended this law in 1994: Could Congress rationally have found that "violent crime in school zones," through its effect on the "quality of education," significantly (or substantially) affects "interstate" or "foreign commerce"?. . . Numerous reports and studies—generated both inside and outside government—make clear that Congress could reasonably have found the empirical connection that its law, implicitly or explicitly, asserts. . . .

[. . .]

Having found that guns in schools significantly undermine the quality of education in our Nation's classrooms, Congress could also have found, given the effect of education upon interstate and foreign commerce, that gun-related violence in and around schools is a commercial, as well as a human, problem. Education, although far more than a matter of economics, has long been inextricably intertwined with the Nation's economy.

[. . .]

In recent years the link between secondary education and business has strengthened, becoming both more direct and more important. Scholars on the subject report that technological changes and innovations in management techniques have altered the nature of the workplace so that more jobs now demand greater educational skills. . . .

Finally, there is evidence that, today more than ever, many firms base their location decisions upon the presence, or absence, of a work force with a basic education.

[. . .]

The economic links I have just sketched seem fairly obvious. Why then is it not equally obvious, in light of those links, that a widespread, serious, and substantial physical threat to teaching and learning *also* substantially threatens the commerce to which that teaching and learning is inextricably tied? That is to say, guns in the hands of six percent of inner-city high school students and gun-related violence throughout a city's schools must threaten the trade and commerce that those schools support. The only question, then, is whether the latter threat is (to use the majority's terminology) "substantial." The evidence of (1) the *extent* of the gun-related violence problem, see *supra*, at 619, (2) the *extent* of the resulting negative effect on classroom learning, see *ibid.*, and (3) the *extent* of the consequent negative commercial effects, see *supra*, at 620–622, when taken together, indicate a threat to trade and commerce that is "substantial." At the very least, Congress could rationally have concluded that the links are "substantial."

[. . .]

In sum, a holding that the particular statute before us falls within the commerce power would not expand the scope of that Clause. Rather, it simply would apply pre-existing law to changing economic circumstances. . . . It would recognize that, in today's economic world, gun-related violence near the classroom makes a significant difference to our economic, as well as our social, well-being.

[. . .]

Respectfully, I dissent.

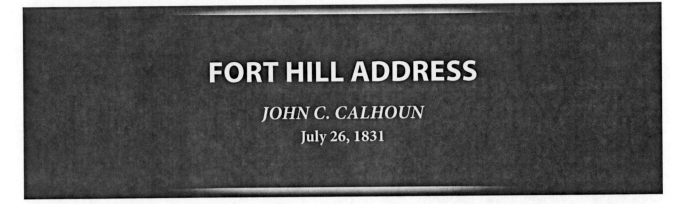

FORT HILL ADDRESS

JOHN C. CALHOUN
July 26, 1831

The question of the relation which the States and General Government bear to each other is not one of recent origin. From the commencement of our system, it has divided public sentiment. Even in the Convention, while the Constitution was struggling into existence, there were two parties as to what this relation should be, whose different sentiments constituted no small impediment in forming that instrument. After the General Government went into operation, experience soon proved that the question had not terminated with the labors of the Convention. The great struggle that preceded the political revolution of 1801, which brought Mr. Jefferson into power, turned essentially on it; and the doctrines and arguments on both sides were embodied and ably sustained—on the one, in the Virginia and Kentucky Resolutions, and the Report to the Virginia Legislature—and on the other, in the replies of the Legislature of Massachusetts and some of the other States. . . .

The great and leading principle is, that the General Government emanated from the people of the several States, forming distinct political communities, and acting in their separate and sovereign capacity, and not from all of the people forming one aggregate political community; that the Constitution of the United States is, in fact, a compact, to which each State is a party, in the character already described; and that the several States, or parties, have a right to judge of its infractions; and in case of a deliberate, palpable, and dangerous exercise of power not delegated, they have the right, in the last resort, to use the language of the Virginia Resolutions, "to interpose for arresting the progress of the evil, and for maintaining, within their respective limits, the authorities, rights, and liberties appertaining to them." This right of interposition, thus solemnly asserted by the State of Virginia, be it called what it may—State-right, veto, nullification, or by any other name—I conceive to be the fundamental principle of our system, resting on facts historically as certain as our revolution itself, and deductions as simple and demonstrative as that of any political, or moral truth whatever; and I firmly believe that on its recognition depend the stability and safety of our political institutions.

I am not ignorant, that those opposed to the doctrine have always, now and formerly, regarded it in a very different light, as anarchical and revolutionary. Could I believe such, in fact, to be its tendency, to me it would be no recommendation. I yield to none, I trust, in a deep and sincere attachment to our political institutions and the union of these States. I never breathed an opposite sentiment; but, on the contrary, I have ever considered them the great instruments of preserving our liberty, and promoting the happiness of ourselves and our posterity; and next to these I have ever held them most dear. Nearly half my life has been passed in the service of the Union, and whatever public reputation I have acquired is indissolubly identified with it. To be too national has, indeed, been considered by many, even of my friends, to be my greatest political fault. With these strong feelings of attachment, I have examined, with the utmost care, the bearing of the doctrine in question; and, so far from

SOURCE: John Calhoun, *Fort Hill Address,* 1831

anarchical or revolutionary, I solemnly believe it to be the only solid foundation of our system, and of the Union itself; and that the opposite doctrine, which denies to the States the right of protecting their reserved powers, and which would vest in the General Government (it matters not through what department), the right of determining, exclusively and finally, the powers delegated to it, is incompatible with the sovereignty of the States, and of the Constitution itself, considered as the basis of a Federal Union. As strong as this language is, it is not stronger than that used by the illustrious Jefferson, who said, to give to the General Government the final and exclusive right to judge of its powers, is to make "its discretion, and not the Constitution, the measure of its powers;" and that, "in all cases of compact between parties having no common judge, each party has an equal right to judge for itself, as well of the infraction as of the mode and measure of redress." Language cannot be more explicit; nor can higher authority be adduced. . . .

It has been well said by one of the most sagacious men of antiquity, that the object of a constitution is, to *restrain the government, as that of laws* is to restrain *individuals.* The remark is correct; nor is it less true, where the government is vested in a majority, than where it is in a single or a few individuals—in a republic, than a monarchy or aristocracy. No one can have a higher respect for the maxim that the majority ought to govern than I have, taken in its proper sense, subject to the restrictions imposed by the Constitution, and confined to objects in which every portion of the community have similar interests; but it is a great error to suppose, as many do, that the right of a majority to govern is a natural and not a conventional right; and, therefore absolute and unlimited. By nature, every individual has the right to govern himself; and governments, whether founded on majorities or minorities, must derive their right from the assent, expressed or implied, of the governed, and be subject to such limitations as they may impose. Where the interests are the same, that is, where the laws that may benefit one, will benefit all, or the reverse, it is just and proper to place them under the control of the majority; but where they are dissimilar, so that the law that may benefit one portion may be ruinous to another, it would be, on the contrary, unjust and absurd to subject them to its will; and such, I conceive to be the theory on which our Constitution rests. . . .

So numerous and diversified are the interests of our country, that they could not be fairly represented in a single government, organized so as to give to each great and leading interest, a separate and distinct voice, as in governments to which I have referred. A plan was adopted better suited to our situation, but perfectly novel in its character. The powers of government were divided, not, as heretofore, in reference to classes, but geographically. One General Government was formed for the whole, to which were delegated all the powers supposed to be necessary to regulate the interests common to all the States, leaving others subject to the separate control of the States, being, from their local and peculiar character, such, that they could not be subject to the will of a majority of the whole Union, without the certain hazard of injustice and oppression. It was thus that the interests of the whole were subjected, as they ought to be, to the will of the whole, while the peculiar and local interests were left under the control of the States separately, to whose custody only, they could be safely confided. This distribution of power, settled solemnly by a constitutional compact, to which all the States are parties, constitutes the peculiar character and excellence of our political system. It is truly and emphatically *American, without example or parallel.*

To realize its perfection, we must view the General Government and those of the States as a whole, each in its proper sphere, sovereign and independent; each perfectly adapted to its respective objects; the States acting separately, representing and protecting the local and peculiar interests; and acting jointly through one General Government, with the weight respectively assigned to each by the

Constitution, representing and protecting the interest of the whole; and thus perfecting, by an admirable but simple arrangement, the great principle of representation and responsibility, without which no government can be free or just. To preserve this sacred distribution, as originally settled, by coercing each to move in its prescribed orbit, is the great and difficult problem, on the solution of which, the duration of our Constitution, of our Union, and, in all probability, our liberty depends. How is this to be effected? . . .

Whenever separate and dissimilar interests have been separately represented in any government; whenever the sovereign power has been divided in its exercise, the experience and wisdom of ages have devised but one mode by which such political organization can be preserved—the mode adopted in England, and by all governments, ancient and modern, blessed with constitutions deserving to be called free—to give to each co-estate the right to judge of its powers, with a negative or veto on the acts of the others, in order to protect against encroachments, the interests it particularly represents: a principle which all of our constitutions recognize in the distribution of power among their respective departments, as essential to maintain the independence of each; but which, to all who will duly reflect on the subject, must appear far more essential, for the same object, in that great and fundamental distribution of powers between the states and General Government. So essential is the principle, that, to withhold the right from either, where the sovereign power is divided, is, in fact, *to annul the division* itself, and to *consolidate*, in the one left in the exclusive possession of the right, *all* powers of government; for it is not possible to distinguish, practically, between a government having all power, and one having the right to take what powers it pleases. Nor does it in the least vary the principle, whether the distribution of power be between co-estates, as in England, or between distinctly organized, but connected governments, as with us. The reason is the same in both cases, while the necessity is greater in our case, as the danger of conflict is greater where the interests of a society are divided geographically than in any other, as has already been shown. . . .

I do not deny that a power of so high a nature may be abused by a State; but when I reflect that the States unanimously called the General Government into existence with all of its powers, which they freely delegated on their part, under the conviction that their common peace, safety, and prosperity required it; that they are bound together by a common origin, and the recollection of common suffering and common triumph in the great and splendid achievement of their independence; and that the strongest feelings of our nature, and among them the love of national power and distinction, are on the side of the Union; it does seem to me that the fear which would strip the States of their sovereignty, and degrade them, in fact, to mere dependent corporations, lest they should abuse a right indispensable to the peaceable protection of those interests which they reserved under their own peculiar guardianship when they created the General Government, is unnatural and unreasonable. If those who voluntarily created the system cannot be trusted to preserve it, what power can?

So, far from extreme danger, I hold that there never was a free State in which this great conservative principle, indispensable to all, was ever so safely lodged. In others, when the co-estates representing the dissimilar and conflicting interests of the community came into contact, the only alternative was compromise, submission, or force. Not so in ours. Should the General Government and a State come into conflict, we have a higher remedy: the power which called the General Government into existence, which gave it all of its authority, and can enlarge, contract, or abolish its powers at its pleasure, may be invoked. The States themselves may be appealed to—three-fourths of which, in fact, form a power, whose decrees are the Constitution itself, and whose voice can silence all discontent. The utmost extent, then, of the power is, that a State, acting in its sovereign capacity, as one of the parties to the constitutional compact, may compel the Government, created by that compact, to submit a question touching its infraction, to the parties who created it; to avoid the supposed dangers of which, it is proposed to resort to the novel, the hazardous, and, I must add, fatal project of giving to the General Government the sole and final right of interpreting the Constitution—thereby reversing the whole system, making that instrument the creature of its will, instead of a rule of action impressed on it at its creation, and annihilating, in fact, the authority which imposed it, and from which the Government itself derives its existence. . . .

Against these conclusive arguments, as they seem to me, it is objected, that, if one of the parties has the right to judge of infractions of the Constitution, so has the other; and that, consequently, in cases of contested powers between a State and the General Government, each would have a right to maintain its opinion, as is the case when sovereign powers differ in the construction of treaties or compacts; and that, of course, it would come to be a mere question of force. The error is in the assumption that the General Government is a party to the constitutional compact. The States, as has been shown, formed the compact, acting as Sovereign and independent communities. The General Government is but its creature; and though, in reality, a government, with all the rights and authority which belong to any other government, within the orbit of its powers, it is, nevertheless, a government emanating from a compact between sovereigns, and partaking, in its nature and object, of the character of a joint commission, appointed to superintend and administer the interests in which all are jointly concerned; but having, beyond its proper sphere, no more power than if it did not exist. To deny this would be to deny the most incontestable facts, and the clearest conclusions; while to acknowledge its truth is, to destroy utterly the objection that the appeal would be to force, in the case supposed. For if each party has a right to judge, then, under our system of government, the final cognizance of a question of contested power would be in the States, and not in the General Government. It would be the duty of the latter, as in all similar cases of a contest between one or more of the principals and a joint commission or agency, to refer the contest to the principals themselves. Such are the plain dictates of both reason and analogy. . . .

CHAPTER 4
CIVIL RIGHTS AND LIBERTIES

BROWN V. BOARD OF EDUCATION

SUPREME COURT OF THE UNITED STATES
347 U.S. 483 (1954)

MR. CHIEF JUSTICE WARREN delivered the opinion of the Court.

[1]

These cases come to us from the States of Kansas, South Carolina, Virginia, and Delaware. They are premised on different facts and different local conditions, but a common legal question justifies their consideration together in this consolidated opinion.

In each of the cases, minors of the Negro race, through their legal representatives, seek the aid of the courts in obtaining admission to the public schools of their community on a nonsegregated basis. In each instance, they had been denied admission to schools attended by white children under laws requiring or permitting segregation according to race. This segregation was alleged to deprive the plaintiffs of the equal protection of the laws under the Fourteenth Amendment. In each of the cases other than the Delaware case, a three-judge federal district court denied relief to the plaintiffs on the so-called "separate but equal" doctrine announced by this Court in *Plessy* v. *Ferguson*, 163 U.S. 537. Under that doctrine, equality of treatment is accorded when the races are provided substantially equal facilities, even though these facilities be separate. In the Delaware case, the Supreme Court of Delaware adhered to that doctrine, but ordered that the plaintiffs be admitted to the white schools because of their superiority to the Negro schools.

The plaintiffs contend that segregated public schools are not "equal" and cannot be made "equal," and that hence they are deprived of the equal protection of the laws. Because of the obvious importance of the question presented, the Court took jurisdiction. Argument was heard in the 1952 Term, and reargument was heard this Term on certain questions propounded by the Court.

Reargument was largely devoted to the circumstances surrounding the adoption of the Fourteenth Amendment in 1868. It covered exhaustively consideration of the Amendment in Congress, ratification by the states, then existing practices in racial segregation, and the views of proponents and opponents of the Amendment. This discussion and our own investigation convince us that, although these sources cast some light, it is not enough to resolve the problem with which we are faced. At best, they are inconclusive. The most avid proponents of the post-War Amendments undoubtedly intended them to remove all legal distinctions among "all persons born or naturalized in the United States." Their opponents, just as certainly, were antagonistic to both the letter and the spirit of the Amendments and wished them to have the most limited effect. What others in Congress and the state legislatures had in mind cannot be determined with any degree of certainty.

An additional reason for the inconclusive nature of the Amendment's history, with respect to segregated schools, is the status of public education at that time. In the South, the movement toward free common schools, supported by general taxation, had not yet taken hold. Education of white children was largely in the hands of private groups. Education of Negroes was almost nonexistent, and practically all of the race were illiterate. In fact, any education of Negroes was forbidden by law in some states. Today, in contrast, many Negroes have achieved outstanding success in the arts and sciences as well as in the business and professional world. It is true that public school education at the time of the Amendment had advanced further in the North, but the effect of the Amendment on Northern States was generally ignored in the congressional debates. Even in the North, the conditions of public education did not approximate those existing today. The curriculum was usually rudimentary; ungraded schools were common in rural areas; the school term was but three months a year in many states; and compulsory school attendance was virtually unknown. As a consequence, it is not surprising that there should be so little in the history of the Fourteenth Amendment relating to its intended effect on public education.

In the first cases in this Court construing the Fourteenth Amendment, decided shortly after its adoption, the Court interpreted it as proscribing all state-imposed discriminations against the Negro race.[5] The doctrine of "separate but equal" did not make its appearance in this Court until 1896 in the case of *Plessy* v. *Ferguson, supra*, involving not education but transportation. American courts have since labored with the doctrine for over half a century. In this Court, there have been six cases involving the "separate but equal" doctrine in the field of public education. In *Cumming* v. *County Board of Education*, 175 U.S. 528, and *Gong Lum* v. *Rice*, 275 U.S. 78, the validity of the doctrine itself was not challenged. In more recent cases, all on the graduate school level, inequality was found in that specific benefits enjoyed by white students were denied to Negro students of the same educational qualifications. . . . In none of these cases was it necessary to re-examine the doctrine to grant relief to the Negro plaintiff. [In] *Sweatt* v. *Painter*, the Court expressly reserved decision on the question whether *Plessy* v. *Ferguson* should be held inapplicable to public education.

In the instant cases, that question is directly presented. Here, unlike *Sweatt* v. *Painter*, there are findings below that the Negro and white schools involved have been equalized, or are being equalized, with respect to buildings, curricula, qualifications and salaries of teachers, and other "tangible" factors. Our decision, therefore, cannot turn on merely a comparison of these tangible factors in the Negro and white schools involved in each of the cases. We must look instead to the effect of segregation itself on public education.

[3]

In approaching this problem, we cannot turn the clock back to 1868 when the Amendment was adopted, or even to 1896 when *Plessy* v. *Ferguson* was written. We must consider public education in the light of its full development and its present place in American life throughout the Nation. Only in this way can it be determined if segregation in public schools deprives these plaintiffs of the equal protection of the laws.

[4]

Today, education is perhaps the most important function of state and local governments. Compulsory school attendance laws and the great expenditures for education both demonstrate our recognition of the importance of education to our democratic society. It is required in the performance of our most basic public responsibilities, even service in the armed forces. It is the very foundation of good citizenship. Today it is a principal instrument in awakening the child to cultural values, in preparing him for later professional training, and in helping him to adjust normally to his environment. In these days, it is doubtful that any child may reasonably be expected to succeed in life if he is denied the opportunity of an education. Such an opportunity, where the state has undertaken to provide it, is a right which must be made available to all on equal terms.

[5]

We come then to the question presented: Does segregation of children in public schools solely on the basis of race, even though the physical facilities and other "tangible" factors may be equal, deprive the children of the minority group of equal educational opportunities? We believe that it does.

In *Sweatt* v. *Painter, supra,* in finding that a segregated law school for Negroes could not provide them equal educational opportunities, this Court relied in large part on "those qualities which are incapable of objective measurement but which make for greatness in a law school." In *McLaurin* v. *Oklahoma State Regents, supra,* the Court, in requiring that a Negro admitted to a white graduate school be treated like all other students, again resorted to intangible considerations: ". . . his ability to study, to engage in discussions and exchange views with other students, and, in general, to learn his profession." Such considerations apply with added force to children in grade and high schools. To separate them from others of similar age and qualifications solely because of their race generates a feeling of inferiority as to their status in the community that may affect their hearts and minds in a way unlikely ever to be undone.

[. . .]

Whatever may have been the extent of psychological knowledge at the time of *Plessy* v. *Ferguson,* this finding is amply supported by modern authority.[11] Any language in *Plessy* v. *Ferguson* contrary to this finding is rejected.

> 11 K. B. Clark, Effect of Prejudice and Discrimination on Personality Development (Midcentury White House Conference on Children and Youth, 1950); Witmer and Kotinsky, Personality in the Making (1952), c. VI; Deutscher and Chein, The Psychological Effects of Enforced Segregation: A Survey of Social Science Opinion, 26 J. Psychol. 259 (1948); Chein, What are the Psychological Effects of Segregation Under Conditions of Equal Facilities?, 3 Int. J. Opinion and Attitude Res. 229 (1949); Brameld, Educational Costs, in Discrimination and National Welfare (MacIver, ed., 1949), 44–48; Frazier, The Negro in the United States (1949), 674–681. And see generally Myrdal, An American Dilemma (1944).

[6]

We conclude that in the field of public education the doctrine of "separate but equal" has no place. Separate educational facilities are inherently unequal. Therefore, we hold that the plaintiffs and others similarly situated for whom the actions have been brought are, by reason of the segregation complained of, deprived of the equal protection of the laws guaranteed by the Fourteenth Amendment. . . .

DISTRICT OF COLUMBIA V. HELLER

SUPREME COURT OF THE UNITED STATES

554 U.S. 570 (2008)

Justice Scalia delivered the opinion of the Court.

We consider whether a District of Columbia prohibition on the possession of usable handguns in the home violates the Second Amendment to the Constitution.

I

The District of Columbia generally prohibits the possession of handguns. It is a crime to carry an unregistered firearm, and the registration of handguns is prohibited. Wholly apart from that prohibition, no person may carry a handgun without a license, but the chief of police may issue licenses for 1-year periods. District of Columbia law also requires residents to keep their lawfully owned firearms, such as registered long guns, "unloaded and dissembled or bound by a trigger lock or similar device" unless they are located in a place of business or are being used for lawful recreational activities.

Respondent Dick Heller is a D. C. special police officer authorized to carry a handgun while on duty at the Thurgood Marshall Judiciary Building. He applied for a registration certificate for a handgun that he wished to keep at home, but the District refused.

[. . .]

II

We turn first to the meaning of the Second Amendment.

A

The Second Amendment provides: "A well regulated Militia, being necessary to the security of a free State, the right of the people to keep and bear Arms, shall not be infringed." In interpreting this text, we are guided by the principle that "[t]he Constitution was written to be understood by the voters; its words and phrases were used in their normal and ordinary as distinguished from technical meaning. . . ." Normal meaning may of course include an idiomatic meaning, but it excludes secret or technical meanings that would not have been known to ordinary citizens in the founding generation.

The two sides in this case have set out very different interpretations of the Amendment. Petitioners and today's dissenting Justices believe that it protects only the right to possess and carry a firearm in connection with militia service. Respondent argues that it protects an individual right to possess a firearm unconnected with service in a militia, and to use that arm for traditionally lawful purposes, such as self-defense within the home.

The Second Amendment is naturally divided into two parts: its prefatory clause and its operative clause. The former does not limit the latter grammatically, but rather announces a purpose. The Amendment could be rephrased, "Because a well regulated Militia is necessary to the security of a free State, the right of the people to keep and bear Arms shall not be infringed." Although this structure of the Second Amendment is unique in our Constitution, other legal documents of the founding era, particularly individual-rights provisions of state constitutions, commonly included a prefatory statement of purpose.

Logic demands that there be a link between the stated purpose and the command. The Second Amendment would be nonsensical if it read, "A well regulated Militia, being necessary to the security of a free State, the right of the people to petition for redress of grievances shall not be infringed." That requirement of logical connection may cause a prefatory clause to resolve an ambiguity in the operative clause. . . . But apart from that clarifying function, a prefatory clause does not limit or expand the scope of the operative clause. Therefore, while we will begin our textual analysis with the operative clause, we will return to the prefatory clause to ensure that our reading of the operative clause is consistent with the announced purpose.

[. . .]

1. Operative Clause.

[. . .]

Putting all of these textual elements together, we find that they guarantee the individual right to possess and carry weapons in case of confrontation. This meaning is strongly confirmed by the historical background of the Second Amendment. We look to this because it has always been widely understood that the Second Amendment, like the First and Fourth Amendments, codified a *pre-existing* right. The very text of the Second Amendment implicitly recognizes the pre-existence of the right and declares only that it "shall not be infringed."

[. . .]

There seems to us no doubt, on the basis of both text and history, that the Second Amendment conferred an individual right to keep and bear arms. Of course the right was not unlimited, just as the First Amendment's right of free speech was not. Thus, we do not read the Second Amendment to protect the right of citizens to carry arms for *any sort* of confrontation, just as we do not read the First Amendment to protect the right of citizens to speak for *any purpose*. Before turning to limitations upon the individual right, however, we must determine whether the prefatory clause of the Second Amendment comports with our interpretation of the operative clause.

2. Prefatory Clause.

The prefatory clause reads: "A well regulated Militia, being necessary to the security of a free State . . . ."

a. "Well-Regulated Militia." In *United States* v. *Miller*, 307 U.S. 174 (1939), we explained that "the Militia comprised all males physically capable of acting in concert for the common defense." That definition comports with founding-era sources.

Petitioners take a seemingly narrower view of the militia, stating that "[m]ilitias are the state-and congressionally-regulated military forces described in the Militia Clauses (art. I, § 8, cls. 15–16)." Although we agree with petitioners' interpretive assumption that "militia" means the same thing in Article I and the Second Amendment, we believe that petitioners identify the wrong thing, namely, the organized militia. Unlike armies and navies, which Congress is given the power to create ("to raise . . . Armies"; "to provide . . . a Navy," Art. I, § 8, cls. 12–13), the militia is assumed by Article I already to be *in existence*. Congress is given the power to "provide for calling forth the Militia," § 8, cl. 15; and the power not to create, but to "organiz[e]" it—and not to organize "a" militia, which is what one would expect if the militia were to be a federal creation, but to organize "the" militia, connoting a body already in existence, cl. 16.

[. . .]

Finally, the adjective "well-regulated" implies nothing more than the imposition of proper discipline and training. . ..

3. Relationship Between Prefatory Clause and Operative Clause.

We reach the question, then: Does the preface fit with an operative clause that creates an individual right to keep and bear arms?

[. . .]

[T]he Second Amendment's prefatory clause announces the purpose for which the right was codified: to prevent elimination of the militia. The prefatory clause does not suggest that preserving the militia was the only reason Americans valued the ancient right; most undoubtedly thought it even more important for self-defense and hunting. But the threat that the new Federal Government would destroy the citizens' militia by taking away their arms was the reason that right—unlike some other English rights—was codified in a written Constitution. Justice Breyer's assertion that individual self-defense is merely a "subsidiary interest" of the right to keep and bear arms . . . is profoundly mistaken. He bases that assertion solely upon the prologue—but that can only show that self-defense had little to do with the right's *codification;* it was the *central component* of the right itself.

Besides ignoring the historical reality that the Second Amendment was not intended to lay down a "novel principl[e]" but rather codified a right "inherited from our English ancestors," petitioners' interpretation does not even achieve the narrower purpose that prompted codification of the right. If, as they believe, the Second Amendment right is no more than the right to keep and use weapons as a member of an organized militia—if, that is, the *organized* militia is the sole institutional beneficiary of the Second Amendment's guarantee—it does not assure the existence of a "citizens' militia" as a safeguard against tyranny. For Congress retains plenary authority to organize the militia, which must include the authority to say who will belong to the organized force. . . . Thus, if petitioners are correct, the Second Amendment protects citizens' right to use a gun in an organization from which Congress has plenary authority to exclude them. It guarantees a select militia of the sort the Stuart kings found useful, but not the people's militia that was the concern of the founding generation.

B

Our interpretation is confirmed by analogous arms-bearing rights in state constitutions that preceded and immediately followed adoption of the Second Amendment. Four States adopted analogues to the Federal Second Amendment in the period between independence and the ratification of the Bill of Rights. . . .

The historical narrative that petitioners must endorse would thus treat the Federal Second Amendment as an odd outlier, protecting a right unknown in state constitutions or at English common law, based on little more than an overreading of the prefatory clause. . . .

III

[N]othing in our opinion should be taken to cast doubt on longstanding prohibitions on the possession of firearms by felons and the mentally ill, or laws forbidding the carrying of firearms in sensitive places such as schools and government buildings, or laws imposing conditions and qualifications on the commercial sale of arms. . . .

IV

We turn finally to the law at issue here. As we have said, the law totally bans handgun possession in the home. It also requires that any lawful firearm in the home be disassembled or bound by a trigger lock at all times, rendering it inoperable.

As the quotations earlier in this opinion demonstrate, the inherent right of self-defense has been central to the Second Amendment right. The handgun ban amounts to a prohibition of an entire class of "arms" that is overwhelmingly chosen by American society for that lawful purpose. The prohibition extends, moreover, to the home, where the need for defense of self, family, and property is most acute. Under any of the standards of scrutiny that we have applied to enumerated constitutional rights,[27] banning from the home "the most preferred firearm in the nation to 'keep' and use for protection of one's home and family," would fail constitutional muster.

[. . .]

It is no answer to say, as petitioners do, that it is permissible to ban the possession of handguns so long as the possession of other firearms (*i.e.*, long guns) is allowed. It is enough to note, as we have observed, that the American people have considered the handgun to be the quintessential self-defense weapon. There are many reasons that a citizen may prefer a handgun for home defense: It is easier to store in a location that is readily accessible in an emergency; it cannot easily be redirected or wrestled away by an attacker; it is easier to use for those without the upper-body strength to lift and aim a long gun; it can be pointed at a burglar with one hand while the other hand dials the police. Whatever the reason, handguns are the most popular weapon chosen by Americans for self-defense in the home, and a complete prohibition of their use is invalid.

We must also address the District's requirement (as applied to respondent's handgun) that firearms in the home be rendered and kept inoperable at all times. This makes it impossible for citizens to use them for the core lawful purpose of self-defense and is hence unconstitutional.

[. . .]

In sum, we hold that the District's ban on handgun possession in the home violates the Second Amendment, as does its prohibition against rendering any lawful firearm in the home operable for the purpose of immediate self-defense. Assuming that Heller is not disqualified from the exercise of Second Amendment rights, the District must permit him to register his handgun and must issue him a license to carry it in the home.

* * *

We are aware of the problem of handgun violence in this country, and we take seriously the concerns raised by the many *amici* who believe that prohibition of handgun ownership is a solution. The Constitution leaves the District of Columbia a variety of tools for combating that problem, including some measures regulating handguns. . . . But the enshrinement of constitutional rights necessarily takes certain policy choices off the table. These include the absolute prohibition of handguns held and used for self-defense in the home. Undoubtedly some think that the Second Amendment is outmoded in a society where our standing army is the pride of our Nation, where well-trained police forces provide personal security, and where gun violence is a serious problem. That is perhaps debatable, but what is not debatable is that it is not the role of this Court to pronounce the Second Amendment extinct.

Justice Stevens, with whom Justice Souter, Justice Ginsburg, and Justice Breyer join, dissenting.

The question presented by this case is not whether the Second Amendment protects a "collective right" or an "individual right." Surely it protects a right that can be enforced by individuals. But a conclusion that the Second Amendment protects an individual right does not tell us anything about the scope of that right.

Guns are used to hunt, for self-defense, to commit crimes, for sporting activities, and to perform military duties. The Second Amendment plainly does not protect the right to use a gun to rob a bank; it is equally clear that it *does* encompass the right to use weapons for certain military purposes. Whether it also protects the right to possess and use guns for nonmilitary purposes like hunting and personal self-defense is the question presented by this case. The text of the Amendment, its history, and our decision in *United States* v. *Miller*, 307 U.S. 174 (1939), provide a clear answer to that question.

The Second Amendment was adopted to protect the right of the people of each of the several States to maintain a well-regulated militia. It was a response to concerns raised during the ratification of the Constitution that the power of Congress to disarm the state militias and create a national standing army posed an intolerable threat to the sovereignty of the several States. Neither the text of the Amendment nor the arguments advanced by its proponents evidenced the slightest interest in limiting any legislature's authority to regulate private civilian uses of firearms. Specifically, there is no indication that the Framers of the Amendment intended to enshrine the common-law right of self-defense in the Constitution.

In 1934, Congress enacted the National Firearms Act, the first major federal firearms law. Sustaining an indictment under the Act, this Court held that, "[i]n the absence of any evidence tending to show that possession or use of a 'shotgun having a barrel of less than eighteen inches in length' at this time has some reasonable relationship to the preservation or efficiency of a well regulated militia, we cannot say that the Second Amendment guarantees the right to keep and bear such an instrument." *Miller*, 307 U.S., at 178. The view of the Amendment we took in *Miller*—that it protects the right to keep and bear arms for certain military purposes, but that it does not curtail the Legislature's power to regulate the nonmilitary use and ownership of weapons—is both the most natural reading of the Amendment's text and the interpretation most faithful to the history of its adoption.

[. . .]

I

The text of the Second Amendment is brief. It provides: "A well regulated Militia, being necessary to the security of a free State, the right of the people to keep and bear Arms, shall not be infringed."

Three portions of that text merit special focus: the introductory language defining the Amendment's purpose, the class of persons encompassed within its reach, and the unitary nature of the right that it protects.

"A well regulated Militia, being necessary to the security of a free State"

The preamble to the Second Amendment makes three important points. It identifies the preservation of the militia as the Amendment's purpose; it explains that the militia is necessary to the security of a free State; and it recognizes that the militia must be "well regulated." In all three respects it is comparable to provisions in several State Declarations of Rights that were adopted roughly contemporaneously with the Declaration of Independence. Those state provisions highlight the importance members of the founding generation attached to the maintenance of state militias; they also underscore the profound fear shared by many in that era of the dangers posed by standing armies. While the need for state militias has not been a matter of significant public interest for almost two centuries, that fact should not obscure the contemporary concerns that animated the Framers.

The parallels between the Second Amendment and these state declarations, and the Second Amendment's omission of any statement of purpose related to the right to use firearms for hunting or personal self-defense, is especially striking in light of the fact that the Declarations of Rights of Pennsylvania and Vermont *did* expressly protect such civilian uses at the time. . . . The contrast between those two declarations and the Second Amendment reinforces the clear statement of purpose announced in the Amendment's preamble. It confirms that the Framers' single-minded focus in crafting the constitutional guarantee "to keep and bear Arms" was on military uses of firearms, which they viewed in the context of service in state militias.

The preamble thus both sets forth the object of the Amendment and informs the meaning of the remainder of its text. Such text should not be treated as mere surplusage, for "[i]t cannot be presumed that any clause in the constitution is intended to be without effect." *Marbury* v. *Madison,* 5 U.S. 137 (1803).

[. . .]

*   *   *

When each word in the text is given full effect, the Amendment is most naturally read to secure to the people a right to use and possess arms in conjunction with service in a well-regulated militia. So far as appears, no more than that was contemplated by its drafters or is encompassed within its terms. Even if the meaning of the text were genuinely susceptible to more than one interpretation, the burden would remain on those advocating a departure from the purpose identified in the preamble and from settled law to come forward with persuasive new arguments or evidence. The textual analysis offered by respondent and embraced by the Court falls far short of sustaining that heavy burden. And the Court's emphatic reliance on the claim "that the Second Amendment . . . codified a *pre-existing* right," is of course beside the point because the right to keep and bear arms for service in a state militia was also a pre-existing right.

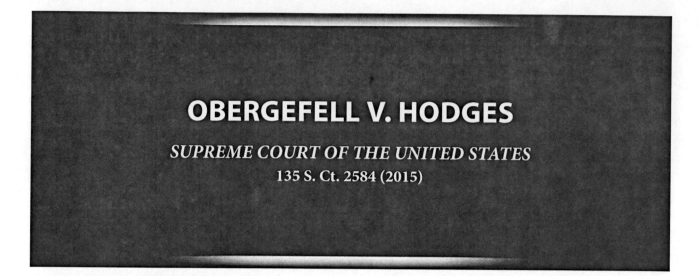

OBERGEFELL V. HODGES

SUPREME COURT OF THE UNITED STATES
135 S. Ct. 2584 (2015)

Justice Kennedy delivered the opinion of the Court.

The Constitution promises liberty to all within its reach, a liberty that includes certain specific rights that allow persons, within a lawful realm, to define and express their identity. The petitioners in these cases seek to find that liberty by marrying someone of the same sex and having their marriages deemed lawful on the same terms and conditions as marriages between persons of the opposite sex.

I

These cases come from Michigan, Kentucky, Ohio, and Tennessee, States that define marriage as a union between one man and one woman. The petitioners are 14 same-sex couples and two men whose same-sex partners are deceased. The respondents are state officials responsible for enforcing the laws in question. The petitioners claim the respondents violate the Fourteenth Amendment by denying them the right to marry or to have their marriages, lawfully performed in another State, given full recognition. . . .

This Court granted review, limited to two questions. The first, presented by the cases from Michigan and Kentucky, is whether the Fourteenth Amendment requires a State to license a marriage between two people of the same sex. The second, presented by the cases from Ohio, Tennessee, and, again, Kentucky, is whether the Fourteenth Amendment requires a State to recognize a same-sex marriage licensed and performed in a State which does grant that right.

II

Before addressing the principles and precedents that govern these cases, it is appropriate to note the history of the subject now before the Court.

A

[. . .]

Petitioner James Obergefell, a plaintiff in the Ohio case, met John Arthur over two decades ago. They fell in love and started a life together, establishing a lasting, committed relation. In 2011, however, Arthur was diagnosed with amyotrophic lateral sclerosis, or ALS. This debilitating disease is progressive, with no known cure. Two years ago, Obergefell and Arthur decided to commit to one another, resolving to marry before Arthur died. To fulfill their mutual promise, they traveled from Ohio to Maryland, where same-sex marriage was legal. It was difficult for Arthur to move, and so the couple were wed inside a medical transport plane as it remained on the tarmac in Baltimore. Three months later, Arthur died. Ohio law does not permit Obergefell to be listed as the surviving spouse on Arthur's death certificate. By statute, they must remain strangers even in death, a state-imposed separation Obergefell deems "hurtful for the rest of time." He brought suit to be shown as the surviving spouse on Arthur's death certificate.

April DeBoer and Jayne Rowse are co-plaintiffs in the case from Michigan. They celebrated a commitment ceremony to honor their permanent relation in 2007. They both work as nurses, DeBoer in a neonatal unit and Rowse in an emergency unit. In 2009, DeBoer and Rowse fostered and then adopted a baby boy. Later that same year, they welcomed another son into their family. The new baby, born prematurely and abandoned by his biological mother, required around-the-clock care. The next year, a baby girl with special needs joined their family. Michigan, however, permits only opposite-sex married couples or single individuals to adopt, so each child can have only one woman as his or her legal parent. If an emergency were to arise, schools and hospitals may treat the three children as if they had only one parent. And, were tragedy to befall either DeBoer or Rowse, the other would have no legal rights over the children she had not been permitted to adopt. This couple seeks relief from the continuing uncertainty their unmarried status creates in their lives.

Army Reserve Sergeant First Class Ijpe DeKoe and his partner Thomas Kostura, co-plaintiffs in the Tennessee case, fell in love. In 2011, DeKoe received orders to deploy to Afghanistan. Before leaving, he and Kostura married in New York. A week later, DeKoe began his deployment, which lasted for almost a year. When he returned, the two settled in Tennessee, where DeKoe works full-time for the Army Reserve. Their lawful marriage is stripped from them whenever they reside in Tennessee, returning and disappearing as they travel across state lines. DeKoe, who served this Nation to preserve the freedom the Constitution protects, must endure a substantial burden.

The cases now before the Court involve other petitioners as well, each with their own experiences. Their stories reveal that they seek not to denigrate marriage but rather to live their lives, or honor their spouses' memory, joined by its bond.

B

The ancient origins of marriage confirm its centrality, but it has not stood in isolation from developments in law and society. The history of marriage is one of both continuity and change. That institution—even as confined to opposite-sex relations—has evolved over time.

For example, marriage was once viewed as an arrangement by the couple's parents based on political, religious, and financial concerns; but by the time of the Nation's founding it was understood to be a voluntary contract between a man and a woman. Under the centuries-old doctrine of coverture, a married man and woman were treated by the State as a single, male-dominated legal entity. As women gained legal, political, and property rights, and as society began to understand that women have their own equal dignity, the law of coverture was abandoned. These and other developments in the institution of marriage over the past centuries were not mere superficial changes. Rather, they worked deep transformations in its structure, affecting aspects of marriage long viewed by many as essential.

These new insights have strengthened, not weakened, the institution of marriage. Indeed, changed understandings of marriage are characteristic of a Nation where new dimensions of freedom become apparent to new generations, often through perspectives that begin in pleas or protests and then are considered in the political sphere and the judicial process.

This dynamic can be seen in the Nation's experiences with the rights of gays and lesbians. . . .

For much of the 20th century, moreover, homosexuality was treated as an illness. . . In the late 20th century, following substantial cultural and political developments, same-sex couples began to lead more open and public lives and to establish families. This development was followed by a quite extensive discussion of the issue in both governmental and private sectors and by a shift in public attitudes toward greater tolerance. As a result, questions about the rights of gays and lesbians soon reached the courts, where the issue could be discussed in the formal discourse of the law.

III

Under the Due Process Clause of the Fourteenth Amendment, no State shall "deprive any person of life, liberty, or property, without due process of law." The fundamental liberties protected by this Clause include most of the rights enumerated in the Bill of Rights. In addition these liberties extend to certain personal choices central to individual dignity and autonomy, including intimate choices that define personal identity and beliefs.

The identification and protection of fundamental rights is an enduring part of the judicial duty to interpret the Constitution. That responsibility, however, "has not been reduced to any formula." Rather, it requires courts to exercise reasoned judgment in identifying interests of the person so fundamental that the State must accord them its respect. That process is guided by many of the same considerations relevant to analysis of other constitutional provisions that set forth broad principles rather than specific requirements. History and tradition guide and discipline this inquiry but do not set its outer boundaries. That method respects our history and learns from it without allowing the past alone to rule the present.

[. . .]

Applying these established tenets, the Court has long held the right to marry is protected by the Constitution. In *Loving* v. *Virginia*, 388 U.S. 1, 12 (1967), which invalidated bans on interracial unions, a unanimous Court held marriage is "one of the vital personal rights essential to the orderly pursuit of happiness by free men. . . ." Over time and in other contexts, the Court has reiterated that the right to marry is fundamental under the Due Process Clause. . . .

It cannot be denied that this Court's cases describing the right to marry presumed a relationship involving opposite-sex partners. The Court, like many institutions, has made assumptions defined by the world and time of which it is a part. . . .

Still, there are other, more instructive precedents. This Court's cases have expressed constitutional principles of broader reach. In defining the right to marry these cases have identified essential attributes of that right based in history, tradition, and other constitutional liberties inherent in this intimate bond. See, *e.g., Lawrence v. Texas*, 539 U.S., at 574 (2003).

This analysis compels the conclusion that same-sex couples may exercise the right to marry. The four principles and traditions to be discussed demonstrate that the reasons marriage is fundamental under the Constitution apply with equal force to same-sex couples.

A first premise of the Court's relevant precedents is that the right to personal choice regarding marriage is inherent in the concept of individual autonomy. This abiding connection between marriage and liberty is why *Loving* invalidated interracial marriage bans under the Due Process Clause. . . . Like choices concerning contraception, family relationships, procreation, and childrearing, all of which are protected by the Constitution, decisions concerning marriage are among the most intimate that an individual can make. . . .

The nature of marriage is that, through its enduring bond, two persons together can find other freedoms, such as expression, intimacy, and spirituality. This is true for all persons, whatever their sexual orientation. . . .

A second principle in this Court's jurisprudence is that the right to marry is fundamental because it supports a two-person union unlike any other in its importance to the committed individuals. This point was central to *Griswold* v. *Connecticut*, which held the Constitution protects the right of married couples to use contraception. 381 U.S., at 485 (1965). . . .

As this Court held in *Lawrence*, same-sex couples have the same right as opposite-sex couples to enjoy intimate association. *Lawrence* invalidated laws that made same-sex intimacy a criminal act. And it acknowledged that "[w]hen sexuality finds overt expression in intimate conduct with another person, the conduct can be but one element in a personal bond that is more enduring." 539 U.S., at 567 (2003). But while *Lawrence* confirmed a dimension of freedom that allows individuals to engage in intimate association without criminal liability, it does not follow that freedom stops there. Outlaw to outcast may be a step forward, but it does not achieve the full promise of liberty.

A third basis for protecting the right to marry is that it safeguards children and families and thus draws meaning from related rights of childrearing, procreation, and education. The Court has recognized these connections by describing the varied rights as a unified whole. . . . Under the laws of the several States, some of marriage's protections for children and families are material. But marriage also confers more profound benefits. By giving recognition and legal structure to their parents' relationship, marriage allows children "to understand the integrity and closeness of their own family and its concord with other families in their community and in their daily lives." Marriage also affords the permanency and stability important to children's best interests.

As all parties agree, many same-sex couples provide loving and nurturing homes to their children, whether biological or adopted. And hundreds of thousands of children are presently being raised by such couples. Most States have allowed gays and lesbians to adopt, either as individuals or as couples, and many adopted and foster children have same-sex parents. This provides powerful confirmation from the law itself that gays and lesbians can create loving, supportive families.

Excluding same-sex couples from marriage thus conflicts with a central premise of the right to marry. Without the recognition, stability, and predictability marriage offers, their children suffer the stigma of knowing their families are somehow lesser. They also suffer the significant material costs of being raised by unmarried parents, relegated through no fault of their own to a more difficult and uncertain family life. The marriage laws at issue here thus harm and humiliate the children of same-sex couples.

That is not to say the right to marry is less meaningful for those who do not or cannot have children. An ability, desire, or promise to procreate is not and has not been a prerequisite for a valid marriage in any State. In light of precedent protecting the right of a married couple not to procreate, it cannot be said the Court or the States have conditioned the right to marry on the capacity or commitment to procreate. The constitutional marriage right has many aspects, of which childbearing is only one.

Fourth and finally, this Court's cases and the Nation's traditions make clear that marriage is a keystone of our social order.

[. . .]

For that reason, just as a couple vows to support each other, so does society pledge to support the couple, offering symbolic recognition and material benefits to protect and nourish the union. Indeed, while the States are in general free to vary the benefits they confer on all married couples, they have throughout our history made marriage the basis for an expanding list of governmental rights, benefits, and responsibilities. These aspects of marital status include: taxation; inheritance and property rights; rules of intestate succession; spousal privilege in the law of evidence; hospital access; medical decisionmaking authority; adoption rights; the rights and benefits of survivors; birth and death certificates; professional ethics rules; campaign finance restrictions; workers' compensation benefits; health insurance; and child custody, support, and visitation rules. Valid marriage under state law is also a significant status for over a thousand provisions of federal law. The States have contributed to the fundamental character of the marriage right by placing that institution at the center of so many facets of the legal and social order.

There is no difference between same- and opposite-sex couples with respect to this principle. Yet by virtue of their exclusion from that institution, same-sex couples are denied the constellation of benefits that the States have linked to marriage. This harm results in more than just material burdens. Same-sex couples are consigned to an instability many opposite-sex couples would deem intolerable in their own lives. As the State itself makes marriage all the more precious by the significance it attaches to it, exclusion from that status has the effect of teaching that gays and lesbians are unequal in important respects. It demeans gays and lesbians for the State to lock them out of a central institution of the Nation's society. Same-sex couples, too, may aspire to the transcendent purposes of marriage and seek fulfillment in its highest meaning.

The limitation of marriage to opposite-sex couples may long have seemed natural and just, but its inconsistency with the central meaning of the fundamental right to marry is now manifest. With that knowledge must come the recognition that laws excluding same-sex couples from the marriage right impose stigma and injury of the kind prohibited by our basic charter.

Objecting that this does not reflect an appropriate framing of the issue, the respondents . . . assert the petitioners do not seek to exercise the right to marry but rather a new and nonexistent "right to same-sex marriage."

[. . .]

If rights were defined by who exercised them in the past, then received practices could serve as their own continued justification and new groups could not invoke rights once denied. This Court has rejected that approach, both with respect to the right to marry and the rights of gays and lesbians.

[. . .]

The right of same-sex couples to marry that is part of the liberty promised by the Fourteenth Amendment is derived, too, from that Amendment's guarantee of the equal protection of the laws. The Due Process Clause and the Equal Protection Clause are connected in a profound way, though they set forth independent principles. Rights implicit in liberty and rights secured by equal protection may rest on different precepts and are not always coextensive, yet in some instances each may be instructive as to the meaning and reach of the other. In any particular case one Clause may be thought to capture the essence of the right in a more accurate and comprehensive way, even as the two Clauses may converge in the identification and definition of the right. . . .

The Court's cases touching upon the right to marry reflect this dynamic. In *Loving* the Court invalidated a prohibition on interracial marriage under both the Equal Protection Clause and the Due Process Clause. The Court first declared the prohibition invalid because of its unequal treatment of interracial couples. It stated: "There can be no doubt that restricting the freedom to marry solely because of racial classifications violates the central meaning of the Equal Protection Clause." 388 U.S., at 12.

[. . .]

Indeed, in interpreting the Equal Protection Clause, the Court has recognized that new insights and societal understandings can reveal unjustified inequality within our most fundamental institutions that once passed unnoticed and unchallenged. . . .

[T]he Equal Protection Clause can help to identify and correct inequalities in the institution of marriage, vindicating precepts of liberty and equality under the Constitution. . . .

It is now clear that the challenged laws burden the liberty of same-sex couples, and it must be further acknowledged that they abridge central precepts of equality. Here the marriage laws enforced by the respondents are in essence unequal: same-sex couples are denied all the benefits afforded to opposite-sex couples and are barred from exercising a fundamental right. Especially against a long history of disapproval of their relationships, this denial to same-sex couples of the right to marry works a grave and continuing harm. The imposition of this disability on gays and lesbians serves to disrespect and subordinate them. And the Equal Protection Clause, like the Due Process Clause, prohibits this unjustified infringement of the fundamental right to marry.

These considerations lead to the conclusion that the right to marry is a fundamental right inherent in the liberty of the person, and under the Due Process and Equal Protection Clauses of the Fourteenth Amendment couples of the same-sex may not be deprived of that right and that liberty. The Court now holds that same-sex couples may exercise the fundamental right to marry. No longer may this liberty be denied to them.

[. . .]

Chief Justice Roberts, with whom Justice Scalia and Justice Thomas join, dissenting.

Petitioners make strong arguments rooted in social policy and considerations of fairness. They contend that same-sex couples should be allowed to affirm their love and commitment through marriage, just like opposite-sex couples. That position has undeniable appeal; over the past six years, voters and legislators in eleven States and the District of Columbia have revised their laws to allow marriage between two people of the same sex.

But this Court is not a legislature. Whether same-sex marriage is a good idea should be of no concern to us. Under the Constitution, judges have power to say what the law is, not what it should be. The people who ratified the Constitution authorized courts to exercise "neither force nor will but merely judgment."

Although the policy arguments for extending marriage to same-sex couples may be compelling, the legal arguments for requiring such an extension are not. The fundamental right to marry does not include a right to make a State change its definition of marriage. And a State's decision to maintain the meaning of marriage that has persisted in every culture throughout human history can hardly be called irrational. In short, our Constitution does not enact any one theory of marriage. The people of a State are free to expand marriage to include same-sex couples, or to retain the historic definition. . . .

Five lawyers have closed the debate and enacted their own vision of marriage as a matter of constitutional law. Stealing this issue from the people will for many cast a cloud over same-sex marriage, making a dramatic social change that much more difficult to accept.

The majority's decision is an act of will, not legal judgment. The right it announces has no basis in the Constitution or this Court's precedent. . . . As a result, the Court invalidates the marriage laws of more than half the States and orders the transformation of a social institution that has formed the basis of human society for millennia, for the Kalahari Bushmen and the Han Chinese, the Carthaginians and the Aztecs. Just who do we think we are?

[. . .]

The majority purports to identify four "principles and traditions" in this Court's due process precedents that support a fundamental right for same-sex couples to marry. In reality, however the majority's approach has no basis in principle or tradition, except for the unprincipled tradition of judicial policymaking that characterized discredited decisions such as *Lochner* v. *New York*, 198 U.S. 45. Stripped of its shiny rhetorical gloss, the majority's argument is that the Due Process Clause gives same-sex couples a fundamental right to marry because it will be good for them and for society. If I were a legislator, I would certainly consider that view as a matter of social policy. But as a judge, I find the majority's position indefensible as a matter of constitutional law.

[. . .]

Allowing unelected federal judges to select which unenumerated rights rank as "fundamental"—and to strike down state laws on the basis of that determination—raises obvious concerns about the judicial role. . . .

Our precedents have required that implied fundamental rights be "objectively, deeply rooted in this Nation's history and tradition," and "implicit in the concept of ordered liberty, such that neither liberty nor justice would exist if they were sacrificed. . . ."

Proper reliance on history and tradition of course requires looking beyond the individual law being challenged, so that every restriction on liberty does not supply its own constitutional justification. The Court is right about that. But given the few "guideposts for responsible decisionmaking in this unchartered area, an approach grounded in history imposes limits on the judiciary that are more meaningful than any based on [an] abstract formula." Expanding a right suddenly and dramatically is likely to require tearing it up from its roots. Even a sincere profession of "discipline" in identifying fundamental rights does not provide a meaningful constraint on a judge, for "what he is really likely to be 'discovering,' whether or not he is fully aware of it, are his own values." The only way to ensure restraint in this delicate enterprise is "continual insistence upon respect for the teachings of history, solid recognition of the basic values that underlie our society, and wise appreciation of the great roles [of] the doctrines of federalism and separation of powers."

[. . .]

Neither *Lawrence* nor any other precedent in the privacy line of cases supports the right that petitioners assert here. Unlike criminal laws banning contraceptives and sodomy, the marriage laws at issue here involve no government intrusion. They create no crime and impose no punishment. Same-sex couples remain free to live together, to engage in intimate conduct, and to raise their families as they see fit. No one is "condemned to live in loneliness" by the laws challenged in these cases—no one. . . .

In sum, the privacy cases provide no support for the majority's position, because petitioners do not seek privacy. Quite the opposite, they seek public recognition of their relationships, along with corresponding government benefits. Our cases have consistently refused to allow litigants to convert the shield provided by constitutional liberties into a sword to demand positive entitlements from the State. Thus, although the right to privacy recognized by our precedents certainly plays a role in protecting the intimate conduct of same-sex couples, it provides no affirmative right to redefine marriage and no basis for striking down the laws at issue here.

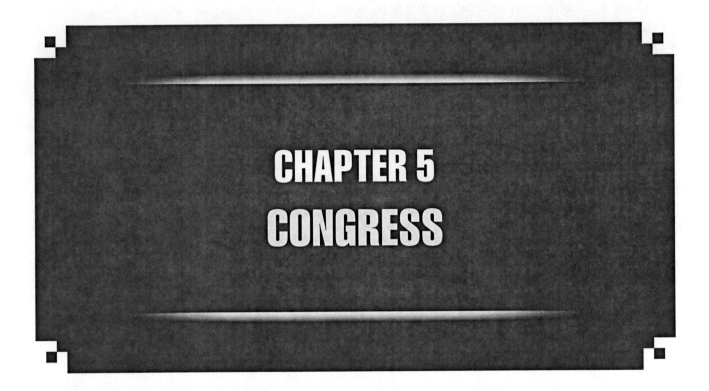

CHAPTER 5
CONGRESS

THE ELECTORAL INCENTIVE

DAVID R. MAYHEW

The discussion to come will hinge on the assumption that United States congressmen[1] are interested in getting reelected—indeed, in their role here as abstractions, interested in nothing else. Any such assumption necessarily does some violence to the facts, so it is important at the outset to root this one as firmly as possible in reality. A number of questions about that reality immediately arise.

First, is it true that the United States Congress is a place where members wish to stay once they get there? Clearly there are representative assemblies that do not hold their members for very long. Members of the Colombian parliament tend to serve single terms and then move on.[2] Voluntary turnover is quite high in some American state legislatures—for example, in Alabama. In his study of the unreformed Connecticut legislature, Barber labeled some of his subjects "reluctants"—people not very much interested in politics who were briefly pushed into it by others.[3] An ethic of "volunteerism" pervades the politics of California city councils.[4] And in the Congress itself voluntary turnover was high throughout most of the nineteenth century.

Yet in the modern Congress the "congressional career" is unmistakably upon us.[5] Turnover figures show that over the past century increasing proportions of members in any given Congress have been holdovers from previous Congresses—members who have both sought reelection and won it. Membership turnover noticeably declined among southern senators as early as the 1850s, among senators generally just after the Civil War.[6] The House followed close behind, with turnover dipping in the late nineteenth century and continuing to decline throughout the twentieth.[7] Average number of terms served has gone up and up, with the House in 1971 registering an all-time high of 20 percent of its members who had served at least ten terms.[8] It seems fair to characterize the modern Congress as an assembly of professional politicians spinning out political careers. The jobs offer good pay and high prestige. There is no want of applicants for them. Successful pursuit of a career requires continual reelection.[9]

A second question is this: even if congressmen seek reelection, does it make sense to attribute that goal to them to the exclusion of all other goals? Of course the answer is that a complete explanation (if one were possible) of a congressman's or any one else's behavior would require attention to more than just one goal. There are even occasional congressmen who intentionally do things that make their own electoral survival difficult or impossible. The late President Kennedy wrote of congressional "profiles in courage."[10] Former Senator Paul Douglas (D., Ill.) tells of how he tried to persuade

DAVID R. MAYHEW, *CONGRESS: THE ELECTORAL CONNECTION* © Yale University Press

Senator Frank Graham (D., N.C.) to tailor his issue positions in order to survive a 1950 primary. Graham, a liberal appointee to the office, refused to listen. He was a "saint," says Douglas.[11] He lost his primary. There are not many saints. But surely it is common for congressmen to seek other ends alongside the electoral one and not necessarily incompatible with it. Some try to get rich in office, a quest that may or may not interfere with reelection.[12] Fenno assigns three prime goals to congressmen— getting reelected but also achieving influence within Congress and making "good public policy."[13] These latter two will be given attention further on in this discussion. Anyone can point to contemporary congressmen whose public activities are not obviously reducible to the electoral explanation; Senator J. William Fulbright (D., Ark.) comes to mind. Yet, saints aside, the electoral goal has an attractive universality to it. It has to be the *proximate* goal of everyone, the goal that must be achieved over and over if other ends are to be entertained. One former congressman writes, "All members of Congress have a primary interest in getting re-elected. Some members have no other interest."[14] Reelection underlies everything else, as indeed it should if we are to expect that the relation between politicians and public will be one of accountability.[15] What justifies a focus on the reelection goal is the juxtaposition of these two aspects of it—its putative empirical primacy and its importance as an accountability link. For analytic purposes, therefore, congressmen will be treated in the pages to come as if they were single-minded reelection seekers. Whatever else they may seek will be given passing attention, but the analysis will center on the electoral connection.

Yet another question arises. Even if congressmen are single-mindedly interested in reelection, are they in a position as individuals to do anything about it? If they are not, if they are inexorably shoved to and fro by forces in their political environments, then obviously it makes no sense to pay much attention to their individual activities. This question requires a complex answer, and it will be useful to begin reaching for one by pondering whether individual congressmen are the proper analytic units in an investigation of this sort. An important alternative view is that parties rather than lone politicians are the prime movers in electoral politics. The now classic account of what a competitive political universe will look like with parties as its analytic units is Downs's *Economic Theory of Democracy*.[16] In the familiar Downsian world parties are entirely selfish. They seek the rewards of office, but in order to achieve them they have to win office and keep it. They bid for favor before the public as highly cohesive point-source "teams." A party enjoys complete control over government during its term in office and uses its control solely to try to win the next election. In a two-party system a voter decides how to cast his ballot by examining the record and promises of the party in power and the previous record and current promises of the party in power and the previous record and current promises of the party out of power; he then calculates an "expected party differential" for the coming term, consults his own policy preferences, and votes accordingly. These are the essential lineaments of the theory.[17] Legislative representatives appear only as modest "intermediaries." If of the governing party they gather information on grassroots preferences and relay it to the government, and they try to persuade constituents back home that the government is doing a worthy job.[18]

How well a party model of this kind captures the reality of any given regime is an empirical question. One difficulty lies in the need for parties as cohesive teams (members whose "goals can be viewed as a simple, consistent preference-ordering").[19] In all non-autocratic regimes governments are made up of a plurality of elective officials—not just one man. How can a group of men be bound together so that it looks something like a Downsian team? Probably nowhere (in a nonautocratic regime) does a group achieve the ultimate fusion of preference-orderings needed to satisfy the model; party government in Britain, for example, proceeds substantially by intraparty bargaining.[20] Nonetheless, it is plain that some regimes fit the model better than others. For some purposes it is quite useful to study

British politics by using parties as analytic units. Britain, to start with, has a constitution that readily permits majoritarian government. But, beyond that, at the roll call stage British M.P.'s act as cohesive party blocs that look something like teams. It is not inevitable that they should do so, and indeed there was a good deal of individualistic voting in the Commons in the mid-nineteenth century.[21] Why do contemporary M.P.'s submit to party discipline? There are at least three reasons why they do so, and it will be profitable here to examine them in order to allow later contrasts with the American regime.

First of all, in both British parties the nominating systems are geared to produce candidates who will vote the party line if and when they reach Parliament. This happens not because nominations are centrally controlled, but because the local nominating outfits are small elite groups that serve in effect as nationally oriented cheerleaders for the Commons party leadership.[22]

Second, British M.P.'s lack the resources to set up shop as politicians with bases independent of party. Television time in campaigns goes to parties rather than to scattered independent politicians.[23] By custom or rule or both, the two parties sharply limit the funds that parliamentary candidates can spend on their own in campaigns.[24] Once elected, M.P.'s are not supplied the kinds of office resources— staff help, free mailing privileges, and the like—that can be used to achieve public salience.[25] These arguments should not be carried too far; M.P.'s are not ciphers, and obviously dissident leaders like Aneurin Bevan and Enoch Powell manage to build important independent followings. But the average backbencher is constrained by lack of resources. It comes as no surprise that individual M.P.'s add little to (or subtract little from) core partisan electoral strength in their constituencies; the lion's share of the variance in vote change from election to election is chargeable to national swings rather than to local or regional fluctuations.[26]

Third, with the executive entrenched in Parliament the only posts worth holding in a Commons career are the ones doled out by party leaders. Up to a third of majority party M.P.'s are now included in the Ministry.[27] "For the ambitious backbencher, the task is to impress ministers and particularly the Prime Minister."[28] Party loyalty is rewarded; heresy is not.

The upshot of all this is that British M.P.'s are locked in. The arrangement of incentives and resources elevates parties over politicians. But the United States is very different. In America the underpinnings of "teamsmanship" are weak or absent, making it possible for politicians to triumph over parties. It should be said that Madisonian structure and Downsian teamsmanship are not necessarily incompatible.[29] Connecticut state government, in which party organizations exercise substantial control over nominations and political careers, comes close to the British model; governorship and state legislative parties are bound together by party organization.[30] But Connecticut is exceptional, or, more accurately, it is at one end of a spectrum toward the other end of which there are states in which parties have little binding effect at all.[31] In American politics the place where Downsian logic really applies is in the election of individuals to executive posts—presidents, governors, and big city mayors. To choose among candidates for the presidency or the New York City mayoralty is to choose among "executive teams"—candidates with their retinues of future high administrators, financial supporters, ghost-writers, pollsters, student ideologues, journalistic flacks, hangers-on, occasionally burglars and spies. In executive elections the candidates are highly visible; they bid for favor in Downsian fashion; they substantially control government (or appear to) and can be charged with its accomplishments and derelictions (President Nixon for inflation, Mayor Lindsay for crime); elections are typically close (now even in most old machine cities); voters can traffic in "expected differentials" (between executive candidates rather than parties). When the late V. O. Key, Jr., wrote *The Responsible Electorate*,[32] a book in the Downsian spirit, he had the empirical good sense to focus on competition between incumbent and prospective presidential administrations rather than more broadly on competition between parties. Indeed, it can be argued that American representative assemblies have declined in power in the twentieth century (especially at the city council level) and executives have risen chiefly because it is the executives who offer electorates something like Downsian accountability.[33]

But at the congressional level the teamsmanship model breaks down. To hark back to the discussion of Britain, the specified resource and incentive arrangements conducive to party unity among M.P.'s are absent in the congressional environment: First, the way in which congressional candidates win party nominations is not, to say the least, one that fosters party cohesion in Congress. For one thing, 435 House members and 98 senators (all but the Indiana pair) are now nominated by direct primary (or can be, in the few states with challenge primaries) rather than by caucus or convention. There is no reason to expect large primary electorates to honor party loyalty. (An introduction of the direct primary system in Britain might in itself destroy party cohesion in the Commons.) For another, even where party organizations are still strong enough to control congressional primaries,[34] the parties are locally rather than nationally oriented; local party unity is vital to them, national party unity is not. Apparently it never has been.[35]

Second, unlike the M.P. the typical American congressman has to mobilize his own resources initially to win a nomination and then to win election and reelection. He builds his own electoral coalition and sustains it. He raises and spends a great deal of money in doing so. He has at his command an elaborate set of electoral resources that the Congress bestows upon all its members. There will be more on these points later. The important point here is that a congressman can—indeed must—build a power base that is substantially independent of party.[36] In the words of a House member quoted by Clapp, "If we depended on the party organization to get elected, none of us would be here."[37]

Third, Congress does not have to sustain a cabinet and hence does not engage the ambitions of its members in cabinet formation in such a fashion as to induce party cohesion. It would be wrong to posit a general one-to-one relation here between party cohesion and cabinet sustenance. On the one hand, there is nothing preventing congressmen from building disciplined congressional parties anyway if they wanted to do so. On the other hand, as the records of the Third and Fourth French republics show, cabinet regimes can be anchored in relatively incohesive parties. Yet, to pose the proposition in statistical rather than deterministic form, the need for an assembly to sustain a cabinet probably raises the likelihood that it will spawn disciplined parties.[38]

The fact is that no theoretical treatment of the United States Congress that posits parties as analytic units will go very far. So we are left with individual congressmen, with 535 men and women rather than two parties, as units to be examined in the discussion to come. The style of argument will be somewhat like that of Downs, but the reality more like that of Namier.[39] Whether the choice of units is propitious can be shown only in the facts marshaled and the arguments embellished around them. With the units nailed down, still left unanswered is the question of whether congressmen in search of reelection are in a position to do anything about it.

Here it will be useful to deal first with the minority subset of congressmen who serve marginal districts or states—constituencies fairly evenly balanced between the parties. The reason for taking up the marginals separately is to consider whether their electoral precariousness ought to induce them to engage in distinctive electoral activities. Marginals have an obvious problem; to a substantial degree they are at the mercy of national partisan electoral swings. But general voter awareness of congressional legislative activities is low.[40] Hence national swings in the congressional vote are normally judgments on what the president is doing (or is thought to be doing) rather than on what Congress is doing. In the familiar case where parties controlling the presidency lose House seats in the midterm, swings seem to be not judgments on anything at all but rather artifacts of the election cycle.[41] More along a judgmental line, there has been an impressive relation over the years between partisan voting for the House and ups and downs in real income among voters. The national electorate rewards the congressional party of a president who reigns during economic prosperity and punishes the party of one who reigns during adversity.[42] Rewards and penalties may be given by the same circuitous route for other states of affairs, including national involvement in wars.[43] With voters behaving the way they do, it is in the electoral interest of a marginal congressman to help insure that a presidential administration of his own party is a popular success or that one of the opposite party is a failure. (Purely from the standpoint of electoral interest there is no reason why a congressman with a safe seat should care one way or another.)

But what can a marginal congressman do to affect the fortunes of a presidency? One shorthand course a marginal serving under a president of his own party can take is to support him diligently in roll call voting; there is ambiguous evidence that relevant marginals do behave disproportionately in this fashion.[44] This strategy may not always be the best one. During the 1958 recession, for example, it may have been wise for marginal Republicans to support Democratic deficit-spending bills over the opposition of President Eisenhower; in the 1958 election Eisenhower's policies seem to have been ruinous for members of his own party. How about marginals of the opposition party? By the same logic it might be advantageous for opposition marginals to try to wreck the economy; if it were done unobtrusively the voters would probably blame the president, not them.

There are a number of intriguing theoretical possibilities here for marginals of parties both in and out of power. Yet marginals seem not to pay much attention to strategies of this sort, whether ingenuous or ingenious. What we are pondering is whether individual marginals can realistically hope to do anything to affect the national component of the variance over time in congressional partisan election percentages.[45] And the answer seems to be no—or at least extraordinarily little. Leaving aside the problem of generating collective congressional action, there is the root problem of knowing what to try to do. It is hard to point to an instance in recent decades in which any group of congressmen (marginals or not) has done something that has clearly changed the national congressional electoral percentage in a direction in which the group intended to change it (or to keep it stationary if that was the intention). There are too many imponderables. Most importantly, presidents follow their own logic. So do events. Not even economists can have a clear idea about what the effects of economic measures will be. The election cycle adds its own kind of perversity; the vigorous enactment of President Johnson's Great Society legislation (by all the survey evidence popular) was followed in 1966 by the largest Republican gain in House popular vote percentage of the last quarter century. Hence there is a lack of usable lore among congressmen on what legislative actions will produce what national electoral effects.[46]

End Notes

1. Where the context does not suggest otherwise, the term *congressmen* will refer to members of both House and Senate.
2. James L. Payne, *Patterns of Conflict in Colombia* (New Haven: Yale University Press, 1968), pp. 19–20.

3. James D. Barber, *The Lawmakers* (New Haven: Yale University Press, 1965), ch. 4.

4. Kenneth Prewitt, "Political Ambitions, Volunteerism, and Electoral Accountability," 64 *American Political Science Review* 5–17 (1970).

5. H. Douglas Price, "The Congressional Career Then and Now," ch. 2 in Nelson W. Polsby (ed.), *Congressional Behavior* (New York: Random House, 1971).

6. Price, "Computer Simulation and Legislative 'Professionalism,'" pp. 14–16.

7. Nelson W. Polsby, "The Institutionalization of the U.S. House of Representatives," 62 *American Political Science Review* 146 (1968).

8. Charles S. Bullock III, "House Careerists: Changing Patterns of Longevity and Attrition," 66 *American Political Science Review* 1296 (1972).

9. Indeed, it has been proposed that professional politicians could be gotten rid of by making reelection impossible. For a plan to select one-term legislators by random sampling of the population, see Dennis C. Mueller et al., "Representative Government via Random Selection," 12 *Public Choice* 57–68 (1972).

10. John F. Kennedy, *Profiles in Courage* (New York: Harper and Row, 1956).

11. Paul H. Douglas, *In the Fullness of Time* (New York: Harcourt Brace Jovanovich, 1972), pp. 238–41.

12. In the case of the late Senator Thomas Dodd (D., Conn.) these two goals apparently conflicted. See James Boyd, *Above the Law* (New York: New American Library, 1968). Using office for financial profit is probably less common in Congress than in some of the state legislatures (e.g. Illinois and New Jersey).

13. Fenno, *Congressmen in Committees*, p. 1.

14. Frank E. Smith (D., Miss.), *Congressman from Mississippi* (New York: Random House, 1964), p. 127. It will not be necessary here to reach the question of whether it is possible to detect the goals of congressmen by asking them what they are, or indeed the question of whether there are unconscious motives lurking behind conscious ones. In Lasswell's formulation "political types" are power seekers, with "private motives displaced on public objects rationalized in terms of public interest." Harold D. Lasswell, *Power and Personality* (New York: Viking, 1948), p. 38.

15. Of other kinds of relations we are entitled to be suspicious. "There can be no doubt, that if power is granted to a body of men, called Representatives, they, like any other men, will use their power, not for the advantage of the community, but for their own advantage, if they can. The only question is, therefore, how can they be prevented?" James Mill, "Government," in *Essays on Government, Jurisprudence, Liberty of the Press, and Law of Nations* (New York: Augustus M. Kelley, 1967), p. 18. Madison's view was that the United States House, by design the popular branch, "should have an immediate dependence on, and an intimate sympathy with, the people. Frequent elections are unquestionably the only policy by which this dependency and sympathy can be effectively secured." *The Federalist Papers*, selected and edited by Roy Fairfield (Garden City, N.Y.: Doubleday Anchor, 1961), no. 52, p. 165.

16. Anthony Downs, *An Economic Theory of Democracy* (New York: Harper and Row, 1957). Downs gives a formal touch to a political science literature of both normative and empirical importance, extending from Woodrow Wilson through E. E. Schattschneider and V. O. Key, Jr.

17. Ibid., chs. 2, 3.

18. Ibid., pp. 88–90. Because the information and opinions supplied by representatives are important in decision making, Downs says that in effect some decision power devolves to the representatives. But there is this constraint: "Theoretically, the government will continue to decentralize its power until the marginal gain in votes from greater conformity to popular desires is outweighed by the marginal cost in votes of lesser ability to co-ordinate its actions." Pp. 89–90.

19. Ibid., p. 26.

20. See, for example, Richard E. Neustadt, "White House and Whitehall," *The Public Interest*, Winter 1966, pp. 55–69.

21. See William O. Aydelotte, "Voting Patterns in the British House of Commons in the 1840's," 5 *Comparative Studies in Society and History*, 134–63 (1963).

22. Austin Ranney, *Pathways to Parliament: Candidate Selection in Britain* (Madison: University of Wisconsin Press, 1965), p. 281; Leon D. Epstein, "British M.P.'s and Their Local Parties: The Suez Case," 54 *American Political Science Review* 385–86 (1960).

23. Jay G. Blumler and Denis McQuail, *Television in Politics* (Chicago: University of Chicago Press, 1969), pp. xi–xxviii.

24. R. T. McKenzie, *British Political Parties* (New York: St. Martin's, 1955), pp. 252–53, 555.

25. "An American Congressman, it is said, collapsed with shock on being shown the writing-rooms and the Library of the Commons full of men writing letters in longhand: members of Parliament answering the constituency mail." Bernard Crick, *The Reform of Parliament* (Garden City, N.Y.: Doubleday, 1965), p. 58; and, generally, Crick, pp. 58–59. Things have changed somewhat since Crick's account, but the contrast is still valid. See also Anthony Barker and Michael Rush, *The Member of Parliament and His Information* (London: Allen and Unwin, 1970). Loewenberg reports that, in West Germany, "the average member of the Bundestag works under Spartan conditions." Gerhard Loewenberg, *Parliament in the German Political System* (Ithaca: Cornell University Press, 1967), p. 53.

26. Donald E. Stokes, "Parties and the Nationalization of Electoral Forces," ch. 7 in William N. Chambers and Walter D. Burnham, *The American Party Systems* (New York: Oxford University Press, 1967), pp. 188–89.

27. Crick, *The Reform of Parliament*, pp. 30–31. Crick adds: "A modern Prime Minister has a patronage beyond the wildest dreams of political avarice of a Walpole or a Newcastle." P. 31.

28. John P. Mackintosh, "Reform of the House of Commons: The Case for Specialization," in Loewenberg (ed.), *Modern Parliaments*, p. 39.

29. Indeed in city studies there is the standard functional case that cohesive parties may arise to deal with problems caused by constitutional diffusion. See, for example, on Chicago, Edward C. Banfield, *Political Influence* (New York: Free Press, 1961), ch. 8. American parties have traditionally been strongest at the municipal level. But something interesting happens to Downs on the way to the city. Where parties are held together by patronage, and where there are no geographically subsidiary governments that can serve as independent political bases, there is a strong tendency for party politics to become monopolistic rather than competitive. Ambitious politicians have little incentive to sustain an opposition party and every incentive to join the ruling party. The same argument generally holds for national politics in mid-eighteenth-century England.

30. See Duane Lockard, *New England State Politics* (Princeton: Princeton University Press, 1965), chs. 9, 10; Joseph I. Lieberman, *The Power Broker* (Boston: Houghton Mifflin, 1966); James D. Barber, "Leadership Strategies for Legislative Party Cohesion," 28 *Journal of Politics* 347–67 (1966).

31. In the California Senate, for example, at least until recently, committee chairmanships were given out to the most senior members regardless of party. Alvin D. Sokolow and Richard W. Brandsma, "Partisanship and Seniority in Legislative Committee Assignments: California after Reapportionment," 24 *Western Political Quarterly* 741–47 (1971).

32. Cambridge: Harvard University Press, 1966.

33. There is Huntington's point that sweeping turnover of a Jacksonian sort now occurs in national politics only at the top executive level. Samuel P. Huntington, "Congressional Responses to the

Twentieth Century," ch. 1 in David B. Truman (ed.), *The Congress and America's Future* (Englewood Cliffs, N.J.: Prentice-Hall, 1965), p. 17.

34. In Chicago, for example. See Leo M. Snowiss, "Congressional Recruitment and Representation," 60 *American Political Science Review* 627–39 (1966).

35. On the fluid behavior of machine congressmen back when there were a good many more of them, see Moisei Ostrogorski, *Democracy and the Organization of Political Parties*, vol. II, *The United States* (Garden City, N.Y.: Doubleday, 1964), pp. 286–89. Tammany Democrats broke party ranks to save Speaker Joseph G. Cannon from Insurgent and Democratic attack in the Sixtieth Congress, a year before his downfall. See Blair Bolles, *Tyrant from Illinois* (New York: Norton, 1951), p. 181.

36. See Charles L. Clapp, *The Congressman: His Work as He Sees It* (Washington, D.C.: Brookings, 1963), pp. 30–31; Robert J. Huckshorn and Robert C. Spencer, *The Politics of Defeat* (Amherst, Mass.: University of Massachusetts Press, 1971), pp. vii, 71–72; David A. Leuthold, *Electioneering in a Democracy* (New York: Wiley, 1968), passim.

37. Clapp, *The Congressman*, p. 351.

38. See the argument in Leon D. Epstein, "A Comparative Study of Canadian Parties," 58 *American Political Science Review* 46–59 (1964).

39. Lewis Namier, *The Structure of Politics at the Accession of George III* (London: Macmillan, 1960). For a Namier passage on assemblies without disciplined parties see p. 17.

40. Donald E. Stokes and Warren E. Miller, "Party Government and the Saliency of Congress," ch. 11 in Angus Campbell et al., *Elections and the Political Order* (New York: Wiley, 1966), p. 199.

41. Angus Campbell, "Surge and Decline: A Study of Electoral Change," ch. 3 in ibid.; Barbara Hinckley, "Interpreting House Midterm Elections: Toward a Measurement of the In-Party's 'Expected' Loss of Seats," 61 *American Political Science Review* 694–700 (1967).

42. Gerald H. Kramer, "Short-Term Fluctuations in U.S. Voting Behavior, 1896–1964," 65 *American Political Science Review* 131–43 (1971). See also the symposium on the Kramer findings in 63 *American Economic Review* 160–80 (May 1973).

43. Kramer, "U.S. Voting Behavior," p. 140. Wars seem to earn penalties.

44. David B. Truman, *The Congressional Party* (New York: Wiley, 1959), pp. 213–18.

45. As in Stokes, "Parties and the Nationalization of Electoral Forces."

46. Nonetheless there are interesting questions here that have never been explored. Do marginal congressmen—or members generally—of the party not in control of the presidency try to sabotage the economy? Of course they must not appear to do so, but there are "respectable" ways of acting. How about Republicans in the Eightieth Congress with their tax cutting in time of inflation? Or Democrats with their spending programs under President Nixon—also in a time of inflation? The answer is probably no. It would have to be shown that the same congressmen's actions differ under presidencies of different parties, and they probably do not. Strategies like this not only require duplicity, they require a vigorous consciousness of distant effects of a sort that is foreign to the congressional mentality.

THE POLARIZATION OF CONTEMPORARY AMERICAN POLITICS[1]

CHRISTOPHER HARE
University of Georgia, Athens

KEITH T. POOLE
University of Georgia, Athens

Political elites of the United States are deeply polarized. Polarization of the Democratic and Republican Parties is higher than at any time since the end of the Civil War. This essay describes how the modern polarization trend emerged and its implications for mass political behavior and public policy outcomes. We contend that contemporary political polarization must be understood in terms of both the ideological divergence of the parties and the expansion of the liberal conservative dimension of conflict to a wider set of social and cultural conflicts in American society. We close with the speculation that the Republican Party has become the more fractured of the parties along the liberal–conservative dimension at both the elite and mass level.

[...] Partisan conflict has grown sharper, unrelenting, and more ideological over recent decades. Contemporary American politics seems to be fiercely contested over a wider range of issues—from traditional battles over the size and scope of government intervention in the economy to social/cultural battles over abortion, contraception, gay marriage, religious liberty, immigration, and gun control. These ideological divides also seem to align more closely with partisan divisions as the ranks of conservative Democrats and liberal Republicans have diminished in both Congress and the electorate.[2]

[...] To assess the nature and extent of polarization, we require some method for the measurement of ideology. Measurement is crucial to the task of studying polarization, as our inferences are entirely reliant on the values we assign to a latent quantity such as ideology. For instance, questions like whether one legislator is more conservative than another or whether a legislator has become more liberal over time depend solely on how we measure those legislators' ideological positions. [...] The importance of measurement becomes immensely clear in a context like the study of political polarization.

In this essay, we apply the NOMINATE statistical procedure to measure the ideological positions of Members of Congress (MCs) and document the dramatic increase in political polarization in the United States since the 1970s. NOMINATE (for Nominal Three-Step Estimation) is an unfolding method[3] based on the spatial theory of voting that jointly estimates the positions of legislators and policy outcomes in latent ideological space from observed roll call voting behavior.[4] The recovered dimensions correspond to ideological divisions within Congress and legislators' scores on these dimensions provide empirical measures of their ideological positions. [...]

Polity, The Polarization of Contemporary American Politics, Hare, C. & Poole, K. Polity (2014) 46: 411. Reprinted with permission of Springer.

[. . .] NOMINATE uses legislators' entire roll call voting records to estimate their ideological locations, rather than just a subset of selected votes, as with interest group ratings. Moreover, the specific DW-NOMINATE (for dynamic, weighted NOMINATE) procedure that we employ uses overlapping cohorts of legislators to "bridge" between legislators who have not served together, thus allowing ideological scores to be compared over time.[5]

This allows us to make explicit comparisons of the ideological positions of, for example, a freshman Senator with a Senator who last served in the 1960s. These sorts of comparisons are necessary for the study of a dynamic trend like polarization.

[. . .] NOMINATE uses legislators' entire roll call voting records to estimate their ideological locations, rather than just a subset of selected votes, as with interest group ratings. Moreover, the specific DW-NOMINATE (for dynamic, weighted NOMINATE) procedure that we employ uses overlapping cohorts of legislators to "bridge" between legislators who have not served together, thus allowing ideological scores to be compared over time.[6] This allows us to make explicit comparisons of the ideological positions of, for example, a freshman Senator with a Senator who last served in the 1960s. These sorts of comparisons are necessary for the study of a dynamic trend like polarization.

The results from DW-NOMINATE indicate that the level of polarization in Congress is now the highest since the end of the Civil War and shows no sign that it will abate. [. . .] Before discussing these measures of polarization, we first briefly review some important characteristics of the political party system that evolved from the British colonial era and have implications for the sources of contemporary polarization.

Polarization in the American Party System

Four traditions—representative democracy, plurality elections, geographic-based representation (the tradition of the representative living with those he represented), and private property rights—were established from the beginning of the British colonies and shaped American political history. They also have important consequences for why and how polarization (and de-polarization) takes place in American politics.

Representative democracy and capitalism in North America evolved together in an environment of almost unlimited natural resources. Private property rights and representative democracy have cooperatively cohabitated since the earliest British colonial settlements and no real European style socialist party ever gained a lasting foothold in the United States. This is what Louis Hartz called the "Liberal Tradition in America."[7] As a consequence, the American political space has long been bracketed on the left.

In addition, because of the nature of the earliest settlements, geography-based representation in representative assemblies became the norm. The sharp break with British tradition was that legislators lived in the district/town that they represented, rather than being assigned by a political party to represent a district. As the political parties were active throughout the United States, regional interests were incorporated within the parties, and that tended to dampen conflict between the parties. For example, before the Civil War, Southern Whigs and Southern Democrats shared an interest in representing the economic concerns of the South, which was based primarily on exporting commodities (namely, cotton, rice, naval stores, and indigo) against the high tariffs often demanded by the nascent manufacturing sectors of the North.

Finally, the adoption of a non-proportional representation electoral system—in line with Duverger's Law—constrained the American political system to two dominant parties.[8] These electoral characteristics, coupled with the emergence of mass-based political parties in the 1820s and the colonial legacy of private property rights, formed the basis of the American political–economic system that has survived into the twenty-first century.

[...]

Beginning in the mid-1970s, the parties in Congress began to move further apart on the liberal–conservative dimension. More Democrats staked out consistently liberal positions, and more Republicans supported wholly conservative ones. In other words, Congress began to polarize. **Figure 5.1** shows the dispersion of the parties along the liberal–conservative dimension between the end of Reconstruction (1879) and 2013 by plotting the 10th and the 90th percentile first-dimension DW-NOMINATE scores in each party. That is, 10 percent of Democrats will have higher (more moderate) scores than the 10th percentile score and 10 percent of Democrats will have lower (more liberal) scores than the 90th percentile score. Eighty percent of Democrats will have scores within this range. As can be seen, the parties began to diverge in the mid-1970s and this trend has continued unabated into the most recent Congress. Certainly, there had been some polarizing trends before the 1970s; namely, Democrats began moving left in response to the Great Depression under Presidential Franklin Roosevelt. However, this leftward drift had stabilized by the end of Presidential Lyndon Johnson's second term. By this point, the Democratic Party largely shifted from proposing new social welfare programs to defending existing ones. However, since the mid-1970s, polarization has steadily increased as the ideological center has hollowed out and the outer edges of the parties—especially the Republican Party—have moved ever further toward the ideological poles. Whether we gauge congressional polarization by the difference of party means, the difference between the parties' 10th percentile scores, or any number of alternative measures, Congress is now more polarized than at any time since the end of the Civil War.

The roots of the modern trend to greater polarization can in part be found in the passage of the 1964 Civil Rights Act and the 1965 Voting Rights Act. Southern Whites began voting for Republican candidates as the process of issue evolution over race played out.[9] Southern Republicans first gained a strong foothold in presidential elections, then in elections for the U.S. Senate and House, and finally most of the southern state legislatures became dominated by Republicans. The old southern Democratic Party has, in effect, disintegrated. The exodus of conservative Southerners from the Democratic Party at both the elite and mass levels has created a more homogenously liberal party. The net effect of these changes is that race—once a regional, second-dimension issue has been drawn into the liberal–conservative dimension because race-related issues are increasingly questions of redistribution.[10]

However, the southern realignment does not fully account for the increase in polarization. The Republican Party became much more conservative across all regions of the United States. The 1964 Goldwater presidential primary campaign was a key turning point.[11] The Goldwater insurgency created a national cadre of activists like Newt Gingrich who slowly shifted the Republican Party to the right across the whole country.

The steady growth in income inequality and changes in immigration trends in the United States over the last half century also have implications for political polarization.[12] Poorer citizens routinely exhibit

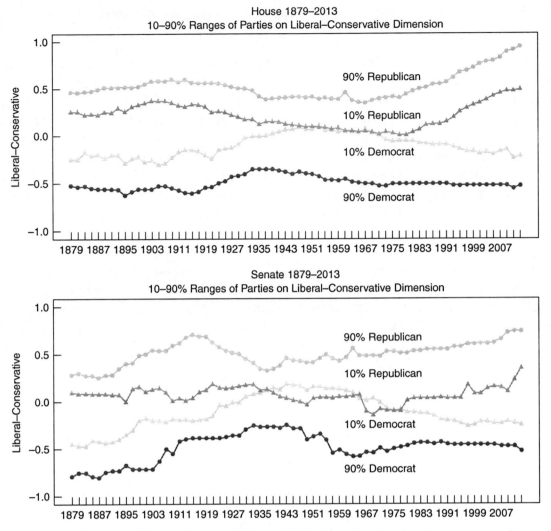

Figure 5.1 Ideological Dispersion of the Parties in Congress

NOTE: Figure shows the DW-NOMINATE ideological scores of the 10th/90th percentile Democratic and Republican legislators in the House and Senate over time.

lower levels of political participation, and the influx of immigrants who are low-income workers and/ or non-citizens has further increased the proportion of non-voters at the bottom end of the income distribution. In effect, this has shifted the position of the median income voter upward along the income distribution and, thus, the active electorate is less supportive than the mass public of government spending on redistributive social welfare policies.[13] This helps explain how the Republican Party has been able to move steadily rightward over the last 40 years without major electoral consequences, whereas Democrats have not been able to move further left than where the party was in the 1960s.

Finally, as we show in the following section, social/cultural issues are increasingly being drawn into the main dimension of conflict, which has usually been nearly exclusively occupied by economic issues. The end result is that the Democratic and Republican parties have become more ideologically homogeneous and are now deeply polarized. Moderates in Congress have virtually disappeared during the past 40 years, as the parties have pulled apart.

[. . .]

Heightened Ideological Constraint and the Changing Conflict Space of American Politics

One of the underappreciated aspects of contemporary political polarization has been how a diverse set of policy conflicts—from abortion to gun control to immigration— has collapsed into the dominant economic liberal–conservative dimension of American politics. That is, not only have the parties moved further apart on this ideological dimension in recent decades, but the meaning of the dimension itself has changed as it now encompasses a wider range of issues. The phenomenon has been termed "conflict extension" by Geoffrey Layman and Tom Carsey, and its occurrence among party activists and strong partisans in the electorate has been thoroughly documented by Layman et al.[14] In this section, we examine the progression of conflict extension in Congress and show that several formerly cross-cutting (i.e., issues that divide the parties internally) issues have been absorbed into the primary liberal–conservative dimension as polarization has expanded.

Of course, the notion that there are now fewer socially or culturally conservative Democrats as well as socially or culturally liberal Republicans in Congress is hardly controversial and probably obvious to any casual observer of contemporary American politics. However, we can more methodologically trace the evolution of "conflict extension" since the 1970s in Congress by examining the over-time fit of roll call votes on non-economic issues to one- and two-dimensional spatial models of ideology estimated by the DW-NOMINATE procedure.

Roll call votes that strongly tap into the primary liberal–conservative divide among legislators represent issues that are good fits to a one-dimensional model. That is, we can correctly classify most legislators' vote choices using only their positions on the first (liberal–conservative) dimension. Roll call votes that correspond to cross-cutting divisions are, of course, not picked up by the dominant liberal–conservative dimension and are poor fits in one dimension. However, the addition of a second dimension greatly improves the fit of these issues to the model. Finally, roll call votes with non-ideological voting patterns are poor fits in both models. An example of a vote with a good one-dimensional fit would be the 2010/2011 votes on the Patient Protection and Affordable Care Act; an example of a vote with a poor one-dimensional fit but a good two-dimensional fit would be the 1964 vote on the Civil Rights Act (before race became absorbed into the first liberal–conservative dimension); and an example of a vote with a poor fit in both models would be the 2008 votes on the $700b financial industry bailout package (TARP).[15]

[. . .]

Discussion

Both components of contemporary political polarization—the growing distance between the parties on the liberal–conservative spectrum and the redefinition of the liberal–conservative dimension itself to encompass a wider set of social and cultural conflicts—have profound implications for American politics. Issues such as abortion and gay marriage tap into fundamental worldview divides, inject added passion into partisan conflict, and make compromise between the two sides more difficult.[16] That this cleavage reinforces an already-widening schism between the parties over questions of economic regulation and redistribution further hampers the ability of the political system to address problems such as regulation of the finance industry, balancing the federal budget, and addressing income inequality.[17]

One of the consequences of polarization has been the movement of policy outcomes away from the ideological center and greater oscillation in policy outcomes between left and right when party control of Congress changes. **Figure 5.2** illustrates both patterns by showing the mean first-dimension (liberal– conservative) DW-NOMINATE score of the House and the Senate overall and of the winning coalitions in each chamber between 1879 and 2013. In other words, Figure 5.2 summarizes the ideological position of the policy outputs of each chamber over time. In both the House and Senate, the chamber means are more stable and closer to the center than the winning coalition means. However, the divergence between the two is largest in polarized eras; namely, the late nineteenth/ early twentieth century and roughly the last 25 years. Note, for example, that the winning coalition means closely track the chamber mean during the 1950s–1970s. This reflects the large number of moderates in each party and the frequency with which winning bipartisan coalitions were formed; hence, legislation needed to appeal to centrist members to win passage. This is not true during periods of ideological polarization when party unity is higher and winning coalitions are built with a majority of the majority party. As one example, Medicare passed the House in 1965 with the support of 237 Democrats and 70 Republicans, while President Obama's health-care reform package passed

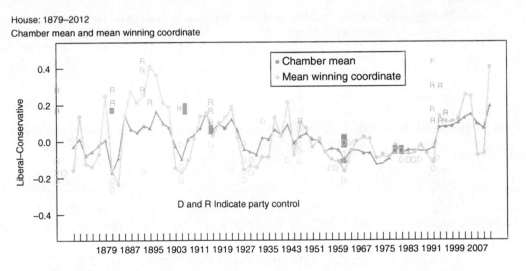

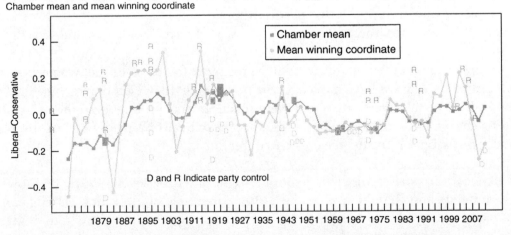

Figure 5.2   Fluctuation in Congressional Policy Outcomes

NOTE: Figure shows the DW-NOMINATE ideological scores of the 10th/90th percentile Democratic and Republican legislators in the House and Senate over time.

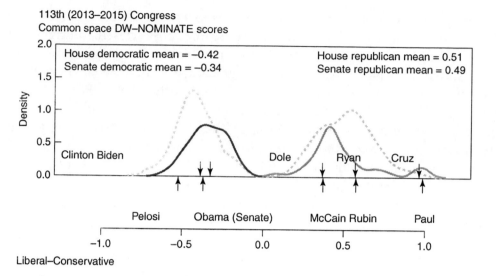

Figure 5.3 Ideological Positions of the Parties in the 113th Congress

NOTE: The House is shown with dotted lines, the Senate with solid lines. Democrats are shown in dark gray, Republicans in light gray.

the House in 2010 without a single Republican vote and despite defections from 34 of the more moderate members of the Democratic caucus.

[...]

Of course, a strong regularity of the American two-party system is that because parties are coalitions of diverse and sometimes competing interests, internal cleavages routinely arise within one or both of the parties. In most cases, these are simply minor stresses that create some intra-party conflict, but at times they can "break" the parties and lead to a realignment. Over the last half century, Democrats have been the more fractured of the two parties with an uneasy marriage of the New Left with the New Deal coalition of unions, the white working class, Southern Democrats, and racial minorities.

However, we speculate that the Republicans will be the more fractured of the two parties moving forward. Republicans in Congress have moved further to the right than Democrats must the left over the last 40 years and the Republican Party now covers greater territory along the right side of the ideological spectrum. That is, contemporary Republicans appear to be primarily divided not over a new issue or regional concerns, but on the degree of their conservatism.[18]

We find evidence in support of this claim at both the elite and mass level. **Figure 5.3** shows the distribution of Democrats and Republicans in the 113th Congress along the first (liberal–conservative) dimension recovered by the DW-NOMINATE Common Space procedure.[19] In both chambers, Republicans are further away from the center and have wider variances than the Democrats. It is difficult to identify distinct ideological clusters of Democratic MCs, but it is easy to do so for Republicans; for instance, moderate-conservatives like Senator John McCain (R-AZ) and former Senator Robert

Dole (R-KS), solid conservatives like Senator Marco Rubio (R-FL) and Representative Paul Ryan (R-WI), and very conservative Republicans with close ties to the Tea Party movement like Senators Rand Paul (R-KY) and Ted Cruz (R-TX). With the possible (though non-trivial) exception of foreign policy and domestic surveillance issues, these groups hold conservative positions over a range of economic and social/cultural issues.[20] The differences seem to lie primarily in the degree of conservatism—for instance, if and how much they would like to cut from entitlement programs and the federal budget to achieve deficit reduction.

We see a similar cleavage among Republicans in the electorate, as well. The Pew Research Center's January 2013 Political Survey includes several measures that we think are useful to examine this divide among Republican Party identifiers and leaners.[21] Namely, the survey asks for attitudes toward the Tea Party (Agree, Disagree, or No Opinion) and whether respondents prefer elected officials who make compromises with people they disagree with or elected officials who stick to their positions. [...]

Conclusion

The study of political polarization is contingent on the measurement of political actors' ideological positions. Poole and Rosenthal's NOMINATE procedure pro-vides a method to estimate ideological scores for MCs that is based on the spatial model of voting and uses legislators' entire voting histories. Crucially, these scores are dynamic and allow for the comparisons of quantities of interest (like the mean score of the Democratic and Republican parties) across time. The application of NOMINATE to the study of polarization in contemporary American politics produces unambiguous and import-ant results: The Democratic and Republican parties in Congress are more polarized than at any time since the end of Reconstruction, and a single liberal–conservative dimension explains the vast majority of legislators' vote choices, including on a wide array of social/cultural issues. We are now firmly entrenched in a political era that is characterized by the ubiquity of unidimensional, polarized political conflict.

End Notes

1. From THE POLARIZATION OF CONTEMPORARY AMERICAN POLITICS, Polity (2014) 46, 411–429. doi:10.1057/pol.2014.10
2. Matthew Levendusky, *The Partisan Sort: How Liberals Became Democrats and Conservatives Became Republicans* (Chicago: University of Chicago Press, 2009).
3. Clyde H. Coombs, *A Theory of Data* (New York: Wiley, 1964).
4. Keith T. Poole and Howard Rosenthal, *Congress: A Political-Economic History of Roll Call Voting* (New York: Oxford University Press, 1997).
5. Nolan McCarty, Keith T. Poole, and Howard Rosenthal, *Income Redistribution and the Realignment of American Politics* (Washington DC: AEI Press, 1997).
6. Nolan McCarty, Keith T. Poole, and Howard Rosenthal, *Income Redistribution and the Realignment of American Politics* (Washington DC: AEI Press, 1997).
7. Louis Hartz, *The Liberal Tradition in America: An Interpretation of American Political Thought Since the Revolution* (New York: Harcourt, Brace & World, 1955). See also Richard Hofstadter, *The American Political Tradition and the Men Who Made It* (New York: Vintage Press, 1948).
8. Maurice Duverger, *Les Partis Politiques* (Paris: Armand Colin, 1951).
9. Edward G. Carmines and James A. Stimson, *Issue Evolution: Race and the Transformation of American Politics* (Princeton: Princeton University Press, 1989).

10. Poole and Rosenthal, *Congress*.
11. Rick Perlstein, *Before the Storm: Barry Goldwater and the Unmaking of the American Consensus* (New York: Hill and Wang, 2001).
12. Thomas Piketty and Emmanuel Saez, "Income Inequality in the United States, 1913–1998," *Quarterly Journal of Economics* 118 (February 2003): 1–39.
13. Nolan McCarty, Keith T. Poole, and Howard Rosenthal, *Polarized America: The Dance of Ideology and Unequal Riches* (Cambridge, MA: MIT Press, 2006).
14. Geoffrey C. Layman and Thomas M. Carsey, "Party Polarization and 'Conflict Extension' in the American Electorate," *American Journal of Political Science* 46 (October 2002): 786–802; Geoffrey C. Layman and Thomas M. Carsey, "Party Polarization and Party Structuring of Policy Attitudes: A Comparison of Three NES Panel Studies," *Political Behavior* 24 (September 2002): 199–236; Thomas M. Carsey and Geoffrey C. Layman, "Changing Sides or Changing Minds? Party Identification and Policy Preferences in the American Electorate," *American Journal of Political Science* 50 (April 2006): 464–77; Geoffrey C. Layman, Thomas M. Carsey, John C. Green, Richard Herrera, and Rosalyn Cooperman, "Activists and Conflict Extension in American Party Politics," *American Political Science Review* 104 (May 2010): 324–46.
15. Nolan McCarty, Keith T. Poole, and Howard Rosenthal, *Political Bubbles: Financial Crises and the Failure of American Democracy* (Princeton: Princeton University Press, 2013).
16. James Davison Hunter, *Culture Wars: The Struggle to Define America* (New York: Basic Books, 1991); Marc J. Hetherington and Jonathan D. Weiler, *Authoritarianism and Polarization in American Politics* (Cambridge: Cambridge University Press, 2009).
17. McCarty, Poole, and Rosenthal, *Polarized America*; McCarty, Poole, and Rosenthal, *Political Bubbles*.
18. Of course, a similar ideological divide could appear in the Democratic Party between the left and center, most likely over economic issues like income inequality and financial regulation. However, at present there is no evidence from NOMINATE of such a divide among congressional Democrats
19. Common Space scores allow for comparisons between the chambers as well as across time by using two sets of overlapping cohorts: legislators who have served in both the House and Senate to bridge across the chambers as well as legislators who have served in multiple Congresses to bridge across time. This allows us to include density plots for the parties in both the House and the Senate as well as compare the position of a former legislator like Senator Robert Dole (R-KS) with the positions of MCs in the 113th Congress.
20. If the most conservative group of congressional Republicans were breaking from other Republicans on new issue dimensions, we would expect that their fit to the existing spatial model would be poorer. However, the correlation between first-dimension DW-NOMINATE Common Space score and Geometric Mean Probability (a measure of fit of legislators' observed choices to the spatial model) is $r = 0.20$ among House Republicans and $r = 0.37$ among Senate Republicans in the 112th Congress and $r = 0.05$ among House Republicans and $r = 0.06$ among Senate Republicans in the 113th Congress. Hence, there is at most a weak relationship between ideological extremity and spatial fit among Republican MCs in the last two Congresses, and to the extent a relationship does exist, it is positive (meaning more conservative legislators are a better fit to the model).
21. Pew Research Center for the People and the Press, January 2013 Political Survey, available for download at: http://www.people-press.org/2013/01/13/january-2013-political-survey/, accessed on June 5, 2014.

CHAPTER 6
THE PRESIDENT

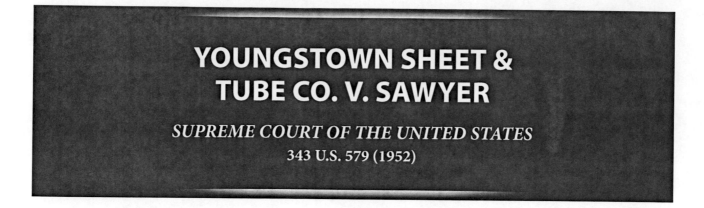

YOUNGSTOWN SHEET & TUBE CO. V. SAWYER

SUPREME COURT OF THE UNITED STATES
343 U.S. 579 (1952)

MR. JUSTICE BLACK delivered the opinion of the Court.

We are asked to decide whether the President was acting within his constitutional power when he issued an order directing the Secretary of Commerce to take possession of and operate most of the Nation's steel mills. The mill owners argue that the President's order amounts to lawmaking, a legislative function which the Constitution has expressly confided to the Congress and not to the President. The Government's position is that the order was made on findings of the President that his action was necessary to avert a national catastrophe which would inevitably result from a stoppage of steel production, and that in meeting this grave emergency the President was acting within the aggregate of his constitutional powers as the Nation's Chief Executive and the Commander in Chief of the Armed Forces of the United States. The issue emerges here from the following series of events:

In the latter part of 1951, a dispute arose between the steel companies and their employees over terms and conditions that should be included in new collective bargaining agreements. Long-continued conferences failed to resolve the dispute. On December 18, 1951, the employees' representative, United Steelworkers of America, C. I. O., gave notice of an intention to strike when the existing bargaining agreements expired on December 31. The Federal Mediation and Conciliation Service then intervened in an effort to get labor and management to agree. This failing, the President on December 22, 1951, referred the dispute to the Federal Wage Stabilization Board to investigate and make recommendations for fair and equitable terms of settlement. This Board's report resulted in no settlement. On April 4, 1952, the Union gave notice of a nation-wide strike called to begin at 12:01 a. m. April 9. The indispensability of steel as a component of substantially all weapons and other war materials led the President to believe that the proposed work stoppage would immediately jeopardize our national defense and that governmental seizure of the steel mills was necessary in order to assure the continued availability of steel. Reciting these considerations for his action, the President, a few hours before the strike was to begin, issued Executive Order 10340, a copy of which is attached as an appendix, *post*, p. 589. The order directed the Secretary of Commerce to take possession of most of the steel mills and keep them running. The Secretary immediately issued his own possessory orders, calling upon the presidents of the various seized companies to serve as operating managers for the United States. They were directed to carry on their activities in accordance with regulations and directions of the Secretary. The next morning the President sent a message to Congress reporting his action. Twelve days later he sent a second message. Congress has taken no action.

Obeying the Secretary's orders under protest, the companies brought proceedings against him in the District Court. Their complaints charged that the seizure was not authorized by an act of Congress or by any constitutional provisions. The District Court was asked to declare the orders of the President and the Secretary invalid and to issue preliminary and permanent injunctions restraining their enforcement. Opposing the motion for preliminary injunction, the United States asserted that a strike disrupting steel production for even a brief period would so endanger the well-being and safety of the Nation that the President had "inherent power" to do what he had done—power "supported by the Constitution, by historical precedent, and by court decisions." The Government also contended that in any event no preliminary injunction should be issued because the companies had made no showing that their available legal remedies were inadequate or that their injuries from seizure would be irreparable. Holding against the Government on all points, the District Court on April 30 issued a preliminary injunction restraining the Secretary from "continuing the seizure and possession of the plants . . . and from acting under the purported authority of Executive Order No. 10340. . . ."

Two crucial issues have developed: *First*. Should final determination of the constitutional validity of the President's order be made in this case which has proceeded no further than the preliminary injunction stage? *Second*. If so, is the seizure order within the constitutional power of the President?

[. . .]

The President's power, if any, to issue the order must stem either from an act of Congress or from the Constitution itself. There is no statute that expressly authorizes the President to take possession of property as he did here. Nor is there any act of Congress to which our attention has been directed from which such a power can fairly be implied. Indeed, we do not understand the Government to rely on statutory authorization for this seizure. . . .

Moreover, the use of the seizure technique to solve labor disputes in order to prevent work stoppages was not only unauthorized by any congressional enactment; prior to this controversy, Congress had refused to adopt that method of settling labor disputes. When the Taft-Hartley Act was under consideration in 1947, Congress rejected an amendment which would have authorized such governmental seizures in cases of emergency. Apparently it was thought that the technique of seizure, like that of compulsory arbitration, would interfere with the process of collective bargaining. Consequently, the plan Congress adopted in that Act did not provide for seizure under any circumstances. Instead, the plan sought to bring about settlements by use of the customary devices of mediation, conciliation, investigation by boards of inquiry, and public reports. . . .

It is clear that if the President had authority to issue the order he did, it must be found in some provision of the Constitution. And it is not claimed that express constitutional language grants this power to the President. The contention is that presidential power should be implied from the aggregate of his powers under the Constitution. Particular reliance is placed on provisions in Article II which say that "The executive Power shall be vested in a President . . ."; that "he shall take Care that the Laws be faithfully executed"; and that he "shall be Commander in Chief of the Army and Navy of the United States."

The order cannot properly be sustained as an exercise of the President's military power as Commander in Chief of the Armed Forces. The Government attempts to do so by citing a number of cases upholding broad powers in military commanders engaged in day-to-day fighting in a theater of war. Such cases need not concern us here. Even though "theater of war" be an expanding concept, we cannot with faithfulness to our constitutional system hold that the Commander in Chief of the Armed Forces has the ultimate power as such to take possession of private property in order to keep labor disputes from stopping production. This is a job for the Nation's lawmakers, not for its military authorities.

Nor can the seizure order be sustained because of the several constitutional provisions that grant executive power to the President. In the framework of our Constitution, the President's power to see that the laws are faithfully executed refutes the idea that he is to be a lawmaker. The Constitution limits his functions in the lawmaking process to the recommending of laws he thinks wise and the vetoing of laws he thinks bad. And the Constitution is neither silent nor equivocal about who shall make laws which the President is to execute. The first section of the first article says that "All legislative Powers herein granted shall be vested in a Congress of the United States. . ."

The President's order does not direct that a congressional policy be executed in a manner prescribed by Congress—it directs that a presidential policy be executed in a manner prescribed by the President. The preamble of the order itself, like that of many statutes, sets out reasons why the President believes certain policies should be adopted, proclaims these policies as rules of conduct to be followed, and again, like a statute, authorizes a government official to promulgate additional rules and regulations consistent with the policy proclaimed and needed to carry that policy into execution. The power of Congress to adopt such public policies as those proclaimed by the order is beyond question. It can authorize the taking of private property for public use. It can make laws regulating the relationships between employers and employees, prescribing rules designed to settle labor disputes, and fixing wages and working conditions in certain fields of our economy. The Constitution does not subject this lawmaking power of Congress to presidential or military supervision or control.

[. . .]

JUSTICE JACKSON, concurring in the judgement of the Court:

Presidential powers are not fixed but fluctuate, depending upon their disjunction or conjunction with those of Congress. We may well begin by a somewhat over-simplified grouping of practical situations in which a President may doubt, or others may challenge, his powers, and by distinguishing roughly the legal consequences of this factor of relativity.

1. When the President acts pursuant to an express or implied authorization of Congress, his authority is at its maximum, for it includes all that he possesses in his own right plus all that Congress can delegate. In these circumstances, and in these only, may he be said (for what it may be worth) to personify the federal sovereignty. If his act is held unconstitutional under these circumstances, it usually means that the Federal Government as an undivided whole lacks power. A seizure executed by the President pursuant to an Act of Congress would be supported by the strongest of presumptions and the widest latitude of judicial interpretation, and the burden of persuasion would rest heavily upon any who might attack it.

[. . .]

2. When the President acts in absence of either a congressional grant or denial of authority, he can only rely upon his own independent powers, but there is a zone of twilight in which he and Congress may have concurrent authority, or in which its distribution is uncertain. Therefore, congressional inertia, indifference or quiescence may sometimes, at least as a practical matter, enable, if not invite,

measures on independent presidential responsibility. In this area, any actual test of power is likely to depend on the imperatives of events and contemporary imponderables rather than on abstract theories of law.

[. . .]

3. When the President takes measures incompatible with the expressed or implied will of Congress, his power is at its lowest ebb, for then he can rely only upon his own constitutional powers minus any constitutional powers of Congress over the matter. Courts can sustain exclusive presidential control in such a case only by disabling the Congress from acting upon the subject. Presidential claim to a power at once so conclusive and preclusive must be scrutinized with caution, for what is at stake is the equilibrium established by our constitutional system.

[. . .]

Into which of these classifications does this executive seizure of the steel industry fit? It is eliminated from the first by admission, for it is conceded that no congressional authorization exists for this seizure. That takes away also the support of the many precedents and declarations which were made in relation, and must be confined, to this category.

[. . .]

Can it then be defended under flexible tests available to the second category? It seems clearly eliminated from that class because Congress has not left seizure of private property an open field but has covered it by three statutory policies inconsistent with this seizure. In cases where the purpose is to supply needs of the Government itself, two courses are provided: one, seizure of a plant which fails to comply with obligatory orders placed by the Government; another, condemnation of facilities, including temporary use under the power of eminent domain. The third is applicable where it is the general economy of the country that is to be protected rather than exclusive governmental interests. None of these were invoked. In choosing a different and inconsistent way of his own, the President cannot claim that it is necessitated or invited by failure of Congress to legislate upon the occasions, grounds and methods for seizure of industrial properties.

[. . .]

This leaves the current seizure to be justified only by the severe tests under the third grouping, where it can be supported only by any remainder of executive power after subtraction of such powers as Congress may have over the subject. In short, we can sustain the President only by holding that seizure of such strike-bound industries is within his domain and beyond control by Congress. Thus, this Court's first review of such seizures occurs under circumstances which leave presidential power most vulnerable to attack and in the least favorable of possible constitutional postures.

[. . .]

That military powers of the Commander in Chief were not to supersede representative government of internal affairs seems obvious from the Constitution and from elementary American history. Time out of mind, and even now in many parts of the world, a military commander can seize private housing to shelter his troops. Not so, however, in the United States, for the Third Amendment says, "No Soldier shall, in time of peace be quartered in any house, without the consent of the Owner, nor in time of war, but in a manner to be prescribed by law." Thus, even in war time, his seizure of needed military housing must be authorized by Congress. It also was expressly left to Congress to "provide for calling forth the Militia to execute the Laws of the Union, suppress Insurrections and repel Invasions . . . ." Such a limitation on the command power, written at a time when the militia rather than a standing army was contemplated as the military weapon of the Republic, underscores the Constitution's policy that Congress, not the Executive, should control utilization of the war power as an instrument of domestic policy. Congress, fulfilling that function, has authorized the President to use the army to enforce certain civil rights. On the other hand, Congress has forbidden him to use the army for the purpose of executing general laws except when *expressly* authorized by the Constitution or by Act of Congress.

[. . .]

The essence of our free Government is "leave to live by no man's leave, underneath the law"—to be governed by those impersonal forces which we call law. Our Government is fashioned to fulfill this concept so far as humanly possible. The Executive, except for recommendation and veto, has no legislative power. The executive action we have here originates in the individual will of the President and represents an exercise of authority without law. No one, perhaps not even the President, knows the limits of the power he may seek to exert in this instance and the parties affected cannot learn the limit of their rights. We do not know today what powers over labor or property would be claimed to flow from Government possession if we should legalize it, what rights to compensation would be claimed or recognized, or on what contingency it would end. With all its defects, delays and inconveniences, men have discovered no technique for long preserving free government except that the Executive be under the law, and that the law be made by parliamentary deliberations.

KOREMATSU V. UNITED STATES

SUPREME COURT OF THE UNITED STATES

323 U.S. 214

December 18, 1944, Decided

MR. JUSTICE BLACK delivered the opinion of the Court.

The petitioner, an American citizen of Japanese descent, was convicted in a federal district court for remaining in San Leandro, California, a "Military Area," contrary to Civilian Exclusion Order No. 34 of the Commanding General of the Western Command, U.S. Army, which directed that after May 9, 1942, all persons of Japanese ancestry should be excluded from that area. No question was raised as to petitioner's loyalty to the United States. The Circuit Court of Appeals affirmed, and the importance of the constitutional question involved caused us to grant certiorari.

It should be noted, to begin with, that all legal restrictions which curtail the civil rights of a single racial group are immediately suspect. That is not to say that all such restrictions are unconstitutional. It is to say that courts must subject them to the most rigid scrutiny. Pressing public necessity may sometimes justify the existence of such restrictions; racial antagonism never can.

In the instant case prosecution of the petitioner was begun by information charging violation of an Act of Congress, of March 21, 1942, 56 Stat. 173, which provides that ". . . whoever shall enter, remain in, leave, or commit any act in any military area or military zone prescribed, under the authority of an Executive order of the President, by the Secretary of War, or by any military commander designated by the Secretary of War, contrary to the restrictions applicable to any such area or zone or contrary to the order of the Secretary of War or any such military commander, shall, if it appears that he knew or should have known of the existence and extent of the restrictions or order and that his act was in violation thereof, be guilty of a misdemeanor and upon conviction shall be liable to a fine of not to exceed $ 5,000 or to imprisonment for not more than one year, or both, for each offense."

Exclusion Order No. 34, which the petitioner knowingly and admittedly violated, was one of a number of military orders and proclamations, all of which were substantially based upon Executive Order No. 9066. That order, issued after we were at war with Japan, declared that "the successful prosecution of the war requires every possible protection against espionage and against sabotage to national-defense material, national-defense premises, and national-defense utilities. . . ."

One of the series of orders and proclamations, a curfew order, which like the exclusion order here was promulgated pursuant to Executive Order 9066, subjected all persons of Japanese ancestry in prescribed West Coast military areas to remain in their residences from 8 p.m. to 6 a.m. As is the case with the exclusion order here, that prior curfew order was designed as a "protection against espionage and against sabotage." In *Hirabayashi* v. *United States*, 320 U.S. 81, we sustained a conviction obtained for violation of the curfew order. The Hirabayashi conviction and this one thus rest on the same 1942 Congressional Act and the same basic executive and military orders, all of which orders were aimed at the twin dangers of espionage and sabotage.

The 1942 Act was attacked in the *Hirabayashi* case as an unconstitutional delegation of power; it was contended that the curfew order and other orders on which it rested were beyond the war powers of the Congress, the military authorities and of the President, as Commander in Chief of the Army; and finally that to apply the curfew order against none but citizens of Japanese ancestry amounted to a constitutionally prohibited discrimination solely on account of race. To these questions, we gave the serious consideration which their importance justified. We upheld the curfew order as an exercise of the power of the government to take steps necessary to prevent espionage and sabotage in an area threatened by Japanese attack.

In the light of the principles we announced in the *Hirabayashi* case, we are unable to conclude that it was beyond the war power of Congress and the Executive to exclude those of Japanese ancestry from the West Coast war area at the time they did. True, exclusion from the area in which one's home is located is a far greater deprivation than constant confinement to the home from 8 p.m. to 6 a.m. Nothing short of apprehension by the proper military authorities of the gravest imminent danger to the public safety can constitutionally justify either. But exclusion from a threatened area, no less than curfew, has a definite and close relationship to the prevention of espionage and sabotage. The military authorities, charged with the primary responsibility of defending our shores, concluded that curfew provided inadequate protection and ordered exclusion. They did so, as pointed out in our *Hirabayashi* opinion, in accordance with Congressional authority to the military to say who should, and who should not, remain in the threatened areas.

In this case the petitioner challenges the assumptions upon which we rested our conclusions in the *Hirabayashi* case. He also urges that by May 1942, when Order No. 34 was promulgated, all danger of Japanese invasion of the West Coast had disappeared. After careful consideration of these contentions we are compelled to reject them.

Here, as in the *Hirabayashi* case, ". . . we cannot reject as unfounded the judgment of the military authorities and of Congress that there were disloyal members of that population, whose number and strength could not be precisely and quickly ascertained. We cannot say that the war-making branches of the Government did not have ground for believing that in a critical hour such persons could not readily be isolated and separately dealt with, and constituted a menace to the national defense and safety, which demanded that prompt and adequate measures be taken to guard against it."

Like curfew, exclusion of those of Japanese origin was deemed necessary because of the presence of an unascertained number of disloyal members of the group, most of whom we have no doubt were loyal to this country. It was because we could not reject the finding of the military authorities that it was impossible to bring about an immediate segregation of the disloyal from the loyal that we sustained the validity of the curfew order as applying to the whole group. In the instant case, temporary exclusion of the entire group was rested by the military on the same ground. The judgment that exclusion of the whole group was for the same reason a military imperative answers the contention that the exclusion was in the nature of group punishment based on antagonism to those of Japanese origin. That there were members of the group who retained loyalties to Japan has been confirmed by investigations made subsequent to the exclusion. Approximately five thousand American citizens of

Japanese ancestry refused to swear unqualified allegiance to the United States and to renounce allegiance to the Japanese Emperor, and several thousand evacuees requested repatriation to Japan.

We uphold the exclusion order as of the time it was made and when the petitioner violated it. In doing so, we are not unmindful of the hardships imposed by it upon a large group of American citizens. But hardships are part of war, and war is an aggregation of hardships. All citizens alike, both in and out of uniform, feel the impact of war in greater or lesser measure. Citizenship has its responsibilities as well as its privileges, and in time of war the burden is always heavier. Compulsory exclusion of large groups of citizens from their homes, except under circumstances of direst emergency and peril, is inconsistent with our basic governmental institutions. But when under conditions of modern warfare our shores are threatened by hostile forces, the power to protect must be commensurate with the threatened danger.

[. . .]

It is said that we are dealing here with the case of imprisonment of a citizen in a concentration camp solely because of his ancestry, without evidence or inquiry concerning his loyalty and good disposition towards the United States. Our task would be simple, our duty clear, were this a case involving the imprisonment of a loyal citizen in a concentration camp because of racial prejudice. Regardless of the true nature of the assembly and relocation centers—and we deem it unjustifiable to call them concentration camps with all the ugly connotations that term implies—we are dealing specifically with nothing but an exclusion order. To cast this case into outlines of racial prejudice, without reference to the real military dangers which were presented, merely confuses the issue. Korematsu was not excluded from the Military Area because of hostility to him or his race. He *was* excluded because we are at war with the Japanese Empire, because the properly constituted military authorities feared an invasion of our West Coast and felt constrained to take proper security measures, because they decided that the military urgency of the situation demanded that all citizens of Japanese ancestry be segregated from the West Coast temporarily, and finally, because Congress, reposing its confidence in this time of war in our military leaders—as inevitably it must—determined that they should have the power to do just this. There was evidence of disloyalty on the part of some, the military authorities considered that the need for action was great, and time was short. We cannot—by availing ourselves of the calm perspective of hindsight—now say that at that time these actions were unjustified.

[. . .]

MR. JUSTICE FRANKFURTER, concurring.

The provisions of the Constitution which confer on the Congress and the President powers to enable this country to wage war are as much part of the Constitution as provisions looking to a nation at peace. And we have had recent occasion to quote approvingly the statement of former Chief Justice Hughes that the war power of the Government is "the power to wage war successfully." *Hirabayashi* v. *United States*. Therefore, the validity of action under the war power must be judged wholly in the context of war. That action is not to be stigmatized as lawless because like action in times of peace would be lawless. To talk about a military order that expresses an allowable judgment of war needs by those entrusted with the duty of conducting war as "an unconstitutional order" is to suffuse a part of the Constitution with an atmosphere of unconstitutionality. The respective spheres of action of military authorities and of judges are of course very different. But within their sphere, military authorities are no more outside the bounds of obedience to the Constitution than are judges within theirs. "The war power of the United States, like its other powers . . . is subject to applicable constitutional limitations," *Hamilton* v. *Kentucky Distilleries Co.*, 251 U.S. 146, 156. To recognize that military orders are "reasonably expedient military precautions" in time of war and yet to deny them constitutional legitimacy makes of the Constitution an instrument for dialectic subleties not reasonably to be attributed to the hard-headed Framers, of whom a majority had had actual participation in war. If a military order such as that under review does not transcend the means appropriate for conducting war, such action by the military is as constitutional as would be any authorized action by the Interstate Commerce Commission within the limits of the constitutional power to regulate commerce. And being an exercise of the war power explicitly granted by the Constitution for safeguarding the national life by prosecuting war effectively, I find nothing in the Constitution which denies to Congress the power to enforce such a valid military order by making its violation an offense triable in the civil courts. . . . To find that the Constitution does not forbid the military measures now complained of does not carry with it approval of that which Congress and the Executive did. That is their business, not ours.

[. . .]

MR. JUSTICE MURPHY, dissenting.

This exclusion of "all persons of Japanese ancestry, both alien and non-alien," from the Pacific Coast area on a plea of military necessity in the absence of martial law ought not to be approved. Such exclusion goes over "the very brink of constitutional power" and falls into the ugly abyss of racism.

In dealing with matters relating to the prosecution and progress of a war, we must accord great respect and consideration to the judgments of the military authorities who are on the scene and who have full knowledge of the military facts. The scope of their discretion must, as a matter of necessity and common sense, be wide. And their judgments ought not to be overruled lightly by those whose training and duties ill-equip them to deal intelligently with matters so vital to the physical security of the nation.

At the same time, however, it is essential that there be definite limits to military discretion, especially where martial law has not been declared. Individuals must not be left impoverished of their constitutional rights on a plea of military necessity that has neither substance nor support. Thus, like other claims conflicting with the asserted constitutional rights of the individual, the military claim must subject itself to the judicial process of having its reasonableness determined and its conflicts with other interests reconciled. "What are the allowable limits of military discretion, and whether or not they have been overstepped in a particular case, are judicial questions." *Sterling* v. *Constantin*, 287 U.S. 378, 401.

The judicial test of whether the Government, on a plea of military necessity, can validly deprive an individual of any of his constitutional rights is whether the deprivation is reasonably related to a public danger that is so "immediate, imminent, and impending" as not to admit of delay and not to permit the intervention of ordinary constitutional processes to alleviate the danger. Civilian Exclusion Order No. 34, banishing from a prescribed area of the Pacific Coast "all persons of Japanese ancestry, both alien and non-alien," clearly does not meet that test. Being an obvious racial discrimination, the order deprives all those within its scope of the equal protection of the laws as guaranteed by the Fifth

Amendment. It further deprives these individuals of their constitutional rights to live and work where they will, to establish a home where they choose and to move about freely. In excommunicating them without benefit of hearings, this order also deprives them of all their constitutional rights to procedural due process. Yet no reasonable relation to an "immediate, imminent, and impending" public danger is evident to support this racial restriction which is one of the most sweeping and complete deprivations of constitutional rights in the history of this nation in the absence of martial law.

It must be conceded that the military and naval situation in the spring of 1942 was such as to generate a very real fear of invasion of the Pacific Coast, accompanied by fears of sabotage and espionage in that area. The military command was therefore justified in adopting all reasonable means necessary to combat these dangers. In adjudging the military action taken in light of the then apparent dangers, we must not erect too high or too meticulous standards; it is necessary only that the action have some reasonable relation to the removal of the dangers of invasion, sabotage and espionage. But the exclusion, either temporarily or permanently, of all persons with Japanese blood in their veins has no such reasonable relation. And that relation is lacking because the exclusion order necessarily must rely for its reasonableness upon the assumption that *all* persons of Japanese ancestry may have a dangerous tendency to commit sabotage and espionage and to aid our Japanese enemy in other ways. It is difficult to believe that reason, logic or experience could be marshalled in support of such an assumption.

That this forced exclusion was the result in good measure of this erroneous assumption of racial guilt rather than bona fide military necessity is evidenced by the Commanding General's Final Report on the evacuation from the Pacific Coast area. In it he refers to all individuals of Japanese descent as "subversive," as belonging to "an enemy race" whose "racial strains are undiluted," and as constituting "over 112,000 potential enemies . . . at large today" along the Pacific Coast. In support of this blanket condemnation of all persons of Japanese descent, however, no reliable evidence is cited to show that such individuals were generally disloyal, or had generally so conducted themselves in this area as to constitute a special menace to defense installations or war industries, or had otherwise by their behavior furnished reasonable ground for their exclusion as a group.

Justification for the exclusion is sought, instead, mainly upon questionable racial and sociological grounds not ordinarily within the realm of expert military judgment, supplemented by certain semi-military conclusions drawn from an unwarranted use of circumstantial evidence.

[. . .]

The main reasons relied upon by those responsible for the forced evacuation, therefore, do not prove a reasonable relation between the group characteristics of Japanese Americans and the dangers of invasion, sabotage and espionage. The reasons appear, instead, to be largely an accumulation of much of the misinformation, half-truths and insinuations that for years have been directed against Japanese Americans by people with racial and economic prejudices—the same people who have been among the foremost advocates of the evacuation. A military judgment based upon such racial and sociological considerations is not entitled to the great weight ordinarily given the judgments based upon strictly military considerations. Especially is this so when every charge relative to race, religion, culture, geographical location, and legal and economic status has been substantially discredited by independent studies made by experts in these matters.

[. . .]

No adequate reason is given for the failure to treat these Japanese Americans on an individual basis by holding investigations and hearings to separate the loyal from the disloyal, as was done in the case of persons of German and Italian ancestry. . . .

I dissent, therefore, from this legalization of racism. Racial discrimination in any form and in any degree has no justifiable part whatever in our democratic way of life. It is unattractive in any setting but it is utterly revolting among a free people who have embraced the principles set forth in the Constitution of the United States. All residents of this nation are kin in some way by blood or culture to a foreign land. Yet they are primarily and necessarily a part of the new and distinct civilization of the United States. They must accordingly be treated at all times as the heirs of the American experiment and as entitled to all the rights and freedoms guaranteed by the Constitution.

MR. JUSTICE JACKSON, dissenting.

Korematsu was born on our soil, of parents born in Japan. The Constitution makes him a citizen of the United States by nativity and a citizen of California by residence. No claim is made that he is not loyal to this country. There is no suggestion that apart from the matter involved here he is not law-abiding and well disposed. Korematsu, however, has been convicted of an act not commonly a crime. It consists merely of being present in the state whereof he is a citizen, near the place where he was born, and where all his life he has lived.

Even more unusual is the series of military orders which made this conduct a crime. They forbid such a one to remain, and they also forbid him to leave. They were so drawn that the only way Korematsu could avoid violation was to give himself up to the military authority. This meant submission to custody, examination, and transportation out of the territory, to be followed by indeterminate confinement in detention camps.

A citizen's presence in the locality, however, was made a crime only if his parents were of Japanese birth. Had Korematsu been one of four—the others being, say, a German alien enemy, an Italian alien enemy, and a citizen of American-born ancestors, convicted of treason but out on parole—only Korematsu's presence would have violated the order. The difference between their innocence and his crime would result, not from anything he did, said, or thought, different than they, but only in that he was born of different racial stock.

Now, if any fundamental assumption underlies our system, it is that guilt is personal and not inheritable. . . .

But the "law" which this prisoner is convicted of disregarding is not found in an act of Congress, but in a military order. Neither the Act of Congress nor the Executive Order of the President, nor both together, would afford a basis for this conviction. It rests on the orders of General DeWitt. And it is said that if the military commander had reasonable military grounds for promulgating the orders, they are constitutional and become law, and the Court is required to enforce them. There are several reasons why I cannot subscribe to this doctrine.

[. . .]

In the very nature of things, military decisions are not susceptible of intelligent judicial appraisal. They do not pretend to rest on evidence, but are made on information that often would not be admissible and on assumptions that could not be proved. Information in support of an order could not be disclosed to courts without danger that it would reach the enemy. Neither can courts act on communications made in confidence. Hence courts can never have any real alternative to accepting the mere declaration of the authority that issued the order that it was reasonably necessary from a military viewpoint.

Much is said of the danger to liberty from the Army program for deporting and detaining these citizens of Japanese extraction. But a judicial construction of the due process clause that will sustain this order is a far more subtle blow to liberty than the promulgation of the order itself. A military order, however unconstitutional, is not apt to last longer than the military emergency. Even during that period a succeeding commander may revoke it all. But once a judicial opinion rationalizes such an order to show that it conforms to the Constitution, or rather rationalizes the Constitution to show that the Constitution sanctions such an order, the Court for all time has validated the principle of racial discrimination in criminal procedure and of transplanting American citizens. The principle then lies about like a loaded weapon ready for the hand of any authority that can bring forward a plausible claim of an urgent need. Every repetition imbeds that principle more deeply in our law and thinking and expands it to new purposes. . . .

My duties as a justice as I see them do not require me to make a military judgment as to whether General DeWitt's evacuation and detention program was a reasonable military necessity. I do not suggest that the courts should have attempted to interfere with the Army in carrying out its task. But I do not think they may be asked to execute a military expedient that has no place in law under the Constitution. I would reverse the judgment and discharge the prisoner.

CHAPTER 7
JUDICIARY

BOUND FOR GLORY? *BROWN* AND THE CIVIL RIGHTS REVOLUTION

GERALD N. ROSENBERG

Education—Elementary and Secondary Schools

Court Action

Brown and its companion case, *Bolling* v. *Sharpe* (1954),[1] were the Court's first modern foray into questions of segregation in the elementary and secondary schools. *Brown* was actually four consolidated cases coming from the states of Kansas (*Brown* v. *Board of Education of Topeka, Kansas* 1951), South Carolina (*Briggs* v. *Elliott* 1952), Virginia (*Davis* v. *County School Board of Prince Edward County, Virginia* 1952), and Delaware (*Gebhardt* v. *Belton* 1952). Its holding, however, was applicable to all public elementary and secondary schools throughout the nation. At the time of the decision (May 17, 1954), seventeen Southern and Border states,[2] plus the District of Columbia, maintained segregated elementary and secondary schools by law and four states outside the region—Arizona, Kansas, New Mexico, and Wyoming—allowed local segregation. Eleven states had no laws on the subject and sixteen states had laws prohibiting segregation, though not all were enforced. Thus, twenty-seven states either prohibited segregated schools outright or had no laws dealing with the question while twenty-one states either required or allowed segregated schools.

Brown had taken several years to decide. Originally argued in 1952, it was re-argued in 1953, before a Court presided over by a new Chief Justice, Earl Warren. The decision was announced in May of 1954. The time delay between initial argument and final decision was due to the complexity of the issues involved and the desire of the new Chief Justice to reach a unanimous decision (Ulmer 1971).[3]

The National Association for the Advancement of Colored People (NAACP) was euphoric over the unanimous decision. Thurgood Marshall, the chief litigator for the black plaintiffs, told reporters that the Supreme Court's interpretation of the law was "very clear." If the decision were violated anywhere "on one morning" Marshall said, "we'll have the responsible authorities in court by the next morning, if not the same afternoon." When asked how long he thought it would take for segregation to be eliminated from public schools, Marshall replied that "it might be 'up to five years' for the entire country." Finally, "he predicted that by the time the 100th anniversary of the Emancipation Proclamation was observed in 1963, segregation in all its forms would have been eliminated from the nation" ("N.A.A.C.P." 1954, 16).

The decision, however, did not include any announcement as to the appropriate relief for the plaintiffs. This was postponed for reargument due to the "considerable complexity" (*Brown* 1954, 495) of the matter. Reargument lasted for four days in April 1955, and the parties to the case, including the United States, were joined by the attorneys general of Arkansas, Florida, Maryland, North Carolina, Oklahoma, and Texas, as *amici curiae* pursuant to the Court's invitation in *Brown* (1954, 495–96).

The remedy was announced on May 31, 1955, slightly more than a year after the initial decision and two and one-half years after the initial argument. The Court in *Brown II* (1955) held that, because local school problems varied, federal courts were in the best position to assure compliance with *Brown I*, an end to legally enforced public-school segregation. The cases were reversed and remanded to the lower courts[4] which were ordered to "take such proceedings and enter such orders and decrees consistent with this opinion as are necessary and proper to admit to public schools on a racially non-discriminatory basis with all deliberate speed the parties to these cases" (1955, 301). The phrase "with all deliberate speed" was picked up by commentators, lawyers, and judges as the applicable standard. Thus, the end result of the *Brown* litigation was a unanimous Supreme Court clearly and unequivocally holding that state-enforced segregation of public schools was unconstitutional and ordering that it be ended "with all deliberate speed."

During the years from 1955 through the passage of the 1964 Civil Rights Act, the Court issued only three full opinions in the area of segregation of elementary and secondary schools. It routinely refused to hear cases or curtly affirmed or reversed lower-court decisions (for a discussion of these cases, see Wasby et al. 1977, 166–73, 192–98). However, in *Cooper v. Aaron* (1958), the first case after *Brown*, the Court spoke strongly.

Cooper v. *Aaron* involved the attempt of Governor Faubus and the Arkansas legislature to block the desegregation of Central High School in Little Rock, Arkansas. The Court convened in a special session for only the fifth time in thirty-eight years to hear the case (Peltason 1971, 187). After reviewing the history of attempts to desegregate the public schools in Little Rock, the Court faced the question of whether violence, or threat of violence, in response to desegregation and resulting in turmoil in the school disruptive of the educational process justified the suspension of desegregation efforts for two and one-half years. In answering in the negative, rejecting the school board's claim and reversing the federal district court, the Supreme Court held that the "constitutional rights of respondents [black students] are not to be sacrificed or yielded to the violence and disorder" which was occurring (1958, 16). This was, as the opinion stated, "enough to dispose of the case" (1958, 17), but the Court continued for several pages to underline its determination that *Brown* be followed. It reminded the parties that Article VI of the Constitution makes the Constitution the "supreme law of the land" (1958, 18). Further, the Court unearthed *Marbury* v. *Madison* (1803) and Chief Justice Marshall's words that "[i]t is emphatically the province and duty of the judicial department to say what the law is" (1803, 177, quoted at 1958, 18). The opinion also pointed out that the decision in "*Brown* was unanimously reached by this Court only after the case had been briefed and twice argued and the issues had been given the most serious consideration." Not stopping here, the justices stressed that twelve justices had considered and approved the *Brown* doctrine (the nine who originally agreed to it and the three who had joined the Court since then) (1958, 19). Finally, in an unprecedented move, all nine justices individually signed the opinion. *Cooper* v. *Aaron* was a massive and unswerving affirmation that desegregation was the law and must be implemented.

The next full opinion in the elementary and secondary education field came in *Goss* v. *Board of Education of Knoxville* (1963). At issue was a desegregation plan that included a provision allowing students to transfer from a school where their race was a minority to one where it predominated. This provision was challenged on the ground that since race was the sole criterion of the plan it would perpetuate rather than alleviate racial segregation, denying plaintiffs the right to attend desegregated schools. The Court agreed, unanimously holding the one-way transfer plan to be violative of the Fourteenth Amendment and contrary to *Brown*.

The third decision, *Griffin* v. *Prince Edward County* was handed down in 1964. The case involved the constitutionality of the closing of Prince Edward County public schools to avoid desegregation and the use of state tuition grants and tax credits to support private segregated education for white children. The Court unanimously[5] found both acts unconstitutional, being essentially devices to avoid the constitutional mandate of desegregation, and denying plaintiffs the equal protection of the law.

Brown I and *II* stated the law and stated clearly that steps had to be taken to end state-enforced segregation. *Cooper* v. *Aaron* emphatically re-iterated it. And *Goss* and *Griffin* unanimously held that patent attempts to avoid desegregation were unconstitutional. The Court had spoken clearly and forcefully.

In the first four years after the passage of the 1964 Civil Rights Act, the Supreme Court remained quiet in the education area. However, the lower federal courts, particularly in the Fourth and Fifth Circuits, became increasingly involved in litigation. In 1965, the Fifth Circuit, in a case from Jackson, Mississippi, upheld desegregation guidelines announced by the U.S. Department of Health, Education, and Welfare (HEW) (to be discussed below). The circuit court "attach[ed] great weight to the standards" established by HEW and warned that it would not allow school districts to avoid HEW requirements by obtaining less stringent desegregation orders from local, and friendly, federal district courts (*Singleton* v. *Jackson Municipal Separate School District* 1965, 731). Similarly, in the *Jefferson County* case, in which a three-judge panel had ordered the defendant school systems to desegregate classrooms, facilities, and staffs by the 1967–68 school year, the Fifth Circuit, quoting *Singleton*, reaffirmed its support for the guidelines (*U.S.* v. *Jefferson County Board of Education* 1966, 847, 848, 851). The court reiterated its concern that the courts not be used to avoid strict HEW standards and stressed that "affirmative action" had to be taken to create a "unitary, non-racial system" (1966, 862, 878).

The Supreme Court re-entered the field in 1968 and issued, for the first time since *Brown*, a detailed opinion on remedies. *Green* v. *County School Board of New Kent County, Va.* (1968), involved a freedom-of-choice plan under which no white child had transferred to the "formerly black school" and only about 15 percent of the black children had transferred to the "formerly white school." In a unanimous opinion, written by Justice Brennan, the Court threw out the freedom-of-choice plan and suggested that such plans would be unlikely to meet constitutional standards. Showing a good deal of impatience, the opinion stated that "the burden on a school board today is to come forward with a plan that promises realistically to work, and promises realistically to work *now*" (1968, 439). In the fall of 1969, in *Alexander* v. *Holmes County* (1969), the Court continued with its impatience, reinstating a July 1969 Fifth Circuit order requiring thirty Mississippi school districts to desegregate by the start of school in September in accordance with *Green*. In a terse, two-page *per curiam* ruling in October, the Court rejected a delay until December, holding that "continued operation of segregated schools under a standard of allowing 'all deliberate speed' for desegregation is no longer constitutionally permissible." Further, the Court held that school districts were required to "terminate dual school systems at once and to operate now and hereafter only unitary schools" (1969, 19, 20).

Finally, in *Swann* v. *Charlotte-Mecklenburg Board of Education* (1971), the Court upheld the power of district judges to include busing as part of a remedial decree. Writing for a unanimous Court, Chief Justice Burger held that "once a right and a violation have been shown, the scope of a district court's equitable powers to remedy past wrongs is broad" (1971, 15). This included, Burger noted, busing, because "desegregation plans cannot be limited to the walk-in school" (1971, 30).

From 1954 through 1971, the Court remained steadfast in its commitment to end public-school segregation. Repeatedly, it reminded parties before it, and the nation, that segregation violated the Constitution. And, as shall soon be shown, for many of those years it was the only branch of the federal government that acted.

Congressional and Executive Branch Action

Congressional and executive branch action in the area of public-school desegregation was virtually non-existent until the passage of the 1964 Civil Rights Act. In stark contrast to the actions of the Supreme Court in *Brown*, the other two branches of the federal government remained essentially passive.

In 1957 Congress passed the first civil rights act since 1875. In the education field the act was most notable for its lack of provisions. While an attempt was made to give the Department of Justice the authority to file suits on behalf of individuals alleging segregation in education, it was unsuccessful. The Eisenhower administration opposed the provision because, in the words of Attorney General William P. Rogers, it "might do more harm than good" (quoted in Sarratt 1966, 72).

Congress passed a second civil rights act in 1960. Unlike the 1957 act, this one gave a fair amount of attention to segregation in education, but as with the earlier act, little of substance was enacted. In particular, the Department of Justice was not given the authority to file desegregation suits on behalf of individuals nor was the federal government given the power to cut off funds to school districts refusing to desegregate.[6] The bill's educational provisions were aimed at violent interference with court-ordered school desegregation and at providing education for children of military personnel stationed in places where the public schools had been closed to avoid desegregation.

The 1964 act was a major departure from its predecessors. The most sweeping civil rights legislation since the Civil War and Reconstruction era, the act touched many fields. In education, Congress finally empowered the attorney general to bring desegregation suits on behalf of individuals.[7] Also, Title VI of the act gave the federal government the power to cut off federal funds to school districts that discriminated on the basis of race.[8] Its key language held:

> No person in the United States shall, on the ground of race, color, or national origin, be excluded from participation in, be denied the benefits of, or be subjected to discrimination under any program or activity receiving Federal financial assistance.

The 1964 act, as I will demonstrate shortly, had a major impact on school desegregation.

Until 1964, executive action was little better. Although the president and the administration can be a "particularly powerful agenda setter" (Kingdon 1984, 208), the power and prestige of the presidency was not employed in support of civil rights until the mid-1960s. Little was done by President Eisenhower in the 1950s and only slowly did Presidents Kennedy and Johnson bring their administrations into the civil rights battle. Their actions, or lack thereof, are highlighted in chapter 3.

In the spring of 1965 Congress enacted the Elementary and Secondary Education Act (ESEA), providing federal aid to school districts with large percentages of low-income children. The act was heavily directed at the South (Orfield 1969, 94), and nearly $1 billion was expended in the first year of operation (Bailey and Mosher 1968, 156). A total of $1.3 billion was authorized for 1966 (Miles 1974, 148) and in fiscal year 1968 alone, $1.5 billion of federal money was sent to the states (USCCR 1970, chapter 1).

Title VI required some kind of government response. The task of formulating procedures fell to HEW and, specifically, to the Office of Education. Action became imperative with the enactment of ESEA in the spring of 1965, because there was now a large pot of federal money available to Southern school districts. While the details of government actions are both fascinating and complicated, brief summary is possible.[9]

HEW acted slowly to implement Title VI. At first, it asked school districts for assurances of non-discrimination. The first regulations, adopted on December 3, 1964, allowed federal aid to school districts that either submitted assurances that their schools were totally desegregated, that were under court orders to desegregate and agreed to abide by such orders, or that submitted voluntary desegregation plans. Further, state agencies were instructed not to renew programs or to authorize new ones until the commissioner of education certified that local districts were in compliance with Title VI. These regulations, however, were vague on what was an acceptable voluntary desegregation plan. In April 1965, guidelines were issued that required the opening of all grades to freedom of choice by the start of the 1967 school year.[10] These guidelines were upheld by the Fifth Circuit in *Singleton*, discussed above. The guidelines were again revised and tightened in March 1966, setting standards for acceptable freedom-of-choice plans. The March 1966 guidelines established standards based on the percentage increase in students transferring from segregated schools. In most cases, the guidelines required a doubling or tripling of the percentage of blacks in "formerly white schools" for the 1966–67 school year. It was these guidelines that the Fifth Circuit upheld in the *Jefferson County* case discussed above. Regulations were further tightened in March 1968 when school districts were ordered to submit plans for complete desegregation by the fall of 1968, or, in some cases, the fall of 1969. The Supreme Court, in *Green*, essentially seconded these result-oriented standards that went past freedom of choice. Thus, by the end of the Johnson administration, HEW had come to officially require complete desegregation as a requirement for receiving federal funds under Title VI.

The Nixon administration appeared to back off from this strict requirement. In a July, 1969, statement, HEW Secretary Finch and Attorney General Mitchell announced modifications of the guidelines in several important ways (USCCR 1969, Appendix C). Chief among them was rejection of the 1969–70 terminal date for all districts as "arbitrary" and "too rigid to be either workable or equitable." In terms of freedom of choice, a plan that "genuinely promises to achieve a complete end to racial discrimination at the earliest possible date" would be acceptable. In addition, the statement pledged the administration to rely more heavily on "stepped-up enforcement activities of [the Department of] Justice" and to "minimize" the number of HEW fund cut-off proceedings. However, the statement did not purport to change the guidelines. "In general," the administration announced, the "terminal date" for acceptable plans "must be the 1969–70 school year." Also, the statement pointed to the courts, holding that "policy in this area will be as defined in the latest Supreme Court and Circuit Court decisions." Finally, the statement quoted approvingly the language from *Green*, quoted above, that desegregation plans must work *now*.[11]

Enforcement proceedings and fund terminations under Title VI were uncommon but not unheard-of. Although by the early 1970s the federal government had "investigated, negotiated with, and arm-twisted over 3,000 districts" (Hochschild 1984, 28), only a small percentage of these districts ended up in enforcement proceedings or had their eligibility for federal funds terminated. Of the approximately 2,800 school districts in the eleven Southern states, 320 were involved in enforcement proceedings from September 15, 1965, through June 30, 1967. While few districts suffered from fund terminations, the period from the passage of Title VI to the end of the Johnson administration saw over 200 such terminations, slightly more than 7 percent of all Southern districts. While terminations were unlikely, the threat was real.[12]

Results and Comparison

The decade from 1954 to 1964 provides close to an ideal setting for measuring the contribution of the courts vis-à-vis Congress and the executive branch in desegregating public schools. For ten years the Court spoke forcefully while Congress and the executive did little. Then, in 1964, Congress and the executive branch entered the battle with the most significant piece of civil rights legislation in nearly ninety years. In 1965, the enactment of ESEA made a billion dollars in federal funds available to school districts that, in accord with Title VI, did not discriminate. This history allows one to isolate the contribution of the courts. If the courts were effective in desegregating public schools, the results should show up before 1964. However, if it was Congress and the executive branch, through the 1964 Civil Rights Act and 1965 ESEA, that made the real difference, then change would occur only in the years after 1964 or 1965.

"In the problem of racial discrimination," Judge Brown once remarked, "statistics often tell much" (*Alabama* v. *U.S.* 1962, 586). Due to the herculean efforts of the Southern Education Reporting Service,[13] supplemented by the U.S. Commission on Civil Rights (USCCR), and later, HEW, fairly good statistics on the progress of school desegregation are available. A summary is presented in Table 7.1 and **Figure 7.1** while state breakdowns are in Appendix 1. The table and graph present the

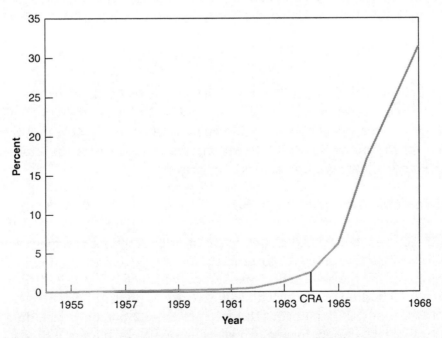

Figure 7.1   Percentage of All Southern Black Schoolchildren Attending School with Whites

Table 7.1   Black Children in Elementary and Secondary School with Whites, 1954–1972, Selected Years

Year	South %	South #	South without Texas and Tennessee %	South without Texas and Tennessee #	Border %	Border #	Border without D.C. %	Border without D.C. #
1954–55	.001	23	.001	20	NA	NA	NA	NA
1955–56	.12	2,782	.002	47	NA	NA	NA	NA
1956–57	.14	3,514	.002	34	39.6	106,878	18.1	35,378
1957–58	.15	3,829	.005	109	41.4	127,677	25.2	57,677
1958–59	.13	3,456	.006	124	44.4	142,352	31.1	73,345
1959–60	.16	4,216	.03	747	45.4	191,114	35.5	117,824
1960–61	.16	4,308	.02	432	49.0	212,895	38.7	131,503
1961–62	.24	6,725	.07	1,558	52.5	240,226	42.8	151,345
1962–63	.45	12,868	.17	4,058	51.8	251,797	43.7	164,048
1963–64	1.2	34,105	.48	11,619	54.8	281,731	46.2	182,918
1964–65	2.3	66,135	1.2	29,846	58.3	313,919	50.1	207,341
1965–66	6.1	184,308	3.8	95,507	68.9	384,992	64.1	275,722
1966–67	16.9	489,900			71.4	456,258		
1968–69	32.0	942,600			74.7	475,700		
1970–71	85.9	2,707,000			76.8	512,000		
1972–73	91.3	2,886,300			77.3	524,800		

SOURCES: Southern Education Reporting Service (1967, 40–44); USCCR (1967); U.S. Department of HEW, Office of Civil Rights (*Directory*, 1968, 1970, 1972).

NOTE: Numbers in the column marked "%" are the percentages of black students, out of all black schoolchildren, attending school with whites.

number of black children attending public school with whites as well as their percentages out of all black schoolchildren in the seventeen states (and the District of Columbia) which required segregation in public schools at the time of *Brown*. While this way of presenting the numbers does not discriminate between token and substantial integration, and thus suggests more desegregation than actually occurred, it does allow for a time-series comparison.

The Border States and the District of Columbia

The Supreme Court appears to have had an important impact on school desegregation in the six border states and the District of Columbia. Unfortunately, reliable figures are not available until the 1956 school year. However, during the eight school years from the fall of 1956 until the passage of the 1964 act, the number of black children in school with whites rose 15.2 percent (39.6 percent to 54.8 percent) in the region as a whole and 28.1 percent (18.1 percent to 46.2 percent) excluding the District of Columbia. However, the lack of data for the two years immediately following *Brown* may understate the change. That is, the change may have been even greater than these numbers suggest, for substantial change may have taken place in the years 1954–56.[14] Thus, the Supreme Court's actions appear to have had an effect.

The passage of the 1964 Civil Rights Act increased the rate of desegregation. During the two school years after enactment of the 1964 act, there was an increase of 14.1 percentage points (54.8 percent to 68.9 percent) in the number of black children in desegregated schools in the region as a whole, nearly equal to the eight-year increase from 1956–57 through 1963–64. Similarly, excluding the District of Columbia, the increase in just two years was 17.9 percentage points. Looking at the border states and D.C. as a whole, in the eight school years starting in 1963 (before enactment of the 1964 and 1965 acts) and continuing through 1970, the number of black children attending desegregated schools jumped 22.0 percentage points (54.8 percent to 76.8 percent), an even greater increase than that recorded in the eight years prior to congressional and executive action. These numbers suggest two points. First, that the Court made a major contribution to desegregation of the public schools in the border states and, second, that the rate of desegregation noticeably increased after the passage of the 1964 and 1965 acts. The seeming successful contribution of the Supreme Court in the border states and the District of Columbia is explored in chapter 3.

The Southern States

The statistics from the Southern states are truly amazing. For ten years, 1954–64, virtually *nothing happened.* Ten years after *Brown* only 1.2 percent of black schoolchildren in the South attended school with whites. Excluding Texas and Tennessee,[15] the percent drops to less than one-half of one percent (.48 percent). Despite the unanimity and forcefulness of the *Brown* opinion, the Supreme Court's reiteration of its position and its steadfast refusal to yield, its decree was flagrantly disobeyed. After ten years of Court-ordered desegregation, in the eleven Southern states barely 1 out of every 100 black children attended school with whites. The Court ordered an end to segregation and segregation was not ended. As Judge Wisdom put it, writing in the *Jefferson County* case, "*the courts acting alone have failed*" (1966, 847; emphasis in original). The numbers show that the Supreme Court contributed virtually *nothing* to ending segregation of the public schools in the Southern states in the decade following *Brown.*

The entrance of Congress and the executive branch into the battle changed this. As Figure 7.1 graphically demonstrates, desegregation took off after 1964, reaching 91.3 percent in 1972 (not shown). In the first year of the act, 1964–65, nearly as much desegregation was achieved as during all the preceding years of Supreme Court action. In just the few months between the end of the 1964–65 school year and the start of the 1965–66 year, nearly three times as many black students entered desegregated schools as had in the preceding decade of Court action. And the years following showed significant increases. While much segregation still existed, and still exists, the change after 1964 is as extraordinary as is the utter lack of impact of the Supreme Court prior to 1964. The actions of the Supreme Court appear irrelevant to desegregation from *Brown* to the enactment of the 1964 Civil Rights Act and 1965 ESEA. Only after the passage of these acts was there any desegregation of public schools in the South.

What accounts for the phenomenal increase in desegregation in the post-1964 years, particularly the 1968–72 period? Was it the action of HEW? The courts? Local school officials? All three? Part of the answer may be found in the responses of nearly 1,000 school superintendents to a U.S. Commission on Civil Rights survey of school districts containing at least some minorities (USCCR 1977a).[16] When superintendents reported that "substantial steps to desegregate" had been taken, the survey asked, among other questions, "which was the single most important source of pressure for initiation of desegregation?" Table 7.2 presents the results. While the survey's coding rules underestimate the effect of HEW,[17] it can be seen that, overall, state-local pressures were mentioned most often, followed by courts and HEW. It can also be seen that while courts were mentioned in only 20 of 154 districts in the years 1954–67, in the 1968–71 period 160 of 343 districts that initiated desegregation pointed to the courts. Those years also recorded 103 mentions of HEW, suggesting that it was quite active too. The survey suggests that while HEW was active, the courts played an important role in desegregation in the 1968–72 period.

In terms of success, the survey found extremely large decreases in segregation between 1968 and 1972 from both court and HEW action and more moderate decreases with local action. It also found that districts desegregating under HEW pressure were less segregated in 1972 than were districts desegregating under court orders (USCCR 1977a, 66). However, districts desegregating under court orders were more segregated to start with, had, on average, higher percentages of minority students, and achieved a somewhat greater decline in segregation than those desegregating under HEW pressure. Yet perhaps because courts faced a tougher task, desegregation in districts under court orders proceeded less smoothly: "school districts that reported school desegregation by court intervention were far more likely to experience disruptions than those that desegregated under HEW or local pressures" (USCCR 1977a, 84).[18]

Table 7.2   Desegregated School Districts, by Primary Source of Intervention, and by Year of Greatest Desegregation, 1901–1974

| | Source of Intervention | | | | | | Total | |
| | Courts | | HEW | | State-Local | | | |
Year	#	%	#	%	#	%	#	%
1901–53	—	—	—	—	6	2	6	1
1954–65	12	6	18	12	52	21	82	13
1966–67	8	4	19	13	45	18	72	12
1968–69	53	26	42	28	34	13	129	21
1970–71	107	52	61	40	46	18	214	35
1972–73	12	6	5	3	38	15	55	9
1974–75	15	7	7	5	31	12	53	9
Total	207	101	152	101	252	99	611	100
Percent of total number of districts	34		25		41			

SOURCE: USCCR (1977a, 26).

NOTE: Percentages do not equal 100 because of rounding.

These findings were corroborated by Giles in a study of 1,362 Southern school districts. Comparing actual levels of segregation in school districts under HEW and court enforcement in 1968 and 1970, Giles concluded that "districts under H.E.W. enforcement were significantly less segregated than court-ordered districts in both 1968 and 1970" (Giles 1975, 88). He also found greater decline in desegregation in court-ordered districts than in those under HEW enforcement.

In sum, although Hochschild overstated the case in concluding that "were it not for the courts there would be little reduction in racial isolation" (Hochschild 1984, 134), she did pinpoint a period of court efficacy in civil rights. Chapter 3 explores the reasons why, with particular emphasis on why the Constrained Court view seems to explain the first decade after *Brown* while the Dynamic Court view appears to do a better job explaining the post-1964 findings.

Higher Education

The story of Court and governmental action regarding segregation of public colleges and universities is shorter but similar to that of lower education. In the late nineteenth century Congress, in the second Morrill Act, allowed segregation if separate black institutions were maintained (Orfield 1969, 11). Congressional action was followed, of course, by Supreme Court approval of the separate but equal doctrine in *Plessy* v. *Ferguson* (1896). However, the Court began to chip away at that doctrine in a number of cases challenging segregation in graduate and professional education.[19] In these cases, states were ordered to admit black applicants to formerly segregated state universities where the state's practice had been to provide them with out-of-state scholarships (*Missouri ex. rel. Gaines* v. *Canada* 1938), and universities were prohibited from treating black students differently than other students once admitted (*McLaurin* v. *Oklahoma Board of Regents* 1950). Attempts to set up "separate but equal" black institutions were dealt a death blow in *Sweatt* v. *Painter* (1950). Sweatt, a black applicant, had been denied admission to the University of Texas Law School because of his color. The state courts upheld the denial but ordered Texas to build a state law school for blacks. In a unanimous opinion, the Supreme Court ordered Sweatt's admission to the University of Texas Law School, holding, in essence, that although any new law school would certainly be separate, it would hardly be equal. Chief Justice Vinson wrote: "The University of Texas Law School possesses to a far greater degree those qualities which are incapable of objective measurement but which make for greatness in a law school" (1950, 634). Although the separate but equal doctrine was not formally rejected, the clear impact of the holding was that lack of equality would compel admission to the previously segregated institution and that proving equality would be a nearly impossible task. It was not long to *Brown*'s declaration that separate educational facilities are inherently unequal.

As with elementary and secondary education, in the years before 1964 Congress and the administration did little to desegregate universities. There was no congressional action until the 1964 Civil Rights Act. President Kennedy, when violence was rampant, did send federal troops to the University of Mississippi in 1963. However, other than utter the occasional platitude, he did little. President Eisenhower had done even less. With the passage of the 1964 Civil Rights Act, however, the executive branch was given the power to bring desegregation suits and cut off federal funds to segregating institutions.

Despite these new powers, the Office of Civil Rights (OCR) did little to enforce the act. Until 1968, for example, there was no compliance review program at all for institutions of higher learning (USCCR 1970, 42). Even after that, there were no clear guidelines or any serious attempt to require compliance

Table 7.3A Blacks at Southern, Predominantly White Public Colleges and Universities, 1963, 1965, 1966

Year	Source of Intervention			
	South		Border	
	# of Students	% of Enrollment	# of Students	% of Enrollment
1963	4,639	NA	NA	NA
1965	12,054	1.9	6,607	2.5
1966	20,788	2.6	14,102	4.9

SOURCES: Sarratt (1966, chap. 5); Southern Education Reporting Service (1965, 3–25; 1967, 3).

Table 7.3B Percentage of Black Enrollment at Southern, Formerly All-White, Public Colleges and Universities, by State, 1970 and 1978

States	1970[a]	1978
Southern		
Alabama	3.3	10.0
Arkansas	4.6	10.4
Florida	2.9	6.0
Georgia	3.1	10.5
Louisiana	5.0	11.5
Mississippi	3.5	9.8
North Carolina	2.4	6.6
South Carolina	2.8	9.0
Tennessee	4.1	9.7
Texas	4.3	5.3
Virginia	2.0	5.2
Border		
Delaware	2.3	3.1
Kentucky	3.1	5.1
Maryland	3.9	10.1
Missouri	2.6	4.5
Oklahoma	3.8	5.0
West Virginia	2.3	2.8

SOURCE: Office for Civil Rights data adapted from Ayres (1984, 125).

[a]1972 data were used for 17 of the 256 traditionally white campuses. They were located in Florida (3), Georgia (2), Maryland (1), Mississippi (1), North Carolina (1), Oklahoma (1), and West Virginia (8).

(USCCR 1974b: 3, chap. 3). By January 1975, for example, there had been only two fund terminations, involving small schools, Bob Jones University and Freewill Baptist Bible College. However, between January 1969 and February 1970, letters requesting desegregation plans were sent to ten states.[20] Even with that action, it appeared to some that the Nixon administration was dragging its feet in applying the law. Thus, a lawsuit was brought by the Legal Defense and Educational Fund, Inc. of the NAACP to force the government to act. In *Adams* v. *Richardson* (1973), decided in early 1973, OCR was ordered to obtain acceptable desegregation plans or commence enforcement proceedings leading to fund terminations.

Results and Comparison

Unlike with elementary and secondary education, few reliable statistics are available for making the comparison in higher education. This qualification being made, it is clear that there was little movement to desegregate universities prior to the 1964 Civil Rights Act. Tables 7.3A and 7.3B summarize the best information available (for state breakdowns, see Appendix 2). Table 7.3A shows that from 1963 to 1966, from before the passage of the 1964 Act to after it, the number of black students attending predominantly white universities in the South increased nearly five-fold. In one year alone, from 1965 to 1966, it increased over 70 percent. In the border states, the number of black students in predominantly white institutions more than doubled from 1965 to 1966. These figures suggest that it was the action of Congress and the executive branch, not the Court, that brought at least some desegregation to higher education. Chapter 3 will explore the reasons behind this finding.

On the other hand, as the 1970 and 1978 data presented in Table 7.3B show, while there was change, the overall percentages were small. That is, despite congressional and executive action, and despite *Adams*, only some progress was made in bringing more than a token number of black students to formerly white public institutions. The response, for example, to OCR's letters to ten states mentioned above was the submission of unacceptable plans from five states and no plans at all from the other five![21] Other examples of inaction abound. In December 1985, a federal judge in Alabama, in a suit involving Auburn University, found that "the state of Alabama has indeed operated a dual system of education; that in certain aspects, the dual system yet exists" (*U.S.* v. *Alabama* 1985). These findings, too, will be discussed in chapter 3.

Voting

Court Action

The right to vote has long been denied American minorities. Although the Fifteenth Amendment guaranteed blacks the right to vote, the failure of Reconstruction and its replacement by Jim Crow laws and practices put an effective end to black voting in the South. By 1903, every Southern state had passed legislation limiting the vote.[22] Throughout the twentieth century the Supreme Court heard and decided a number of cases in which it held unconstitutional various state attempts to prevent blacks from voting. As early as 1915, the so-called "Grandfather Clause," limiting voters to those who could prove that their ancestors had the right to vote (i.e., whites), was held unconstitutional (*Guinn & Beal* v. *U.S.* 1915).[23] This, of course, was but one of many different ways states attempted (and succeeded) to disenfranchise blacks.

The best-known Supreme Court cases dealing with voting are the Texas Primary Cases. In Texas, as in the rest of the South, the Democratic primary was the real election, with the general election being merely a required procedural formality. The Democratic parties of all eleven Southern states, aware of the realities of political life, banned blacks from voting in Democratic primaries (USCCR 1968, 7). This exclusion was challenged as violative of the Fourteenth Amendment in *Nixon* v. *Herndon* in 1927, and the Supreme Court struck it down. Texas responded by enacting legislation giving the state executive committee of each party the power to prescribe voting qualifications for its own members. The Democratic Party Executive Committee then required that its members be white. Mr. Nixon again brought suit, challenging this new bar to his ability to vote. In *Nixon* v. *Condon* (1932), the Supreme Court, citing *Nixon* v. *Herndon*, struck down the law, holding that the power to determine membership qualifications resides in the party in convention assembled. Thus, executive committee action was state action violative of the Fourteenth Amendment. Undaunted, and relying on the loophole in the *Condon* opinion, the Texas Democratic party in its convention voted to exclude blacks. This exclusion was upheld by the Supreme Court in *Grovey* v. *Townsend* (1935), where the Court held that since the action had been taken by the "representatives of the party in convention assembled," it was "not state action" (1935, 48) and therefore was constitutional. This position was reversed nine years later in *Smith* v. *Allwright* (1944), where the Court essentially held that primary and general elections are one process and that denying blacks the right to vote in primaries could be held to be state action. The final Texas Primary Case, *Terry* v. *Adams* (1953), involved the Jaybird Democratic Association, purportedly a self-governing voluntary private club whose nominees, it just so happened, "nearly always" (1953, 463) ran unopposed in the Democratic primaries. The Jaybirds, of course, denied membership to blacks. The Court, realizing that the Jaybird election was the real election in Texas (1953, 469), accordingly struck down the exclusion.

The Court also acted to invalidate other blatant attempts to disenfranchise black voters. One case came from Tuskegee, Alabama, where the Alabama legislature had redrawn the city boundaries to exclude nearly all black residents. The local newspapers made much of the "joke" that Tuskegee's blacks had suddenly "moved out of town" (cited in Wasby et al. 1977, 225). In *Gomillion* v. *Lightfoot* (1960), the Court saw past the facially neutral character of the statute and threw out the redistricting plan.

The Court, then, with one exception subsequently reversed, consistently upheld the right of blacks to take part in the electoral process. It continually struck down attempts by state legislatures to prohibit blacks from participating in a meaningful way in the electoral process.

Congressional and Executive Branch Action

Until 1957, congressional and executive branch action in voting discrimination was, as in other civil rights areas, virtually non-existent. As with education, the Supreme Court was left to speak alone.

In 1957, Congress passed its first civil rights act in eighty-two years. The act had several voting rights provisions, the most important of which authorized the Justice Department to initiate suits on behalf of blacks deprived of voting rights. The act also prohibited intimidation of voting in federal elections, including primaries, and established the Civil Rights Commission with power to gather evidence on violations of voting rights.

In 1960, Congress passed its second civil rights act of the century. Among its voting-rights provisions were the requirements that voting records be preserved for twenty-two months and that the attorney general be given access to them. An important provision allowed for judicial appointment of referees to temporarily replace local registrars. However, the process required before such appointments could be made was cumbersome.[24] Thus, both the 1957 and 1960 acts required that courts be a vital part of the process. And little change was made by the 1964 act, which concentrated on other aspects of discrimination.

Finally, in 1965, Congress passed the Voting Rights Act, making a major break with the past. The 1965 act, unlike the prior acts, provided for direct federal action to enable blacks to vote. Federal examiners could be sent to election districts to list eligible voters where tests or devices were required as a precondition for voting or registering and where less than 50 percent of the total voting-age population was registered. The act also suspended all literacy tests in the jurisdictions it covered and directed the attorney general to file suit challenging the constitutionality of the poll tax.[25] The 1965 Voting Rights Act, as will be seen shortly, had a major impact on black registration.

Administration action in voting rights was slight. Eisenhower's reticence in civil rights was noted earlier, and the voting-rights area was no exception. As of 1959, the Eisenhower Justice Department had instituted only three suits under the 1957 act.[26] And while the passage of the 1957 and 1960 acts was important, the Eisenhower administration hardly used them.

The Kennedy administration did make use of the powers it had under the 1957 and 1960 acts by filing scores of voting rights suits. However, it failed to push for major modification of the existing statutes. While its record was a vast improvement over that compiled by the Eisenhower administration, the major effort did not come until the Johnson administration and the 1965 Voting Rights Act.

Until 1957 the Court spoke alone in prohibiting racial discrimination in voting rights. Congress joined in with the 1957, 1960, and 1964 acts with small, but growing, executive support. Finally, Congress and the executive branch forcefully acted to prohibit discrimination in voting with the passage and implementation of the 1965 Voting Rights Act.

Results and Comparison

Voting rights provide a good comparison of the relative contribution of the courts and the other two branches of the government to civil rights. Until 1957, the Court acted alone. It was joined half-heartedly by the other branches in 1957 and strongly in 1965. **Figure 7.2** shows the change in the estimated number of black registered voters over the years and Table 7.4 contains the raw data. Striking is the large jump in the number and the percentage of blacks registered to vote from just prior to the passage of the 1965 act to just after it. As Table 7.4 records, the number of registered blacks in the eleven Southern states in this period jumped from approximately 2 million to 2.9 million, an increase of nearly 900,000, or 45 percent. In the first few months after the passage of the act more than 300,000 blacks were registered (Rodgers and Bullock 1972, 30). No other time period shows such an increase. Prior to 1957, when only the Court acted, only 1 out of every 4 blacks was registered to vote in the South where nearly 3 out of every 4 whites were. Nearly three-quarters as many blacks registered to vote merely in the two years after passage of the act as had been registered in all the years prior to 1957. The gains in some states were enormous. Mississippi, for example, showed a nine-fold increase in three years (see Appendix 3 for state figures). There can be no doubt that the major

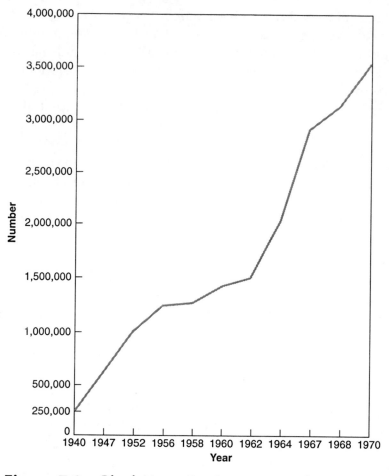

Figure 7.2 Black Voter Registration in the Southern States

increase in the registration of blacks came from the action of Congress and the executive branch through the 1965 Voting Rights Act.

The best case that can be made for Court influence is that the increases from 1940 to 1956 were due to the holdings of the Texas Primary Cases, particularly *Smith* v. *Allwright* in 1944 and *Terry* v. *Adams* in 1953. However, as the U.S. Civil Rights Commission pointed out, the end of World War II brought home many black servicemen who, having risked their lives for America, were determined to exercise the right to vote. Also, the black literacy rate had been continually growing, from 33 percent in 1898 to 82 percent by 1960 (USCCR 1961b: 1, 42). And, as chapter 5 details, blacks had been moving in large numbers from the rural South to the urban South, where registration was sometimes possible, and to the North, where there were few, if any, registration barriers. Although the issue of what accounted for the increase in the percentage of blacks registered to vote between 1940 and 1956 is by no means clear, what is clear is that important societal changes were taking place, independently of the Court, that surely affected registration.[27]

The lack of impact of governmental action prior to the 1965 act can also be seen by the lack of direct results of proceedings initiated with the courts under the 1957 and 1960 acts. In 1963, for example,

Table 7.4 Black Voter Registration in the Southern States, 1940–1970, Selected Years

Year	Estimated # of Black Registered Voters	% of Voting-Age Blacks Registered
1940	250,000	5
1947	595,000	12
1952	1,008,614	20
1956	1,238,038	25
1958	1,266,488	25
1960	1,414,052	28
1962	1,480,720	29.4
1964	2,005,971	40.0
1967	2,903,284	57.6
1968	3,112,000	58.7
1970	3,506,000	66.9

SOURCES: Garrow (1978, 19); Jaynes and Williams (1989, 233); Lawson (1976, 285); Matthews and Prothro (1963a, 27); USCCR (1968, 12, 13, 222, 223).

NOTE: As the U.S. Commission on Civil Rights states: "Registration figures themselves vary widely in their accuracy." For another set of figures which differ, but present the same general pattern, see Voter Education Project (1966); Watters and Cleghorn (1967).

the U.S. Civil Rights Commission concluded that five years of litigation under the acts had "not provided a prompt or adequate remedy for wide-spread discriminatory denials of the right to vote." It cited the efforts in 100 counties in eight states where, despite the filing of thirty-six voting rights suits by the Department of Justice, registration increased a measly 3.3 percent between 1956 and 1963, from approximately 5 percent to 8.3 percent (USCCR 1963a, 13, 14–15). Another study found that eight years of litigation under the two acts in the forty-six most heavily segregated Southern counties resulted in the registration of only 37,146 blacks out of 548,358 eligibles, a mere 6.8 percent (Note 1966, 1088 n.108). Even administration officials came to the conclusion that litigation was fruitless (Garrow 1978, 34, 67). For example, Deputy Attorney General Katzenbach concluded that the weakness of litigation to produce change "meant essentially that you had to bring a separate lawsuit for each person who was discriminated against, and there were thousands. It would take years to get them registered to vote" (quoted in Hampton 1990, 212). And Attorney General Robert F. Kennedy, testifying before Congress in 1962, noted that the "problem is deep rooted and of long standing. It demands a solution which cannot be provided by lengthy litigation on a piecemeal, county-by-county basis" (U.S. Cong. 1962, 264). These figures and statements provide further evidence that Court action was ineffective in combating discrimination in voting rights.

On the other hand, there is evidence in addition to the figures that suggests the important direct effect of the 1965 act. In July 1966, about one year after the passage of the 1965 act, the Voter Education Project of the Southern Regional Council studied the effects on registration of sending federal examiners to Southern counties. The findings show substantially higher levels of black registration in counties where federal examiners were working than in those where they were not. For example, comparing counties where federal examiners were present to those where they were not, the study found increases in the percentage of blacks registered of 22.6 percent in South Carolina (71.4 percent versus 48.8 percent), 18.3 percent in Alabama (63.7 percent versus 45.4 percent), and 17 percent in Mississippi (41.2 percent versus 24.2 percent) (USCCR 1968, 155). Coupled with the huge increase in black registration immediately after the 1965 act, these figures buttress the attribution of those changes to the 1965 Act (see also USCCR 1965).

In sum, the bottom line in voting is that the actions of the Court contributed little to the increase in black registration. When major change did occur, it was clearly attributable to the actions of Congress and the executive.

End Notes

1. *Bolling* was directed at the schools of the District of Columbia under the control of the federal government. Thus, the holding was based on the Fifth Amendment. In other respects, it was similar to *Brown*.
2. The Southern states: Alabama, Arkansas, Florida, Georgia, Louisiana, Mississippi, North Carolina, South Carolina, Tennessee, Texas, Virginia. The Border states: Delaware, Kentucky, Maryland, Missouri, Oklahoma, West Virginia. These references are used throughout this study.
3. However, Johnson (1979) has found that unanimity does *not* affect the treatment Supreme Court opinions receive in lower courts. Thus, the effort to achieve unanimity in *Brown* may not have been worth it, particularly if it resulted in compromise over the implementation decision.
4. The Delaware case, *Gebhardt* v. *Belton*, was affirmed and remanded to the Delaware Supreme Court for proceedings consistent with *Brown*.
5. Justices Clark and Harlan dissented from the remedy portions of the opinion.
6. In its first report, the U.S. Commission on Civil Rights (USCCR) had split 3–3 in recommending federal power to cut off funds from segregated institutions of higher learning. One member, Commissioner Johnson, supported such power for secondary and elementary schools as well (USCCR 1959, 328–30).
7. Empowering the attorney general to bring suits had not only been proposed as early as the 1957 act, but also had been recommended by the U.S. Commission on Civil Rights in its 1961 and 1963 reports (USCCR 1961b: 2, 181; USCCR 1963a, 69).
8. A partial fund cut-off had been officially recommended by the U.S. Commission on Civil Rights (1961b: 2, 181) as early as 1961. Also, amendments to congressional legislation requiring non-discrimination in the distribution of federal funds had been introduced since the 1940s. On this point, see discussion in chapter 4.
9. For more detail, see Orfield (1969, chaps. 2 and 3); Note (1967); USCCR (1970). The summary that follows is based primarily on these sources.
10. Freedom of choice allowed students to attend any school in the district.
11. It must be noted, however, that in August 1969, the administration petitioned the Fifth Circuit to relax the final date for complete desegregation in thirty Mississippi school districts from September 1, 1969, to December 1, 1969. This action led to the Supreme Court decision in *Alexander* v. *Holmes County*, discussed in the text.
12. Edelman (1973, 39 n.29); Orfield (1969, 115); USCCR (1974b 3: 128; 1970, 37).
13. The Southern Education Reporting Service described itself as an impartial fact-finding agency

led by a board of directors of Southern newspaper editors and educators, and funded with a grant from the Ford Foundation.

14. For example, there was no desegregation in the District of Columbia prior to 1954.

15. Tennessee and Texas had the smallest percentage of black enrollment in public schools of any of the eleven Southern states. Thus, resistance to desegregation may have been weaker.

16. The survey covered 47 percent of all school districts with at least 5 percent minority enrollment and enrollments of 1,500 or more. Seventy-seven percent (996) of the superintendents surveyed responded.

17. When there was more than one box checked for "primary" pressure, the survey's coding rule was that "courts took priority over HEW" (Appendix A, 118). The commission also suggests that "many districts that describe their desegregation as locally initiated may have been influenced by HEW" (13).

18. Data on disruptions and violence can be found in USCCR (1977a, 85ff.).

19. The leading cases are *Missouri ex. rel. Gaines* v. *Canada* (1938); *Sipuel* v. *Oklahoma Board of Regents* (1948); *Sweatt* v. *Painter* (1950); *McLaurin* v. *Oklahoma Board of Regents* (1950).

20. The states were Arkansas, Florida, Georgia, Louisiana, Maryland, Mississippi, North Carolina, Oklahoma, Pennsylvania, and Virginia.

21. Florida, Louisiana, Mississippi, North Carolina, and Oklahoma did not submit plans.

22. Kousser (1974, 32). For a good history of state action denying blacks the right to vote, see USCCR (1959, 55–97). For a discussion of some of the state tactics employed in the context of why litigation failed to remedy the discrimination, see chapter 3.

23. A similar case, also from Oklahoma, was *Lane* v. *Wilson* (1939).

24. For a good description, see USCCR (1961b: 1, 77–78).

25. The poll tax had been made unconstitutional in federal elections by the enactment of the Twenty-fourth Amendment in 1964. Subsequently, the poll tax was held unconstitutional in state elections as violative of the equal protection clause of the Fourteenth Amendment in *Harper* v. *Virginia Board Of Elections* (1966).

26. USCCR (1961b: 1, 75). Not surprisingly, the administration lost all three cases.

27. This point is expanded upon in chapter 5.

MARBURY V. MADISON

SUPREME COURT OF THE UNITED STATES
5 U.S. 137
February 24, 1803, Decided

[During the first transfer of power from one party to another, the Federalists, led by President Adams, created a host of new judicial positions and appointed loyal Federalist to the positions. Upon assuming office, the Democrats, led by President Jefferson, refused to deliver a commission for Marbury to be a minor judge in the District of Columbia, a commission that was mistakenly not delivered by President Adam's Secretary of State John Marshall. Marshall was subsequently appointed Chief Justice of the Supreme Court and delivered the opinion of the Court in this case.

Marbury sought a writ of mandamus, an order issued by a court to a lower court or official commanding performance of a duty.]

OPINION BY: MARSHALL

[. . .]

At the last term on the affidavits then read and filed with the clerk, a rule was granted in this case, requiring the secretary of state to show cause why a mandamus should not issue, directing him to deliver to William Marbury his commission as a justice of the peace of the county of Washington, in the district of Columbia.

No cause has been shown, and the present motion is for a mandamus. The peculiar delicacy of this case, the novelty of some of its circumstances, and the real difficulty attending the points which occur in it, require a complete exposition of the principles, on which the opinion to be given by the court, is founded.

These principles have been, on the side of the applicant, very ably argued at the bar. In rendering the opinion of the court, there will be some departure in form, though not in substance, from the points stated in that argument.

In the order in which the court has viewed this subject, the following questions have been considered and decided.

1st. Has the applicant a right to the commission he demands?

2dly. If he has a right, and that right has been violated, do the laws of his country afford him a remedy?

3dly. If they do afford him a remedy, is it a mandamus issuing from this court?

The first object of enquiry is,

1st. Has the applicant a right to the commission he demands?

[Marshall says that Marbury's commission was official when it was signed by the President and that he therefore has a right to it. Actual physical delivery of the appointment is not necessary for this right to accrue to Marbury.]

[. . .]

2dly. If he has a right, and that right has been violated, do the laws of his country afford him a remedy?

 The very essence of civil liberty certainly consists in the right of every individual to claim the protection of the laws, whenever he receives an injury. One of the first duties of government is to afford that protection. In Great Britain the king himself is sued in the respectful form of a petition, and he never fails to comply with the judgment of his court.

[. . .]

The government of the United States has been emphatically termed a government of laws, and not of men. It will certainly cease to deserve this high appellation, if the laws furnish no remedy for the violation of a vested legal right.

[Therefore, according to Marshall, issuing the writ of mandamus does not interfere with the duties of the President.]

[. . .]

[Marshall proceeds to consider whether the writ of mandamus sought by Marbury can be granted by the Supreme Court.]

The act to establish the judicial courts[1] of the United States authorizes the supreme court "to issue writs of mandamus, in cases warranted by the principles and usages of law, to any courts appointed, or persons holding office, under the authority of the United States."

The secretary of state, being a person holding an office under the authority of the United States, is precisely within the letter of the description; and if this court is not authorized to issue a writ of mandamus to such an officer, it must be because the law is unconstitutional, and therefore absolutely incapable of conferring the authority, and assigning the duties which its words purport to confer and assign.

The constitution vests the whole judicial power of the United States in one supreme court, and such inferior courts as congress shall, from time to time, ordain and establish. This power is expressly extended to all cases arising under the laws of the United States; and consequently, in some form, may be exercised over the present case; because the right claimed is given by a law of the United States.

In the distribution of this power it is declared that "the supreme court shall have original jurisdiction in all cases affecting ambassadors, other public ministers and consuls, and those in which a state shall be a party. In all other cases, the supreme court shall have appellate jurisdiction."

It has been insisted, at the bar, that as the original grant of jurisdiction, to the supreme and inferior courts, is general, and the clause, assigning original jurisdiction to the supreme court, contains no negative or restrictive words; the power remains to the legislature, to assign original jurisdiction to that court in other cases than those specified in the article which has been recited; provided those cases belong to the judicial power of the United States.

If it had been intended to leave it to the discretion of the legislature to apportion the judicial power between the supreme and inferior courts according to the will of that body, it would certainly have been useless to have proceeded further than to have defined the judicial powers, and the tribunals in which it should be vested. The subsequent part of the section is mere surplusage, is entirely without meaning, if such is to be the construction. If congress remains at liberty to give this court appellate jurisdiction, where the constitution has declared their jurisdiction shall be original; and original jurisdiction where the constitution has declared it shall be appellate; the distribution of jurisdiction, made in the constitution, is form without substance.

Affirmative words are often, in their operation, negative of other objects than those affirmed; and in this case, a negative or exclusive sense must be given to them or they have no operation at all.

It cannot be presumed that any clause in the constitution is intended to be without effect; and therefore such a construction is inadmissible, unless the words require it.

If the solicitude of the convention, respecting our peace with foreign powers, induced a provision that the supreme court should take original jurisdiction in cases which might be supposed to affect them; yet the clause would have proceeded no further than to provide for such cases, if no further restriction on the powers of congress had been intended. That they should have appellate jurisdiction in all other cases, with such exceptions as congress might make, is no restriction; unless the words be deemed exclusive of original jurisdiction.

When an instrument organizing fundamentally a judicial system, divides it into one supreme, and so many inferior courts as the legislature may ordain and establish; then enumerates its powers, and proceeds so far to distribute them, as to define the jurisdiction of the supreme court by declaring the cases in which it shall take original jurisdiction, and that in others it shall take appellate jurisdiction; the plain import of the words seems to be, that in one class of cases its jurisdiction is original, and not appellate; in the other it is appellate, and not original. If any other construction would render the clause inoperative, that is an additional reason for rejecting such other construction, and for adhering to their obvious meaning.

To enable this court then to issue a mandamus, it must be shown to be an exercise of appellate jurisdiction, or to be necessary to enable them to exercise appellate jurisdiction.

It has been stated at the bar that the appellate jurisdiction may be exercised in a variety of forms, and that if it be the will of the legislature that a mandamus should be used for that purpose, that will must be obeyed. This is true, yet the jurisdiction must be appellate, not original.

It is the essential criterion of appellate jurisdiction, that it revises and corrects the proceedings in a cause already instituted, and does not create that cause. Although, therefore, a mandamus may be directed to courts, yet to issue such a writ to an officer for the delivery of a paper, is in effect the same as to sustain an original action for that paper, and therefore seems not to belong to appellate, but to original jurisdiction. Neither is it necessary in such a case as this, to enable the court to exercise its appellate jurisdiction.

The authority, therefore, given to the supreme court, by the act establishing the judicial courts of the United States, to issue writs of mandamus to public officers, appears not to be warranted by the constitution; and it becomes necessary to enquire whether a jurisdiction, so conferred, can be exercised.

The question, whether an act, repugnant to the constitution, can become the law of the land, is a question deeply interesting to the United States; but, happily, not of an intricacy proportioned to its interest. It seems only necessary to recognize certain principles, supposed to have been long and well established, to decide it.

That the people have an original right to establish, for their future government, such principles as, in their opinion, shall most conduce to their own happiness, is the basis, on which the whole American fabric has been erected. The exercise of this original right is a very great exertion; nor can it, nor ought it to be frequently repeated. The principles, therefore, so established, are deemed fundamental. And as the authority, from which they proceed, is supreme, and can seldom act, they are designed to be permanent.

This original and supreme will organizes the government, and assigns, to different departments, their respective powers. It may either stop here; or establish certain limits not to be transcended by those departments.

The government of the United States is of the latter description. The powers of the legislature are defined, and limited; and that those limits may not be mistaken, or forgotten, the constitution is written. To what purpose are powers limited, and to what purpose is that limitation committed to writing, if these limits may, at any time, be passed by those intended to be restrained? The distinction, between a government with limited and unlimited powers, is abolished, if those limits do not confine the persons on whom they are imposed, and if acts prohibited and acts allowed, are of equal obligation. It is a proposition too plain to be contested, that the constitution controls any legislative act repugnant to it; or, that the legislature may alter the constitution by an ordinary act.

Between these alternatives there is no middle ground. The constitution is either a superior, paramount law, unchangeable by ordinary means, or it is on a level with ordinary legislative acts, and like other acts, is alterable when the legislature shall please to alter it.

If the former part of the alternative be true, then a legislative act contrary to the constitution is not law: if the latter part be true, then written constitutions are absurd attempts, on the part of the people, to limit a power, in its own nature illimitable.

Certainly all those who have framed written constitutions contemplate them as forming the fundamental and paramount law of the nation, and consequently the theory of every such government must be, that an act of the legislature, repugnant to the constitution, is void.

This theory is essentially attached to a written constitution, and is consequently to be considered, by this court, as one of the fundamental principles of our society. It is not therefore to be lost sight of in the further consideration of this subject.

If an act of the legislature, repugnant to the constitution, is void, does it, notwithstanding its invalidity, bind the courts, and oblige them to give it effect? Or, in other words, though it be not law, does it constitute a rule as operative as if it was a law? This would be to overthrow in fact what was established in theory; and would seem, at first view, an absurdity too gross to be insisted on. It shall, however, receive a more attentive consideration.

It is emphatically the province and duty of the judicial department to say what the law is. Those who apply the rule to particular cases, must of necessity expound and interpret that rule. If two laws conflict with each other, the courts must decide on the operation of each.

So if a law be in opposition to the constitution; if both the law and the constitution apply to a particular case, so that the court must either decide that case conformably to the law, disregarding the constitution; or conformably to the constitution, disregarding the law; the court must determine which of these conflicting rules governs the case. This is of the very essence of judicial duty.

If then the courts are to regard the constitution; and the constitution is superior to any ordinary act of the legislature; the constitution, and not such ordinary act, must govern the case to which they both apply.

Those then who controvert the principle that the constitution is to be considered, in court, as a paramount law, are reduced to the necessity of maintaining that courts must close their eyes on the constitution, and see only the law.

This doctrine would subvert the very foundation of all written constitutions. It would declare that an act, which, according to the principles and theory of our government, is entirely void; is yet, in practice, completely obligatory. It would declare, that if the legislature shall do what is expressly forbidden, such act, notwithstanding the express prohibition, is in reality effectual. It would be giving to the legislature a practical and real omnipotence, with the same breath which professes to restrict their powers within narrow limits. It is prescribing limits, and declaring that those limits may be passed at pleasure.

That it thus reduces to nothing what we have deemed the greatest improvement on political institutions—a written constitution—would of itself be sufficient, in America, where written constitutions have been viewed with so much reverence, for rejecting the construction. But the peculiar expressions of the constitution of the United States furnish additional arguments in favor of its rejection.

The judicial power of the United States is extended to all cases arising under the constitution.

Could it be the intention of those who gave this power, to say that, in using it, the constitution should not be looked into? That a case arising under the constitution should be decided without examining the instrument under which it arises?

This is too extravagant to be maintained.

In some cases then, the constitution must be looked into by the judges. And if they can open it at all, what part of it are they forbidden to read, or to obey?

There are many other parts of the constitution which serve to illustrate this subject.

It is declared that "no tax or duty shall be laid on articles exported from any state." Suppose a duty on the export of cotton, of tobacco, or of flour; and a suit instituted to recover it. Ought judgment to be rendered in such a case? ought the judges to close their eyes on the constitution, and only see the law.

The constitution declares that "no bill of attainder or ex post facto law shall be passed."

If, however, such a bill should be passed and a person should be prosecuted under it; must the court condemn to death those victims whom the constitution endeavors to preserve?

"No person," says the constitution, "shall be convicted of treason unless on the testimony of two witnesses to the fame overt act, or on confession in open court."

Here the language of the constitution is addressed especially to the courts. It prescribes, directly for them, a rule of evidence not to be departed from. If the legislature should change that rule, and declare one witness, or a confession out of court, sufficient for conviction, must the constitutional principle yield to the legislative act?

From these, and many other selections which might be made, it is apparent, that the framers of the constitution contemplated that instrument, as a rule for the government of courts, as well as of the legislature.

Why otherwise does it direct the judges to take an oath to support it? This oath certainly applies, in an especial manner, to their conduct in their official character. How immoral to impose it on them, if they were to be used as the instruments, and the knowing instruments, for violating what they swear to support!

The oath of office, too, imposed by the legislature, is completely demonstrative of the legislative opinion on the subject. It is in these words, "I do solemnly swear that I will administer justice without respect to persons, and do equal right to the poor and to the rich; and that I will faithfully and impartially discharge all the duties incumbent on me as according to the best of my abilities and understanding, agreeably to the constitution, and laws of the United States."

Why does a judge swear to discharge his duties agreeably to the constitution of the United States, if that constitution forms no rule for his government? if it is closed upon him, and cannot be inspected by him?

If such be the real state of things, this is worse than solemn mockery. To prescribe, or to take this oath, becomes equally a crime.

It is also not entirely unworthy of observation, that in declaring what shall be the supreme law of the land, the constitution itself is first mentioned; and not the laws of the United States generally, but those only which shall be made in pursuance of the constitution, have that rank.

Thus, the particular phraseology of the constitution of the United States confirms and strengthens the principle, supposed to be essential to all written constitutions, that a law repugnant to the constitution is void; and that courts, as well as other departments, are bound by that instrument.

The rule must be discharged.

CONFIRMATION HEARING FOR ROBERT BORK, NOMINEE TO THE U.S. SUPREME COURT

(September, 1987)

[Robert Bork was nominated to the U.S. Supreme Court by Ronald Reagan in 1987. Liberal interest groups immediately objected to Bork's position on a number of issues, including abortion rights (provided for by the Supreme Court's decision in *Roe v. Wade* and earlier cases, such as *Griswold v. Connecticut*, that established a right to privacy), as well his position on the rights of minorities and women. Bork's testimony in the Senate confirmation hearing was unusually candid, partially because of a long trail of written legal work on these issues prior to his nomination. Bork's nomination was ultimately rejected by the Senate by a vote of 42–58. The seat to which Bork was nominated was ultimately filled by Justice Anthony Kennedy. Excerpts from Bork's testimony are provided below.]

Opening Statement of Senator Edward M. Kennedy

Senator KENNEDY. Good morning, Judge Bork. From the beginning, America has set the highest standards for our highest Court. We insist that a nominee should have outstanding ability and integrity. But we also insist on even more: that those who sit on the Supreme Court must deserve the special title we reserve for only nine federal judges in the entire country, the title that sums up in one word the awesome responsibility on their shoulders—the title of "Justice."

Historically, America has set this high standard because the Justices of the Supreme Court have a unique obligation: to serve as the ultimate guardians of the Constitution, the rule of law, and the liberty and the quality of every citizen. To fulfill these responsibilities, to earn the title of "Justice," a person must have special qualities:

A commitment to individual liberty as the cornerstone of American democracy.

A dedication to equality for all Americans, especially those who have been denied their full measure of freedom, such as women and minorities.

A respect for justice for all whose rights are too readily abused by powerful institutions, whether by the power of government or by giant concentrations of power in the private sector.

A Supreme Court Justice must also have respect for the Supreme Court itself, for our constitutional system of government, and for the history and heritage by which that system has evolved, including the relationship between the federal government and the States, and between Congress and the President.

Indeed, it has been said that the Supreme Court is the umpire of the federal system because it has the last word about justice in America. Above all, therefore, a Supreme Court nominee must possess the special quality that enables a justice to render justice. This is the attribute whose presence we describe by the words such as fairness, impartiality, open-mindedness, and judicial temperament, and whose absence we call prejudice or bias.

These are the standards by which the Senate must evaluate any judicial nominee. And by these standards, Robert Bork falls short of what Americans demand of a man or woman as a Justice on the Supreme Court. Time and again, in his public record over more than a quarter of a century, Robert Bork has shown that he is hostile to the rule of law and the role of the courts in protecting individual liberty.

He has harshly opposed—and is publicly itching to overrule—many of the great decisions of the Supreme Court that seek to fulfill the promise of justice for all Americans.

He is instinctively biased against the claims of the average citizen and in favor of concentrations of power, whether that is governmental or private.

And in conflicts between the legislative and executive branches of government, he has repeatedly expressed a clear contempt for Congress and an unbridled trust in the power of the President.

Mr. Bork has said many extreme things in his comments of a lifetime in the law. We already have a more extensive record of his work and writings than perhaps we have had for any other Supreme Court nominee in history.

It is easy to conclude from the public record of Mr. Bork's published views that he believes women and blacks are second-class citizens under the Constitution. He even believes that, in the relation to the executive, Members of Congress are second-class citizens, yet he is asking the Senate to confirm him.

The strongest case against this nomination is made by the words of Mr. Bork himself. In an article he wrote in 1963, during the battle to desegregate lunch counters, motels, hotels, and other public accommodations in America, he referred to the civil rights principle underlying that historic struggle as a principle of unsurpassed ugliness.

Ten years later, he recanted his opposition, but in the time since then he has consistently demonstrated his hostility towards equal justice for all.

As recently as June of this year, he ridiculed a Supreme Court decision prohibiting sex discrimination and suggested that the extension of the equal protection clause to women trivializes the Constitution.

In Robert Bork's America, there is no room at the inn for blacks and no place in the Constitution for women, and in our America there should be no seat on the Supreme Court for Robert Bork. Mr. Bork has been equally extreme in his opposition to the right to privacy. In an article in 1971, he said, in effect, that a husband and wife have no greater right to privacy under the Constitution than a smokestack has to pollute the air.

President Reagan has said that this controversy is pure politics, but that is not the case. I and others who oppose Mr. Bork have often supported nominees to the Supreme Court by Republican Presidents, including many with whose philosophy we disagree. I voted for the confirmation of Chief Justice Burger and also Justices Blackmun, Powell, Stevens, O'Connor and Scalia. But Mr. Bork is a nominee of a different stripe. President Reagan has every right to take Mr. Bork's reactionary ideology into account in making the nomination, and the Senate has every right to take that ideology into account in acting on the nomination.

Opening Statement of Senator Orrin G. Hatch

Senator HATCH. [. . .] [I]t is hard to understand why your nomination would generate controversy. The answer is found in one word, which is tragic in this judicial context, and that word is "politics." Judge Bork is experiencing the kind of innuendo and intrigue that usually accompanies a campaign for the U.S. Senate. Many Senators are experienced at running that kind of campaign but it has no place in a judicial nominating proceeding. Federal judges are not politicians and ought not to be judged like politicians.

The great danger I see in the impending ideological inquisition is injury to the independence and integrity of the Supreme Court and the whole federal judiciary. When we undertake to judge a judge according to political rather than legal criteria, we have stripped the judicial office of all that makes it a distinct separated power. If the general public begins to measure judges by a political yardstick and if the judges themselves begin to base their decisions on political criteria, we will have lost the reasoning processes of the law which have served us so well to check political excesses and fervor over the past 200 years. I would ask any American if they would wish to have their life, liberty and property resting on the decisions of judges who are more worried about what the newspaper might say about the case than they are about life, liberty or property.

Recognizing precisely this danger, the Senate has refused to employ political litmus tests while confirming 53 justices over this past century. Senate precedent does not support subjecting judicial nominees to ideological inquisitions. [. . .]

Despite the lessons of Senate precedent and the Constitution and despite the political damage to the independence and integrity of the judiciary, we are likely to witness a bruising political campaign before your nomination comes to a final vote in the Senate. It is not difficult to outline in advance the type of campaign it will be. In the first place, you will be labelled. Even though political litmus tests do not work well with judges, you will be branded an extreme conservative. Of course, this will require some explanation as to why you voted with your Carter-appointed colleague, Judge Ruth Ginzburg—who is a great judge, by the way—in 90 percent of the cases in which you both sat [. . .]

The next tactic will be to extract a few quotes from 15-year-old articles while you were a law professor and ignore your judicial actions. For example, we have already heard allegations that you might allow censorship of free speech. In fact, anyone who wants to know your views on censorship would merely need to read your Lebron decision where you held that the D.C. Metro authorities violated Mr. Lebron's free speech rights by refusing to let him hang a poster that was extremely critical of President Reagan. In fact, those posters are going up today. You were even willing to allow the embarrassment of the President who appointed you to uphold his rights. In my mind, actions speak louder than words.

Another tactic will be to selectively use evidence. For instance, we have already seen criticism that your Dronenburg decision denied homosexuals a special constitutional protection. The evidence that these critics consistently ignore is that the Supreme Court reached precisely the same decision and the same result in the Bowers v. Hardwick case.

Still another tactic, familiar to political campaigns is to accuse you of ethical violations. In that vein, we have heard too much recently about the so-called Saturday Night Massacre. In fact, this was one of your finest hours. You were not the cause of Watergate but you were part of the solution. As a precondition of carrying out the President's order, you gained a commitment that the investigation would go forth without further interference. You had to make a difficult decision on the spur of the moment. Even then you had to be convinced by Attorney General Richardson not to resign, but the evidence that your decision was correct is history. Because you preserved the investigation, the President was later forced to resign and several others were prosecuted. The performance that you gave, it seems to me, deserves commendation, not criticism.

Opening Statement of Robert H. Bork, to be Associate Justice of the U.S. Supreme Court

Judge BORK. Mr. Chairman, thank you very much, and distinguished members of the Judiciary Committee. [. . .]

As you have said, quite correctly, Mr. Chairman, and as others have said here today, this is in large measure a discussion of judicial philosophy, and I want to make a few remarks at the outset on that subject of central interest.

That is, my understanding of how a judge should go about his or her work. That may also be described as my philosophy of the role of a judge in a constitutional democracy. The judge's authority derives entirely from the fact that he is applying the law and not his personal values. That is why the American public accepts the decisions of its courts, accepts even decisions that nullify the laws a majority of the electorate or of their representatives voted for.

The judge, to deserve that trust and that authority, must be every bit as governed by law as is the Congress, the President, the State Governors and legislatures, and the American people. No one, including a judge, can be above the law. Only in that way will justice be done and the freedom of Americans assured.

How should a judge go about finding the law? The only legitimate way, in my opinion, is by attempting to discern what those who made the law intended. The intentions of the lawmakers govern whether the lawmakers are the Congress of the United States enacting a statute or whether they are those who ratified our Constitution and its various amendments.

Where the words are precise and the facts simple, that is a relatively easy task. Where the words are general, as is the case with some of the most profound protections of our liberties—in the Bill of Rights and in the Civil War Amendments—the task is far more complex. It is to find the principle or value that was intended to be protected and to see that it is protected.

As I wrote in an opinion for our court, the judge's responsibility "is to discern how the framers' values, defined in the context of the world they knew, apply in the world we know."

If a judge abandons intention as his guide, there is no law available to him and he begins to legislate a social agenda for the American people. That goes well beyond his legitimate power.

He or she then diminishes liberty instead of enhancing it. [. . .]

Times come, of course, when even a venerable precedent can and should be overruled. The primary example of a proper overruling is Brown v. Board of Education, the case which outlawed racial segregation accomplished by government action. Brown overturned the rule of separate but equal laid down 58 years before in Plessy v. Ferguson. Yet Brown, delivered with the authority of a unanimous Court, was clearly correct and represents perhaps the greatest moral achievement of our constitutional law.

Nevertheless, overruling should be done sparingly and cautiously. Respect for precedent is a part of the great tradition of our law, just as is fidelity to the intent of those who ratified the Constitution and enacted our statutes. That does not mean that constitutional law is static. It will evolve as judges modify doctrine to meet new circumstances and new technologies. Thus, today we apply the first amendment's guarantee of the freedom of the press to radio and television, and we apply to electronic surveillance the fourth amendment's guarantee of privacy for the individual against unreasonable searches of his or her home. [. . .]

My philosophy of judging, Mr. Chairman, as you pointed out, is neither liberal nor conservative. It is simply a philosophy of judging which gives the Constitution a full and fair interpretation but, where the Constitution is silent, leaves the policy struggles to the Congress, the President, the legislatures and executives of the 50 States, and to the American people.

[. . .]

Senator HATCH. . . . . I think when you get into the complexities, I think the American people would basically say "I might disagree with Judge Bork on the philosophy on some of these cases, but I cannot disagree on the jurisprudence or the actual application of law." I think most people would feel that way. By the way, this discussion leads to another important case governed by the so-called privacy doctrine, and that is the case of Roe v. Wade. You have been criticized for having been critical of this abortion case called Roe v. Wade. Can you explain your apprehensions about this particular case?

Judge BORK. It is not apprehension so much, Senator, as it is—If Griswold v. Connecticut established or adopted a privacy right on reasoning which was utterly inadequate, and failed to define that right so we know what it applies to, Roe v. Wade contains almost no legal reasoning. We are not told why it is a private act—and if it is, there are lots of private acts that are not protected—why this one is protected. We are simply not told that. We get a review of the history of abortion and we get a review of the opinions of various groups like the American Medical Association, and then we get rules. That's what I object to about the case. It does not have legal reasoning in it that roots the right to an abortion in constitutional materials.

[. . . .]

Senator HATCH. I think it would be helpful to examine the character of the legal scholarship that has voiced apprehensions similar to yours on this case, since you have been criticized by some of my colleagues as being outside of the mainstream, because of your criticisms of the so-called Roe v. Wade case. For example, Gerald Gunther of the Stanford Law School cites Roe as an instance of the "bad legacy of substantive due process and ends-oriented" judging. Professor Archibald Cox of Harvard notes that the "court failed to establish the legitimacy of the decision by not articulating a precept of sufficient attractiveness to lift the ruling above the level of a political judgment."

By the way, let's pause here. What do you suppose Archibald Cox meant when he said that the decision was not legitimate?

Judge BORK. I suppose he means it comes out of no—so far as he can see—comes out of no legitimate constitutional materials, which are primarily text, history and constitutional structure.

Senator HATCH. Do you agree with that?

Judge BORK. Yes.

[. . .]

Judge BORK. I think I have listened to arguments in every case, Senator, and sometimes I don't think somebody is going to be able to make it in an argument, and sometimes they do make it, despite my initial doubts. But as I have mentioned to you, I would ask for a grounding of the privacy right and a definition of it in a traditional, constitutional reasoning way. As I say, if that can't be done, I will ask for a rooting of the right to an abortion, or some right to an abortion of some scope, in traditional, legal, constitutional materials. And if that can't be done, then I would like to hear argument on stare decisis and whether or not this is the kind of case that should or should not be overruled.

[. . .]

Senator DECONCINI. But we are talking here about a little bit different use or I believe a constitutional right of privacy. Let me just pursue with you. You said yesterday, relating to a question that Senator Hatch asked you regarding Roe v. Wade and the ninth amendment, its application—and correct me please—you said something that nobody really knows what that amendment means. Is that correct?

Judge BORK. I do not know. I know of only one historical piece. There may be more. You know, this is not a subject I have researched at great length, but most people say they do not know what it means.

Senator DECONCINI. Do you know what it means?

Judge BORK. It could be—you know, I can speculate.

Senator DECONCINI. Do you have an opinion on the ninth amendment?

Judge BORK. The most sensible conclusion I heard was the one offered in the Virginia Law Review, which was that the enumeration, as the ninth amendment says—

Senator DECONCINI. Enumeration in the Constitution of certain rights shall not be construed to deny or disparage others retained by the people.

Judge BORK. That is right, Senator. And I think the ninth amendment therefore may be a direct counterpart to the 10ᵗʰ amendment. The 10th amendment says, in effect, that if the powers are not delegated to the United States, it is reserved to the States or to the people. And I think the ninth amendment says that, like powers, the enumeration of rights shall not be construed to deny or disparage rights retained by the people in their State Constitutions. That is the best I can do with it.

Senator DECONCINI. Yes. You feel that it only applies to their State constitutional rights.

Judge BORK. Senator, if anybody shows me historical evidence about what they meant, I would be delighted to do it. I just do not know.

Senator DECONCINI. I do not have any historical evidence. What I want to ask you is purely hypothetical, Judge. Do you think it is unconstitutional, in your judgment, for the Supreme Court to consider a right that is not enumerated in the Constitution

Judge BORK. Well, no.

Senator DECONCINI. To be found under article IX?

Judge BORK. There are two parts to that. First, there are some rights that are not enumerated but are found because of the structure of the Constitution and government. That is fine with me. I mean that is a legitimate mode of constitutional analysis. I do not think you can use the ninth amendment unless you know something of what it means. For example, if you had an amendment that says "Congress shall make no" and then there is an ink blot and you cannot read the rest of it and that is the only copy you have, I do not think the court can make up what might be under the ink blot if you cannot read it.

Senator DECONCINI. Let me ask you this question: If you had to speculate, what do you think Madison or some of the framers had in mind as to unenumerated rights?

Judge BORK. They might have had in mind—this is pure speculation, which I do not think is—

Senator DECONCINI. I understand. I said this is all hypothetical.

Judge BORK. All right. They might have had in mind what I just said about the enumeration of these does not entitle judges to override the state constitutional rights. They also might have had in mind perhaps a fixed category of what they regarded as natural rights, although if they did have in mind a category of natural rights, I am a little surprised they did not spell it out and put it into the Constitution, because they specified all the other rights. There is no evidence that I know of that this was to be a dynamic category of rights, that is that under the ninth amendment the court was free to make up more Bill of Rights. There is no evidence of that at all that I know of. And I think that had that been their objective, they could have spelled it out a lot better, and a lot of the constitutional debates we had right after the Constitution was formed, and John Marshall began applying the Constitution and so forth, would have been irrelevant debates because the court is just entitled to make up constitutional rights.

Senator DECONCINI. Would you say that in your judgment it would be unconstitutional for the Supreme Court to find a right—we will not say what it is, but Right A—

Judge BORK. If a Supreme Court makes

Senator DECONCINI [continuing]. Because it is not enumerated here.

Judge BORK. If the Supreme Court makes up a new right for which there is not historical evidence, then I think it has exceeded its powers under the Constitution.

Senator DECONCINI. That is vis-a-vis your criticism of the Griswold case.

Judge BORK. Yes, insofar as they did not explain adequately where it came from and what it was.

Senator DECONCINI [continuing]. The structure of the decision. How would you as a Supreme Court judge address a similar case dealing with an area that you now feel is not enumerated or a constitutionally right set out? Where would you find that right if you decided that you felt you wanted to come to that same conclusion as you indicated on the Griswold decision? You wanted that conclusion

Judge BORK. No. I wanted that conclusion as a political matter. You know, I make a sharp distinction between a judicial function and a legislative function. If I were a legislator, I would vote against that statute instantly.

[. . .]

Senator DECONCINI. Do you see anything else in the Constitution?

Judge BORK. I have not gone through this exercise, Senator, so I am just speculating. I suppose the most likely form of attack might be the equal protection attack. I do not know.

[. . .]

Senator DECONCINI. . . . . In a recent interview you were quoted saying that "The role that men and women should play in society is a highly complex business, and it changes as our culture changes. What I am saying (10 years ago) was that it was shift in constitutional methods of government to have judges deciding all of those enormously sensitive, highly political, highly cultural issues", end of quote. That was June 1, 1966, the Judicial Notice.

Now what troubles me, Judge, is why are the questions concerning sex discrimination any more difficult or any more complex and undeserving of constitutional, judicial resolution than other questions routinely subject to the court constitutional analysis, questions such as the discrimination on the basis of race that we have discussed here? It leaves me with a big void here that—and I know that you have tried to explain it and I have paid attention yesterday, but I did not get it.

Judge BORK. YOU are comparing, I take it, Senator DeConcini, my—

Senator DECONCINI. Yes, that is 1986. I am sorry.

Judge BORK [continuing]. My remarks about the Equal Rights Amendment with my views of the equal protection clause. Is that what you are saying?

Judge BORK. Yes. All right. My objection to the Equal Rights Amendment was that legislatures would have nothing to say about these complex cultural matters, and had no chance to express a judgment. People would go straight to court and challenge any distinction, and the court would have to write the complete body of what is allowable, discrimination or whatever it is. A reasonable basis test allows a little more play in the joints, I think, for the court to listen to the legislatures and look at the society and bring evidence in and so forth. If you want to say that the

Equal Rights Amendment really would enact the same thing as the reasonable basis test, then my objection to the Equal Rights Amendment drops out.

Senator DECONCINI. What troubles me is that—

Judge BORK. But nobody said that, Senator.

Senator DECONCINI [continuing]. You are saying to me, as I understand, what you are saying to me is that this reasonable test is something that the court has made up, that you are willing to use, and I do not see any distinction in that amendment. It seems to me far greater to say, "Yes, it applies to women, just as it applies to the races."

Judge BORK. I said that, but it cannot apply just as it does to the races. It is possible to say

Senator DECONCINI. You say it can apply just as it does to the races.

Judge BORK. It cannot apply—

Senator DECONCINI. It cannot.

Judge BORK [continuing]. To gender just as it does to race. It is possible to say, for example, that there shall be no segregated toilet facilities anywhere as to race. I do not think anybody wants to say that as to gender. Differences have to be accommodated. That is why the difference.

Senator DECONCINI. But is not that a bogus argument? We are not talking about unisex toilets here. We are talking about—

Judge BORK. No.

Senator DECONCINI [continuing]. Fundamental rights that women for too, too long have not been provided.

Judge BORK. That is right.

Senator DECONCINI. And we are talking about your interpretation of whether or not on the Supreme Court you are going to look towards that equality for women, whether we have the Equal Rights Amendment or not. And if you have a reasonable standard that comes into play for women, because I am referring just to women or for sex—let us just say the women—but you do not apply that reasonable standard to racial matters

Judge BORK. I do. Senator, I do. It is exactly the same standard.

Senator DECONCINI. You do have the standard?

Judge BORK. Yes, exactly the same standards, a reasonable basis test, and there is no reasonable basis to segregate the races by toilet facilities. There is a reasonable basis to segregate the genders by those facilities. And when I said to you that you cannot treat gender exactly the same as you do race, all I meant was some distinctions are reasonable as to gender, such as the one we mentioned, some are not reasonable, the same one would not be reasonable as to race.

CHAPTER 8
BUREAUCRACY

CONGRESSIONAL OVERSIGHT OVERLOOKED: POLICE PATROLS VERSUS FIRE ALARMS[1]

MATHEW D. MCCUBBINS, THOMAS SCHWARTZ
University of Texas at Austin

Scholars have often remarked that Congress neglects its oversight responsibility. We argue that Congress does no such thing: what appears to be a neglect of oversight really is the rational preference for one form of oversight-which we call fire-alarm oversight-over another form-police-patrol oversight. Our analysis supports a somewhat neglected way of looking at the strategies by which legislators seek to achieve their goals.

Scholars often complain that Congress has neglected its oversight responsibility: despite a large and growing executive branch, Congress has done little or nothing to oversee administrative compliance with legislative goals. As a consequence, we are told, Congress has largely lost control of the executive branch: it has allowed the executive branch not only to grow but to grow irresponsible. In popular debate as well as congressional scholarship, this neglect of oversight has become a stylized fact: widely and dutifully reported, it is often bemoaned, sometimes explained, but almost never seriously questioned.[2]

[However, we argue that it is a preference for one form of oversight over another less-effective form of oversight]. [. . .] And we develop a simple model of congressional choice of oversight policy, offer evidence to support the model, and draw from it further implications regarding bureaucratic discretion and regulatory legislation. [. . .]

The Model

[. . .] Our model of congressional choice of oversight policy rests on a distinction between two forms or techniques of oversight:

Police-Patrol Oversight   Analogous to the use of real police patrols, police-patrol oversight is comparatively centralized, active, and direct: at its own initiative, Congress examines a sample of executive-agency activities, with the aim of detecting and remedying any violations of legislative goals and, by its surveillance, discouraging such violations. [. . .]

Fire-Alarm Oversight [. . .]   fire-alarm oversight is less centralized and involves less active and direct intervention than police-patrol oversight: instead of examining a sample of administrative decisions, looking for violations of legislative goals, Congress establishes a system of rules, procedures, and informal practices that enable individual citizens and organized interest groups to examine administrative decisions (sometimes in prospect), to charge executive agencies with violating congressional goals, and to seek remedies from agencies, courts, and Congress itself. [...] Congress's role consists in creating and perfecting this decentralized system and, occasionally, intervening in response to complaints. Instead of sniffing for fires, Congress places fire-alarm boxes on street corners, builds neighborhood fire houses, and sometimes dispatches its own hook-and-ladder in response to an alarm.

The distinction between police-patrol and fire-alarm oversight should not be confused with the distinction that sometimes is drawn between *formal* and *informal* oversight, which differ in that formal oversight activities have oversight as their principal and official purpose, whereas informal oversight activities are incidental to other official functions, such as appropriations hearings. Both can involve direct and active surveillance rather than responses to alarms. (See Dodd and Schott, 1977; Ogul, 1977.)

Our model consists of three assumptions:

Technological Assumption   Two forms of oversight are available to Congress: police-patrol oversight and fire-alarm oversight. Congress can choose either form or a combination of the two, making tradeoffs between them in two circumstances: (1) When writing legislation, Congress can include police-patrol features, such as sunset review, or fire-alarm features, such as requirements for public hearings. (2) When it evaluates an agency's performance, Congress can either call oversight hearings to patrol for violations of legislative goals or else wait for alarms to signal potential violations.

Motivational Assumption   A congressman seeks to take as much credit as possible for the net benefits enjoyed by his potential support- ers-by citizens and interest groups, within his constituency and elsewhere, whose support can help him win reelection. [...]

Institutional Assumption   Executive agencies act as agents of Congress and especially of those subcommittees on which they depend for authorizations and appropriations.

[...]

We will argue, however, that if the Motivational Assumption were replaced by the assumption that congressmen act strictly as statesmen, our conclusions regarding oversight would still be derivable, although in a somewhat different way. Our analysis has less to do with specific legislative goals than with optimal strategies for enforcing compliance with legislative goals of any sort.

Consequences

Three important consequences

Consequence 1   To the extent that they favor oversight activity of any sort, congressmen tend to prefer fire-alarm oversight to police-patrol oversight.

Our argument for Consequence 1 is that a congressman's objective, according to the Motivational Assumption, is to take as much credit as possible for net benefits enjoyed by his potential supporters and that he can do so more efficiently under a policy of fire-alarm oversight than under a police-patrol policy, for three reasons:

First, congressmen engaged in police-patrol oversight inevitably spend time examining a great many executive-branch actions that do not violate legislative goals or harm any potential supporters, at least not enough to occasion complaints. They might also spend time detecting and remedying arguable violations that nonetheless harm no potential supporters. For this they receive scant credit from their potential supporters. According to the Motivational Assumption, then, their time is largely wasted, so they incur opportunity costs. But under a fire-alarm policy, a congressman does not address concrete violations unless potential supporters have complained about them, in which case he can receive credit for intervening. [. . .]

Second, under a realistic police-patrol policy, congressmen examine only a small sample of executive-branch actions. As a result, they are likely to miss violations that harm their potential supporters, and so miss opportunities to take credit for redressing grievances, however fair the sample. Under a fire-alarm policy, by contrast, potential supporters can in most cases bring to congressmen's attention any violations that harm them and for which they have received no adequate remedy through the executive or judicial branch.

Third, although fire-alarm oversight can be as costly as police-patrol oversight, much of the cost is borne by the citizens and interest groups [. . .] A congressman's responsibility for such costs is sufficiently remote that he is not likely to be blamed for them by his potential supporters.

Consequence 2   Congress will not neglect its oversight responsibility. It will adopt an extensive and somewhat effective (even if imperfect) oversight policy.

This is because one of the two forms of oversight-the fire-alarm variety-serves congressmen's interests at little cost. When his potential supporters complain of a violation of legislative goals, a congressman gains credit if he eliminates the cause of the complaint. [. . .]

Consequence 3   Congress will adopt an extensive and somewhat effective policy of fire-alarm oversight while largely neglecting police-patrol oversight.

This just summarizes Consequences 1 and 2.

Misperception

[. . .] Here are the three main explanations found in the literature, along with a brief critical comment on each:

Complexity   Because public-policy issues are so complex, Congress has had to delegate authority over them to a large, complex, technically expert bureaucracy, whose actions it is unable effectively to oversee (Lowi, 1969; Ogul, 1977; Ripley, 1969; Seidman, 1975; Woll, 1977).

Comment- [. . .] A striking example is the tax code (Jaffe, 1973, pp. 1189–90). What is more, there is no evident reason why Congress should respond to the complexity of issues by creating a large, expert bureaucracy without also creating a large, expert congressional staff-one sufficiently large and expert, not only to help decide complex issues, but to help oversee a large, expert bureaucracy.

Good Government   [. . .] Because these agencies are designed to serve the public interest, whereas Congress is influenced by special-interest lobbies, oversight not only is unnecessary but might be regarded as political meddling in processes that ought to remain nonpolitical (Lowi, 1969).

Comment- Whatever the original intent, it is no longer plausible in most cases to suppose that the public interest is best served by a bureaucracy unaccountable to Congress and, therefore, unaccountable to the electorate.

Decentralization   Because congressional decisions are made, for the most part, by [many] small, relatively autonomous subcommittees with narrow jurisdictions, general oversight committees tend to be weak (Dodd and Schott, 1979).

[. . .] Subcommittee specialization should enhance congressional over-sight over individual agencies. Subcommittees controlling authorizations and appropriations might be in a better position to do oversight than so-called oversight committees.

[. . .]

[Previous scholars on congressional neglect of oversight were narrowly defining "oversight"] to mean police-patrol oversight, contrary to our Technological Assumption.

To this we have three replies: First, [. . .] No technique for accomplishing this task can be ruled out by definition. Second, the definitional equation of oversight with police-patrol oversight reflects the odd view that it is less important for Congress to make a serious attempt to detect and remedy violations of legislative goals than to employ a specific technique for doing so. Third, it would be odd to have a name for one way of detecting and remedying executive-branch violations of legislative goals but none for the general task of detecting and remedying such violations.

It has also been suggested to us that fire-alarm activities were never conceived or intended to be a form of oversight, whatever their effects. [. . .] Still, there is no evident reason for congressmen to engage in most fire-alarm activities unless they aim thereby to detect and remedy certain administrative violations of legislative goals. [. . .]

The Greater Effectiveness of Fire-Alarm Oversight

[There are two qualifications for fire alarm oversights to be better than police patrol oversight]. First, we do not contend that the most effective oversight policy is likely to contain no police-patrol features, only that fire-alarm techniques are likely to predominate. Second, only that it is likely to secure greater compliance with legislative goals; whether such compliance serves the public interest depends on what those goals are.

[The primary reasons for better effectiveness are-]

First, legislative goals often are stated in such a vague way that it is hard to decide whether any violation has occurred unless some citizen or group registers a complaint. Such a complaint gives Congress the opportunity to spell out its goals more clearly-just as concrete cases and controversies give courts the opportunity to elucidate legal principles that would be hard to make precise in the abstract.

Second, whereas a fire-alarm policy would almost certainly pick up any violation of legislative goals that seriously harmed an organized group, a police-patrol policy would doubtless miss many such violations, since only a sample of executive-branch actions would be examined.

[...]

Evidence

[...]

1. Under a fire-alarm system, complaints against administrative agencies are often brought to the attention of congressional subcommittees by lobbyists for organized groups, and to the attention of administrative agencies by congressional subcommittees. The functioning of this "sub-governmental triangle" has been well documented (Dodd and Oppenheimer, 1977; Fenno, 1966, 1973a,b; Goodwin, 1970; Ornstein, 1975; Ripley, 1969; Huitt, 1973; Matthews, 1960; Ripley and Franklin, 1976).

2. Congress has passed legislation to help comparatively disorganized groups to press their grievances against the federal government. McConnell (1966) shows how the Agriculture, Labor, and Commerce Departments act as lobbyists for farm, labor, and small-business interests. Congress has also created new programs, such as the Legal-Services Corporation, to organize and press the claims of comparatively voiceless citizens.

3. Constituent-service activities are not limited to unsnarling procedural knots. As part of the fire-alarm system, district staff and casework help individuals and groups-some of them otherwise powerless-to raise and redress grievances against decisions by administrative agencies. [...]

4. Often the fire-alarm system allows for the redress of grievances by administrative agencies and courts; Congress itself need not always get involved. To facilitate such redress, Congress has passed several laws, notably the Administrative Procedures Act of 1946 and the Environmental Procedures Act of 1969, that have substantially increased the number of groups with legal standing before administrative agencies and district courts regarding bureaucratic controversies (Lowi, 1969).[3] [...]

5. There are numerous cases in which violations of legislative goals were brought to the attention of Congress, which responded with vigorous remedial measures. For example, Congress dismantled the Area Redevelopment Administration (ARA) in 1963, even though it had just been authorized in 1961. [...]

6. The general impression that Congress neglects oversight, we have argued, really is a perception that Congress neglects police-patrol over-sight. That impression and the evidence adduced to support it constitute further evidence for Consequences 1 and 3: they show that congressmen tend to prefer an oversight policy in which fire-alarm techniques predominate.

Further Implications: Has Bureaucratic Discretion Increased?

Although Congress may, to some extent, have allowed the bureaucracy to make law, it may also have devised a reasonably effective and non-costly way to articulate and promulgate its own legislative goals-a way that depends on the fire-alarm oversight system. It is convenient for Congress to adopt broad legislative mandates and give substantial rule-making authority to the bureaucracy. The problem with doing so, of course, is that the bureaucracy might not pursue Congress's goals. But citizens and interest groups can be counted on to sound an alarm in most cases in which the bureaucracy has arguably violated Congress's goals. Then Congress can intervene to rectify the violation. Congress has not necessarily relinquished legislative responsibility to anyone else. It has just found a more efficient way to legislate.

[...]

The ostensible shifting of legislative responsibility to the executive branch may simply be the responsible adoption of efficient legislative techniques and the responsible acceptance of human cognitive limits-both facilitated by the fire-alarm system.

Further Implications: The Choice of Regulatory Policy

When it decides regulatory issues, Congress tends to choose one of two types of regulatory instrument: command-and-control instruments and incentive-based instruments. Congress faces a similar choice when it decides, not how to regulate society, but how to regulate the regulators-when it decides, in other words, on oversight policy. For police-patrol oversight is similar to command-and-control regulatory instruments, while fire-alarm oversight is similar to incentive-based instruments. Offhand one might suppose that just as congressmen tend to prefer fire-alarm to police-patrol oversight policies, so they would tend to prefer incentive-based to command-and-control regulatory policies. Our observations, of course, do not support this supposition (Breyer, 1982; Fiorina, 1982a; Joskow and Noll, 1978; McCubbins, 1982a; McCubbins and Page, 1982; Schultze, 1977). [...]

Conclusion

The widespread perception that Congress has neglected its oversight responsibility is a widespread mistake. Congressional scholars have focused their attention on police-patrol oversight. What has appeared to many of them to be a neglect of oversight is really a preference-an eminently rational one-for fire-alarm oversight. That a decentralized, incentive-based control mechanism has been found more effective, from its users' point view, than direct, centralized surveillance should come as no surprise. Besides criticizing the received wisdom regarding congressional over-sight, we hope to have highlighted a neglected way of looking at congressional behavior. Sometimes Congress appears to do little, leaving important policy decisions to the executive or judicial branch. But appearances can deceive. A perfectly reasonable way for Congress to pursue its objectives is by ensuring that fire alarms will be sounded, enabling courts, administrative agencies, and ultimately Congress itself to step in, whenever executive compliance with congressional objectives is called in question. In examining congressional policies and their impact, do not just ask how clear, detailed, or far-sighted congressional legislation is. Ask how likely it is that fire alarms will signal putative violations of legislative goals and how Congress is likely to respond to such alarms.

References

Arrow, Kenneth. 1963. *Social choice and individual values.* 2nd ed. New York: Wiley.

Baldwin, John. 1975. *The regulatory agency and the public corporation: The Canadian air transport industry.* Cambridge, Mass.: Ballinger.

Bibby, John. 1966. Committee characteristics and legislative oversight of administration. *Midwest Journal of Political Science*, 10 (February 1966): 78–98.

_____. 1968. Congress' neglected function. In *Republican papers*, edited by Melvin Laird. New York: Praeger.

Breyer, Stephen. 1982. *Regulation and its reform*. Cambridge, Mass.: Harvard University Press.

Cain, Bruce, John Ferejohn, and Morris Fiorina. 1979a. The roots of legislator popularity in Great Britain and the United States. Social Science Working Paper No. 288, California Institute of Technology, Pasadena, Calif.

_____. 1979b. Casework service in Great Britain and the United States. California Institute of Technology, Pasadena, Calif. Mimeo.

Calvert, Randall, Mark Moran, and Barry Weingast. 1982. Congressional influence over policymaking: The case of the FTC. Paper presented at the annual meeting of the American Political Science Association, Chicago, September 1982.

Dodd, Lawrence, and Bruce Oppenheimer, eds. 1977. *Congress reconsidered*. New York: Praeger.

Dodd, Lawrence, and Richard Schott. 1979. *Congress and the administrative state*. New York: Wiley.

Fenno, Richard, Jr. 1966. *The power of the purse*. Boston: Little, Brown.

_____. 1973a. *Congressmen in committees*. Boston: Little, Brown.

_____. 1973b. The internal distribution of influence: The house. In *The Congress and America's future*, 2nd ed, edited by David Truman, pp. 52–76. Englewood Cliffs, N.J.: Prentice-Hall.

_____. 1978. *Home style*. Boston: Little, Brown.

Ferejohn, John. 1974. *Pork barrel politics*. Stanford: Stanford University Press.

_____. 1981. A note on the structure of administrative agencies. California Institute of Technology, Pasadena, Calif. Mimeo.

Fiorina, Morris, 1977a. Congress: *Keystone of the Washington establishment*. New Haven: Yale University Press.

_____. 1977b. Control of the bureaucracy: A mismatch of incentives and capabilities. Social Science Working Paper No. 182, California Institute of Technology, Pasadena, Calif.

_____. 1982a. Legislative choice of regulatory forms: Legal process or administrative process? *Public Choice* 39 (September 1982): 33–66.

_____. 1982b. Group concentration and the delegation of legislative authority. California Institute of Technology, Pasadena, Calif. Mimeo.

Fiorina, Morris, and Roger Noll. 1978. Voters, bureaucrats and legislators: A rational choice perspective on the growth of bureaucracy, *Journal of Public Economics* 9 (June 1978): 239–54.

_____. 1979a. Voters, legislators and bureaucracy: Institutional design in the public sector. In *Problemi di administrazione publica, Centro di formazione e studi per il Messogiorno*, Naples, Italy, Formes 4 (2): 69–89.

_____. 1979b. Majority rule models and legislative election. *Journal of Politics* 41: 1081–1104.

Goodwin, George, Jr. 1970. *The little legislatures*. Amherst: University of Massachusetts Press.

Harris, Joseph. 1964. *Congressional control of administration*. Washington, D.C.: Brookings.

Hess, Stephen. 1976. *Organizing the presidency*. Washington: Brookings.

Huitt, Ralph. 1973. The internal distribution of influence: The Senate. In *The Congress in America's future*, 2nd ed., edited by David Truman, pp. 77–101. Englewood Cliffs, N.J.: Prentice-Hall.

Huntington, Samuel. Congressional responses to the twentieth century. In *The Congress in America's future*, 2nd ed., edited by David Truman, pp. 5–31. Englewood Cliffs, N.J.: Prentice-Hall, 1973.

Jaffe, Louis. 1973. The illusion of the ideal administration. *Harvard Law Review*, 86: 1183–99.

Joskow, Paul. 1974. Inflation and environmental concern: Structural change is the process of public utility price regulation. *Journal of Law and Economics*, 17 (October 1974): 291–327.

Joskow, Paul, and Roger Noll. 1978. Regulation in theory and practice: An overview. California Institute of Technology, Social Science Working Paper No. 213, Pasadena, Calif.

Lees, John D. 1977. Legislatures and oversight: A review article on a neglected area of research. *Legislative Studies Quarterly* (May 1977): 193–208.

Levi, Edward. 1948. *Legal reasoning.* Chicago: University of Chicago Press.

Lowi, Theodore. 1969. *The end of liberalism.* New York: Norton.

Matthews, Donald. 1960. *U.S. Senators and their world.* Chapel Hill: University of North Carolina Press.

Mayhew, David. 1974. Congress: *The electoral connection.* New Haven: Yale University Press.

McConnell, Grant. 1966. *Private power and American democracy.* New York: Vintage Books.

McCubbins, Mathew. 1982a. Rational individual behavior and collective irrationality: The legislative choice of regulatory forms. Ph.D. dissertation, California Institute of Technology, Pasadena, Calif.

_____. 1982b. On the form of regulatory intervention. Paper presented at the 1983 Annual Meeting of the Public Choice Society, Savannah, Georgia, March 24–26, 1983.

McCubbins, Mathew, and Talbot Page. 1982. On the failure of environmental, health and safety regulation. Paper presented at the 1983 Annual Meeting of the Midwest Political Science Association, Chicago, Illinois, April 20–23, 1983.

Mitnick, Barry. 1980. *The political economy of regulation.* New York: Columbia University Press.

Oakeshott, Michael. 1973. Political education. In *Rationalism in politics*, edited by Michael Oakeshott, pp. 110–36. New York: Basic Books, 1962. Reprinted *in Freedom and authority*, edited by Thomas Schwartz, 362–80. Encino, Calif.: Dickenson.

Ogul, Morris. 1976. *Congress oversees the bureaucracy.* Pittsburgh: University of Pittsburgh Press.

Ogul, Morris. 1977. Congressional oversight: Structure and incentives. *In Congress reconsidered*, edited by Lawrence Dodd and Bruce Oppenheimer, pp. 207–221. New York: Praeger.

Ornstein, Norman, ed. 1975. *Congress in change.* New York: Praeger.

Parker, Glenn, and Roger Davidson. 1979. Why do Americans love their congressmen so much more than their Congress? *Legislative Studies Quarterly* 4 (February 1979): 53–62.

Pearson, James. 1975. Oversight: A vital yet neglected congressional function. *Kansas Law Review* 23: 277–88.

Plott, Charles. 1967. A notion of equilibrium and its possibility under majority rules. *American Economic Review* 57 (September 1967): 787–806.

Ripley, Randall 1969. *Power in the Senate.* New York: St. Martin's.

Ripley, Randall. 1971. *The politics of economic and human resource development.* Indianapolis: Bobbs-Merrill.

_____. 1978. *Congress: Process and policy.* 2nd ed. New York: Norton.

Ripley, Randall, and Grace Franklin. 1976. *Congress, the bureaucracy and public policy.* Homewood, Ill.: Dorsey.

Scher, Seymour. 1963. Conditions for legislative control. *Journal of Politics* 25 (August 1963): 526–51.

Schultze, Charles. 1977. *The public use of private interest.* Washington, D.C.: Brookings.

Schwartz, Thomas. 1970. On the possibility of rational policy evaluation. *Theory and Decision* 1 (October 1970): 89–106.

_____. 1981. The universal-instability theorem. *Public Choice* 37 (no. 3): 487–501.

_____. 1982a. A really general impossibility theorem. *Quality and Quantity* 16 (December 1982): 493–505.

_____. 1982b. The porkbarrel paradox. University of Texas, Austin, Tex. Mimeo.

Seidman, Harold. 1975. *Politics, position, and power: The dynamics of federal organization.* New York: Oxford.

U.S. Senate. Committee on Government Operations. 1977. *Study on federal regulation, vol. II, congressional oversight of regulatory agencies.* Washington, D.C.: Government Printing Office.

Weingast, Barry, and Mark Moran. 1981. Bureaucratic discretion of congressional control: Regulatory policymaking by the Federal Trade Commission. Washington University, St.

Louis: Center of the Study of American Business. Mimeo. Woll, Peter. 1977. *American bureaucracy.* New York: Norton.

End Notes

1. *Partial funding for this research was provided by grants from the University Research Institute, University of Texas. We are grateful to Bruce Cain, Charles Cnudde, Morris Fiorina, Paul Kens, David Prindle, and especially Roger Noll for a number of valuable criticisms and suggestions.

2. See Bibby, 1966, 1968; Dodd and Schott, 1979; Fiorina, 1977a,b, 1982b; Hess, 1976; Huntington, 1973; Lowi, 1969; Mitnick, 1980; Ogul, 1976, 1977; Ripley, 1978; Scher, 1963; Seidman, 1975; Woll, 1977. The following remarks by Pearson (1975) succinctly exemplify this view: "Paradoxically, despite its importance, congressional oversight remains basically weak and ineffective" (p. 281). "Oversight is a vital yet neglected congressional function" (p. 288).

3. Ferejohn (1974) provides a good example of how the decision-making procedures of the Army Corps of Engineers were expanded to include wilderness, wildlife, and environ-mental group interests by the passage of the 1969 Environmental Procedures Act.

GOVERNANCE AND
THE BUREAUCRACY PROBLEM

KENNETH J. MEIER

LAURENCE J. O'TOOLE JR.

One of the most important and persisting challenges of modern government is how to reconcile the demands of democracy with the imperatives of bureaucracy. In many countries around the world, politicos and pundits bash "bureaucracy," frequently in the name of popular governance (Suleiman 2003). Bureaucrats, meanwhile, often look to protect their decision making from uninformed or polemical interference by amateurs who seek influence without having the expertise or experience to handle technically complex policy issues.

Bureaucracies are hierarchical institutions that can provide the capacity and expertise to accomplish complex social tasks, but they are frequently characterized as undemocratic and even threatening to democracy. Democracies are systems of government that are based, directly or indirectly, on the principle of popular control. They attend in differing measures to principles of majority rule and deference to the perspectives of intense interests among the public. But as such, they need not necessarily show keen attention to the values of efficiency, effectiveness, or specialized expertise.[1] Bureaucracy may be thought of as government's tool to exercise coercion as an instrument for productive action. As institutional forms designed to emphasize different values, bureaucracy and democracy sit in an uneasy relationship with each other.

In the classic terms of German sociologist Max Weber (1946), bureaucracies can serve any master. As an abstract institutional form, bureaucracy is thus indifferent to whether that master is authoritarian or democratic. In the United States, Woodrow Wilson suggested the American importation of Prussian bureaucratic approaches (although he urged, rather ambiguously, that Americans should "distil away" the "foreign gases" [1887, 219]). Current reform advocates urge similar action; the latest bureaucratic approaches, including the "New Public Management," continue to stir interest internationally and are borrowed wholesale across dozens of nations worldwide without any concern for democratic issues. Still, in debates from Beijing to Boston, proponents of popular government argue that bureaucracy and its administrative apparatus limit the promise of democracy. Relying on bureaucracy in governance, therefore, can generate challenges to legitimacy in democratic systems (Nye, Zelikow, and King 1997).

Underscoring the bureaucracy problem is the institution's use of expertise and judgment to exercise what are deemed political powers—the determination of who gets what, when, and how—by unelected and insulated decision makers. This well-known feature of bureaucratic decision making is regularly

Meier, Kenneth J., and Laurence J. O'Toole Jr. *Bureaucracy in a Democratic State: A Governance Perspective.* pp 1–20. © 2006 The Johns Hopkins University Press. Reprinted with permission of Johns Hopkins University Press.

pilloried by politicians (Hall 2002), and the drumbeat of bureaucratic criticism in popular culture encourages the development of skeptical and negative public perspectives on bureaucracy. Nevertheless, decades of research have demonstrated that excising this discretion from the bureaucracy is impossible. Its inevitability poses an apparent threat to democracy.

This book reexamines and reframes this classic question.[2] Several reasons justify such a project. First, while specialists in bureaucracy and public management have extolled the value and contributions of public bureaucracy to governance, they have generally been unsuccessful in clarifying the role and place of bureaucratic discretion in terms of democratic governance itself (e.g., Wamsley et al. 1990). Second, a substantial literature under the rubric of "political control of the bureaucracy" (e.g., Moe 1985; Scholz, Twombley, and Headrick 1991; Scholz and Wood 1999; and Wood and Waterman 1994) has provided some empirical evidence that elected officials influence and perhaps even "control" some of the actions of bureaucracy, but this line of work exhibits some serious limitations. The subject therefore needs to be examined afresh. Third, the evolution of both popularly controlled and bureaucratic institutions of governance continues. In fact, the classic portrait of "bureaucracy" as the institutional form for turning policy preferences into action offers a distorted image of today's realities of governance, which often involve networked combinations of public, private, and nonprofit organizations jointly implementing public programs. These changes mean that the political-control literature underestimates the difficulty of controlling bureaucracy because analysts have not recognized current developments in program design and because typical formulations of the issue have not adequately considered the full range of existing bureaucratic forms.

As this volume demonstrates, while the bureaucracy-democracy challenge remains important across nations and circumstances, the issue cannot be effectively analyzed in the abstract. A clear understanding of how the challenge can actually be addressed, and where its most tendentious elements may lie, must follow from an engagement with the specifics of a particular political system and its bureaucratic institutions. Many kinds of regimes treat the democratic ideal seriously, and "bureaucracy" appears in quite distinct forms in different policy fields, levels of government, and national contexts. These differences matter greatly in any effort to assess the performance of a system. In short, the issue must be engaged by framing it in one or more particular governing systems (Hood 2002).

In this volume, we conduct such an empirically grounded analysis. In doing so, we seek correctives to the difficulties identified above and sketch what we regard as a more accurate and useful perspective on both the particular context and the general issue. Before delving into those specifics, however, we first situate the coverage in the broad bureaucracy-democracy problematic as it has typically been understood among the social sciences and show that most of the discourse can be seen as consistent with one of two partial, albeit abstract, perspectives. We then indicate why a more context-specific approach is necessary. We outline a particular kind of setting for systematic analysis and frame the subsequent coverage in terms of the developing literature on governance. Finally, we sketch the plan of this book.

Bureaucracy-Democracy Tension: A Continuing Legacy

The difficult relationship between the institution of bureaucracy and the ideal of democracy has been a broad and persistent theme across the social sciences. In sociology, a field that has dissected the institution of bureaucracy for nearly a century, the power implied by the expertise and near-permanence of such structures has been a prime topic of analysis. Bureaucrats facing political leaders are like experts confronting dilettantes, as Weber (1946) indicated. Early astute analyses pointed to a bureaucratic dynamic in which power slowly accretes to insiders at the center of the organizational action: the "iron law of oligarchy" (Michels 1999). This pessimistic insight hypothesizes a tendency for organized arrangements to move in a less accessible and less democratic direction over time, despite contrary preferences expressed during institutional design. Studies of informal organization, as well, and of actions taken by administrators under pressure to generate support from external events, echo a similar thesis: bureaucracies engage in co-optive strategies to protect themselves and aid their survival. Even the most well-intentioned and "democratic" approaches to administration can produce results in which powerful interests exert disproportionate control over bureaucratic action, and broader but more diffuse majoritarian preferences are cast aside (Selznick 1949). Bureaucratic politics and luck, some have argued, rather than responsiveness or even effectiveness, can account for the survival rates of most government bureaus (Kaufman 1985; Pfeffer and Salancik 1978).[3]

Economists have also grappled with bureaucracy, albeit in quite a different fashion. Here the focus has been less on democracy and more on efficiency, although some public-choice analysts would argue that these two concepts converge (Ostrom 1989). Stimulated by analyses of "nonmarket failure" in bureaucratic institutions, economists have identified a range of possible problems entailed by bureaucratic forms, and some of these are directly relevant to the bureaucracy-democracy theme. For instance, economic analysis based on an assumption that bureaucrats are self-interested actors explores the ways that bureaucratic behavior is likely to generate "rent seeking" as opposed to public-interested action. Information asymmetries have been explored by economists, and the results of such analyses have buttressed the sociologists' point about the power of expertise (Niskanen 1971; but see Blais and Dion 1991). The contract notion from principal-agent theory has been especially influential.[4] Political leaders as principals, it is argued, inevitably face a slippage of control when dealing with bureaucrats as agents. The latter constitute a constant threat to principals' control—and thus to democratic governance. This is one reason that many economists prefer market-based policy instruments to bureaucratically managed programs. Another argument voiced by economists that also touches upon the bureaucracy-democracy challenge is that the extensive variety among individual citizen preferences is unlikely to be satisfied by means of a rule-governed, centrally directed bureaucratic apparatus. The implication is that even were the bureaucracy entirely altruistic, it could not possibly deal in a sufficiently variegated fashion with the full range of citizens' or clients' utility functions (Ostrom 1989; Tiebout 1956). Bureaucracies seek regularity and consistent application of rules. Clearly, a bureaucratic process will meet only some citizens' utility functions as a result of this regularity and consistency.

The sociological and economic treatments of the bureaucracy-democracy problematic are provocative. Still, the main lines of analysis rely on either a depiction of selected general tendencies or a heavily deductive argument with little grounding in the actual empirical settings of interest. More direct treatments of the bureaucracy-democracy challenge have been developed in the fields of political science and public administration. These are sketched next and serve as particularly important foci for analysis and critique in the ensuing coverage.

Political science has long considered the feasibility of achieving democracy and has debated, for instance, the extent to which pluralistic or corporatist political systems impede or facilitate popular control. In most of political science, democracy has been interpreted operationally as popular electoral control of political decision makers (for a classic statement, see Schumpeter 1950). This definition is typically interpreted to include such features as political competition, basic individual rights, and transparent mechanisms of accountability within the political system. In this light, bureaucracy can be seen as a potential challenge—particularly to the extent that major decision making devolves to it and to the extent that various protections insulate it from control by the people. As Mosher put the issue in his important study, "The accretion of specialization and of technological and social complexity seems to be an irreversible trend, one that leads to increasing dependence upon the protected, appointive public service, thrice removed from direct democracy. Herein lies the central and underlying problem . . . : How can a public service so constituted be made to operate in a manner compatible with democracy?" (1982, 5).[5]

As we attempt to demonstrate in this book, *all* institutions of governance—not merely those outside the electoral system and separate from the "political" branches—can appropriately be assessed for their contribution to democracy. Political science, on the other hand, has typically viewed bureaucracy ipso facto as a problem because of its independence from political overseers.

The main model of the democratic ideal operating in political science has been some version of "overhead democracy" (Redford 1969). The public chooses political leaders in competitive elections, with successful leaders then assuming power and responsibility for enacting and executing policy. Successful leaders—that is, those able to attract popular approval for their program of action—can thus be rewarded with reelection, whereas those seen as failures can be unseated at periodic intervals. In this depiction, those with responsibility to lead must have control over the bureaucracy. Otherwise, bureaucratic autonomy would subvert the political will and make a mockery of the democratic principle. In key respects, therefore, the conventional political science framing of the issue has much in common with principal-agent ideas in economics.

From the perspective of mainstream political science, bureaucracy is inherently problematic for democracy. The "solution" follows directly from the logic of overhead democracy: to ensure that political leaders are effectively able to direct, constrain, and control the bureaucracy. A significant stream of empirical research has sprung up around this topic, particularly in the United States, with the goal of seeing whether bureaucracy is in fact responsive to the policy initiatives from above. We examine this literature in some detail in chapter 2. For now it is sufficient to note that the political science approach is to assume a particular form for the resolution of the issue. That is, control by political leaders is essential. Reconciling democracy and bureaucracy means maximizing control by politicos over bureaucrats. As we shall see, however, bureaucracy itself can sometimes facilitate democracy, and political leaders can sometimes impede it (Meier 1997).

The field of public administration has also long considered the bureaucracy-democracy issue. The U.S. literature is particularly noteworthy. From its coming of age as a self-aware field near the beginning of the twentieth century, American public administration has grappled with the place of administrative institutions in a democratic regime. Woodrow Wilson's (1887) early essay on the field represented a classic argument for distinguishing politics from administration. Advocating for this dichotomy, both normatively and in terms of specific reforms to effectuate it (council-manager city governments, civil service reform, etc.), was a widely adopted way of trying to handle the problem. In this approach, democratic norms were applicable in the political realm, whereas bureaucracy was to be structured and overseen internally by scientifically driven principles of administration, which should be identical for all governments, whether democratic or autocratic (Waldo 1948; for an alternative interpretation, see Bertelli and Lynn 2006).

This tidy manner of resolving the problem and defanging bureaucratic independence was the conventional wisdom in this field for decades. The perspective had only one problem, but that was fatal: It bore no relationship to the real world. Analysts could talk about the separation of politics from administration, and vice versa, but researchers and practitioners began to proclaim in the 1930s and 1940s that the reality was much more a seamless web (Appleby 1949; Herring 1936; Simon 1947).[6] The collapse of the dichotomy was followed by a succession of efforts to find a more effective way of reconciliation. As demonstrated in chapter 2, some of these initiatives have helped in developing important insights on the issue. Nonetheless, none of the reformulations in and of themselves adequately handle the challenge.

Between the 1940s and the late 1960s, the dominant normative stance in the field was what might be termed administrative pluralism. If politics is no stranger to the bureaucracy, the argument went, that fact does not necessarily entail a threat to democracy. Rather, administrators properly socialized in the requisites of democratic governance can use their discretion to grease the wheels of the system by facilitating the virtually endless rounds of bargaining characteristic of pluralistic democracy. In this depiction public administrators, as the lead bureaucrats, are necessary, albeit benign, partners in pluralistic politics (Appleby 1949; Kaufman 1956; Long 1949).

During the late 1960s and the 1970s, in particular, U.S.-style pluralism came under heavy criticism, and the role of the bureaucracy was part of the issue. Analysts and activists argued that the U.S. political system systematically benefits well-organized and well-financed special interests at the expense of the general public and that the bureaucracy is complicit in this pattern (Lowi 1969). Bureaucratic decision makers typically forge alliances with the most powerful interest groups and legislative committees to stabilize their jurisdictions and facilitate smooth policy making and implementation. The critique is aimed at the relatively closed character of policy making—agribusiness is in on the action but not, say, tenant farmers—and the injustice that results. If professions are conspiracies against the laity, as George Bernard Shaw once said, then the bureaucracy, in league with its allies, might be considered a conspiracy against the public.

In the field of public administration, as in other parts of the social sciences, this normative stance represented a theme of the political left. A version of it that made a distinctive mark was the so-called New Public Administration,[7] whose proponents advocated a view of the administrator as free, and obliged, to make a social-equity stand on behalf of the poorly represented rather than the well-represented special interests (Frederickson 1980; Marini 1971). Some advocates would go so far as to say that the bureaucracy should right the undemocratic wrongs of the political system. The general stance, in any event, is for the democratically inspired exercise of discretionary decision making.

The New Public Administration has been challenged as having been not very new (Mosher 1992) and, in particular, as itself threatening the basic tenets of democratic governance by interposing bureaucratic notions of the public's needs in place of those determined by means of the explicitly political process (Thompson 1975). Still, in one form or another, some such approach has remained attractive to many in the field of public administration. Most who focus primarily on public bureaucracy are inclined to interpret the bureaucracy in relatively positive terms and public bureaucrats as contributors to the public weal (e.g., Denhardt 1993). One of the best-known volumes in this specialty, *The Case for Bureaucracy* (Goodsell 2004), explicitly aims to debunk virtually all aspects of the negative stereotype. Goodsell claims that, particularly in the United States, the "problem" has been vastly overblown. And in the "Blacksburg Manifesto," coauthored by several scholars at the Virginia

Institute of Technology, Wamsley and colleagues argue that "the Public Administration" is an extraordinarily positive institution that heals some of the defects in the American constitutional design (1990; see also Wamsley and Wolf 1996). While some critics challenge this argument and emphasize its implicitly undemocratic tenets (Cooper 1990; Kaufman 1990), a significant part of the scholarly community in public administration remains inclined to believe that bureaucracy as an institution offers support for democratic principles.

A portion of the field lies outside this fold. In the 1980s and thereafter, economics has influenced public administration, and public-choice arguments about reframing the bureaucracy-democracy issue have taken root (Ostrom 1989; see also the discussion of the New Public Management, below). Nonetheless, the modal view is much like this: Overhead democracy is a simplistic rendering of the issue; and bureaucracy itself, if infused with appropriate values,[8] can support democratic governance.

While scholars of public administration can be faulted for not treating the potential conflict between bureaucracy and democracy as seriously as it deserves—and for too often dealing with the issue in its abstracted form (as do researchers in other fields as well)—some particularly helpful work has been done. An example of this kind of effort is the maturing scholarship on "representative bureaucracy." Those aspects of public administration research that do contribute in a helpful fashion to framing and addressing the bureaucracy-democracy question are discussed systematically in chapter 2.

Top-Down and Bottom-Up Democratic Ideas

This brief review shows that across numerous social sciences, the bureaucracy-democracy theme has been considered to be an issue worthy of significant attention. How the topic is framed and analyzed has varied by discipline and also within discipline. If one considers the full set of perspectives, however, two broad logics can be seen. Each of these, in general terms, sketches a way of conceptualizing the challenge, as well as a strategy for addressing the issue. Outlining the two reveals some commonalities across a range of approaches and also sets the core issue in a context that this volume systematically examines.

One basic approach to the bureaucracy-democracy problem is to conceive of the democratic impulse as essentially emanating from "above." The "top" of the political system, in this view, consists of the central or most formally authoritative positions and organs of the governing system: those directly chosen by the electorate and those entailing the broadest and most encompassing jurisdiction. Because of the direct link to the public via periodic competitive elections, bodies like parliaments and elected chief executives have a special claim to represent the agenda of the people. One challenge facing these political leaders, then, is to monitor and control the bureaucracy so that the agents do not replace the democratically chosen principals as the key decision makers.

This depiction is in clear harmony with the political control literature of political science. It also fits the perspective of the new economics of organization. In some of its refinements, it can incorporate the notion of multiple principals as well (Chubb 1985). Although some top-down proponents are particularly positive about parliamentary systems (Finer 1941), in the United States the separation-of-powers design renders the top-down perspective more complicated. At the national level, there is no single constitutionally privileged "top." Similarly, a federal system that permits autonomous state and local elected officials adds additional complications to the perspective.

Outside the United States, other variants on a top-down design include neocorporatist systems, which frame policy agreements as legitimately the province of the "top" conceived as political officials, in conjunction with the key sectoral leadership, like business and labor peak-associational decision makers. The views of individual firms and industries, as well as of laborers and particular unions, are channeled to the top of their respective sectors, where agreements are forged across the social partners, who then have a common interest in monitoring and controlling execution by the bureaucracy.

Why would the bureaucracy respond to the "top"? The main theme in top-down depictions is a reliance on coercion, at least as a default condition (even if not often exercised or visible). In addition, although less often emphasized by analysts of political systems, socialization could play a role. Inculcating bureaucrats with agency missions, emphasizing responsiveness to political authority, and socializing civil servants into the mores of a top-down democratic ethos could also be important forces. The principal-agent approach narrowly frames the response in terms of the incentives offered by the principal, although in practice even the actual incentives are often not specified.

The other broad notion of democratic governance reflected in the set of perspectives sketched earlier is what might be called bottom-up democracy. The reference is not to some naive version of grassroots or direct democracy, nor to an injunction to maximize discretion in the hands of the administrative "bottom," the legions of street-level bureaucrats. Rather, the logic is that popular control is most effectively achieved through channels other than the political "top." In other words, the bureaucracy as a political institution might best be checked by direct popular oversight (citizens' review boards monitoring police departments, clients controlling some aspects of agency decisions) or by institutional arrangements that deviate from a standard monocratic authority structure and instead incorporate incentives for bureaucratic actors to be directly attuned to popular preferences.

One way that these might operate is via openness of the bureaucracy itself to pressure and control by organized interests that may care greatly about the actions of administrative units. Some analysts have been critical of "excessive" influence through such pluralistic channels (Lowi 1969); but the advocates of administrative pluralism, mentioned earlier in this chapter, saw the democratic ideal advanced by interest groups becoming directly involved in the "pulling and hauling" that characterizes the decision-making process of public bureaucracies.

Other versions of such generally bottom-up institutional designs are sympathetic to the public-choice perspective, including the use of quasi-markets. Such systems ideally transmit signals from consumers of policy, or at least public services, to bureaucratic producers in such a way that the latter are strongly encouraged to follow preferences as conveyed by consumer choice or consumption patterns. The notion here is to use marketlike forces to shape bureaucratic behavior rather than rely upon command and control by standard political authority. Public-choice advocates therefore argue that quasi-market forces can simultaneously improve both governmental efficiency and democracy, with the latter being defined operationally largely in terms of maximizing the match between consumer preferences and governmental production or supply (Ostrom 1989).

Recent reform efforts rely on a modified version of this argument and, in effect, combine features of top-down and bottom-up logics. Thus the so-called New Public Management (NPM), as it has been advocated in several countries, argues in favor of "liberating" government bureaucratic managers as they do their job, thereby reducing some of the direct administrative controls upon them, largely by tapping market forces to encourage greater attention to the production and provision of services.

Treating the citizen like a customer is part of the perspective. Liberating the managers, furthermore, has typically been encouraged at the same time that renewed attention to productivity by political leaders has been emphasized. Whether in the U.S. variant of this reform movement, especially popular during the Clinton-Gore presidency through the National Performance Review, or as developed in the United Kingdom, New Zealand, Australia, and a number of other countries, the main emphasis has been on the bottom-up portion of the logic, with government bureaucrats largely cast as efficient contract administrators. This emphasis suggests that it would be a mistake to conclude that the NPM is mostly a bundle of technocratic initiatives, divorced from the political realm. Rather, it appeals broadly in part because of its apparent connection with a key theme of the democratic ethos.[9]

In general, why would the bureaucracy actually respond to bottom-up pressures? Political pressure or economic incentives are typically singled out as major parts of the explanation. Political pressures from clientele can be aggregated to provide political support for bureaucracies in their dealings with electoral institutions; efficiently delivering such services can contribute to being able to increase the total volume of services and thus also add to political support (Meier 2000). Furthermore, as students of bureaucracies like the U.S. Department of Agriculture or the Tennessee Valley Authority have pointed out, socialization of the bureaucrats can also play an important role. Agencies staffed by people trained to consider the public, or certain relevant portions of the public, as their primary constituents are likely to be deferential to direct pressures and inputs from those groups.

These two broad perspectives on democracy and bureaucracy both have some merit. In general, nonetheless, they can be faulted on at least three grounds. First, proponents of one tend to caricature or ignore the other. In particular, political scientists focused on the issue of political control of the bureaucracy seem to have the issue, or aspects of the issue, half right. They treat well and carefully the top-down accountability challenges, but they ignore the ways in which the pressures and incentives from the other direction can aid the cause of democracy. In this latter regard, they pay little attention to the actual incentives operating on the bureaucracy, or they assume that bureaucratic values and socialization constitute threats to democracy. They also tend to assume that the legitimacy of the actions of unelected decision makers are automatically suspect, whereas the actions of elected and politically appointed leaders are necessarily legitimate—this despite widespread evidence that the legitimacy of explicitly political institutions of government is equally (or more) questionable in the eyes of the public (see, e.g., Inglehart 1997; Orren 1997). In this regard, they may misspecify the challenge.

Second, proponents of each perspective tend to ignore the disadvantages of an exclusive emphasis on its features. For example, the transaction costs of leading the administrative apparatus are already very high even without wholehearted efforts to exert detailed control (i.e., to "micromanage") the bureaucracy. Proponents of a top-down variant of democracy have generally not dealt with such important constraints (for a formal demonstration that principal-agent control cannot be effected by the use of incentives alone, even within a single bureaucratic organization, see Miller 1992). Further, the bureaucratic hyperresponsiveness sometimes implicitly endorsed as an element of democratic control—with the bureaucracy expected, in effect, to respond "how high?" to any political injunction to "jump"—distorts the considered meaning of democracy. Bureaucratic institutions and their programs themselves represent institutionalized aspects of responsible government that are politically designed, in part, to provide some stability and regularity to governance; drastic shifts in governmental direction in response to episodic blips of public opinion are not consistent with most careful treatments of democratic governance (note Madison's reference to the "permanent and aggregate interests of the majority" in *Federalist*, no. 10).

Advocates of bottom-up democratic governance generally avoid dealing with the deliberative and collective aspects of democratic consensus building and control, either by focusing on individuals' utility—public-choice approaches—or by assuming that administrative agencies are appropriately general forums for the resolution of public problems—the administrative pluralists or the Blacksburg proponents. The requisites of political control are typically insufficiently depicted and inadequately worked into the logic of bottom-up democratic governance within bureaucratic systems.

The third problem with these perspectives is that they are overly broad and abstract. The arguments in support of overhead democracy tend to be framed to head off the anticipated difficulties of the ideal-typical bureaucracy, sketched generally and in forms that are not much advanced from the Weberian picture formulated nearly a century ago. Whether actual, functioning administrative agencies much resemble the abstract depiction is not a research question among such analysts. Some forms of bottom-up argument are more empirically grounded in the realities of bureaucratic operations, including the values of bureaucrats in particular settings and the access of stakeholders to bureaucratic decision makers in concrete situations (see chap. 2). Still, these perspectives tend to treat politicians and political control from the top in an overly general and abstract fashion—as if political control does or should have little to do with effective democratic governance.

A key premise of this book is that neither line of reasoning about democracy and bureaucracy offers a fully satisfactory picture, that elements of each must be incorporated clearly into the analytical picture in any assessment of how well any actual governing system comports with the democratic principle. The top-down arguments framed in the logic of political control offer an important piece of the puzzle, but an incomplete one. Bottom-up analysts alert us to crucial modes and channels of popular influence but likewise omit elements that must be included. Any valid perspective must necessarily be grounded in the empirical features of actual governing systems.

As one moves from abstract theory to a particular governance setting, the problem becomes more complex because one is no longer dealing with the ideal-typical "bureaucracy" or with unambiguous commitment to an abstractly general "democracy". Bureaucratic units shaped by particular political and cultural forces populate the institutional landscape. A German ministry is an organization very different, in many dimensions, from a postsocialist Russian bureaucracy, and these are both far cries from bureaus of the U.S. Department of Agriculture. These differences—in patterns of bureaucratic recruitment and socialization, decision making, links to interest groups and arrays of formal and informal advisory committees, degrees of decentralization and rule-boundedness, and so forth— definitely matter in any assessment of the fit between bureaucracy and democracy. Some versions of bureaucracy and some contexts are much likelier to facilitate popular influence than others.

Similarly, Westminster-style institutions of top-down popular control reflect a very different realization of "democracy" than do separation-of-powers forms. Grassroots channels of influence over bureaucrats—as visible, for instance, in hundreds of U.S. intergovernmental grant programs—reflect yet another reformulation of "democracy."

We argue, therefore, that the bureaucracy-democracy challenge is central, but it must be addressed in an empirically grounded fashion for any valid conclusions to be drawn. Many varieties of democracy and many kinds of bureaucracy inevitably mean that many different assessments are possible. Understanding the particular challenges and vulnerabilities of a governing system requires analyzing how its particular institutions and patterns of action operate. In this volume, we embed the bureaucracy-democracy discussion in one specific kind of context (the United States) to facilitate this kind of assessment, and further productive discourse on this theme must, we argue, be similarly embedded.

This argument does not mean, however, that the conclusion to be drawn about bureaucracy and democracy consists of the maxim "It all depends." Rather, we suggest that significant advance on this question requires context-specific analyses framed within a more general theoretical perspective, so that different contexts and institutions can ultimately be compared systematically and explicitly. For that reason, we also situate our analysis in a more general way by clarifying what is meant by a governance perspective and then employing it in an approach to understanding public program performance in a governance setting. The next section covers these topics briefly and explains the empirical settings on which the analysis of this book is conducted. The section following then sketches the plan of the volume.

A Governance Perspective: A General Approach and An Empirical Setting

A governance approach seeks to integrate political and bureaucratic forces at multiple levels to indicate how programs are designed, adopted, implemented, and evaluated in terms of both effectiveness and democracy. Such a point of view clearly recognizes that only with effective implementing institutions can societies generate the fairness and slack resources that permit democracies with their large transaction costs to exist and prosper. Governing institutions, in turn, operate at multiple levels of government and take a variety of forms; a governance perspective (see Heinrich and Lynn 2000; Kettl 2002; Kooiman 2003; Pierre and Peters 2000; Rhodes 1997) sensitizes one to the fuller array of these. Some are traditional electoral institutions such as legislatures; others operate outside of government— interest groups, political parties, social movements, private organizations. Similarly, implementing institutions, commonly denoted simply as "bureaucracy," actually take a wide range of forms, from the traditional government agency, to nonprofit organizations, private organizations, or elaborate networks composed of all of these forms.

In this book we frequently use the shorthand "bureaucracy" to reference the institutional arrangements used for implementation in a governance system. We do so for two reasons: for economy of expression and also to connect our analysis to the longstanding and important line of debate and research on bureaucracy and democracy (for further coverage see the appendix). As emphasized earlier, however, the actual institutional arrangements operating in any given governance setting can vary considerably. One particularly important dimension of such institutional arrangements is the extent to which, at one extreme, public programs are carried out through a classic and stable hierarchy, on the one hand, or through a set of actors tied together in a less hierarchical and less stable fashion: a "network." Networks consist of two or more actors linked by some degree and type of interdependence, in which the actors are not connected simply by a set of superior-subordinate relations. We refer to the full range of these as "bureaucracy"; but, as will be clear in later chapters, the range of variation in such arrangements is much broader than that encompassed by the usual types of administrative agencies, each separately managing its own straightforwardly structured programs.

This perspective sets the contemporary debate on bureaucracy and democracy in the context of twenty-first century governance arrangements. Governance is a broad topic; governance models range from relatively loosely structured logics of governance (Lynn, Heinrich, and Hill 2001) to highly specific models that specify sets of testable hypotheses (see the appendix; O'Toole and Meier 1999).

Rather than examine the literature in detail, for purposes of establishing the context for this book a relatively simple heuristic will be adequate. Governance systems cover three basic functions: the aggregation of preferences, decisions on policy options, and the implementation of policies. Each merits discussion in turn.

The aggregation of preferences, whether of the general public or of highly motivated elites, is accomplished through processes of representation. Although the most common form of representation occurs when legislators take mass public values and express them in the policy-making process, additional representational processes can also be noted. In addition to representation via legislatures and elected chief executives, similar functions can be performed when other institutions, such as interest groups, political parties, private firms, and nonprofit organizations, represent interests. This broader notion is important for our purposes since it suggests that bureaucratic institutions can also serve a representational function. In fact, at least two such forms can be identified: active representation, in which the representational role is explicitly established in authorizing legislation or other initiating pronouncements (e.g., the U.S. Department of Agriculture, which was created to serve the interests of farmers), or more passive representation, the incorporation of values or common experiences by those who populate the administrative apparatus. We examine the bureaucratic representational function empirically later in this book.

The governance perspective is also sensitive to the point that the locus of decision making can vary. Policies can be established in what may be considered the traditional way, by legislative action, but a governance perspective also attends to the point that policies can be made when government defers action to nonstate actors. From this perspective, policy decisions can be made by private-sector organizations whenever government decides not to decide. Policy decisions can also be delegated to elected executives, bureaucratic organizations, or networks comprising a wide variety of actors (see chap. 3). Although a more traditional perspective might trace such decisions to legislative action or inaction, in many cases bureaucracies initiate policies without legislative approval (e.g., airline deregulation, the nonbank loophole in financial regulation) or networks self-organize and set policies (e.g., early AIDS policy; see chap. 3).

Implementation, or generating tangible results from such systems, has perhaps seen the greatest influence of the governance perspective. This impact has become increasingly visible as the institutional arrangements involved in delivering governance have evolved (in academic recognition if not in practice) from solitary government bureaucracies, to more variable networks of multiple organizations, or parts of organizations, including government agencies at the same or different levels of government, nonprofit organizations and associations, and private-sector companies. The clusters of networked units may be charged with varying types and levels of coordination, or they may self-organize to do so even if not explicitly required. Because achievement of public policy objectives takes place within a context of culture, laws, and traditions, some policies might even be relatively self-implementing. Many others will rely on some co-production with citizens, whether the institutional implementing apparatus is a bureaucratic agency or a more complex network.

The governance perspective treats these three functions not as a linear progression from preference aggregation to decision making to implementation, but rather as a set of interrelated and temporally overlapping functions. In addition to the obvious feedback that develops from policy implementation, which can influence both decisions and the aggregation of preferences, each of the elements in this triad of functions influences both of the others. In other words, all the relationships are reciprocal. A wide variety of political institutions or combination of institutions can perform any of the three functions. One important advantage of a governance perspective is that it encourages a consideration of how the various key processes are actually carried out, rather than examining only formal arrangements and formally stipulated tasks.

Many empirical contexts could be useful as settings for the systematic analysis of the bureaucracy and democracy theme. We choose to emphasize evidence from the United States; as a developed nation with substantial commitment to public programs and a long history of serious attention to democracy, it is an appropriate context. At the same time, exploring the bureaucracy-democracy issue for the United States is no substitute for systematic attention to the issue elsewhere. To be productive, analysis must be grounded in the particular democratic and bureaucratic features of a given governance setting. In some respects, particularly with regard to its administrative experience, the United States is a highly unusual case (Stillman 1991); and Europeans or Latin Americans, for example, need to adapt this kind of analysis to the circumstances that are played out in a variety of other cases.

Within the United States, many interesting settings could be candidates for analyses. The Tennessee Valley Authority is a national agency with a substantial history of attention to democratic values, as is the U.S. Department of Agriculture. The former has been known to interpret democracy heavily in terms of local preferences and grass-roots democracy (Lilienthal 1944; Selznick 1949); the latter has emphasized attention to its core sectoral constituency using bottom-up processes of preference aggregation, decision making, and implementation by and among the agricultural community, with some management from above. Many other national bureaus could provide instructive material. Further, there are more than eighty-five thousand governments within the United States, all but fifty-one of which are local.

In this volume, we offer some limited but systematically framed and gathered data from the national level to elucidate some aspects of the bureaucracy-democracy challenge. The bulk of the empirical coverage, however, is drawn from the local level, and in particular from that uniquely American form of special governmental form, school districts. On issues of democracy and bureaucracy, the governance of school systems is a key forum; public education represents a significant channel of socialization and civic development. How such systems perform can be considered one of the critical challenges of democratic governance. Of the more than fourteen thousand U.S. school districts, we select the thousand-plus districts of the state of Texas for detailed examination. While a focus on so many different governance systems precludes detailed attention to any one of them, the tradeoff is sensible. Analyzing bureaucracy and democracy in many different governance systems, each providing similar and important public services in the same state at the same time, provides ideal research settings for systematic analyses of some of the key aspects of this topic as outlined earlier. Texas is a large, diverse state, and the availability of high-quality and detailed data on many of the most salient issues gives us a chance to make some empirical headway.

Plan of the Volume

Thus far we have framed the subject to be tackled in this book in terms of attention to it by various social sciences and reform perspectives, empirical settings, and dimensions. We have also connected the issue to the contemporary discussion of governance (see the appendix for our formal model of the governance process).

Chapter 2 emphasizes the political-control theme, which has been such an important part of the dialogue on bureaucracy and democracy in political science. We use four alternative streams of literature to show that the standard political-science control framework is incomplete and at times even inaccurate. The chapter demonstrates conclusively that political control is only one of many environmental inputs to bureaucracy and that "political control" or overhead democracy is only one relevant form of democratic governance.

Chapter 3 begins the empirical analyses. Most studies of political control of the bureaucracy assume a simple principal-agent model; even more complicated models, which allow for multiple principals, only examine a single, unitary bureaucracy. This chapter demonstrates that traditional models of political control are inaccurate and underestimate the problems of top-down political control. The analysis presents national U.S. empirical findings to show that public programs are increasingly implemented not by single, hierarchical bureaucracies but by complex inter-governmental and interorganizational networks. In such networks, the ability of a lead bureaucratic agency to coerce compliance is limited. Instead, bureaucracies must use resources, political skills, and strategic efforts to entice other governments, private organizations, and citizen groups to cooperate to implement policy. Such relationships imply that while Congress may have some hierarchical influence over a federal bureaucracy, the bureaucracy often does not have sufficient institutional control over other relevant policy actors to carry out the intent of Congress. These networks characterize a wide range of U.S. policies, thus validating the importance of a governance perspective and implying that top-down political control faces a structural system that is not especially amenable to such control.

Chapter 4 then asks and provides an answer to the following important question: If one were to examine a more "ideal" structural situation (ideal, that is, from the standpoint of the logic of political control), how effective would overhead control actually be? Here the treatment moves to the subnational level for some systematic exploration of the factors that shape bureaucratic results in these relatively simple and straightforward settings. The chapter argues that political control itself can only be assessed when one knows the goals of both the politicians and the bureaucrats. This assertion is justified with two different theories: representative bureaucracy and spatial modeling. The chapter then provides a critical test by using school districts and the interests of Latino citizens to demonstrate how little control political institutions have over one set of implementing institutions. The chapter probes various methods of political control, such as relying on political appointments and setting general policies, in addition to undertaking simple majoritarian efforts. All prove to be marginally effective. In short, even in situations of optimal structure, from the standpoint of advocates of political control, top-down control is problematic. At the same time bureaucracy appears to be highly responsive to citizen demands; this responsiveness, however, is a function of bureaucratic values, not political-control efforts. This chapter thus develops the bottom-up theme from what began as a top-down portrayal.

Chapter 5 sets up a second situation in which political control over bureaucracy should be at a maximum: the use of standardized testing to hold schools accountable. In such circumstances political principals tend to be unified, monitoring is done relatively cheaply and openly by parents and the media, and bureaucratic shirking should be minimized. Even in such ideal situations, however, bureaucracies can "cheat"—that is, use their own devices to comply with the letter of account-ability schemes but avoid the substantive intent of political controllers—in clever and difficult-to-counter ways. The analysis and findings are then linked to a theoretical framework that predicts when an implementing organization facing multiple goals is likely to cheat in this manner and when it is not.

Two implications follow. First, in a situation that should be optimal for political control, bureaucracies can subvert that control by relying on techniques that emphasize their expertise. Second, bureaucracies can adopt such strategies not because their objective is to subvert political control but because their professional values lead them to believe that such testing policies will have major deleterious effects on students. The bottom line is that in a situation that appears to be ideal for political control, there is substantial evidence of bureaucratic discretion and that a professionalized implementing institution is no guarantor of democratic governance.

The concluding chapter interprets these empirical findings within the context of contemporary governance research. The basic themes are two. First, top-down political control of the bureaucracy has only modest impact at best on the activities of bureaucracy in the United States. The book shows that overhead democracy in such settings is not an effective way to ensure the responsiveness of bureaucracy in a democracy. If overhead democracy is limited in these "ideal" situations, its impact in more challenging situations, circumstances that are clearly not uncommon, is substantially less. Second, at the same time bureaucracy in the United States can be highly sensitive to the needs and desires of citizens. Shared values and commitments to democratic norms, along with political control, produce a bureaucracy that is often responsive to the American people. These themes are then used to speculate on the role of bureaucracy in a democratic society, both in the United States and elsewhere. A brief review of contemporary notions of bureaucratic reform, in the context of the present analysis, suggests that caution be used before adopting wholesale some of the most popular current notions for "reinventing government." In fact, the requisites of democracy require an extended critique and reappraisal of such ideas.

End Notes

1. In the abstract, democracy is a form of government resting on the popular will and thus has no linkage to questions of effectiveness or efficiency (Dahl 1970). In the practical world, however, we know of no modern democracy that does not also have an effective bureaucracy. Suleimari (2003) contends that effective policy provides legitimacy for democratic governments. Meier (1997) argues that only bureaucracy can provide the efficiency needed to absorb the large transaction costs of democracy.

2. One dimension of the issue that will not be covered in this volume is the democratization of decision making *within* the bureaucracy. Researchers in organizational development and change have long explored the impact of more participatory schemes within bureaucratic systems (Golembiewski 1995), and a long tradition of research and debate has considered democratic themes as they might apply to the design and operation of the permanent civil service. As Waldo noted decades ago, it is simply not credible to claim that "autocracy during working hours is the price to be paid for democracy after hours" (1952, 87). Still, redistributing influence within public agencies, while important, is not the same as democratizing a political system (Mosher 1982).

3. Many scholars might feel that the ability to co-opt the environment is an essential component of any definition of bureaucratic effectiveness.

4. This body of work receives considerable attention later in this book.

5. "Reliance upon popularly elected representatives is one step removed from direct participative democracy. A second step occurs when officers so chosen select and delegate powers to other officers, appointed and removable by them. . . . A third step away from direct democracy is taken with the designation of personnel who are neither elected nor politically appointive and removable, but rather are chosen on bases of stated criteria . . . and, once appointed, are protected from removal on political grounds" (Mosher 1982, 4–5).

6. A careful reading of Goodnow (1900), conceded to be one of the originators of the dichotomy, shows that he did not propose the dichotomy as an empirical reality but rather suggested that it was a normative idea.

7. The ideas of the New Public Administration are not all of a piece (O'Toole 1977), despite efforts to offer an overarching interpretation (Frederickson 1980).

8. Several different kinds of values have been seen as attractive or crucial by theorists. A number of these are examined in the next chapter.

9. The ideas sketched in the last two paragraphs are revisited later, after several chapters of empirical analysis.

CHAPTER 9
PUBLIC OPINION

CORN-PONE OPINIONS

MARK TWAIN

Fifty years ago, when I was a boy of fifteen and helping to inhabit a Missourian village on the banks of the Mississippi, I had a friend whose society was very dear to me because I was forbidden by my mother to partake of it. He was a gay and impudent and satirical and delightful young black man—a slave—who daily preached sermons from the top of his master's woodpile, with me for sole audience. He imitated the pulpit style of the several clergymen of the village, and did it well, and with fine passion and energy. To me he was a wonder. I believed he was the greatest orator in the United States and would some day be heard from. But it did not happen; in the distribution of rewards he was overlooked. It is the way, in this world.

He interrupted his preaching, now and then, to saw a stick of wood; but the sawing was a pretense -he did it with his mouth; exactly imitating the sound the bucksaw makes in shrieking its way through the wood. But it served its purpose; it kept his master from coming out to see how the work was getting along. I listened to the sermons from the open window of a lumber room at the back of the house. One of his texts was this:

"You tell me whar a man gits his corn pone, en I'll tell you what his 'pinions is."

I can never forget it. It was deeply impressed upon me. By my mother. Not upon my memory, but elsewhere. She had slipped in upon me while I was absorbed and not watching. The black philosopher's idea was that a man is not independent, and cannot afford views which might interfere with his bread and butter. If he would prosper, he must train with the majority; in matters of large moment, like politics and religion, he must think and feel with the bulk of his neighbors, or suffer damage in his social standing and in his business prosperities. He must restrict himself to corn-pone opinions— at least on the surface. He must get his opinions from other people; he must reason out none for himself; he must have no first-hand views.

I think Jerry was right, in the main, but I think he did not go far enough.

1. It was his idea that a man conforms to the majority view of his locality by calculation and intention. This happens, but I think it is not the rule.
2. It was his idea that there is such a thing as a first-hand opinion; an original opinion; an opinion which is coldly reasoned out in a man's head, by a searching analysis of the facts involved, with the heart unconsulted, and the jury room closed against outside influences. It may be that such an opinion has been born somewhere, at some time or other, but I suppose it got away before they could catch it and stuff it and put it in the museum.

SOURCE: Mark Twain, *Corn-Pone Opinions,* 1923

I am persuaded that a coldly-thought-out and independent verdict upon a fashion in clothes, or manners, or literature, or politics, or religion, or any other matter that is projected into the field of our notice and interest, is a most rare thing—if it has indeed ever existed.

A new thing in costume appears—the flaring hoopskirt, for example—and the passers-by are shocked, and the irreverent laugh. Six months later everybody is reconciled; the fashion has established itself; it is admired, now, and no one laughs. Public opinion resented it before, public opinion accepts it now, and is happy in it. Why? Was the resentment reasoned out? Was the acceptance reasoned out? No. The instinct that moves to conformity did the work. It is our nature to conform; it is a force which not many can successfully resist. What is its seat? The inborn requirement of self-approval. We all have to bow to that; there are no exceptions. Even the woman who refuses from first to last to wear the hoop skirt comes under that law and is its slave; she could not wear the skirt and have her own approval; and that she must have, she cannot help herself. But as a rule our self-approval has its source in but one place and not elsewhere—the approval of other people. A person of vast consequences can introduce any kind of novelty in dress and the general world will presently adopt it—moved to do it, in the first place, by the natural instinct to passively yield to that vague something recognized as authority, and in the second place by the human instinct to train with the multitude and have its approval. An empress introduced the hoopskirt, and we know the result. A nobody introduced the bloomer, and we know the result. If Eve should come again, in her ripe renown, and reintroduce her quaint styles—well, we know what would happen. And we should be cruelly embarrassed, along at first.

The hoopskirt runs its course and disappears. Nobody reasons about it. One woman abandons the fashion; her neighbor notices this and follows her lead; this influences the next woman; and so on and so on, and presently the skirt has vanished out of the world, no one knows how nor why, nor cares, for that matter. It will come again, by and by and in due course will go again.

Twenty-five years ago, in England, six or eight wine glasses stood grouped by each person's plate at a dinner party, and they were used, not left idle and empty; to-day there are but three or four in the group, and the average guest sparingly uses about two of them. We have not adopted this new fashion yet, but we shall do it presently. We shall not think it out; we shall merely conform, and let it go at that. We get our notions and habits and opinions from outside influences; we do not have to study them out.

Our table manners, and company manners, and street manners change from time to time, but the changes are not reasoned out; we merely notice and conform. We are creatures of outside influences; as a rule we do not think, we only imitate. We cannot invent standards that will stick; what we mistake for standards are only fashions, and perishable. We may continue to admire them, but we drop the use of them. We notice this in literature. Shakespeare is a standard, and fifty years ago we used to write tragedies which we couldn't tell from—from somebody else's; but we don't do it any more, now. Our prose standard, three quarters of a century ago, was ornate and diffuse; some authority or other changed it in the direction of compactness and simplicity, and conformity followed, without argument. The historical novel starts up suddenly, and sweeps the land. Everybody writes one, and the nation is glad. We had historical novels before; but nobody read them, and the rest of us conformed—without reasoning it out. We are conforming in the other way, now, because it is another case of everybody.

The outside influences are always pouring in upon us, and we are always obeying their orders and accepting their verdicts. The Smiths like the new play; the Joneses go to see it, and they copy the Smith verdict. Morals, religions, politics, get their following from surrounding influences and atmospheres, almost entirely; not from study, not from thinking. A man must and will have his own approval first of all, in each and every moment and circumstance of his life—even if he must repent of a self-approved act the moment after its commission, in order to get his self-approval again: but, speaking in general terms, a man's self-approval in the large concerns of life has its source in the approval of the peoples about him, and not in a searching personal examination of the matter. Mohammedans are Mohammedans because they are born and reared among that sect, not because they have thought it out and can furnish sound reasons for being Mohammedans; we know why Catholics are Catholics; why Presbyterians are Presbyterians; why Baptists are Baptists; why Mormons are Mormons; why thieves are thieves; why monarchists are monarchists; why Republicans are Republicans and Democrats, Democrats. We know it is a matter of association and sympathy, not reasoning and examination; that hardly a man in the world has an opinion upon morals, politics, or religion which he got otherwise than through his associations and sympathies. Broadly speaking, there are none but corn-pone opinions. And broadly speaking, corn-pone stands for self-approval. Self-approval is acquired mainly from the approval of other people. The result is conformity. Sometimes conformity has a sordid business interest—the bread-and-butter interest—but not in most cases, I think. I think that in the majority of cases it is unconscious and not calculated; that it is born of the human being's natural yearning to stand well with his fellows and have their inspiring approval and praise—a yearning which is commonly so strong and so insistent that it cannot be effectually resisted, and must have its way. A political emergency brings out the corn-pone opinion in fine force in its two chief varieties—the pocketbook variety, which has its origin in self-interest, and the bigger variety, the sentimental variety—the one which can't bear to be outside the pale; can't bear to be in disfavor; can't endure the averted face and the cold shoulder; wants to stand well with his friends, wants to be smiled upon, wants to be welcome, wants to hear the precious words, "He's on the right track!" Uttered, perhaps by an ass, but still an ass of high degree, an ass whose approval is gold and diamonds to a smaller ass, and confers glory and honor and happiness, and membership in the herd. For these gauds many a man will dump his life-long principles into the street, and his conscience along with them. We have seen it happen. In some millions of instances.

Men think they think upon great political questions, and they do; but they think with their party, not independently; they read its literature, but not that of the other side; they arrive at convictions, but they are drawn from a partial view of the matter in hand and are of no particular value. They swarm with their party, they feel with their party, they are happy in their party's approval; and where the party leads they will follow, whether for right and honor, or through blood and dirt and a mush of mutilated morals.

In our late canvass half of the nation passionately believed that in silver lay salvation, the other half as passionately believed that that way lay destruction. Do you believe that a tenth part of the people, on either side, had any rational excuse for having an opinion about the matter at all? I studied that mighty question to the bottom—came out empty. Half of our people passionately believe in high tariff, the other half believe otherwise. Does this mean study and examination, or only feeling? The latter, I think. I have deeply studied that question, too—and didn't arrive. We all do no end of feeling, and we mistake it for thinking. And out of it we get an aggregation which we consider a boon. Its name is Public Opinion. It is held in reverence. It settles everything. Some think it the Voice of God.

CHAPTER 10
POLITICAL PARTIES AND INTEREST GROUPS

PROSPECTS FOR PARTISAN REALIGNMENT: LESSONS FROM THE DEMISE OF THE WHIGS

What America's last major party crack-up in the 1850s tells us about the 2010s

PHILIP A. WALLACH

Summary

Everything in American politics feels unsettled after the dizzying 2016 election, including the future of America's two major political parties. Both Democrats and Republicans are struggling with internal divisions, and a major realignment is imaginable. In this paper, Philip Wallach sheds light on the current political moment by showing its parallels with 1848–1854, during which the Whig party rapidly went from majority status to extinction.

Introduction

For all the understandable nostalgia we now feel for the simpler political times of, say, 2014, there is no avoiding it: American politics is as thrilling today as it has been in generations. What had seemed immovable is now fluid, and the future is maddeningly obscure. Perhaps the greatest part of our uncertainty is trying to imagine what will become of our two major parties, both of which face profound uncertainty in the months and years to come.

In the wake of Republicans' victories this past November, many are convinced that the GOP is healthier and sturdier than it has been in a century. To even consider the party's demise in this context may seem a strange and futile exercise, then. But to the extent that any moment in America's political history can provide lessons about the chaotic present, the period from 1848 until 1856, during which the Whig Party self-destructed and disappeared, has much to teach us. It featured surging nativism, profound uncertainty for both major parties, the demise of the Whig Party, and the rise of several others, including the GOP. And it began with a political outsider sweeping in to take one of the two major party's nominations, and then leading them to a narrow victory in the presidential election.

In this piece, which relies heavily on Michael F. Holt's enormous and compelling history, *The Rise and Fall of the American Whig Party* (Oxford University Press, 2003), I work through the factors that contributed to the Whigs' demise and examine which of them apply to the predicaments of contemporary Republicans and Democrats. There are a striking number of rhymes. Then, as now, the issues that provided the traditional lines of contestation between the two major parties were losing potency while new divisions were taking their place. The end result then was a shift to a new party system—accompanied by Civil War.

Plenty of factors in our own political landscape make such a dramatic break with the past seem unlikely, at least in the immediate future. Both Democrats and Republicans in 2016 are better insulated from outside competition than the parties of the 1850s. Nevertheless, dramatic change is possible, either with or without the formal demise of a major party, and a look at history clarifies what portents in the years to come would indicate an imminent partisan restructuring.

I. Factors leading to the demise of the Whigs and the restructuring of the 1850s

America's founding fathers envisioned a legislature without organizing parties, but once in motion, our constitutional system soon generated competition between organized groups. The first party system pitted Hamilton's Federalists against Jefferson's Democratic-Republicans and ended in the so-called "era of good feelings" following the War of 1812, when the animating conflicts of those early years faded away. By the late 1820s, the outlines of a second party system were emerging, with Andrew Jackson's Democrats facing off against a coalition of the president's opponents led by Henry Clay, which would ultimately form the Whig Party.

To use Holt's felicitous metaphor, during the twenty-some years that American politics was structured around the conflict between Democrats and Whigs (roughly 1833–1855), each party contained centrifugal forces pulling its coalition apart that had to be counteracted by centripetal forces holding it together.

The story of Whigs' downfall, as Holt chronicles it, is complicated and defies a single explanation. Many factors, reinforcing each other over more than a decade, worked to erode the foundations of Whiggery until the party finally underwent a dramatic collapse from 1853 to 1855. Rather than attempting to retell this history chronologically, this paper attempts to isolate factors that can then be looked for in the present with as much parallelism as is possible.

We will turn to the decline of the forces holding the Whigs together first, and then to the growth of forces pulling them apart.

A. Decline in importance of traditional lines of contestation

As the Whig Party coalesced in the 1830s, it defined itself in opposition to Andrew Jackson and Martin Van Buren's Democrats, with three issues paramount. First, the tariff: Whigs were the party of protective tariffs, Democrats the party of free trade. Second, the broader issue of government involvement in the economy: Whigs were committed to an active government role in banking and internal infrastructure development (first canals and roads, later railroads), encouragement of business activity through bankruptcy laws, and regulation of social behavior, while Democrats argued that government involvement in these endeavors was likely to be harmful and corrupting. Third, reacting to perceptions of Jackson's Caesarism, Whigs saw themselves as champions of Congress, the rule of law, and the republican tradition of enlightened representative government. These were the leading issues that organized electoral competition, not only in presidential elections, but in the full range of local and congressional elections during the 1830s and 1840s. When Democratic policies seemed to produce calamity, as they arguably did in the run-up to the Panic of 1837, Whigs gained from offering a sharply differentiated set of policies.

By the 1850s, there was a significant narrowing of differences between the parties on the issues of the tariff (which settled at middling rates), banking (where Whigs made peace with the demise of the Second National Bank and its replacement by the Independent Treasury), and infrastructure (Democrats became backers of support for railroads and rivers and harbors improvements). Meanwhile, Jackson left office in 1837 and died in 1845, and while Whigs did their best to paint his Democratic successors Van Buren and Polk as similarly prone to executive overreach, this message resonated far less than it did under the reign of "King Andrew I." By the administration of Franklin Pierce, beginning in 1853, the anti-Caesarism that had bound Whigs together in the past was a feeble echo incapable of counteracting more salient issues pushing toward division. By then, many Whigs (including one letter-writer Holt quotes) had come to see politics as impoverished, a mere "scramble for the spoils & a fight about Men rather than measures."

B. Profusion of intra-party factions

The two party coalitions that dominated national political life from the 1830s until the 1850s both contained a diverse range of opinion and priorities. This was especially important on the key issue of slavery. Both Democrats and Whigs were bisectional parties—drawing support from both the North and South—that managed to contain a variety of views about the future of slavery, from Southern champions of the peculiar institution to compromisers seeking middle ground, especially on the contentious issue of the future of slavery in the western territories, to out-and-out abolitionists.

The delicate balance that allowed Whigs and Democrats to compete exclusively on non-slavery issues came apart beginning in the 1840s, in large part because of the need to decide on the future of slavery in the territories acquired in the Mexican War. Worried that new slave states carved from these lands would permanently tip the balance in favor of the South, many Northerners opposed any extension of slavery into the territories. The Compromise of 1850 attempted to push slavery decisively off the agenda and was passed with bipartisan and bisectional support, but the coalition that had backed it proved unable to maintain majority support.

As a result, intraparty factional conflict dominated both parties during this period. Democrats had anti-slavery Barnburners pitted against conservative pro-Compromise Hunkers and their Southern allies; Whigs had anti-slavery Sewardites and "Conscience Whigs" fighting pro-Compromise "Silver Grays" and Southerners.

Pro-compromisers in both Whig and Democratic parties came to see each other as more important allies than their copartisans. In Holt's telling they are sympathetic figures, given that they believed the Union between North and South was in danger of giving way to violent conflict. Commitment to the Compromise was used as a litmus test for many voters in 1852, such that a major focus for Whigs in the contest for their nomination was whether their candidate would take a formal "finality" pledge that declared the compromise sacrosanct. To the extent that the parties failed to adapt to the centrality of slavery, voters turned to other alternatives (see Section I.D).

Although slavery was undoubtedly the most important issue dividing Whigs from each other, two other schisms that opened up in the party in the 1850s proved nearly as damaging to Whigs' ability to hang together. The first of these was prohibition of alcohol. The temperance movement was energized by Maine's passage of a statewide ban on the sale of alcoholic beverages in 1851, and the divide between wets and drys in the Whig Party proved to be a deep and largely unbridgeable one. Whig politicians could try to ignore the issue or skillfully prevaricate, but, more and more, they found themselves alienating some part of their political base, whatever choice they made.

The second, not wholly unrelated issue was the rise of anti-Catholic nativism. The 1840s and 1850s saw a major influx of Catholic immigrants, mainly from Germany and Ireland. "Native" Protestant Americans, many of whom were traditionally Whig voters, were suspicious of these immigrants' "popery," their foreign languages, their association with corrupt urban political machines, and also their wet politics. Many Whig politicians thus embraced openly nativist positions as a way of shoring up their base. Others, however, felt that remaining competitive with Democrats necessitated courting these new Americans. During his 1852 presidential campaign, Winfield Scott pursued this course. Scott was Episcopalian, and had one daughter who had converted to Catholicism and joined a nunnery, and thus he seemed to be in a position to court Catholic voters in the 1852 election. But his efforts to do so yielded few votes, and meanwhile rankled anti-Catholic nativists within the Whig ranks. Nativists would soon begin to look outside the Whig Party for candidates who took the urgency of their concerns seriously and propel the Know-Nothing movement to national prominence.

C. Outsider infiltration and broken conventions

A major element of the Whig party's degeneration was the lack of continuity in its leadership, especially in the crucial realm of presidential politics. This was undoubtedly both the result of a dissolving coalition and itself a further source of problems.

Two of the most striking examples of this tendency come from the party's two vice-presidents who ascended to the presidency only to find themselves at odds with large segments of their parties, and without their party's nomination in the next presidential election. With John Tyler, this situation came early in the party's development, and could be explained by Tyler coming from a group of Virginia states' rights conservatives whose fit in the Whig coalition was awkward and ultimately impermanent. Millard Fillmore, on the other hand, had a long history among the Whigs but was caught in the crossfire of the fights over the future of slavery and the Compromise of 1850 (which he had signed shortly after becoming president).

But the identity of the party's presidential nominees in 1848 and 1852 offer perhaps the most striking instances in which the party abandoned continuity. As the party looked for a champion going into the presidential election of 1848, a majority of its members opted to put their trust in a man who had no political history in the party at all. General Zachary Taylor, hero of the Mexican War, seemed to be "a new Cincinnatus, a man who, like the revered Washington, stood above party." There were even those who were enthusiastic about rebranding the party, abandoning the "Whig" label in favor of "Taylor Republicans."

Taylor, in fact, was no political naif, but he skillfully exploited the public's impression that he was above politics and adapted himself to the political realities of the day without yoking himself to Whigs' historical positions. For Whigs in areas without long histories of party success, like U.S. Representative Abraham Lincoln of Illinois, Taylor's personal reputation seemed to offer the best means of broadening the Whig Party's base; Lincoln became one of Taylor's earliest and most ardent backers.

But where Whigs were more deeply rooted, Taylor's candidacy was often quite divisive. In the last months of the election, Taylor was forced to respond to Whig voters' potentially demobilizing concerns that he was not truly one of their own. He did so by belatedly insisting that all had long known him to be "a Whig in principle," and explained that his general anti-party disposition meant nothing more than that he would refrain from abusing the powers of his office on behalf of partisan maneuvering. In an age when candidates abstained from nearly all forms of active campaigning, this proved to be enough.

But Taylor did not simply act as a normal Whig upon taking office. Instead, in his distribution of the all-important spoils of victory, in the form of federal offices across the country, he snubbed the backers of Henry Clay and other Whig regulars, tearing open lasting rifts in the Whig coalition and demoralizing the party for midterm elections. He made some abortive and ultimately counterproductive attempts to realize the vision of a Taylor Republicanism more inclusive than Whiggery. By choosing four Southerners and only two Northerners for his cabinet, moreover, he exacerbated the party's difficult sectional tensions.

Then, of course, Taylor's death in July 1850 generated further challenges for his adopted party by elevating his Vice President, Millard Fillmore, to the presidency. Fillmore, who hailed from Buffalo, was strongly associated with the conservative, pro-Compromise wing of the Whig Party, and was already bitter rivals with William Henry Seward, New York's Whig Governor from 1839–1842 and its Senator since 1849. Fillmore and Seward's factional rivalry, which often revolved around the future of slavery, intensified throughout Fillmore's presidency, leading to a bruising fight over the Whig presidential nomination in 1852, when Fillmore squared off against the Seward-backed General Winfield Scott.

Scott's appeal had much in common with Taylor's: his military reputation gave him the potential to run in part on his personal biography rather than by taking stands on divisive issues. While he had been more clearly tied to the Whig Party than Taylor had, he likewise lacked a long political history that would constrain his maneuverability. With the convention delegates mostly split between backers of Fillmore and Scott, but with a significant contingent favoring (pro-Compromise) Daniel Webster, a seemingly unbreakable deadlock made the Whig's 1852 convention in Baltimore drag on for six long days. Only on the *53rd* ballot did Scott emerge with the nomination—and he suffered a serious lack of enthusiasm over the course of the campaign, which ended in his winning just 42 electoral votes from four states. Down-ballot Whigs fared no better. The deep fissure in the party that the convention exposed would ruin the party before the next presidential election, in large part because of the rise of non-Whig alternatives to the (pro-Compromise) Democrats.

D. Ferment of third party activity

The Whig-Democrat bisectional system had always left those whose first priority was purging the evil of slavery from the country without a place in the country's central political debates. As a result, the abolitionist Liberty Party organized in 1840 and managed to take 2.3 percent of the presidential vote in 1844. By 1848, it had been subsumed by the Free Soil Party, a larger and somewhat more realistic coalition that brought in anti-slavery Whigs and Democratic Barnburners alike and prioritized blocking slavery's expansion into the territories. The Free Soil Party was able to recruit Martin Van Buren, the former president, to head their ticket in the election of 1848, and he won 10 percent of the popular vote and came in second place in Vermont and New York (then the nation's most populous state). In the 31st Congress (1849–50), Free Soilers elected nine House members and two U.S.

senators, including Ohio's Salmon P. Chase, who managed to win the support of an anti-Whig coalition in the state's legislature. The Compromise of 1850 satisfied some of those who had voted Free Soil in 1848, and thus the party regressed in the 1852 election, with presidential candidate John Hale of New Hampshire winning just under five percent of the vote that year.

But the Free Soil Party roared back to relevance in 1854 when their leaders quickly branded the Kansas-Nebraska Act a "bold scheme against American liberty" that would forever consign America to the mercy of the Slave Power and thereby framed the ensuing debate over the measure. As Holt puts it: "By exaggerating and impugning southern responsibility for the bill, by portraying it as a southern assault on the liberty and future economic prospects of Northern whites . . . the tiny group of Free Soil congressmen had a far more devastating impact on the Whig party than even they probably intended." Voters in the North rapidly assembled "anti-Nebraska coalitions" using various labels, including "People's" parties and, significantly, "Republicans." These were styled as temporary vehicles needed to resolve an urgent matter, but the new organizations that formed soon "co-opted Whigs' mission to defend republicanism by portraying themselves as better able to do so."

Pro-Compromise (and later pro-Nebraska) Whigs sometimes looked in precisely the opposite direction, looking for ad hoc coalitions meant to prioritize preservation of the union over any other political priority. Unionist parties drawing from both Democrats and Whigs were especially strong in Georgia, Mississippi, and New York, and won some distinguished backers. First Henry Clay, and then Daniel Webster, the Whigs' two elder giants, flirted with the idea of resuscitating their presidential hopes with the backing of a new Union party in 1852. The Unionist movement proved to be short-lived, soon to be undermined by the strength of pro-Compromise Democrats who aimed at preserving the Union largely on the South's terms. But for Northern Whigs devoted to the Compromise, increasingly at odds with other Northern Whigs, the promise of some non-Whig, non-Democrat party designed to avert national catastrophe lingered on, eventually merging with the next strain of third party activity that revolved around nativism.

Nativist politicians, sometimes styled as "Native Americans," had throughout the 1840s won seats in state legislatures, especially from the Philadelphia area; other times, they peeled off enough votes from Whigs that Democrats were able to win. But these modest beginnings gave little intimation of the way that their concerns would spread in the 1850s. As immigration increased along with a sense of rapid social change, so too did the appeal of an anti-Catholic party on a national scale.

It is hard to exaggerate how rapid and widespread the expansion of Know-Nothingism was in the 1850s. Founded as the secret "Order of the Star-Spangled Banner" in 1849, Know-Nothings built up a vast hierarchical organization of lodges and established themselves as the dominant force in many parts of the country. Officeholders of both parties, but especially Whigs, found that their political fortunes depended on having themselves secretly inducted into the rapidly growing order. As long as Know-Nothings remained officially secret, they seemed to offer a kind of symbiotic relationship with the Whig Party rather than posing a direct threat. But members of the movement, active in both the North and South, soon desired a more public arm of their movement, leading to the founding of parties variously called "Native American," "American," or "American Union," in 1854 and 1855.

Before long, many ambitious office-seekers realized that Whiggery no longer provided as attractive a path to power as the Know-Nothings' various splinter parties, which soon would hold their own conventions. This group eventually came to include Millard Fillmore, the Whig ex-president spurned by his party in 1852, who seemed to be the old party's best hope of survival. Fillmore was inducted into the Know-Nothings in January 1855. He hoped that the Know-Nothings could play the role of a non-Whig, pro-Union party that earlier Whig leaders like Webster had flirted with. As such, he directed his energies and his followers in the 1856 election to desert the Whigs en masse in favor of the American Party. Fillmore went on to win 21.5 percent of the popular vote (and Maryland's eight electoral votes) in the 1856 election. By then, Free Soilers and anti-Compromise Whigs had fused into the beginnings of the modern Republican Party.

In short, although Whigs assumed that politics in the 1850s would be zero-sum between Democrats and Whigs, such that internal Democratic problems would automatically strengthen their traditional opposition, in reality they found voters alienated from Democrats turning to the upstart parties that defined their opposition in terms more clearly centered around the issues most salient to voters of the 1850s. Anti-Nebraska coalitions portrayed Whigs as insufficiently committed to protecting white Northerners from the menace of the slave power, and Know-Nothings asserted that Whigs failed to understand the threat to American liberty posed by the influx of foreigners. Both significantly weakened the party without Whig leaders realizing exactly how precarious their party's position had become. Whig leaders hoped to wait until politics allowed them to return to familiar grounds of conflict; but instead, politics moved on and consigned their party to the ash heap of history.

E. Widespread contemplation of party dying, public abandonment by notables

The last features of the Whig Party's death worth noting relate to its final collapse. Although there had been signs of unbridgeable gaps between factions and mounting minor party alternatives for several years, before the election of 1852 the Whig Party outwardly seemed to be as strong as it had ever been; indeed, many contemporaries were sure it was on the cusp of a great success. Things went wrong in a remarkably short time.

First, both Clay and Webster died in 1852. These two presences had been emblematic of Whigs' early anti-Jacksonian glories, and their absence deprived the Whigs of their most potent symbols. Then, after Scott's bruising loss of 1852, worse than almost anyone had anticipated, some of the Whigs' most important second-tier figures decided to abandon the party. The influential New York City publisher Horace Greeley, whose *New York Tribune* had been one of the Whigs' most influential organs, publicly denounced the party in 1853. Then Truman Smith, a Whig representative from Connecticut who had acted as party's de facto national chairman since 1842, walked away from the party and declared himself ready "to have Whiggery charred and burned." A number of influential Whigs decided simply to withdraw from politics rather than face what seemed to them the impossible task of holding together Northern and Southern Whigs.

Through 1853 and 1854, many of the party faithful fought on to preserve what was for them a cherished institution. But the signs of strain were evident. In Whigs' correspondences, which Holt masterfully excerpts, the idea that the party might die steadily spread until it began to seem more likely than not. Some Whigs thought that they could keep their piece of the party alive by denationalizing—in other words, by ceasing to hope for the survival of the national Whigs and instead seeking the continuance of Southern Whigs or Northern Whigs. But Know-Nothings capitalized on the explicitly populist, anti-party moment; not only were religious Catholics suspected, but so were "political jesuits" fighting for the old order.

In October 1855, Senator William Henry Seward of New York, who had finally directed his supporters away from the Whig party and into the rapidly growing Republican Party, gave the Whig Party its eulogy: "Let, then, the Whig party pass. It committed a grievous fault, and grievously hath it answered it. Let it march out of the field, therefore, with all the honors."

II. How many of these factors apply to the modern GOP or Democrats?

Having examined the demise of the Whigs, we now turn to the state of our contemporary parties and examine how many of the same factors are present today.

A. Decline in importance of traditional lines of contestation

At least since Ronald Reagan's victory in the presidential election of 1980, American politics has been defined by a stable and fairly coherent conflict between conservative Republicans and liberal Democrats (acknowledging that these terms have idiosyncratic, historically contingent meanings as used in American politics). But recently it has become difficult to know exactly what these terms encapsulate in the present moment. And with Donald Trump's historic 2016 victory and the rise of 21st century populism as a force, it is clear that neither party can be fully described in these terms any longer.

The GOP has been described as a sturdy three-legged stool: a coalition of social, economic, and defense conservatives. This conservative fusionism—which was hardly synonymous with a GOP that contained self-described liberals through the 1970s—came to be identified with the party itself during Ronald Reagan's presidency. Even as the Cold War has receded into memory, veneration of Reagan's iconic leadership has served the purpose of reaffirming the relevance of the party's old self-definition.

After the events of 2016, however, it is hard to see adhering to the old formula as a viable strategy for assembling a majority of Republican voters. Not only the decline of the Cold War, but also the overwhelmingly negative perceptions of George W. Bush's Iraq War, have made foreign policy hawkishness a hard position to sell voters on. The kind of militarized isolationism dominant among Republicans in the 1920s, however, is hardly a dominant alternative. Social issues have become a contentious source of division within the party, especially gay marriage, which young Republicans often support even as their elders declare their willingness to resist it indefinitely. (Opposition to abortion is, conversely, one issue that still tends to glue the party together.)

Economic issues show perhaps the deepest crack. The party's elites (both the business and ideological variants) remain staunchly committed to a vision of lowered taxes and a retrenched welfare state, but its rank-and-file voters seem quite ambivalent about both prongs of this agenda. On taxes, marginal federal income tax rates for the wealthy hardly strike the average voter as manifestly unjust, as they might have when they were around 70 percent in the Carter era. The federal estate tax applies only to the rich. And although Democrats and Republicans are at odds over taxation of the wealthy, President Obama famously promised to spare the American middle classes from any tax increases and then delivered on that promise, diminishing the difference between the two parties. Although most Republican candidates seeking the party's presidential nomination in recent years have highlighted their commitment to tax cuts, there is something increasingly perfunctory about these gestures, which seem designed to appeal to the party's donor base but no longer seem to be a clear boon to its electoral fortunes. There are at least stirrings of new approaches within the GOP which would seek to shift the burden of taxation onto wealthy investors.

On the spending side, Republicans remain committed to deficit reduction and entitlement reform, at least as a matter of professed principle. But, in spite of having Rep. Paul Ryan—then the Budget Committee Chairman most associated with aspirations of major entitlement reform—on the ticket in 2012, Republicans ran away from entitlement reform in that election, with Mitt Romney framing Obamacare as an objectionable attack on Medicare because of projected spending reductions. In 2016, Donald Trump won the nomination promising to defend the welfare state, at least for the right sort of people (a pattern very much in line with populist parties across Europe). Certainly, he has echoed the familiar Republican call to repeal and replace "Obamacare"—but it remains to be seen whether "Trumpcare" will really turn out to be so radically different (or, for that matter, whether the "repeal" might turn out to be largely imaginary). The rhetorical differences on government health-care provision seem to be considerably stronger than the real policy differences (with the important exception of Medicaid).

As Ross Douthat describes it, the vision of "true conservatism" that sees a strictly limited role for the federal government in economic matters seems to have fallen by the wayside, and "Trumponomics" is ascendant, at least for now. That the latter is such a muddle, and so hard to distinguish from Democrats' positions on many issues, is precisely the point. The battle between "free marketeers" and backers of "industrial policy" is gone, leaving us with both sides denouncing "crony capitalism" and both seeing large roles for government intervention.

The diminished importance of economic issues in organizing partisan conflict is also clear in patterns of voter support in 2016. Democrats have traditionally been the party of labor—that is, of members of private and public sector labor unions. But over the last half century, membership in traditional labor unions has gone from approximately one-in-three to one-in-ten, and the strong preference for Democrats among union households has shrunk nearly to insignificance. And whereas a higher income has traditionally been an excellent predictor of a propensity to support Republicans, the relationship between income levels and support for Trump was quite weak, with education levels becoming a much stronger predictor.

In this way, reminiscent of the 1840s and 50s, the forces binding Democrats and Republicans to their own coalition partners have weakened, making it harder to identify exactly which policy beliefs distinguish the members of each party.

B. Increased importance of issues dividing party, profusion of intra-party factions

Meanwhile, intra-party tensions have soared and named factions proliferated, especially in the years after the financial crisis of 2008. Taking each party in turn:

Republicans have seen the emergence of the Tea Party and Freedom Caucus, Reform Conservatives, #NeverTrump, the alt-right, and others (and the corresponding epithets these factions hurl at each other: "RINO" and "cuckservative" on one side, "authoritarian" or "demagogic" on the other). This split is reflected clearly in the media environment, which then further reifies it. Talk radio and anti-establishment news sites such as Breitbart Media increasingly distrust and denounce not only the conservative end of the mainstream media environment (e.g., *The Wall Street Journal*, or traditional

Republican bastions like the *Cincinnati Enquirer*) but also some of the outlets seen as staunchly conservative but insufficiently anti-establishment, such as *National Review* and Fox News.

Keeping a multiplicity of factions within the Republican coalition is, of course, nothing new to the current period. Back when it was a permanent congressional minority, the party featured active liberal and moderate factions that coexisted with conservatives in an uneasy peace—one that eventually ended in conservatives driving them out, as recounted by Geoffrey Kabaservice's great *Rule and Ruin*. Internationalist and isolationist factions of the party were historically in tension, also, and that rift looks like it might become salient once again.

But today's surge in populism poses what looks to be the greatest challenge to Republicans' ability to coexist within the same caucus in many years. Donald Trump has embraced populism and distanced himself from conservatism in remarkably forthright ways, including at one point declaring, "This is called the Republican party, it's not called the Conservative party." Reliable supply-side economist Stephen Moore, an advisor to Trump, stirred controversy by confidently telling congressional Republicans: "Just as Reagan converted the GOP into a conservative party, Trump has converted the GOP into a populist working-class party." If Trump were to fail to deliver on his promise to transform his party in a populist direction, that would come as a massive disappointment to many of his most ardent supporters.

Some of the most combative conservatives in Congress have tried to convince themselves that their worldviews actually mesh well with Trump's, such that they have a bright partnership ahead of them. But it is hard to see how this honeymoon will last, given that a number of prominent issues clearly divide populists of various stripes and traditional business-friendly interests, which have long been at the heart of the GOP coalition but now look suspect to many of its voters.

The first of these, of course, is immigration. There has been a wave of political energy behind the idea of ejecting illegal immigrants and securing the nation's borders that Republican leaders and donors largely resisted in recent years. In many ways, the spread of nativist sentiment in the 2000s and 2010s recalls the rapid rise of Know-Nothingism in the 1850s; in both cases, the level of foreign-born residents in the country reached double-digit percentages and sparked widespread anxieties among "native" Americans.

Immigration is an especially difficult policy problem for the Republican coalition to handle because of the way it divides the grassroots from business leaders. A serious policy to reduce illegal immigration would be targeted at American employers—whose interest in cheap labor often leads them to support easing the conditions of immigration into the country. Corporate interests wary of alienating any portion of their customer base also tend to embrace an inclusive idea of Americanism, whereas right populists angrily charge that such ideas have diluted our understanding of what makes America a great country.

Questions of international trade create a similar divide. Businesses largely favor free movement of capital across international lines, the better to expand their markets and structure their businesses for maximum efficiency. Middle Americans (and especially Trump supporters) have come to see this way of thinking as profoundly detrimental to their own interests, and want trade policies tailored to protect their livelihoods and penalize outsourcing. Notably, divisions over trade do not correspond neatly to the partisan divide in recent years; again, a populist vs. business dimension seems more important, such that "neoliberals" in the Democrats' coalition and free marketeers in the GOP have more in common with each other than with their populist copartisans.

This is even more clear for issues relating to "cronyism," the political theme most ascendant in recent years. Many of the pronouncements of anti-establishment Republicans denouncing the corrupt self-dealing of Beltway insiders could easily come out of the mouths of left populists such as Elizabeth Warren or Bernie Sanders. True, the particular bêtes noires for these groups are quite distinct, but their intense suspicions of each other often look like the narcissism of small differences. Republican insiders, on the other hand, turned out in 2008 to support the Troubled Asset Relief Program (TARP) legislation along with a majority of Democrats, a fact that continues to enrage many Republican backbenchers years later.

Insider vs. outsider is a recurrent theme in American politics, but it looms especially large given Donald Trump's victory. In many ways, Trump seems poised to heighten its importance, having spent as much time in the final weeks of his campaign picking fights with other Republicans as he did differentiating his agenda from the Democrats'. The same goes for pro-Trump media, which stoked immense fury at all of those Republicans who refused to back Trump.

By no means was Trump the start of Republicans' problems in keeping their coalition unified. Open plotting by hardline elements led to the resignation of House Speaker John Boehner, a remarkable development with few historical precedents. Before Trump's victory, it seemed likely that his successor, Paul Ryan, could meet the same fate after coming to be seen as a traitor by many Trump supporters for his lukewarm support of the party's nominee.

Victory in 2016 has put off these reckonings, at least for a short time. There are already plenty of attempts to reconcile apparently conflicting worldviews within the GOP coalition. But the tensions will undoubtedly be reactivated with a fury once the party is forced to take consequential stands on concrete issues that divide them. If nothing else, those Republicans who remain committed to fiscal conservatism will have to decide whether they can cooperate with an administration likely to swell the federal deficit very early in Trump's presidency.

For **Democrats**, the split between populists and the party's establishment has also widened since the financial crisis. Self-described progressives seek to frame things in terms of a civil war between true reformers struggling for the greater good and a party apparatus hopelessly compromised by its close ties to corporate interests. (A recent symbolic vote on whether Americans should be allowed to purchase Canadian pharmaceuticals provides a good illustration.) While President Obama was, at least in some ways, able to straddle this divide because of the aura created by his heady 2008 rise to the presidency, his anointed successor, Hillary Clinton, proved to be quite incapable of continuing that feat. Her seemingly inexorable march to the party's nomination ended up exposing a deep divide in the party's base over fundamental issues, which her leading challenger, Bernie Sanders, highlighted.

In many ways, Democrats' internal divisions closely parallel Republicans'. On trade and immigration, in particular, there is a profound divergence in worldviews between haves and have-nots. The increasingly reified "WWC"—white working class—seems to be alienated from a party that was once its comfortable home, in large part because of its feelings that cosmopolitan elites care more about advancing global development (and their own financial stakes in it) than about preserving high-quality jobs for their countrymen (whom those elites largely see as undeserving of sympathy relative to historically oppressed minorities).

Such questions of economic solidarity feed into parallel questions of cultural solidarity that have simmered for many years, but seem to have come to a boil recently: whether and how Democrats should put racial identity politics or an aggressive campaign for multicultural diversity at the center of their self-image. During the George W. Bush administration, culture war issues seem to have been a unifying issue for Democrats. "Defense against the religious right" could unite a wide variety of people who felt threatened by evangelical ambitions. But somewhere along the line, the culture war objective for many Democrats shifted; as Mark Tushnet rather gleefully put it, those on the left needed to "abandon defensive crouch liberalism" in favor of stamping out all opposition. "Showing the bigots just how wrong they are, and stopping all of their insidious forms of discrimination in all corners of life" turns out not to be a particularly unifying agenda, especially outside of the nation's major cities.

Of course, much of the difference between the Bush years and the Obama years can be explained by going from out-party to in-party, with all of the attendant burdens of responsibility for governing, and the task of banding together in cultural opposition to Trump will probably be an easier one. But these issues retain the potential to be seriously divisive, especially given some Democrats' insistence that identity-related issues should be the party's top political priority. It remains to be seen if the party can find a way to contain both camps.

C. Outsider infiltration and broken conventions

To many staunch Republicans, the idea that Donald Trump could be their party's nominee, and then president, was unthinkable as recently as late 2015. Trump was widely opposed by movement conservatives, who doubted his commitment to their principles, and seen as someone driven into the Republican Party by opportunism more than anything else. This was entirely understandable, given that in an early primary debate Trump refused to pledge that he would support the GOP nominee (and it is remarkable that this question even needed to be asked). Trump's victory in winning the party's nomination was accompanied by dramatic signs of discontinuity with the party's recent history. Perhaps most strikingly, both Presidents Bush and Mitt Romney withheld their support for Trump, with George H.W. Bush going so far as to let it be known he would vote for Hillary Clinton.

But here we are.

Trump's emergence was not, to be fair, the first sign that the institutional party was incapable of producing leaders its own base would warm to. In 2008, Sarah Palin gave voice to populist elements of the party that were clearly in tension with its pro-TARP congressional leaders (which included nominee John McCain). In 2012, little-known businessman Herman Cain led primary polls at one point. That year, Ron Paul, who ran as the Libertarian Party's presidential nominee in 1988 and has always styled himself as a critic of Republicans' Washington leadership, took 118 delegates into the Republican convention, shaking party insiders enough for them to significantly reconfigure their nomination rules. In 2016, alongside Trump, Dr. Ben Carson garnered huge amounts of early support in national polls preaching a message of citizens ousting a corrupted party leadership.

In the end, Trump's populist takeover of the party was effected fairly smoothly thanks to his string of primary victories over his fragmented opposition. The 2016 Republican National Convention in Cleveland will not go down as a broken one in which the party left in shambles. But there was just a whiff of that old-time convention-floor pandemonium when anti-Trump delegates sought a roll call vote on the question of whether delegates should be unbound by their states' primary results and allowed to vote their consciences. Shouting to have their point of order recognized, the Utah delegation, co-headed by Senator Mike Lee, staged a dramatic moment of resistance to Trump, though ultimately its protests were ignored. In itself, this moment does not amount to much, but it is possible that it is a harbinger of open intraparty warfare yet to come. Certainly this is more drama than featured in most modern conventions, which tend to be carefully scripted affairs.

We will have to wait and see whether the Republican Convention of 2020 might wind up being as divisive as the 1852 Whig Convention was—of course, everything will depend on which divisions within the party deepen, and which are successfully managed, during Trump's presidency.

Democrats have not experienced a similarly charged convention since 1980 (or, in a parallel universe, since the run of Tanner '88); by the time they got to their national convention in Philadelphia in July 2016, the drama of intraparty struggles so evident during the primary contest had been contained. But the successfully stage-managed convention atmosphere belied the extraordinarily lively platform fight that preceded it, which featured struggles over whether to support a national $15 minimum wage, a single-payer national health insurance program, a carbon tax, and other progressive priorities.

Sanders' candidacy deserves some attention as a symptom of outsider infiltration into a party system. Sanders has defined himself as a socialist throughout his political career and always run as an independent, and even as he sought the Democratic Party's presidential nomination he refused to clearly label himself as a member of the party. That he could nevertheless run so strongly, in spite of nearly united support of the Democratic leadership, says a great deal about the party's vulnerability. One might see Democrats' ability to fend off and then ultimately coopt Sanders as a sign of good organizational health, but doing so was extraordinarily costly in terms of ongoing partisan cohesion. Indeed, the struggle spawned a super-PAC devoted to opposing the eventual Democratic nominee from the left and left a trail of disaffected young voters (which contributed to a smaller margin of victory for Democrats among that group).

Lingering organizational tensions within the Democratic party continue to play out in public. First, there was a fierce struggle over who will be the next chair of the Democratic National Committee. Progressive favorite Representative Keith Ellison, backed by Sanders, was opposed by the outgoing administration, which saw him as likely to pick unnecessarily divisive fights during a period in which the party needs to expand its tent. Meanwhile, former Speaker Nancy Pelosi faced an unexpectedly strong challenge for her leadership of House Democrats. Representative Tim Ryan, from a quintessential Rust Belt district in northeast Ohio, mounted a challenge to Pelosi, questioning whether a San Francisco liberal could adequately represent Democrats for middle-Americans coping with the long hangover of deindustrialization. Although he took only 63 votes compared to 134 for Pelosi, this was the strongest performance by any challenger to the former Speaker she has experienced in 15 years as House Democrats' leader. Showing how hard it is to serve all of the diverse elements of their coalition, Senate Democrats under new Minority Leader Charles Schumer will have a remarkably large 10-person leadership team—including Bernie Sanders, who still says he is not a Democrat—during the 115th Congress.

D. Ferment of third party activity

A decisive factor in the Whigs' decline was the rise of third party alternatives, including the Liberty and Free Soil parties focused on slavery and the American Party channeling nativist energy. The emergence of these parties meant that anti-Democratic energy did not necessarily accrue to the Whigs' benefit. The weakness of third parties in our contemporary moment is, conversely, the best thing going for today's two parties. The election of 2016 featured historic levels of antipathy for the nominees of both major parties, but in the end relatively few people were driven to support minor party alternatives.

Holt stresses the importance of a structural element of voting that helped doom the Whigs. In the 1850s, the Australian Ballot had not yet proliferated in America; since there were no official pre-printed ballots, every voter could cast a different ballot. That meant that third parties could make fast inroads much more quickly: simply by providing their own ballots with their own candidates, they could empower voters to support their party up and down the ticket at no greater cost than printing.

Today, in contrast, ballot access laws require political parties to collect thousands (or, in some states, hundreds of thousands) of verified signatures in order for their candidates to be among the choices voters can select from. Third parties are, therefore, at an immense disadvantage. People generally have some sense of this fact, which leads to a widespread sense that politics outside of the two leading parties is inherently unserious and, indeed, a waste of time. This makes it harder for outside parties to gain any traction, which in turn reinforces ballot access restrictions, and duopoly persists effectively unchallenged. We should therefore be cautious about over-reading signs of third party ferment in the current moment.

That said, there have been some signs recently that Americans are willing to look beyond Democrats and Republicans—and when we think about the potential for serious reconfiguration that could doom one of the two existing parties, we must certainly think of both in tandem. For the reconfiguration of the 1850s to happen, Whigs had to fracture and split apart, but Democrats also had to alienate sufficient numbers of northerners to swell the ranks of new parties.

Today's third largest party is the Libertarian Party (LP), which consistently manages the feat of getting its presidential candidate on every state ballot and which, in 2016, attracted its most ever votes, with nearly 4.5 million Americans (about 3.3 percent) supporting their duo of ex-Republican governors, Gary Johnson of New Mexico and William Weld of Massachusetts. That the Libertarians could attract, and agree to nominate, two serious politicians with fairly good reputations shows that the party has made some real strides toward political competitiveness in recent years.

But by other metrics, the LP seems to have missed its moment to emerge as a serious political contender; the breadth of its support is lacking, though hardly negligible. Johnson and Weld got only one endorsement from a sitting federal legislator (Scott Rigell of Virginia, on his way to retirement). They managed to get three percent of the vote in only a third of U.S. Senate races (AK, AR, CO, GA, IL, IN, KS, NC, ND, OK, PA, WI) and put a candidate on the ballot in only around a quarter of all U.S. House races. The national party listed only 602 candidates for any office (state or local) nationally (for reference, there are 7,299 seats in the country's 98 partisan state legislative bodies). As of this past May, the LP was reported to have just 13,000 dues-paying members and a (recently much-increased) membership of over 400,000. There are trends moving in the right direction for the LP, but they do not seem on track to become a full service national political party in the near future. And 2016, in many ways, seemed like their best chance.

The Green Party, which Ralph Nader headed in his infamous 2000 run, is even more of an after-thought than the Libertarian Party. Though its presidential ticket did get almost 1.5 million votes (one percent of the national total), it had very little support from any notables, either in politics or in other walks of life. Just two of its U.S. Senate candidates passed three percent support (in AZ and MD) and it had just 295 candidates nationwide. Considering that Nader received almost 2.9 million votes in 2000, the Green Party seems unlikely to break through into national strength.

Two other recent developments seem more significant to potential party reconfiguration. First was Michael Bloomberg's exploration of a presidential campaign. Facing the possibility that both Republicans and Democrats would select populist candidates in the 2016 cycle, Bloomberg—mega-billionaire and former Mayor of New York City—seriously considered a run in which he would position himself as a practical, business-friendly alternative with the ability to transcend the bitter partisanship of recent years and get things done. Ultimately, he decided that Hillary Clinton was likely to win the Democratic nomination, that she was a responsible enough choice, and that his own presence in the race could help deliver the election to Trump. Bloomberg's flirtation raises an important question about the future of business interests in a political system tending toward structured conflict between left- and right-populists. If they can effectively coopt one of the two main parties, constraining the power of its populists, they may be happy enough backing it. If not, however, they might have considerable power to disrupt things by backing (and funding) some third party capable of winning political offices in business centers and grabbing a pivotal position between Ds and Rs. There are at least stirrings of such centrist political organizing, though it is unclear whether they will gain much traction.

Second, we saw a muted but suggestive reaction against Trump from the right. Given that the hetero-dox and unpredictable Trump took control of the Republican Party, many wondered if hardline conservatives could rally around a "#NeverTrump" candidate who would claim the mantle of "True Republicanism" or the like. This movement failed to draft Mitt Romney, widely seen as its best hope, and seemed to be simply sputtering out. Finally Evan McMullin, a 40-year-old with experience in the CIA and as a congressional staffer, belatedly entered the campaign in August 2016 with the idea of rallying this crowd to support him. Although he had very little institutional support, McMullin was on 11 states' ballots and made a surprisingly strong run in Utah, where his roots in the Mormon community helped him win 21 percent of votes. With a shoestring budget and without an especially distinctive platform, McMullin collected some 725,000 votes, including that of Senator Lindsay Graham of South Carolina. McMullin's run suggests the potential for Trump's singular style to drive a wedge through the Republican coalition.

All this said, political organizing outside the confines of the Democratic or Republican Parties remains rather tame as of this writing. Institutional reforms to encourage such activity is minimal, though not non-existent: third-party-friendly Maine's citizens just adopted ranked-choice voting for all of its statewide (and U.S. Congress) elections, which will allow a kind of provisional support for a third party candidate without costing voters their sense of efficacy should the race turn out to be between a Democrat and Republican. The nation's largest state, California, continues its experiment with nonpartisan blanket primaries, with unclear results as of yet. If there is to be a major disruption of our party system, ferment of third parties well beyond present levels will be the best indicator.

III. Factors working on behalf of party stability and survival

When considering whether all of the centrifugal factors considered above are likely to prove decisive, fracturing the familiar coalitions we have known, we must also consider countervailing centripetal factors that push toward stability, of which there are several.

For the GOP, the first of these is its current strong organizational position when looking across all levels of American government, which is the strongest it has been since 1928. Republicans are about to have control over the White House, House of Representatives, and Senate for the first time since 2006, and their Democratic opposition is roiled by internal dissent. Although Trump's support and their Senate majority are both tenuous, they are arguably in a much better position to absorb shocks in the coming years than Whigs were in after the election of 1848.

Several other factors help make the GOP's position today considerably more secure than the Whig party's in the 1850s, and should also help to cement Democrats' position even in spite of their current disadvantages. First, the national political conversation is much more dominant of state and local ones today than it was in the nineteenth century, both because of the increase in the federal government's power and because of the structure of our modern media industry. That makes it less likely that local groups with divergent priorities will strike off in their own directions, and thus makes it less likely for third party alternatives to the two national parties to develop. The increased role for political money channeled through the two national parties likewise makes it hard to escape the duopoly. Also arguably suppressing third party organizing is social media's facilitation of anonymous contact between like-minded people, which encourages them to discharge their energies in a fairly non-disruptive way relative to the face-to-face political organizing featured in the mid-19th century. At least for now, 4chan and Reddit pale in comparison to Know-Nothingism.

Second, America currently has historic levels of interparty mistrust and even loathing that go much deeper than policy differences. Some of this is about racial attitudes, which many political scientists now see as the single most reliable variable for predicting Americans' political affiliations. Donald Trump's appeal across middle America has been interpreted as being strongly or even primarily racial; a popular trope after the election was that "Whites Without College Degrees Voted Like an Ethnic Bloc" to deliver his victory. To the extent that persistent racial resentments organize our current political environment, they offer a potential source of party unity for Republicans that could override other kinds of intraparty tensions—though, given the trajectory of American demographic change, over the long run relying on racial and ethnic fears is obviously a double-edged sword.

Even apart from race, there is a sense that our "Big Sorted" country really does feature two distinct types, "Reds" and "Blues," each with an assigned political party. If that persists and deepens, our two existing party containers will endure, and the only question will be what kinds of policy agendas they are filled with. Cross-partisan resentments can sustain a two party system, at least in the short run, if no clear cross-cutting issue emerges to create new lines of political competition. Partisan self-identification ticked upward in 2016 and ticket-splitting appeared to continue its decline.

Third, and probably most importantly, there is no cross-cutting issue mobilizing as many Americans today as slavery did in the 1850s. Slavery aroused intense passions and also created policy differences that were quite readily comprehensible to any engaged citizen: although many controversial political tactics were quite arcane, the main questions of whether slavery should be allowed anywhere or in the nation's growing territories were quite cut and dry and easily moralized. Immigration policy, which probably inspires the most intense cross-cutting passions today, raises questions that are far more complex: what enforcement and deportation targets should be prioritized, what kind of border control will be most effective, what kind of penalties should be targeted against employers who hire illegals. Though these undoubtedly do lead to acrimonious feelings for engaged citizens, it is hard to imagine them as the engine of massive political realignment, let alone civil war.

And yet it was difficult for Whigs, in the wake of Zachary Taylor's election, to imagine that their party, still basking in an unexpected victory, could become obsolete over the next eight years. There are many reasons why the GOP and Democrats may avoid that fate. But it is failure of historical and political imagination to think they are necessarily immune.

CHAPTER 11
ELECTIONS AND PARTICIPATION

CITIZENSHIP AND THE TRANSFORMATION OF AMERICAN SOCIETY

RUSSELL J. DALTON
University of California, Irvine

Every age since the ancient Greeks fashioned an image of being political [is] based upon citizenship

Engin Isin, *Being Political*

What does it mean to be a "good citizen" in today's society?

In an article on the 2005 annual UCLA survey of college freshmen, the *Los Angeles Times* presented an interview with a California university student who had spent his semester break as a volunteer helping to salvage homes flooded by Hurricane Katrina.[1] The young man had organized a group of student volunteers, who then gave up their break to do hard labor in the devastated region far from their campus. He said finding volunteers willing to work "was easier than I expected." Indeed, the gist of the article was that volunteering in 2005 was at its highest percentage in the 25 years of the college survey.

Later I spoke with another student who also had traveled to the Gulf Coast. Beyond the work on Katrina relief, he was active on a variety of social and political causes, from problems of development in Africa, to campus politics, to the war in Iraq. When I asked about his interest in political parties and elections, however, there was stark lack of interest. Like many of his fellow students, he had not voted in the last election. He had not participated at all in the 2004 campaign, which was his first opportunity to vote. This behavior seems paradoxical considering the effort involved; it's just a short walk from the campus to the nearest polling station, but almost a two thousand mile drive along Interstate 10 to New Orleans.

These stories illustrate some of the ways that the patterns of citizenship are changing. Many young people in America—and in other Western democracies as well—are concerned about their society and others in the world. And they are willing to contribute their time and effort to make a difference. They see a role for themselves and their government in improving the world in which we all live. At the same time, they relate to government and society in different ways than their elders. Research in the United States and other advanced industrial democracies shows that modern-day citizens are the most educated, most cosmopolitan, and most supportive of self-expressive values than any other public in the history of democracy.[2] So from both anecdotal and empirical perspectives, most of the social and political changes in the American public over the past half-century would seem to have strengthened the foundations of democracy.

Despite this positive and hopeful view of American, however, a very different story is being told today in political and academic circles. An emerging consensus among political analysts would have us believe that the foundations of citizenship and democracy are crumbling. Just recently, a new study cosponsored by the American Political Science Association and the Brookings Institution begins:

> *American democracy is at risk. The risk comes not from some external threat but from disturbing internal trends: an erosion of the activities and capacities of citizenship. Americans have turned away from politics and the public sphere in large numbers, leaving our civic life impoverished. Citizens participate in public affairs less frequently, with less knowledge and enthusiasm, in fewer venues, and less equally than is healthy for a vibrant democratic polity.*[3]

A host of political analysts now bemoans what is wrong with America and its citizens.[4] Too few of us are voting, we are disconnected from our fellow citizens and lacking in social capital, we are losing our national identity, we are losing faith in our government, and the nation is in social disarray. The *lack* of good citizenship is the phrase you hear most often to explain these disturbing trends.

What you also hear is that the young are the primary source of this decline. Authors from Robert Putman to former television news anchor Tom Brokaw extol the civic values and engagement of the older, "greatest generation" with great hyperbole.[5] Putnam holds that the slow, steady, and ineluctable replacement of older, civic-minded generations by the disaffected Generation X is the most important reason for the erosion of social capital in America.[6] Political analysts and politicians seemingly agree that young Americans are dropping out of politics, losing faith in government, and even becoming disenchanted with their personal lives.[7] Perhaps not since Aristotle held that "political science is not a proper study for the young" have youth been so roundly denounced by their elders.

Here we have two very different images of American society and politics. One perspective says American democracy is "at risk" in large part because of the changing values and participation patterns of the young. The other view points to new patterns of citizenship that have emerged among the young, the better educated, and other sectors of American society. These opposing views have generated sharp debates about the vitality of our democracy, and they are the subject of this book.

Perhaps the subtitle for this volume should be: "The good news is . . . the bad news is wrong." Indeed, something is changing in American society and politics. But is it logical to conclude, as many do, that if politics is not working as it did in the past, then our entire system of democracy is at risk? To understand what is changing, and its implications for American democracy, it is more helpful first to ask that simple but fundamental question:

What does it mean to be a good citizen in America today?

Take a moment to think of how you would answer. What are the criteria you would use? Voting? Paying taxes? Obeying the law? Volunteer work? Public protests? Being concerned for those in need? Membership in a political party? Trusting government officials?

This book examines how the American public answers this question—and the fact is, people answer it in different ways. This study will argue that the changing definition of what it means to be a good citizen—what I call the *norms of citizenship*—provides the key to understanding what is really going on.

Let's begin the analysis by examining the social restructuring of American society (**Figure 11.1**). Changing living standards, occupational experiences, generational change, the entry of women into the labor force, expanding civil rights, and other societal changes are producing two reinforcing effects. First, people possess new skills and resources that enable them to better manage the complexities of politics—people today are better educated, have more information available to them, and enjoy a higher standard of living. This removes some of the restrictions on democratic citizenship that might have existed in earlier historical periods when these skills and resources were less commonly available. Second, social forces are reshaping social and political values. Americans are more assertive and less deferential to authority, and they place more emphasis on participating in the decisions affecting their lives. The expansion of these self-expressive values has a host of political implications.[8]

These social changes have a direct effect on the norms of citizenship, if for no other reason than that citizenship norms are the encapsulation of the nation's political culture. They essentially define what people think is expected of them as participants in the political system, along with their expectations of government and the political process.

Most definitions of citizenship typically focus on the traditional norms of American citizenship—voting, paying taxes, belonging to a political party—and how these are changing. I call this **duty-based citizenship** because these norms reflect the formal obligations, responsibilities, and rights of citizenship as they have been defined in the past.

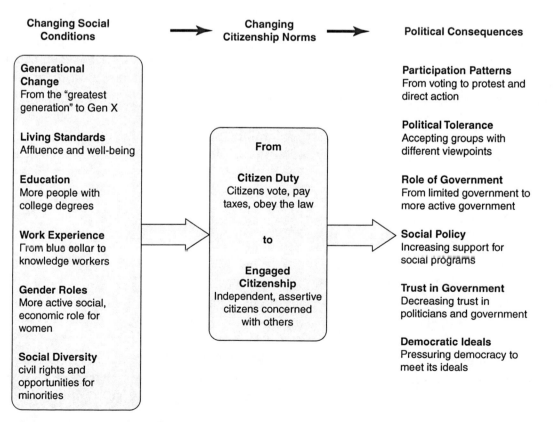

▶ *Changing Social Conditions reshape the norms of what it means to be a good citizen, and this affects how citizens act and think about politics.*

Figure 11.1   The Changing American Public

However, it is just as important to examine new norms that make up what I call **engaged citizenship.** These norms are emerging among the American public with increasing prominence. Engaged citizenship emphasizes a more assertive role for the citizen and a broader definition of the elements of citizenship to include social concerns and the welfare of others. As illustrated by the Katrina volunteers, many Americans believe they are fully engaged in society even if they do not vote or conform to traditional definitions of citizenship. Moreover, the social and political transformation of the United States over the past several decades has systematically shifted the balance between these different norms of citizenship. Duty-based norms are decreasing, especially among the young, but the norms of engaged citizenship are increasing.

Figure 11.1 illustrates the point that social and demographic changes affect citizenship norms, which in turn affect the political values and behavior of the public. For instance, duty-based norms of citizenship stimulate turnout in elections and a sense of patriotic allegiance to the elected government, while engaged citizenship may promote other forms of political action, ranging from volunteerism to public protest. These contrasting norms also shape other political values, such as tolerance of others and public policy priorities. Even respect for government itself is influenced by how individuals define their own norms of citizenship.

American politics and the citizenry are changing. Before anyone can deliver a generalized indictment of the American public, it is important to have a full understanding of how citizenship norms are changing and the effects of these changes. It is undeniable that the American public at the beginning of the twenty-first century is different from the American electorate in the mid-twentieth century. However, some of these differences actually can benefit American democracy, such as increased political tolerance and acceptance of diversity in society and politics. Other generational differences are just different—not a threat to American democracy unless these changes are ignored or resisted. A full examination of citizenship norms and their consequences will provide a more complex, and potentially more optimistic, picture of the challenges and opportunities facing American democracy today.

In addition, it is essential to place the American experience in a broader cross-national context. Many scholars who study American politics still study *only* American politics. This leads to an introspective, parochial view of what is presumably unique about the American experience and how patterns of citizenship may, or may not be, idiosyncratic to the United States. American politics is the last field of area-study research in which one nation is examined by itself. Many trends apparent in American norms of citizenship and political activity are common to other advanced industrial democracies. Other patterns may be distinctly American. Only by broadening the field of comparison can we ascertain the similarities and the differences.

The shift in the norms of citizenship does not mean that American democracy does not face challenges in response to new citizen demands and new patterns of action. Indeed, the vitality of democracy is that it must, and usually does, respond to such challenges, and this in turn strengthens the democratic process. But it is my contention that political reforms must reflect a true understanding of the American public and its values. By accurately recognizing the current challenges, and responding to them rather than making dire claims about political decay, American democracy can continue to evolve and develop. The fact remains, we cannot return to the politics of the 1950s, and we probably should not want to. But we can improve the democratic process if we first understand how Americans and their world are really changing.

The Social Transformation of America

I recently took a cab ride from Ann Arbor, Michigan, to the Detroit airport, and the cab driver retold the story of the American dream as his life story. Now, driving a cab is not a fun job; it requires long hours, uncertainty, and typically brings in a modest income. The cab driver had grown up in the Detroit area. His relatives worked in the auto plants, and he drove a cab as a second job to make ends meet. We started talking about politics, and when he learned I was a university professor, he told me of his children. His son had graduated from the University of Michigan and had begun a successful business career. He was even prouder of his daughter, who was finishing law school. "All this on a cab driver's salary," he said with great pride in his children.

If you live in America, you have heard this story many times. It is the story of American society. The past five decades have seen this story repeated over and over again because this has been a period of exceptional social and political change.[9] There was a tremendous increase in the average standard of living as the American economy expanded. The postwar baby boom generation reaped these benefits, and, like the cab driver's children, were often the first in their family to attend college. The civil rights movement of the 1960s and 1970s ended centuries of official governmental recognition and acceptance of racial discrimination. The women's movement of the 1970s and 1980s transformed gender roles that had roots in social relations since the beginning of human history. (A generation ago, it was unlikely that the cab driver's daughter would have attended law school regardless of her abilities.) America also became a socially and ethnically diverse nation—even more so than its historic roots as an immigrant society had experienced in the past. Changes in the media environment and political process have transformed the nature of democratic politics in America, as citizens have more information about how their government is, or is not, working for them, and more means of expressing their opinions and acting out their views.

In *The Rise of the Creative Class*, Richard Florida has an evocative discussion of how a time traveler from 1950 would view life in the United States if he or she was transported to 1900, and then again to 2000.[10] Florida suggests that *technological* change would be greater between 1900 and 1950, as people moved from horse-and-buggy times all the way to the space age. But *cultural* change would be greater between 1950 and 2000, as America went from a closed social structure to one that gives nearly equal status to women, blacks, and other ethnic minorities. Similarly, I suspect that if Dwight D. Eisenhower and Adlai E. Stevenson returned to observe the next U.S. presidential election, they would not recognize it as the same electorate as the people they encountered in their 1952 and 1956 campaigns for the Oval Office.

In the same respect, many of our scholarly images of American public opinion and political behavior are shaped by an outdated view of our political system. The landmark studies of Angus Campbell, Philip Converse, Warren Miller, and Donald Stokes remain unrivaled in their theoretical and empirical richness in describing the American public.[11] However, they examined the electorate of the 1950s. At an intellectual level, we may be aware of how the American public and American politics have changed since 1952, but since these changes accumulate slowly over time, it is easy to overlook their total impact. The electorate of 1956, for instance, was only marginally different from the electorate of 1952; and the electorate of 2004 is only marginally different from that of 2000. As these gradual changes accumulated over fifty years, however, a fundamental transformation in the socio-economic conditions of the American public occurred, conditions that are directly related to citizenship norms.

None of these trends in and of themselves is likely to surprise the reader. But you may be struck by the size of the total change when compared across a long span of time.

Perhaps the clearest evidence of change, and the carrier of new experiences and new norms, is the generational turnover of the American public. The public of the 1950s largely came of age during the Great Depression or before, and had lived through one or both world wars—experiences that had a strong formative influence on images of citizenship and politics. We can see how rapidly the process of demographic change transforms the citizenry by following the results of the American National Election Studies, which have tracked American public opinions over the past half-century. **Figure 11.2** charts the generational composition of the public. In the electorate of 1952, 85 percent of Americans had grown up before the outbreak of World War II (born before 1926). This includes the "greatest generation" (born between 1895 and 1926) heralded by Tom Brokaw and other recent authors. Each year, with mounting frequency, a few of this generation leave the electorate, to be replaced by new citizens. In 1968, in the midst of the flower-power decade of the 1960s, the "greatest generation" still composed 60 percent of the populace. But by 2004, this generation accounts for barely 5 percent of the populace. In their place, a third of the contemporary public are post-World War II baby boomers, another third is the flower generation of the 1960s and early 1970s, and a full 20 percent are the Generation-Xers who have come of age since 1993 (born after 1975).

The steady march of generations across time has important implications for norms of citizenship. Anyone born before 1926 grew up and became socialized in a much different political context, where citizens were expected to be dutiful, parents taught their children to be obedient, political skills were limited, and social realities were dramatically different from contemporary life. These citizens carry the living memories of the Great Depression, four-term president Franklin Delano Roosevelt and World War II and its aftermath—and so they also embody the norms of citizenship shaped by these experiences.

The baby boom generation experienced a very different kind of life as American social and economic stability was reestablished after the war. In further contrast, the 1960s generation experienced a nation

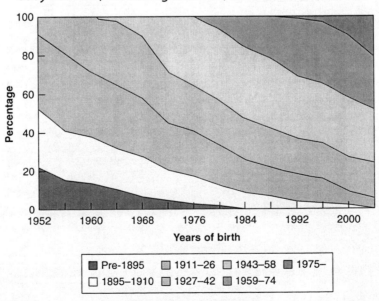

➤ *With the passage of time, the older "greatest generation" that experienced WWII is leaving the electorate to be replaced by baby boomers, the 1960s generation, and now Gen X and Gen Y.*

Figure 11.2   Generational Change

SOURCE: American National Election Study (ANES) Cumulative File, 1952–2004.

in the midst of traumatic social change—the end of segregation, women's liberation, and the expansion of civil and human rights around the world. The curriculum of schools changed to reinforce these developments, and surveys show that parents also began emphasizing initiative and independence in rearing their children.[12] And most recently, Generation X and Generation Y are coming of age in an environment where individualism appears dominant, and both affluence and consumerism seem overdeveloped (even if unequally shared). If nothing else changed, we would expect that political norms would change in reaction to this new social context.

Citizenship norms also reflect the personal characteristics of the people. Over the past several decades, the politically relevant skills and resources of the average American have increased dramatically. One of the best indicators of this development is the public's educational achievement. Advanced industrial societies require more educated and technically sophisticated citizens, and modern affluence has expanded educational opportunities. University enrollments grew dramatically during the latter half of the twentieth century. By the 1990s, graduate degrees were almost as common as bachelor's degrees were in mid-century.

These trends have steadily raised the educational level of the American public (**Figure 11.3**). For instance, two-fifths of the American public in 1952 had a primary education or less, and another fifth had only some high school. In the presidential election that year, the Eisenhower and Stevenson campaigns faced a citizenry with limited formal education, modest income levels, and relatively modest sophistication to manage the complexities of politics. It might not be surprising that these individuals would have a limited definition of the appropriate role of a citizen. By 2004, the educational composition of the American public had changed dramatically. Less than a tenth have less than a high school degree, and more than half have at least some college education—and most of these have earned one or

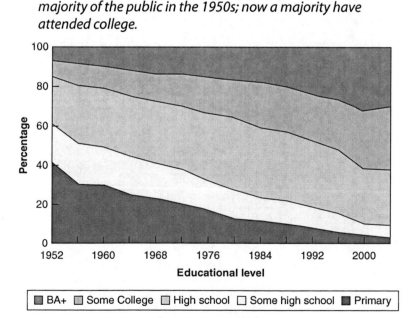

➤ *Citizens with less than a high school education were a majority of the public in the 1950s; now a majority have attended college.*

Figure 11.3 Educational Change

SOURCE: ANES Cumulative File, 1952–2004.

more degrees. The contemporary American public has a level of formal schooling that would have been unimaginable in 1952.

There is no direct, one-to-one relationship between years of schooling and political sophistication. Nonetheless, research regularly links education to a citizen's level of political knowledge, interest, and sophistication.[13] Educational levels affect the modes of political decision-making that people use, and rising educational levels increase the breadth of political interests.[14] A doubling of the public's educational level may not double the level of political sophistication and political engagement, but a significant increase should and does occur. The public today is the most educated in the history of American democracy, and this contributes toward a more expansive and engaged image of citizenship.

In addition, social modernization has transformed the structure of the economy from one based on industrial production and manufacturing (and farming), to one dominated by the services and the information sectors. Instead of the traditional blue-collar union worker, who manufactured goods and things, the paragon of today's workforce has shifted to the "knowledge worker" whose career is based on the creation, manipulation, and application of information.[15] Business managers, lawyers, accountants, teachers, computer programmers, designers, database managers, and media professionals represent different examples of knowledge workers.

If one takes a sociological view of the world, where life experiences shape political values, this shift in occupation patterns should affect citizenship norms. The traditional blue-collar employee works in a hierarchical organization where following orders, routine, and structure are guiding principles. Knowledge workers, in contrast, are supposed to be creative, adaptive, and technologically adept, which presumably produces a different image of what one's role should be in society. Richard Florida calls them the "creative class" and links their careers to values of individuality, diversity, openness, and meritocracy.[16]

These trends are a well-known aspect of American society, but we often overlook the amount of change they have fomented in politics over the past five decades. **Figure 11.4** plots the broad employment patterns of American men from 1952 until 2004. (We'll track only males at this point to separate out the shift in the social position of women, which is examined below). In the 1950s, most of the labor force was employed in working class occupations, and another sixth had jobs in farming. The category of professionals and managers, which will stand here as a surrogate for knowledge workers (the actual number of knowledge workers is significantly larger), was small by comparison. Barely a quarter of the labor force held such jobs in the 1950s.

Slowly but steadily, labor patterns have shifted. By 2000–2004, blue-collar workers and knowledge workers are almost at parity, and the proportions of service and clerical workers have increased (some of whom should also be classified as knowledge workers). Florida uses a slightly more restrictive definition of the creative class, but similarly argues that their proportion of the labor force has doubled since 1950.[17] Again, if nothing else had changed, we would expect that the political outlook of the modern knowledge worker would be much different than in previous generations.

The social transformation of the American public has no better illustration than the new social status of women. At the time Angus Campbell and colleagues published *The American Voter* in 1960, women

➤ *Fewer American males are employed in the blue collar or agricultural occupations, while professional and service employment has increased.*

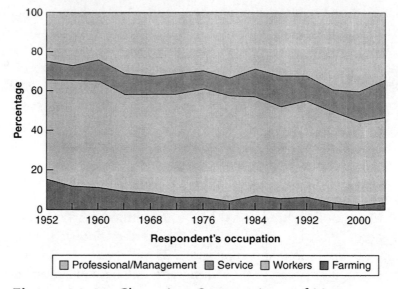

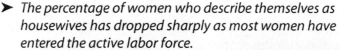

Figure 11.4   Changing Occupations of Men

SOURCE: ANES Cumulative File, 1952–2004; men only.

exercised a very restricted role in society and politics. Women were homemakers and mothers—and it had always been so. One of the co-authors of *The American Voter* noted that their interviewers regularly encountered women who thought the interviewer should return when her husband was home to answer the survey questions, since politics was the man's domain.

➤ *The percentage of women who describe themselves as housewives has dropped sharply as most women have entered the active labor force.*

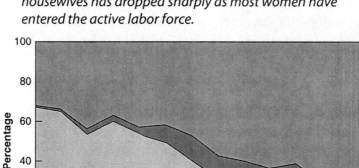

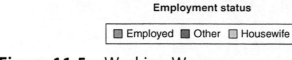

Figure 11.5   Working Women

SOURCE: ANES Cumulative File, 1952–2004; women only, retires not included.

The women's movement changed these social roles in a relatively brief span of time. Women steadily moved into the workplace, entered universities, and became more engaged in the political process. Employment patterns illustrate the changes. **Figure 11.5** tracks the percentage of women who were housewives, in paid employment, or another status across the past five decades.[18] In 1952, two-thirds of women described themselves as housewives. The image of June Cleaver, the stay-at-home-mom on the popular TV show *Leave it to Beaver*, was not an inaccurate portrayal of the middle class American woman of that era. By 2004, however, three-quarters of women were employed and only a sixth described themselves as housewives. The professional woman is now a staple of American society and culture. The freedom and anxieties of the upwardly mobile women in *Friends* and *Sex and the City* are more typical of the contemporary age.

The change in the social status of women also affects their citizenship traits. For instance, the educational levels of women have risen even more rapidly than men. By 2000, the educational attainment of young men and women were essentially equal. As women enter the workforce, this should stimulate political engagement; no longer is politics a male preserve. For instance, although women are still underrepresented in politics, the growth in the number of women officeholders during the last half of the twentieth century is quite dramatic.[19] Rather than being mere spectators or supporters of their husbands, women are now engaged on their own and create their own political identities. Though gender inequity and issues of upward professional mobility remain, this transformation in the social position of half the public has clear political implications.

Race is another major source of political transformation within the American electorate. In the 1950s, the American National Election Studies found that about two-thirds of African-Americans said they were not registered to vote, and few actually voted. By law or tradition, many of these Americans were excluded from the most basic rights of citizenship. The civil rights movement and the transformation of politics in the South finally incorporated African-Americans into the electorate.[20] In the presidential elections of 2000 and 2004, African-Americans voted at rates equal to or greater than white Americans. In other words, almost a tenth of the public was excluded from citizenship in the mid-twentieth century, and these individuals are now both included and more active. Moreover, Hispanic and Asia-Americans are also entering the electorate in increasing numbers, transforming the complexion of American politics. If Adlai Stevenson could witness the Democratic National Convention in 2008, he would barely recognize the party that nominated him for president in both 1952 and 1956.

Though historically seismic, these generational, educational, gender, and racial changes are not the only ingredients of the social transformation of the United States into an advanced industrial society.[21] The living standards of Americans have grown tremendously over this period as well, providing more resources and opportunities to become politically engaged. The great internal migration of Americans from farm to city during the mid-twentieth century stimulated changes in life expectations and lifestyles. The urbanization—and, more recently, the "suburbanization"—of American society has created a growing separation of the home from the workplace, a greater diversity of occupations and interests, an expanded range of career opportunities, and more geographic and social mobility. The growth of the mass media and now the Internet create an information environment that is radically different from the experience of the 1950s: information is now instantaneous, and it's available from a wide variety of sources. The expansion of transportation technologies has shrunk the size of the nation and the world, and increased the breadth of life experiences.[22]

These trends accompany changes in the forms of social organization and interaction. Structured forms of organization, such as political parties run by backroom "bosses" and tightly run political machines, have given way to voluntary associations and ad hoc advocacy groups, which in turn become less formal and more spontaneous in organization. Communities are becoming less bound by geographical proximity. Individuals are involved in increasingly complex and competing social networks that divide their loyalties. Institutional ties are becoming more fluid; hardly anyone expects to work a lifetime for one employer anymore.

None of these trends are surprising to analysts of America society, but too often we overlook the size of these changes and their cumulative impact over more than fifty years. In fact, these trends are altering the norms of citizenship and, in turn, the nature of American politics. They have taken place in a slow and relatively silent process over several decades, but they now reflect the new reality of political life.

BOWLING ALONE OR PROTESTING WITH A GROUP

RUSSELL J. DALTON
University of California, Irvine

A participatory public has been a defining feature of American politics and a strength of the U.S. political system. Tocqueville, for example, was impressed by the participatory tendencies of Americans when he toured the nation in the 1830s:

> *The political activity that pervades the United States must be seen to be understood. No sooner do you set foot upon American ground than you are stunned by a kind of tumult; . . . here the people of one quarter of a town are meeting to decide upon the building of a church; there the election of a representative is going on; a little farther, the delegates of a district are hastening to the town in order to consult upon some local improvements; in another place, the laborers of a village quit their plows to deliberate upon a project of a road or a public school. . . . To take a hand in the regulation of society and to discuss it is [the] biggest concern and, so to speak, the only pleasure an American knows.*[1]

Thomas Jefferson emphasized the importance of participation to the functioning of the democratic process. Social scientists maintain that political participation "is at the heart of democratic theory and at the heart of the democratic political formula in the United States."[2] Without public involvement in the process, democracy lacks both its legitimacy and its guiding force.

Studies of political participation in the 1960s and 1970s stressed the public's high activity levels. The political culture encouraged people to participate: Americans were active in voluntary associations, engaged in political discussion, and involved political affairs.[3] Tocqueville's description of America apparently still applied in the mid-twentieth century.

And yet, a considerable body of contemporary research argues that political participation is declining among the public. Although education levels, socio-economic status, and access to political information and the other resources of democratic citizenship have increased substantially over the past several decades (as described in Chapter 1), this has apparently not stimulated participation. Fewer Americans seem engaged in elections, and other evidence points to a drop in campaign activity.[4] William J. Bennett, the former Education Secretary under President Ronald Reagan, and former Senator Sam Nunn, Democrat of Georgia, observed that "too many of us lack confidence in our capacity to make basic moral and civic judgments, to join with our neighbors to do the work of community, to make a difference. Never have we had so many opportunities for participation, yet rarely have we felt so powerless."[5] In his influential book that provides the title for this chapter, *Bowling Alone*, Robert Putnam similarly concludes: "declining electoral participation is merely the most visible symptom of a broader disengagement from community life. Like a fever, electoral abstention is even more important as a sign of deeper trouble in the body politic than as a malady itself. It is not just from the voting booth that Americans are increasingly AWOL."[6]

Moreover, most analysts view the young as a primary source of this decline. Authors from Tom Brokaw to Robert Putnam extol the civic values and engagement of the older, "greatest generation" with great hyperbole. At the same time, the young are described as the "Doofus generation" or the "invisible generation," even by sympathetic journalists who are members of Generation X. Political analysts and politicians seemingly agree that young Americans are dropping out of politics, producing the erosion of political activity.[7]

Is the situation really so dire? Other evidence points to increases in several forms of political action, especially among the young.[8] Ronald Inglehart, for example, described a much more optimistic image of contemporary citizen engagement: "One frequently hears references to growing apathy on the part of the public . . . These allegations of apathy are misleading: mass publics *are* deserting the old-line, oligarchical political organizations that mobilized them in the modernization era—but they are becoming more active in a wide range of elite-challenging forms of political action."[9] This is starkly different from the decline in civic engagement literature.

Many political causes still motivate the young, such as helping the less fortunate in America, addressing poverty in Africa (and America), or improving the global (and American) environment. So there is at least some countervailing evidence that Americans are changing their style of political action rather than dropping out from politics entirely. And these trends are most apparent among the young. From this perspective, America is witnessing a change in the nature of citizenship and political participation that is leading to a renaissance of democratic participation—rather than a general decline in participation.

We suggest that the norms of citizenship may provide the key to resolving this debate. Duty-based norms of citizenship can stimulate political engagement, especially turnout in elections. The decline of these norms thus may contribute to the erosion of electoral participation. In contrast, engaged citizens apparently are not so drawn to elections, but prefer more direct forms of political action, such as working with public interest groups, boycotts, or contentious actions. Let's first examine how political participation patterns are changing over time. Then, we can find out how the modes of citizenship are linked to the patterns of participation.

What Could You Do To Influence the Government?

Instead of starting with the common assumption that participation is synonymous with voting in elections, let's begin with a citizen-centered view of participation. How do people think of their

Table 11.1 How One Can Try to influence the Government

➤ *Americans increasingly perceive more ways to influence the government, and direct contact and pro-tests have increased the most.*

Ways to Influence Government	Local Government		National Government	
	1959	1981	1959	1981
Work with informal, unorganized group	60	48	30	25
Work with formal group	4	6	4	8
Contact politicians, officials	23	55	60	84
Voting, partycontact	16	15	8	14
Protest, demonstrate, petition	1	33	<1	16
Other means	3	10	1	3
Can do nothing	18	17	22	14
Total	124%	183%	125%	165%

NOTE: Each column totals more than 100 percent because up to three responses were possible in each survey.

SOURCES: Civic Culture Study (1959), Political Action II Study (1981).

participation options? If one wants to influence politics, how should this be done? Answers to these questions reflect a combination of the tools an individual thinks will be effective and what he or she feels prepared to do. To tap these opinions, we use a standardized survey question that asks about participation options:

> *Suppose a regulation was being considered by (your local community) which you considered very unjust or harmful; what do you think you could do? Suppose a law was being considered by Congress which you considered to be very unjust or harmful: what do you think you could do?*

This question was first asked in 1959 as part of the cross-national *Civic Culture* study. Table 11.1 shows that most Americans felt relatively efficacious; only 18 percent said they could do nothing about a bad local regulation and only 22 percent said they could do nothing about a bad national law. When this question was repeated in the 1980s, the level of efficacy held stable for local politics, and increased for national politics. This is a first suggestion that political engagement is not decreasing in America.

The expanding repertoire of political action is even more apparent in responses to how people would be politically active. Many people say they would work through informal groups, neighbors, or friends to influence policy, especially at the local level where the possibility of face-to-face co-operation is greater. This is the type of collective action that represents Tocqueville's image of participation in America. Although responses are slightly less frequent in 1981, this remains a common form of proposed political action.[10]

By the second time point, however, participation means more avenues of influence. In 1959, protests, demonstrations, petitions, and other examples of contentious politics barely were apparent in

Americans' thinking about politics; they were mentioned by 1 percent or less of the public. In 1981, 33 percent mention some direct action related to local government and 16 percent for national government. Most of these responses (26 percent and 12 percent respectively) involve circulation of petitions, but this still means that a substantial percentage cite protests, demonstrations, and boycotts as a primary means of political influence.

The tendency to think of political influence as direct contact has grown even more over this time span. Both contacting a local government official and a national government official have increased by more than 20 percent across these two decades. Direct contacting becomes the most frequently proposed method of political action for local government (55 percent) and national government (84 percent). This trend reflects two reinforcing patterns. First, people today are less deferential to elites and more likely to assert their own political views. Second, people possess the resources and skills to take direct, individual action, such as writing a letter to an official or calling his or her office. And even these data are relatively old; in the modern context of e-mail and faxes, direct contacting has become even simpler for the individual.[11]

Table 11.1 also illustrates the role of voting in the participation repertoire. In 1959, voting or working with a party in some other way was the third most frequently cited means of influence for both local and national government. The percentages citing elections and parties did not change dramatically in the next two decades—but other forms of action expanded. Voting is important, but citizens are now much more likely to say they would turn to other methods when trying to influence government.

In other words, people see expanding options for how they can influence government. Moreover, the growth in the participation repertoire has come primarily in forms of direct action—such as contacting and protest—that typify a style of participation that is much different from the institutionalized and infrequent means of electoral participation of prior years. If more recent data were available, we expect these trends would be even stronger.

The Myth of the Disengaged American

American citizens see new avenues of political action available to them—but do they use these opportunities? Surprisingly, comprehensive data on the participation patterns of Americans are relatively rare.[12] For instance, the American National Election Study has a rich battery of items on campaign activity that extends back to the 1950s, but the study does not regularly monitor non-electoral participation. The Political Action/World Values Surveys regularly ask about protest activities, but not about voting, campaign activity, contacting, or other activities. Even when a survey includes a large battery of participation items, the wording of questions changes in ways that make time comparisons suspect.[13] Several recent studies have presented trends from the Roper and DDB surveys, but these are lower quality commercial polls with changing methodology over time. Unfortunately, there is no definitive source for data on American participation patterns over the last several decades, and so we must combine a variety of sources to track activity patterns.

It's important to start the analyses as early as possible in order to describe patterns before the inflection point of the early 1970s, when some researchers maintain that participation began to erode. With a long time span, we also can better see the long term consequences of social change in the American public, effectively weeding out types of engagement that stem from the ebb and flow of specific events or specific election campaigns.

The first comprehensive assessment of participation in the United States was Sidney Verba's and Norman Nie's classic, *Participation in America*. They surveyed Americans in 1967 and asked about their involvement in a range of political activities. This study identified four distinct **modes of political action** that citizens use: voting, campaign activity, communal activity (working with an informal group in the community), and contacting officials. They found that people tend to specialize in activities that match their motivations and goals. Those who are involved in campaigns, for example, perform a variety of campaign activities; those who are active in community groups are more likely to engage in other community activities. A host of subsequent studies has built upon this framework.

In 1987 Verba, Schlozman, and Brady replicated the 1967 participation battery, also asking a different set of participation questions.[14] Let's begin with these 1967–87 surveys, then extend the series with more recent data from the 2000 Social Capital Survey and the 2004 Comparative Study of Electoral Systems survey (CSES).[15] The questions in these recent surveys are not always identical to the Verba-Nie questions, but they are the most comparable set of current participation measures. We can also supplement these data with other surveys to provide more evidence of trends.

Table 11.2 describes participation patterns over time. As a starting point, the 1967 Verba-Nie survey asked about general interest in politics. Two-thirds of the public said they were very or somewhat interested in politics.[16] Indeed, in the midst of the Vietnam War and the civil rights controversies of the 1960s, this should have been a time of broad political interest. Twenty years later, however, rather than a subsequent drop in interest, political interest held steady in 1987, and it remained at this higher level when the question was repeated in 2000.[17] Meanwhile, the Gallup Poll/Pew Center find a slight increase in political interest between 1952 and 2000.[18] This evidence is an indication that Americans have not become politically disengaged.

As one would expect, voting in elections was common in the 1967 survey; two-thirds of the respondents said they regularly voted in presidential elections, and half said they always voted in local elections. However, both statistics had dropped significantly when these questions were repeated in 1987. Other research generally describes a decrease in turnout since the early 1960s among the voting age public (VAP).[19] However, new studies show that when turnout statistics are recalculated to adjust for the growing proportion of the American public that is not eligible to vote, the decline in turnout is more modest among this voting eligible public (VEP).[20] **Figure 11.6** presents both the VAP and VEP trends over time. Still, initiatives such as simplified registration requirements (such as voter registration while getting a drivers license) and mail voting have not fundamentally altered the downward slide in turnout.

Participation in campaigns extends electoral participation beyond voting. Fewer people are routinely active in campaigns because campaign work requires more initiative, more time, and arguably more political sophistication. Along with the additional effort, however, campaign activity can provide more political influence to the individual citizen and convey more information than voting. Campaign activities are important to parties and candidates, and candidates generally are more sensitive to, and

Table 11.2 Trends in Political Participation, 1967–2004

➤ *Participation in elections and voting has decreased, but most other activities have increased or held fairly constant.*

Question	1967	1987	2000	2004
Are you interested in politics and national affairs?	66	66	66	—
Voting				
Report voting in the last presidential election	66	58	—	—
Official vote statistics in last presidential election (voting age public)	62	53	47	49
What about local elections—do you always vote in those?	47	35	—	—
Campaign Activity				
Do you *ever* try to show (2004: convince) people why they should vote for one of the parties or candidates?	28	32	—	44
Have you done (other) work for one of the parties or candidates?	26	27	—	—
In the *past three or four years,* have you attended any political meetings or rallies? (2000: last year)	19	19	16	—
In the *past three or four years,* have you contributed money to a political party or candidate or to any other political cause?	13	23	—	—
Contacting				
Have you *ever* personally gone to see, or spoken to, or written to some member of local government or some other person of influence in the community about some needs or problems?	21	34	—	28[a]
Contact state/national government	20	31		
Community Action				
Have you *ever* (2000: last year; 2004: past five years) worked with others in this community to try to solve some community problems?	30	34	38	36
Protest				
Have you participated in any demonstrations, protests, boycotts, or marches *in past two years* (2004: past five years)?	—	6	7	7

[a] Over the past five years or so, have you done any of the following things to express your views about something the government should or should not be doing: contacted a politician or government official either in person, or in writing, or some other way?

SOURCES: 1967 *Participation in America* Study; 1987 NORC General Social Survey; 2000 Social Capital Survey; 2004 Comparative Study of Electoral Systems survey; IDEA Turnout database.

aware of, the policy interests of their activists. Several analysts argue that campaign activity has also followed a downward spiral.[21]

The Verba-Nie survey asked several questions on campaign activity. In 1967, about a quarter of the public had tried to influence the vote of others or worked for a party; somewhat smaller numbers attended a campaign rally or contributed to a campaign. By 1987, campaign activity had actually

> *Turnout is presidential and congressional elections has been trending slightly downward since the 1960s.*

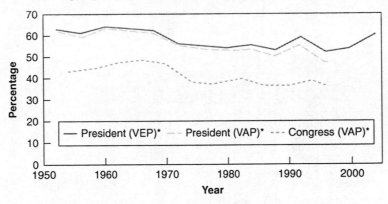

Figure 11.6   Levels of Voter Turnout

* Voting-age public (VAP) includes all adults in the potential electorate; voting-eligible public (VEP) excludes non-citizens, felons, and others without the right to vote.

SOURCE: U.S. Election Project at George Mason Unviersity (http://elections.gmu.edu/voter_turnout.htm).

increased slightly for most of these indicators, despite the decreasing numbers who said they voted.[22] The 2000 Social Capital Survey asked about attending a rally or political meeting in the past 12 months (the survey was done in August/September before the election); yet participation is almost equal to the less restrictively worded question from the 1967/87 surveys. The 2004 CSES questions are not phrased in identical terms, but they suggest that campaign activity has at least held constant.

The American National Election Study (ANES) has more extensive time trends on campaign activity (Table 11.3). The ANES asks about working for a party, going to a meeting, giving money, displaying campaign material, and persuading others how to vote. Between 1952 and 2004, there are ebbs and flows in campaign involvement related to specific campaigns, with a slight downward drift except for the 2004 election.[23] Displaying a campaign button or a bumper sticker was more popular in the 1950s, but today personal discussion about the campaign is actually more common. (One suspects that in contemporary elections more people forward election related e-mails and Web sites than place placards on their lawns.) Except for the upward bounce in 2004, a marked trend does not appear over this fifty-two-year period. Although there is some conflict between different survey trends, the ANES and Verba-Nie comparisons suggest a relatively flat level of campaign activity over time.[24] Even if fewer people vote, election campaigns still engage a significant share of the American public.

A third mode of political action is personally contacting a politician, government official, or media person about a political issue. This is a fairly demanding form of action, requiring an individual to identify a political target and formulate a statement of his or her own policy preferences.

Table 11.3 Trends in American Campaign Activity

▶ *Campaign activity has fluctuated over time without a clear consistent trend, and participation in 2004 was unusually high.*

Activity	1952	1956	1960	1964	1968	1972	1976	1980	1984	1988	1992	1996	2000	2004
Work for a party or candidate	3	3	6	5	6	5	4	4	4	3	3	2	3	3
Go to a meeting	7	7	8	8	9	9	6	8	8	7	8	5	5	8
Give money	4	10	12	11	9	10	16	8	8	9	7	7	6	10
Wear a button or have a bumper sticker	–	16	21	17	15	14	8	7	9	9	11	10	10	21
Persuade others how to vote	28	28	34	31	33	32	37	36	32	29	38	27	34	49
Participate in two or more activities	–	16	21	17	16	17	16	12	12	12	14	11	11	30

SOURCE: American National Election Study, 1952–2004.

Table 11.2 shows that in 1967 a fifth of the public had contacted a member of the local government or a member of the state/national government. By 1987 both questions show that a third of the public had contacted politicians at both levels. Indeed, other evidence suggests that more and more people use this method of individualized participation, which allows them to select the issue agenda, the timing and means of communication, and the content of the message to policy makers.[25] The CSES did not contain an identically worded question, but still finds high levels of individual contacting.[26] A century ago, active citizens marched en masse to the polls with their ballots held high over the heads and voted as their ward captain or union leader told them. Today, they sit in the comfort of their home and write politicians about the issues of the community and the nation.

A fourth mode of action is working with others to address political issues—communal activity. Communal participation can take many forms. It often involves group efforts to deal with social or community problems, ranging from issues of schools or roads to protecting the local environment. From the PTA to local neighborhood committees, this is democracy in action. The existence of such autonomous group action defines the character of a civil society that theorists from Jefferson and Tocqueville to the present have considered a foundation of the democratic process. Today, participation in citizen groups can include involvement in public interest groups with broad policy concerns, such as environmental interest groups, women's groups, or consumer protection.

Group based participation has long been cited as a distinctive aspect of the American political culture, but it is difficult to measure without representative survey data. Verba and Nie asked if individuals had ever worked with others in their community to solve some local problem; 30 percent were active in 1967. By 1987, participation in community groups had increased to 34 percent. The 2000 Social Capital Survey found that 38 percent had participated on a community project, even though the time frame was now restricted to the previous twelve months.[27] The CSES survey asked the question with a longer time frame that is closer to the 1967/87 surveys, and found that 36 percent of Americans said they had worked on a community project. This question is perhaps the closest to the Tocquevillian image of grassroots democracy in America, so it is very significant that informal collective action has become more common among Americans.

Protest is another form of participation. Protest not only expands the repertoire of political participation, but it is a style of action that differs markedly from electoral politics. Protest can focus on specific issues or policy goals—from protecting whales to protesting the policies of a local government—and can convey a high level of political information with real political force. Voting and campaign work seldom focus on a single issue because parties represent a package of policies. Sustained and effective protest is a demanding activity that requires initiative, political skills, and cooperation with others. Thus, the advocates of protest argue that citizens can increase their political influence by adopting a strategy of direct action.

Although protest and similar activities are part of democratic politics, early participation surveys did not ask these items. This partially reflected the low level of protest in the 1950s and early 1960s, as well as the contentious nature of these activities. The 1967 survey, for instance, did not include a question on protest even though the survey occurred in the midst of one of the most turbulent periods of recent American history. In the 1987 survey, 6 percent said they had participated in a demonstration, protest or boycott in the past two years. More than a decade later, 7 percent said they had participated in a protest in 2000 Social Capital Survey (in past year) and in the 2004 CSES survey (in past five years). If we expanded the definition of protest to include political consumerism, internet activism, and other new forms of action, the increase in contentious politics would be even more dramatic.[28]

The Political Action/World Values Survey (WVS) asked about participation in several types of contentious action (**Figure 11.7**).[29] In the mid-1970s about half of Americans said they had signed a petition; now this is over four-fifths of the public. Participation in demonstrations, boycotts, and unofficial strikes has roughly doubled over this time span. This WVS series may exaggerate the trend in protest because it asks if the respondent had ever participated in these activities, instead of asking about participation over a discrete time span. However, if we could extend our time series back to the quieter times of the 1950s and early 1960s, the growth of protest activity would undoubtedly be dramatic. Protest has become so common that it is now the extension of conventional political action by other means.

Finally, the Internet is creating a form of political activism that did not previously exist. The Internet provides a new way for people to connect to others, to gather and share information, and to attempt to influence the political process.[30] For instance, congressional reports state that e-mails are now the most common form of communications from constituents, and they are growing most rapidly.[31] Moveon.org became a vital tool to connect like-minded individuals during the 2004 Democratic primaries, and its methods have broadened into a new practice of political communication and mobilization. While Web sites were unheard of in the 1992 campaign (except, perhaps, to Al Gore), they are now a standard feature of electoral politics. The potential of the Internet is illustrated on the Facebook.com Web site, where young adults communicate and can

➤ *Participation in various forms of protest activity are increasing.*

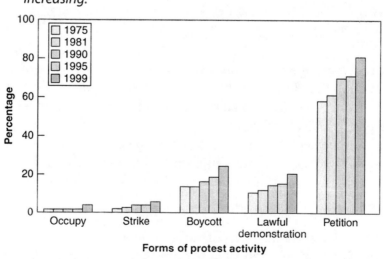

Figure 11.7 Protest Activity

NOTE: Figure entries are the percentage who say they have done the activity.

SOURCE: 1975 Plitical Action Study; 1981, 1990, 1995, and 1999 World Values Survey.

link themselves to affinity groups that reflect their values as a way to meet other like-minded individuals. In Fall 2006 the top ten advocacy groups on Facebook included nearly half a million members in total.[32] The Web is the medium of the young—and often an unknown world to their grandparents.

Because it is so new, the Internet was not part of the classic studies of American participation during the latter part of the twentieth century. The 2005 CDACS survey found that 17 percent of Americans had visited a political Web site in the previous year, 13 percent had forwarded a political e-mail, and 7 percent had participated in other political activities over the Internet. The 2004 GSS found that just over 5 percent say they participated in an Internet political forum. Those in the CDACS who had done any of these activities exceeded the percentage of those who had donated money to any political group, worked for a party or candidate, or displayed campaign materials over the same time period. The numbers are still modest, and the uses are still growing, but the Internet is adding to the tools of political activism, especially among the young.

Old Repertoires and New Repertoires

Why have the participation patterns of Americans changed? There is no single answer because several factors shape the decision whether to participate, and then the choice of how to participate. However, something in this network of factors has changed.

Political activity makes time and cognitive demands upon the citizen. To be fully informed about the candidates and issues of an election is a challenging task, even if the act of voting is relatively simple. The demands increase substantially for other types of political activity, especially individualized, direct forms of action. For instance, to write a letter to a member of Congress or to speak at a city council meeting typically requires an even deeper knowledge of politics, more personal initiative, and a significant time commitment.

Participation research thus stresses the importance of social status as a predictor of political activity. Better education, upper status occupations, and higher incomes provide the resources of time and money that facilitate political action. In addition, these social traits normally indicate a set of cognitive abilities and organizational skills that facilitate activity. Thus, the participation literature commonly describes social status as the "standard model" to explain political participation.[33] This reality still holds true today; the various surveys used in this volume generally display a positive correlation between social status and various forms of action.

Consequently, the increase in social status and other political resources discussed in Chapter 1 should stimulate political engagement. In large part, this has occurred—especially for individualized and direct forms of action, such as protests and direct contacting. However, this has not happened for voting and participation in electoral campaigns. Fewer people are following elections and casting a ballot, and the drop-off in voting is proportionately greater among the young.[34] The voting decline literature thus misses a larger reality because it focuses only on elections and campaigns. Similarly, arguments that complexity is pushing voters away from voting conflicts with evidence that more people are participating in forms of activity that require more initiative, skills, and resources than voting.

Rather, Americans are changing the ways they choose to participate. Voting is a form of action for those with limited skills, resources and motivations—the simplicity of voting explains why more people vote than any other single political activity. As political skills and resources expand, citizens realize the limits of voting as a means of political influence (see Table 11.1) and participate through individualized, direct, and more policy-focused methods. In addition, the growth of self-expressive values encourages participation in activities that are citizen initiated, less constrained, directly linked to government, and more policy oriented. In short, changing skills and norms encourage Americans to engage in more demanding and more assertive means of political action.

Age also influences participation patterns. As a baseline model, we should expect increasing political involvement with age, as individuals assume more family and career responsibilities and become integrated into their political communities. This is generally known as the "life cycle model" of participation.[35]

In addition, participation patterns may shift across generations. Several scholars have argued that the young are dropping out of politics. For instance, William Damon states: "Young people across the world have been disengaging from civic and political activities to a degree unimaginable a mere generation ago. The lack of interest is greatest in mature democracies, but it is evident even in many emerging or troubled ones. Today there are no leaders, no causes, no legacy of past trials or accomplishments that inspire much more than apathy or cynicism from the young."[36]

Are the young really this bad? Although many young people seem disengaged with voting, and alienated from electoral politics—so too are many older Americans. Volunteerism and other forms of direct action seem especially common among younger Americans.[37] When life cycle and generational effects are reinforcing, older Americans are more likely to participate in voting or belonging to a political party or related group.[38] However, in other instances a generational shift toward non-electoral forms of participation is so strong that it may reverse the normal life cycle pattern. Cliff Zukin and his colleagues recently examined the full repertoire of political action among the young, and they rejected the general claim of youth disengagement: "First and foremost, simple claims that today's youth . . . are apathetic and disengaged from civic live are simply wrong."[39]

Therefore, both social modernization and generational change may be reshaping the participation patterns of Americans. To display the interaction of both factors, I defined six "generational units" in terms of age and educational level. I divided the General Social Survey sample into two equally sized groups according to educational level. I also divided the sample into three equally sized age cohorts (aged 18–34, 35–51, 51 and over).[40]

Figure 11.8 presents the patterns of voting and party activity for these six generational units. For example, the top panel in the figure displays the percentage of each generational unit who said they voted in 2000—this defines the center point for each of the six "bubbles" in the figure. The width of the bubble for each group is proportionate to its share of the overall public. For instance, the better educated group among the oldest cohort is smaller than the lesser educated group; and this pattern is reversed for the youngest cohort.[41] The bubble graph displays both the relative participation levels of different generational units and differences in the size of these units.

Figure 11.8 shows that turnout is significantly lower among the young, whatever their educational level. However, rising educational levels mean that the better educated (who participate more)

Voted in 2000 Election

➤ *Voting is more common among older age groups and the better educated within each age group.*

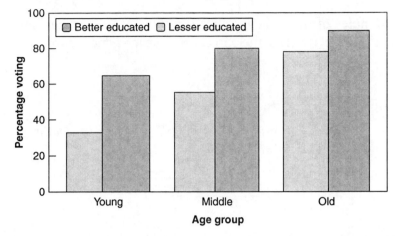

Political Parties

➤ *Party membership increases with age, especially among better educated.*

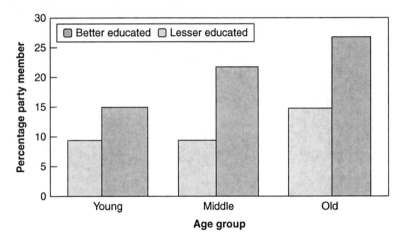

Figure 11.8   Voting and Party Work by Generation

NOTE: The width of the bars represent the proportion of the sample in each population while the height of the bars represent percentage who have participated in an activity for each group.

SOURCE: 2004 General Social Survey.

constitute a growing percentage of younger cohorts. The increase in educational levels among the young has not reversed the general decline in turnout, but it moderates this downward trend.[42] Another way to visualize this effect is that the greater mass of the lesser educated among the older voters pulls down the average participation of the oldest generation, and the greater mass of the better educated among the youngest cohort pulls up the participation rates of the young overall. The same pattern appears for working with political parties. In fact, the movement away from party involvement among the young is greatest among the better educated, as they shift their focus to other forms of political action.

Figure 11.9 shows examples of the new participation tools of the young—and they follow a much different pattern. The top panel displays the percentage of each generational unit that has boycotted a

Boycotted a Product

➤ *Boycotting is more common among the young and by the better educated in each age group.*

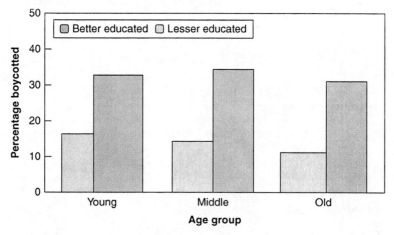

Attended a Demonstration

➤ *Demonstrating rises among the young and is much more common among the better educated.*

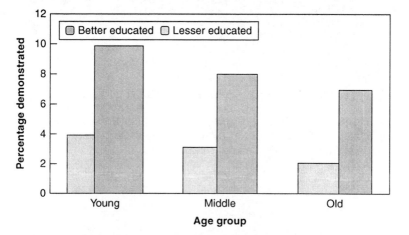

Figure 11.9   Boycotts and Demonstrations by Generation

NOTE: The width of the bars represent the proportion of the sample in each population while the height of the bars represent percentage who have participated in an activity for each group.

SOURCE: 2004 General Social Survey.

product for political reasons in the past year. This activity is more common among the young and among the better educated—so these two effects reinforce each other. For instance, only 12 percent of the oldest, less-educated cohort has engaged in these activities, compared with 33 percent among the better educated youth. If one simply compared all the young (26 percent who had boycotted) to all the old (21 percent), the reinforcing effect of generational change and educational change would not be so apparent.

The lower panel in the figure displays protest participation. Again, the simple differences between young and old are fairly small, but when age differences are reinforced by increasing educational levels that encourage contentious action, the overall contrast is much greater.[43]

CITIZENS UNITED V. FEC

SUPREME COURT OF THE UNITED STATES
558 U.S. 310 (2010)

Justice **Kennedy** delivered the opinion of the Court.

Federal law prohibits corporations and unions from using their general treasury funds to make independent expenditures for speech defined as an "electioneering communication" or for speech expressly advocating the election or defeat of a candidate. 2 U.S.C. § 441b. Limits on electioneering communications were upheld in *McConnell* v. *Federal Election Comm'n*, 540 U.S. 93, 203–209 (2003). The holding of *McConnell* rested to a large extent on an earlier case, *Austin* v. *Michigan Chamber of Commerce*, 494 U.S. 652 (1990). *Austin* had held that political speech may be banned based on the speaker's corporate identity.

In this case we are asked to reconsider *Austin* and, in effect, *McConnell*. It has been noted that "*Austin* was a significant departure from ancient First Amendment principles," *Federal Election Comm'n* v. *Wisconsin Right to Life, Inc.*, 551 U.S. 449 (2007) (Scalia, J., concurring in part and concurring in judgment). We agree with that conclusion and hold that *stare decisis* does not compel the continued acceptance of *Austin*. The Government may regulate corporate political speech through disclaimer and disclosure requirements, but it may not suppress that speech altogether. We turn to the case now before us.

[. . .]

III

The First Amendment provides that "Congress shall make no law . . . abridging the freedom of speech." Laws enacted to control or suppress speech may operate at different points in the speech process. . . .

The law before us is an outright ban, backed by criminal sanctions. Section 441b makes it a felony for all corporations—including nonprofit advocacy corporations—either to expressly advocate the election or defeat of candidates or to broadcast electioneering communications within 30 days of a primary election and 60 days of a general election. Thus, the following acts would all be felonies under § 441b: The Sierra Club runs an ad, within the crucial phase of 60 days before the general election, that exhorts the public to disapprove of a Congressman who favors logging in national forests; the National Rifle Association publishes a book urging the public to vote for the challenger because the incumbent U. S. Senator supports a handgun ban; and the American Civil Liberties Union creates a Web site telling the public to vote for a Presidential candidate in light of that candidate's defense of free speech. These prohibitions are classic examples of censorship.

Section 441b is a ban on corporate speech notwithstanding the fact that a PAC created by a corporation can still speak. . . . A PAC is a separate association from the corporation. So the PAC exemption from § 441b's expenditure ban, § 441b(b)(2), does not allow corporations to speak. Even if a PAC could somehow allow a corporation to speak—and it does not—the option to form PACs does not alleviate the First Amendment problems with § 441b. PACs are burdensome alternatives; they are expensive to administer and subject to extensive regulations. For example, every PAC must appoint a treasurer, forward donations to the treasurer promptly, keep detailed records of the identities of the persons making donations, preserve receipts for three years, and file an organization statement and report changes to this information within 10 days. . . .

And that is just the beginning. PACs must file detailed monthly reports with the FEC, which are due at different times depending on the type of election that is about to occur. . . .

PACs have to comply with these regulations just to speak. This might explain why fewer than 2,000 of the millions of corporations in this country have PACs . . . PACs, furthermore, must exist before they can speak. Given the onerous restrictions, a corporation may not be able to establish a PAC in time to make its views known regarding candidates and issues in a current campaign.

Section 441b's prohibition on corporate independent expenditures is thus a ban on speech. As a "restriction on the amount of money a person or group can spend on political communication during a campaign," that statute "necessarily reduces the quantity of expression by restricting the number of issues discussed, the depth of their exploration, and the size of the audience reached." *Buckley* v. *Valeo*, 424 U.S. 1, 19 (1976). Were the Court to uphold these restrictions, the Government could repress speech by silencing certain voices at any of the various points in the speech process. . . . If § 441b applied to individuals, no one would believe that it is merely a time, place, or manner restriction on speech. Its purpose and effect are to silence entities whose voices the Government deems to be suspect.

Speech is an essential mechanism of democracy, for it is the means to hold officials accountable to the people. . . . The right of citizens to inquire, to hear, to speak, and to use information to reach consensus is a precondition to enlightened self-government and a necessary means to protect it. The First Amendment "has its fullest and most urgent application' to speech uttered during a campaign for political office." *Eu* v. *San Francisco County Democratic Central Comm.*, 489 U.S. 214, 223, (1989. . . .

For these reasons, political speech must prevail against laws that would suppress it, whether by design or inadvertence. Laws that burden political speech are "subject to strict scrutiny," which requires the Government to prove that the restriction "furthers a compelling interest and is narrowly tailored to achieve that interest." While it might be maintained that political speech simply cannot be banned or restricted as a categorical matter . . . the quoted language . . . provides a sufficient framework for protecting the relevant First Amendment interests in this case. We shall employ it here.

Premised on mistrust of governmental power, the First Amendment stands against attempts to disfavor certain subjects or viewpoints. Prohibited, too, are restrictions distinguishing among different speakers, allowing speech by some but not others. As instruments to censor, these categories are interrelated: Speech restrictions based on the identity of the speaker are all too often simply a means to control content.

Quite apart from the purpose or effect of regulating content, moreover, the Government may commit a constitutional wrong when by law it identifies certain preferred speakers. By taking the right to speak from some and giving it to others, the Government deprives the disadvantaged person or class of the right to use speech to strive to establish worth, standing, and respect for the speaker's voice. The Government may not by these means deprive the public of the right and privilege to determine for itself what speech and speakers are worthy of consideration. The First Amendment protects speech and speaker, and the ideas that flow from each.

The Court has upheld a narrow class of speech restrictions that operate to the disadvantage of certain persons, but these rulings were based on an interest in allowing governmental entities to perform their functions. . . . The corporate independent expenditures at issue in this case, however, would not interfere with governmental functions, so these cases are inapposite. These precedents stand only for the proposition that there are certain governmental functions that cannot operate without some restrictions on particular kinds of speech. By contrast, it is inherent in the nature of the political process that voters must be free to obtain information from diverse sources in order to determine how to cast their votes. At least before *Austin*, the Court had not allowed the exclusion of a class of speakers from the general public dialogue.

We find no basis for the proposition that, in the context of political speech, the Government may impose restrictions on certain disfavored speakers. Both history and logic lead us to this conclusion.

A

1

The Court has recognized that First Amendment protection extends to corporations. . . .

This protection has been extended by explicit holdings to the context of political speech. Under the rationale of these precedents, political speech does not lose First Amendment protection "simply because its source is a corporation." Corporations and other associations, like individuals, contribute to the 'discussion, debate, and the dissemination of information and ideas' that the First Amendment seeks to foster" (quoting *Bellotti,* 435 U.S. at 783).

The Court has thus rejected the argument that political speech of corporations or other associations should be treated differently under the First Amendment simply because such associations are not "natural persons. . . ."

At least since the latter part of the 19th century, the laws of some States and of the United States imposed a ban on corporate direct contributions to candidates. Yet not until 1947 did Congress first prohibit independent expenditures by corporations and labor unions. . . .

For almost three decades thereafter, the Court did not reach the question whether restrictions on corporate and union expenditures are constitutional. . . .

B

The Court is. . .confronted with conflicting lines of precedent: a pre-*Austin* line that forbids restrictions on political speech based on the speaker's corporate identity and a post-*Austin* line that permits them. No case before *Austin* had held that Congress could prohibit independent expenditures for political speech based on the speaker's corporate identity. Before *Austin*, Congress had enacted legislation for this purpose, and the Government urged the same proposition before this Court. . . .

In its defense of the corporate-speech restrictions in § 441b, the Government. . .argues instead that [an]other compelling interests support *Austin*'s holding that corporate expenditure restrictions are constitutional: an anticorruption interest. . . .

[. . .]

What we have said also shows the invalidity of other arguments made by the Government. . . . [T]he Government falls back on the argument that corporate political speech can be banned in order to prevent corruption or its appearance. In *Buckley*, the Court found this interest "sufficiently important" to allow limits on contributions but did not extend that reasoning to expenditure limits. . . .

The practices *Buckley* noted would be covered by bribery laws. . .if a *quid pro quo* arrangement were proved. The Court, in consequence, has noted that restrictions on direct contributions are preventative, because few if any contributions to candidates will involve *quid pro quo* arrangements. The *Buckley* Court, nevertheless, sustained limits on direct contributions in order to ensure against the reality or appearance of corruption. That case did not extend this rationale to independent expenditures, and the Court does not do so here.

[. . .]

When *Buckley* identified a sufficiently important governmental interest in preventing corruption or the appearance of corruption, that interest was limited to *quid pro quo* corruption. . . . The fact that speakers may have influence over or access to elected officials does not mean that these officials are corrupt. . . .

The appearance of influence or access, furthermore, will not cause the electorate to lose faith in our democracy. By definition, an independent expenditure is political speech presented to the electorate that is not coordinated with a candidate. . . . The fact that a corporation, or any other speaker, is willing to spend money to try to persuade voters presupposes that the people have the ultimate influence over elected officials. This is inconsistent with any suggestion that the electorate will refuse "'to take part in democratic governance'" because of additional political speech made by a corporation or any other speaker.

[. . .]

[I]t is our law and our tradition that more speech, not less, is the governing rule. An outright ban on corporate political speech during the critical preelection period is not a permissible remedy. Here Congress has created categorical bans on speech that are asymmetrical to preventing *quid pro quo* corruption.

Dissent

Justice **Stevens,** with whom Justice **Ginsburg,** Justice **Breyer,** and Justice **Sotomayor** join, concurring in part and dissenting in part.

The real issue in this case concerns how, not if, the appellant may finance its electioneering. Citizens United is a wealthy nonprofit corporation that runs a political action committee (PAC) with millions of dollars in assets. Under the Bipartisan Campaign Reform Act of 2002 (BCRA), it could have used those assets to televise and promote *Hillary: The Movie* wherever and whenever it wanted to. It also could have spent unrestricted sums to broadcast *Hillary* at any time other than the 30 days before the last primary election. Neither Citizens United's nor any other corporation's speech has been "banned." All that the parties dispute is whether Citizens United had a right to use the funds in its general treasury to pay for broadcasts during the 30-day period. The notion that the First Amendment dictates an affirmative answer to that question is, in my judgment, profoundly misguided. Even more misguided is the notion that the Court must rewrite the law relating to campaign expenditures by *for-profit* corporations and unions to decide this case.

The basic premise underlying the Court's ruling is its iteration, and constant reiteration, of the proposition that the First Amendment bars regulatory distinctions based on a speaker's identity, including its "identity" as a corporation. While that glittering generality has rhetorical appeal, it is not a correct statement of the law. Nor does it tell us when a corporation may engage in electioneering that some of its shareholders oppose. It does not even resolve the specific question whether Citizens United may be required to finance some of its messages with the money in its PAC. The conceit that corporations must be treated identically to natural persons in the political sphere is not only inaccurate but also inadequate to justify the Court's disposition of this case.

In the context of election to public office, the distinction between corporate and human speakers is significant. Although they make enormous contributions to our society, corporations are not actually members of it. They cannot vote or run for office. Because they may be managed and controlled by nonresidents, their interests may conflict in fundamental respects with the interests of eligible voters. The financial resources, legal structure, and instrumental orientation of corporations raise legitimate concerns about their role in the electoral process. Our lawmakers have a compelling constitutional basis, if not also a democratic duty, to take measures designed to guard against the potentially deleterious effects of corporate spending in local and national races.

The majority's approach to corporate electioneering marks a dramatic break from our past. Congress has placed special limitations on campaign spending by corporations ever since the passage of the Tillman Act in 1907. . . . The Court today rejects a century of history when it treats the distinction between corporate and individual campaign spending as an invidious novelty born of *Austin* v. *Michigan Chamber of Commerce*, 494 U.S. 652 (1990).

III

[. . .]

The ruling rests on several premises. First, the Court claims that *Austin* and *McConnell* have "banned" corporate speech. Second, it claims that the First Amendment precludes regulatory distinctions based on speaker identity, including the speaker's identity as a corporation. Third, it claims that *Austin* and *McConnell* were radical outliers in our First Amendment tradition and our campaign finance jurisprudence. Each of these claims is wrong.

The So-Called "Ban"

Pervading the Court's analysis is the ominous image of a "categorical ba[n]" on corporate speech. This characterization is highly misleading, and needs to be corrected.

In fact it already has been. Our cases have repeatedly pointed out that, "[c]ontrary to the [majority's] critical assumptions," the statutes upheld in *Austin* and *McConnell* do "not impose an *absolute* ban on all forms of corporate political spending." For starters, both statutes provide exemptions for PACs, separate segregated funds established by a corporation for political purposes. . . .

Administering a PAC entails some administrative burden, but so does complying with the disclaimer, disclosure, and reporting requirements that the Court today upholds. . .and no one has suggested that the burden is severe for a sophisticated for-profit corporation. . . . Like all other natural persons, every shareholder of every corporation remains entirely free under *Austin* and *McConnell* to do however much electioneering she pleases outside of the corporate form. The owners of a "mom & pop" store can simply place ads in their own names, rather than the store's.

[. . .]

So let us be clear: Neither *Austin* nor *McConnell* held or implied that corporations may be silenced; the FEC is not a "censor". . . [T]he majority's incessant talk of a "ban" aims at a straw man.

BLIND RETROSPECTION: ELECTORAL RESPONSES TO DROUGHTS, FLOODS, AND SHARK ATTACKS

CHRISTOPHER H. ACHEN
Larry M. Bartels

And Moses stretched forth his rod over the land of Egypt, and the Lord brought an east wind upon the land all that day, and all that night; and when it was morning, the east wind brought the locusts. And the locusts went up over all the land of Egypt, and rested in all the coasts of Egypt: very grievous were they; before them there were no such locusts as they, neither after them shall be such. For they covered the face of the whole earth, so that the land was darkened; and they did eat every herb of the land, and all the fruit of the trees which the hail had left: and there remained not any green thing in the trees, or in the herbs of the field, through all the land of Egypt.

Then Pharaoh called for Moses and Aaron in haste; and he said, I have sinned against the Lord your God, and against you.

—Exodus 10:13–16 (King James Version)

When collective misfortune strikes a society, someone must be blamed. For ancient Israel, disasters were God's punishment for sin—perhaps the ruler's sin, perhaps the people's. Theology did not single out the guilty party, but it structured the search and set limits on what counted as a credible explanation.

In the theology of classical Egypt, pharaohs were divine beings responsible for making the Nile flood annually. Some scholars believe that when it failed to do so, as happened repeatedly in the First Intermediate Period (ca. 2200 BCE), the resulting famines and political disorder shortened the pharaoh's reign, and perhaps his life as well (Bell 1971; Hassan 1994). Not surprisingly, there are records of Egyptian court officials wishing their pharaoh a good Nile flood.

Through the centuries, rulers and their potential challengers have been well aware of the potential political significance of natural disasters. Poor weather and bad harvests have been given substantial credit for the rise of the Populists in Kansas (Miller 1925) and Nebraska (Dixon 1898, 637; Barnhart 1925) in the 1890s. More recently, one Republican presidential campaign official said in 1992 that "it wouldn't be so bad" if Hurricane Andrew left Florida and instead "blew on up to Kentucky and the rust-belt states" where incumbent George H. W. Bush had less chance to win electoral votes (Schneider 1995, 96).

When disasters take on truly catastrophic dimensions, not just the ruler but the entire regime may face a crisis of legitimacy. Islamic missionaries in Java and Sumatra successfully blamed Dutch rule for the 1883 volcanic explosion on Krakatoa (Winchester 2003, 317–338). An earlier catastrophic eruption in 11th-century Arizona apparently triggered social upheavals among the people living nearby; their Hopi descendants still preserve folk memories of the event, which they interpret as retribution for their ancestors' "morally imbalanced and corrupt" culture (Gidwitz 2004, 52). Similarly, the European famine of the early 14th century led to outbreaks of heresy and heretic burning in Silesia (Jordan 1996). Later in the 14th century the Black Death, which may have killed one-third or more of the population of Europe, generated numerous spontaneous religious and political movements to threaten church and government (Herlihy 1997, 64): "The plague also discredited the leaders of society, its governors, priests, and intellectuals, and the laws and theories supported by them. These elites were obviously failing in their prime social function, the defense of the common welfare, in the name of which they enjoyed their privileges."

The argument that natural disasters threaten rulers and regimes is not new. However, the base of evidence on which it rests, while impressively broad historically, is also uncomfortably thin. In this chapter we take up the challenge of providing more precise and comprehensive evidence about the political impact of natural disasters. We focus on modern history and electoral politics, where the data are sufficiently detailed and reliable to trace the political consequences of hard times.

Contemporary democratic rulers have little aura of divinity about them, nor have they faced epic famines or medieval plagues. Nonetheless, we find that when election time comes, the electorate continues to hold rulers responsible for calamities and disasters that are clearly beyond their control. We go beyond that simple correlation, however, to argue a deeper point. While voters' reactions to natural disasters are of importance in their own right, our interest here is in what they can tell us about democratic accountability more broadly. From that perspective, electoral responses to natural disasters are just particularly illuminating instances of the broader phenomenon of retrospective voting.

Our assertion is that voters' retrospections are blind, not just in natural disasters but in hardships of all kinds. When they are in pain they are likely to kick the government, so long as they can justify doing so with whatever plausible cultural constructions are available to them. Only if no such constructions are available, or if no ambitious challengers emerge to articulate them, will people take out their frustrations on other scapegoats, or just suffer. In most cases, incumbents will pay at the polls for bad times, whether or not objective observers can find a rational basis for blame.

Our analysis begins with the unjustly neglected electoral impact of shark attacks.

Shark Attacks in New Jersey: The Voters Bite Back

On the four-day Fourth of July weekend in 1916, the beaches of New Jersey were packed with crowds happy to escape the summer heat of nearby cities.[1] On Saturday, July 1, a young Ivy League graduate from Philadelphia, Charles Vansant, was swimming just beyond the breakers in four feet of water at Beach Haven when he was attacked by a shark. Skillful lifeguards managed to get him to shore, but he died soon after from blood loss. Five days later, a young Swiss bellhop named Charles Bruder, a strong swimmer like Vansant, ventured out past the lifelines at Spring Lake beach, some 45 miles north of Beach Haven. He, too, was attacked by a shark. Though rescued by lifeguards in a small boat, he died of his wounds before reaching shore.

In the days after the two deaths, nearly all of the diminished numbers of Jersey Shore swimmers stuck close to shore. However, no one worried about boys swimming in a creek on July 12 in the town of

Matawan, about two miles from open water. Yet one was attacked and killed by a shark, as was a young man from the town who dove in to recover the boy's body. Down-stream, another group of boys were swimming at the same time in ignorance of the attacks. Within half an hour, one of them had his leg mauled by a passing shark. However, he was quickly pulled from the water, reached the local hospital, and survived.

By this time, the mounting panic reached a crescendo. Even the distant *San Francisco Chronicle* trumpeted the shark attacks in a July 14 front-page headline: "EAST COAST BEGINS WAR ON RAVENOUS MAN-EATERS" (Fernicola 2001, 87). Steel mesh was being installed at beaches. Bounties were offered, and sharks were killed in sizable numbers along the shore. Finally, one great white shark was hauled in near Matawan Creek with what appeared to be human bones in its stomach. Perhaps for that reason, the attacks stopped, ending the most serious string of shark-related fatalities in American history.

Before the attacks, no arm of government had patrolled for sharks or set up barriers against them in New Jersey, since there had never been a recorded shark attack in the history of the state. Indeed, prominent American scientists doubted that unprovoked shark attacks on human beings ever occurred, certainly not as far north as New Jersey (Fernicola 2001, 22).[2] The general climate of skepticism led the *New York Times* to bury its article about the first attack on page 18, headlined "Dies after Attack by Fish"—no doubt a consolation to the New Jersey resort owners, who were anxious to avoid publicity.[3]

In the aftermath of the attacks, the federal government was called on for help. The resorts were losing money rapidly, with $250,000 in reservations cancelled within a week. Some resorts had 75% vacancy rates in the midst of their high season (Capuzzo 2001, 274). Losses may have amounted to as much as $1 million for the season altogether, a sizable sum in 1918 (Fernicola 2001, 174). Letters poured into congressional offices from the affected communities demanding federal action, though there was little any government agency could do. Fernicola (2001, 70) described the atmosphere, as the shark attacks entered popular imagery and became a metaphor for other political crises as well: "Newspaper cartoons now portrayed Wilson's chances for re-election in November, using the shark fin as the symbol for his potential loss. The black fin labeled 'defeat' was shown slicing through shark-infested north-east regions. Other political cartoons of the day showed lawyers, represented by sharks heading toward a beleaguered sailboat, embossed with 'Union Bank.' At the stern of the bank boat, a chewed and legless victim dangled over the gunnel depicting 'deposits.'"

As it happened, the Secretary of the Treasury, William McAdoo, had a summer home in Spring Lake and was in residence at the time of the second attack. Joseph Tumulty, Wilson's powerful aide for political affairs, had a summer home in Asbury Park, about five miles north of Spring Lake. President Wilson himself, a former president of Princeton University and former governor of New Jersey, had been looking for a summer White House in New Jersey as well, and chose a hotel in Asbury Park, moving there shortly after the attacks ended. Thus the attacks received immediate federal attention. Wilson held a cabinet meeting to discuss the attacks (Fernicola 2001, 70), but the Bureau of Fisheries could suggest nothing beyond killing sharks at random and warning bathers. "No certainly effective preventive measure could be recommended," they said (Capuzzo 2001, 277). The president could only direct the Coast Guard to inspect the beaches and patrol the water. However, the shark attacks ended and autumn arrived before much could be done.

By election time in November, Wilson was back at his Asbury Park head-quarters, but other election issues, notably potential U.S. entry into World War I, took over the headlines (Link 1954, 247–251). In the end, Wilson lost nearly all the northeastern and Great Lakes states, including New Jersey, but managed to squeak out his reelection by adding most of the Great Plains, Mountain States, and West to the Democrats' customary Solid South.

Did the shark attacks influence the presidential election in the affected areas of New Jersey? Hitherto, sharks have not been suspects in any electoral analysis. Nonetheless, if our argument is correct, they should have reduced Wilson's vote. First, the attacks caused several deaths plus considerable emotional and financial distress to shore communities. Second, the election occurred just a few months after the summer's events, increasing the likelihood that they would be fresh in the minds of the voters as they went to the polls. Third, high federal officials were present at the scene from the beginning, reinforcing the notion that the federal government should have done *something* to deal with the crisis. The fact that no government has any influence over sharks would, from our perspective, have been irrelevant to the voters.

The evidence for a shark effect turns out to be rather strong. We now turn to the first piece of that evidence, using election returns from New Jersey counties.[4] The Wilson vote in 1916 is the outcome to be explained. Our key explanatory factor is an indicator for "beach counties," defined as Monmouth, Ocean, Atlantic, and Cape May counties. These were, and are, the classic "Jersey Shore" counties listed in the guidebooks, whose beach areas are heavily dependent upon summer tourism. They are the places in which the shark attacks would have had the most pronounced economic effects. The attacks themselves took place in Monmouth (three deaths) and Ocean (one).

We include two additional factors in our county-level analysis. The first is the Wilson vote in 1912, a measure of both partisanship and candidate appeal, including favorite son effects. Wilson's 1912 vote predicts his 1916 showing well, despite the fact that 1912 was a three-way race with former president Teddy Roosevelt running as a Progressive.[5] By contrast, the four presidential elections prior to 1912 (and their mean) were less correlated with the 1916 vote, and they added nothing to the accuracy of the statistical analysis once 1912 was included.[6]

One other control variable is needed to capture an important change in New Jersey politics between 1912 and 1916. Having supported Wilson for governor in 1910, the New Jersey bosses turned against him shortly after his election.[7] They initially opposed his nomination for president in 1912, but fell in line once it became inevitable (Link 1947, chaps. 8–9 and 427–428). After he became president, however, Wilson's control of the New Jersey Democratic Party, once nearly complete, slipped away (Blum 1951, 39, 76; Link 1947, 288). For example, the infamous Jersey City political boss Frank Hague supplanted a progressive Wilson ally during this period (McKean 1940, chap. 3; Connors 1971, chap. 3). To take account of Wilson's reduced power over the bosses in 1916, we include a control variable for "machine counties," defined as those counties with at least 30,000 voters in 1916 and 60% or more "foreign" citizens in the census of 1910.[8] The counties so defined are Bergen, Hudson, Essex, and Union, adjacent to each other and just across the state line from New York City.

Two of these machine counties, Hudson (Jersey City) and Essex (Newark), were particularly well known for boss control. In fact, alone among New Jersey's counties, Wilson never did get so much as partial control of the Essex Democratic machine, which was under the thumb of James Smith, Wilson's bitter political enemy, throughout this period (Blum 1951, 39–40; Link 1947, 288, 424). For that reason, Wilson's 1912 vote in Essex was so low relative to its electoral history that the county becomes a substantial outlier in predicting the 1916 vote, even beyond its status as a machine county. Simply put, Essex County in this electoral period does not act like the rest of New Jersey at the polls; we therefore excluded it from our analysis. The other 20 New Jersey counties make up our sample.

Table 11.5 presents the results of a statistical analysis estimating the difference in Wilson's 1916 presidential vote share between beach counties and non-beach counties, controlling for machine counties and for Wilson's 1912 vote share. All of the parameter estimates are substantively significant and sensibly sized, and each of them is statistically significant beyond the .01 level. The analysis accounts for Wilson's 1916 vote share with an average error of just 1.7 percentage points, and the correlation between actual and predicted 1916 vote shares is .97.[9]

The estimated negative effect on Wilson's vote in the beach counties is a little more than three percentage points, with a 95% confidence interval confined between 1.3 and 5.2. The shark attacks indeed seem to have had an impact. The statistical significance of the estimate is due to the very consistent effect across the beach counties, as may be seen from **Figure 11.10**. This figure shows the statistical relationship between Wilson's 1916 vote share and his 1912 vote share with the machine county variable controlled. The linear relationships are estimated separately for beach and non-beach counties, with Essex excluded. As the graph shows, the beach counties are each depressed nearly the same amount from their expected 1916 vote, and the consistency of the effect bolsters the plausibility of the specification visually while tightening the standard errors statistically.[10]

We explored a variety of other statistical specifications using different measures of partisanship. None worked as well as Wilson's 1912 vote share, and the estimated effect of the shark attacks remained fairly constant—two to four percentage points—so long as the 1912 vote share was included. We also tried including measures of the proportion German, the proportion Irish, and the total proportion

Table 11.5 The Effect of Shark Attacks on the 1916 New Jersey Presidential Vote	
Beach county	−3.2
	(1.0)
Machine county	−5.7
	(1.1)
Wilson 1912 vote (three-way fraction)	0.95
	(0.06)
Intercept	4.5
	(2.8)
Standard error of regression	1.7
Adjusted R^2	.94
N	20

Parameter estimates from ordinary least squares regression analysis (with standard errors in parentheses) of Woodrow Wilson's vote share (two-party %) in New Jersey counties, 1916.

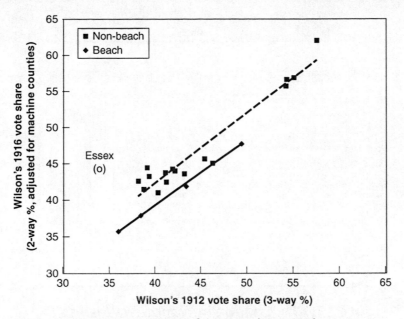

Figure 11.10   Support for Woodrow Wilson in New Jersey Counties, 1916 versus 1912

"foreign," since speculation was rampant at the time of the 1916 election that these communities would be unhappy with Wilson over his potential entry into World War I on the British side or over the British suppression of the 1916 Easter Rising in Dublin. We found no effects of this sort, which is consistent with the conclusions of analysts of the national vote at the time.[11] Similarly, weighting the counties by their total 1916 turnout, or using the change in Wilson's vote share from 1912 to 1916 as the dependent variable, or both, never reduced the estimated impact of the sharks by more than a tenth of a percentage point. In fact, all the turnout-weighted estimates were larger by a few tenths of a percentage point. Thus the shark effect stands up well under a variety of alternative statistical specifications.[12]

We also undertook two additional investigations with different samples. First, we examined the vote in the first two shore townships where the attacks took place.[13] Both Beach Haven and Spring Lake were small, stable communities, making comparison sensible.[14] **Figure 11.11** shows the vote change for Wilson between 1912 and 1916 in these two communities, and compares it with the change in their respective counties and in New Jersey as a whole. Both townships show remarkable drops in Wilson's support, 11 points in Beach Haven and 9 in Spring Lake—far more than the modest decline in the Wilson vote in their counties. It is apparent that something drastically reduced enthusiasm for Woodrow Wilson in these two townships.

We also investigated whether Beach Haven and Spring Lake were typical of beach areas. To answer this question, we examined the townships in Ocean County near the water. Ocean was chosen because it has many beach communities, nearly all on a bank of land (Long Beach Island) clearly separated from the mainland. Thus there is no difficulty in separating those eight communities right on the beach, whose economies were damaged by the shark attacks, from the eleven towns near the beach but not on it, whose economies were less susceptible to harm.[15] New Jersey was growing rapidly in this era; to ensure that vote shares in 1912 and 1916 would be meaningfully comparable, we dropped townships whose vote totals grew or shrank by more than 25% in this four-year period.[16] This left us

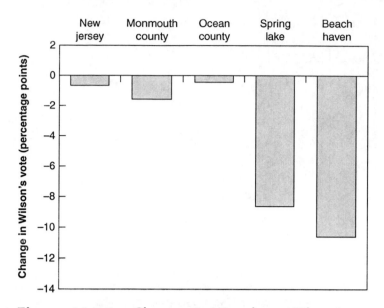

Figure 11.11 Change in Woodrow Wilson's Vote Share (1912–1916) in Counties and Townships with Shark Attacks

with 14 towns, 4 of them on the beach and 10 nearby. These two sets of communities had very similar overall Democratic percentages for Wilson in 1912 (37.1% at the beach and 33.5% in the near-beach), making them comparable.

In each area, we compared Wilson's vote percentages in 1912 and 1916. If our argument is correct, the beach voters should show the largest drop in support for Wilson, while the near-beach voters should have been largely unaffected. As shown in **Figure 11.12**, the actual vote change turns out to be a drop of 13.3 percentage points in the beach area, compared to a tiny loss of half a percentage point in the

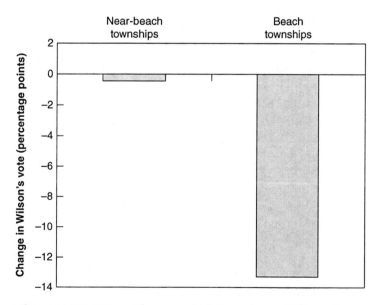

Figure 11.12 Change in Woodrow Wilson's Vote Share (1912–1916) in Ocean County Townships

near-beach area, an easily statistically significant difference.[17] Again, we find that disaffection for Wilson was widespread in the beach areas where livelihoods were most directly affected by the shark attacks, far different from the otherwise comparable areas next door, where Wilson's vote was nearly constant.

In summary, then, every indication in the New Jersey election returns is that the horrifying shark attacks during the summer of 1916 reduced Wilson's vote in the beach communities by about ten percentage points. An effect of that size may sound modest to those unfamiliar with American electoral experience, but by those standards it is a near-earthquake. (A full earthquake, the Great Depression, reduced Herbert Hoover's vote in New Jersey by 12 percentage points, from 59.8% in 1928 to 47.6% in 1932.)

In the case of the shark attacks, retrospection was surely blind. Shark attacks are random events in the purest sense of the term, and they have no governmental solution. If bathers insist on swimming in the ocean, governments then and now cannot save them, as subsequent attacks in New Jersey in 1960 and regular encounters in Florida, California, South Africa, and Australia demonstrate (Fernicola 2001, chap. 5). Nor could the aftermath of the 1916 attacks be repaired by governmental action. The truth could not be covered up. The vacationers could not be compelled to come to the beach, nor could the sharks be forced to stay away. The government was helpless. Yet the voters punished anyway.[18]

From the perspective of a century later, of course, it is obvious that extending federal welfare benefits and unemployment compensation would have helped. But these social programs did not exist at the time, they could not have been put in place quickly, and no one would expect them to be enacted in response to a single local disaster in any case. Thus the idea that the voters blamed Wilson for failing to extend federal disaster assistance, as some readers have suggested to us, is a form of historical presentism—a serious misreading of circumstances at the time.

A Century of Droughts and Floods

Any single instance of blind retrospection, no matter how dramatic, may be dismissed as coincidence or anomaly. Our argument is that voters *consistently* and *systematically* punish incumbents for conditions beyond their control. To assess that broader argument we turn to a comprehensive analysis of electoral responses to droughts and floods by voters in presidential elections through-out the 20th century. We show that voters do indeed punish the incumbent party at the polls for presiding over dry or wet spells.

The data on droughts and floods employed in our analysis consist of monthly readings from 1897 to 2000 of hydrological conditions in each of 344 climate divisions covering the contiguous 48 U.S. states.[19] Each observation summarizes daily data from several weather stations within each climate division. We measure wet and dry spells using the Palmer Hydrological Drought Index (PHDI), an index of long-term moisture supply.[20] A PHDI reading of zero represents an ideal moisture level; negative values represent droughts and positive values represent wet spells.[21]

We aggregate the monthly data for each climate division by computing the absolute value of the sum of monthly PHDI readings from May through October of each calendar year. For simplicity we refer to the result of this calculation as a "drought index," but it is important to bear in mind that the absolute values reflect both wet and dry spells.[22] We further aggregate the data to the level of states by computing a simple average of the annual absolute PHDI values for the climate divisions in each state.[23]

The result of these calculations is an index of climatic pain running from 0.04 to 49.08, with a mean value of 11.03 and a standard deviation of 6.29. Low values of the index are good and high values are bad for voters and thus, according to our account, for incumbent presidents. Our 4,992 observations (for each of 48 states in each of 104 years) include 649 (13%) with absolute PHDI values in excess of 18, the equivalent of a full year of "severe" drought or wetness; 203 observations (4%) have absolute PHDI values in excess of 24, the equivalent of a full year of "extreme" drought or wetness.

We investigate electoral responses to droughts and floods by conducting statistical analyses of popular support for incumbent party candidates in 26 presidential elections (from 1900 through 2000). Thus our analysis is not based on a single, possibly idiosyncratic drought or flood. Rather, we examine an entire century of wet and dry spells, relying upon the random occurrence of numerous droughts and floods to distinguish their common effects from potentially confounding specific circumstances. Our analyses employ state-level voting data and six different versions of our drought index.[24] In each case, we expect droughts and floods to depress the incumbent party's popular vote share. Table 11.6 presents the key results.

In order to allow for other factors affecting the incumbent party's fortunes in each state in each election, we take account of the incumbent party's vote share in the same state in each of the previous two presidential elections, the percentage of the population living in rural areas, and an indicator variable for southern states. The effects of all of these factors are allowed to vary from one election to the next, so that there are 130 coefficients in each regression model in addition to those reported in Table 11.6— an intercept for each election, a coefficient for the lagged incumbent vote in each election, and so on. Only the effects of drought are assumed to be constant across elections.

Table 11.6	Droughts, Floods, and Presidential Elections, 1900–2000					
	Drought index			**Rural drought index**		
	(1)	(2)	(3)	(4)	(5)	(6)
Election-year drought index	−0.060 (0.031)	−0.052 (0.034)	—	−0.176 (0.083)	−0.140 (0.082)	—
(Election−1) drought index	—	−0.043 (0.029)	—	—	−0.116 (0.088)	—
(Election−2) drought index	—	0.016 (0.036)	—	—	0.023 (0.102)	—
(Election−3) drought index	—	−0.043 (0.040)	—	—	−0.024 (0.102)	—
Time weighted drought index	—	—	−0.104 (0.045)	—	—	−0.273 (0.122)
Standard error of regression	3.61	3.60	3.60	3.61	3.61	3.60
Adjusted R^2	.88	.88	.88	.88	.88	.88
N	1,233	1,233	1,233	1,233	1,233	1,233

Parameter estimates (with standard errors in parentheses) from ordinary least squares regression analyses of incumbent vote (%) by state; states weighted by turnout; observations clustered by election year. Election-specific intercepts and election-specific effects of lagged incumbent vote, twice-lagged incumbent vote, % rural and South not shown.

The simplest version of our analysis, reported in the first column of Table 11.6, employs the absolute PHDI value for each state in each election year as the primary explanatory factor. The negative estimated effect indicates that, on average, voters punished incumbent parties for droughts and wet spells; the t-statistic for this parameter estimate is -1.9, so the effect of wet and dry spells on election outcomes cannot easily "be dismissed by the dubious as a coincidence" (Barnhart 1925, 529).[25] Nor is the estimated effect trivial in magnitude. It implies that wet or dry conditions in a typical state and year (an average absolute PHDI value of 11) cost the incumbent party 0.7 percentage points, while "extreme" droughts or wet spells (absolute PHDI values of 24 or more) cost incumbents about 1.5 percentage points.

The second column of Table 11.6 reports the results of a slightly more complicated analysis in which the drought index values for all four years of each president's term appear as separate explanatory factors. Here, the estimated effect of election year drought is quite similar to the estimated effect in the first column, and drought values in two of the three preceding years appear to have additional (albeit slightly smaller) negative effects. In the third column we employ a time-weighted cumulative drought index in which drought conditions in each year of a president's term get twice as much weight as those in the preceding year.[26] Once again, the effect of droughts and wet spells on the incumbent party's vote share is clearly negative (in this case with a t-statistic of -2.3) and of considerable magnitude (costing the incumbent party about 1.1 percentage points in a typical state and year).

The remaining three columns of Table 11.6 repeat the analyses reported in the first three columns, but with each drought variable multiplied by the proportion of the population living in rural areas in each state and year. The resulting rural drought indices allow for the possibility that wet and dry spells may be particularly consequential in rural areas where farming, ranching, and forestry are major economic activities. However, allowing for the difference in scales between the original and rural drought indices, the pattern of estimated effects turns out to be quite similar. For example, the estimated effect of election year rural drought in the fourth column implies that the incumbent party lost 0.6% of the vote in a typical state and year (as compared with 0.7% in the first column).

The strength and consistency of these results across a variety of analyses employing different versions of our drought index should leave little doubt that droughts and wet spells *in general* had a negative effect on electoral support for the president's party.[27] Climatic distress is a pervasive risk to the reelection chances of every incumbent, and no more controllable than the rain.

An important disadvantage of the summary results presented in Table 11.6 is that they conceal a great deal of potentially interesting variation in effects across election years, some of which may be attributable to more or less effective governmental responses and some of which may reflect other factors. For example, as noted by Barnhart (1925, 536–539), insufficient rainfall has less impact on livestock ranchers than on farmers. Thus we expect that some droughts will have substantial economic and political impacts and others less so, depending on where they occurred. That variation is conveyed by **Figure 11.13**, which presents separate estimated effects of election-year drought on the incumbent party's vote share in each election.

The estimated effects of droughts and wet spells are clearly quite variable, with almost half of the election-specific estimates more than twice as large—and a few as much as five times as large—as the corresponding overall estimates in Table 11.6. A detailed examination of those varying responses might shed very useful light on the psychology and sociology of voters' attributions of

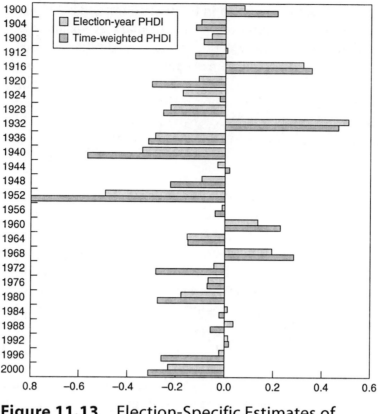

Figure 11.13 Election-Specific Estimates of Drought and Flood Effects, 1900–2000

responsibility for natural disasters. However, that sort of detailed examination is beyond the scope of the present study.

Rather than attempting to provide a detailed analysis of climatic retrospection in each election, we propose here merely to emphasize that our analysis of droughts and floods cannot be dismissed as a bit of Dust Bowl antiquarianism. We do so by examining the electorate's response to droughts and floods in the 2000 presidential election. The 2000 election occurred under relatively unfavorable climatic conditions for the incumbent party. The average absolute PHDI value was about 10% higher than the historical average, with severe drought in parts of the South and West and excessive wetness in the Dakotas and New York and Vermont.[28]

Table 11.7 presents our analysis of the impact of climatic conditions on the 2000 presidential vote. We consider three different versions of our drought index, with statistical controls for previous Democratic votes, percentage rural, and an indicator variable for southern states. All three versions of the statistical analysis fit the data very well, with average errors of less than two percentage points in the predicted Democratic vote share and adjusted R^2 values in excess of .90.

The results of these analyses suggest a great deal of continuity with previous partisan voting patterns, albeit with some significant defections from the Democratic ticket in rural states. The three versions of our drought index all have strong negative estimated effects on the Democratic vote, with

Table 11.7 The Effect of Drought on the 2000 Presidential Vote

	(1)	(2)	(3)
Election-year drought index	−0.231 (0.073)	—	—
Rural drought index	—	−0.546 (0.259)	—
Time-weighted drought index	—	—	−0.310 (0.103)
1996 Clinton vote (%)	0.915 (0.113)	0.896 (0.119)	0.802 (0.115)
1992 Clinton vote (%)	0.206 (0.121)	0.237 (0.127)	0.291 (0.120)
Rural (%)	−0.098 (0.026)	−0.032 (0.040)	−0.116 (0.027)
South	−0.60 (0.76)	−0.96 (0.79)	−1.57 (0.68)
Intercept	−0.14 (3.33)	−3.14 (3.40)	3.40 (3.86)
Standard error of regression	1.94	2.06	1.96
Adjusted R^2	.92	.91	.92
N	48	48	48

Parameter estimates (with standard errors in parentheses) from ordinary least squares regression analyses of Democratic vote (%) by state; states weighted by turnout.

t-statistics ranging from −2.1 to −3.2. The magnitudes of these estimated effects suggest that the Democrats' national vote share was from 1.6 to 3.6 percentage points lower than it would have been had voters not been inclined to make the incumbent party feel their climatic pain. The aggregate effect implied by the best-fitting model, employing the simple election year drought index, falls in the middle of that range at 2.7 percentage points.

This estimate implies that 2.8 million people voted against Al Gore in 2000 because their states were too dry or too wet. As it turned out, Gore could have used those votes. Attributing them to the various states in proportion to their drought scores suggests that climatic retribution cost Gore seven states—Arizona, Louisiana, Nevada, Florida, New Hampshire, Tennessee, and Missouri—and almost three times as many electoral votes as Florida's infamous "butterfly ballot" (Wand et al. 2001). Voters responded to climatic distress in 2000, as they have repeatedly throughout the past century, by punishing the incumbent government at the polls.

Holding Incumbents Responsible: Why So Much Punishment?

When voters endure natural disasters they generally vote against the party in power, even if the government could not possibly have prevented the problem. In our experience, this simple fact induces in many readers a powerful urge to defend the sophistication and rationality of the electorate. Here we take up their arguments.

First, it is possible that voters did not blame the government for the disasters themselves, but did blame it for *exacerbating* or failing to *ameliorate* the damage. In that case, retrospection might not be blind. The point is not a new one. As Barnhart (1925, 540) wrote of 19th-century Nebraska,

> To suggest that the farmer held the politician responsible for the short-age of rainfall would be an unwarranted exaggeration of the thoughtlessness of the voters. But it is quite another matter to suggest that the drouth in Nebraska made a bad set of agricultural conditions worse and that the politicians were held responsible for some of the conditions. Perhaps some held them responsible for most of them. The situation of many farmers forced them to think about the things that had brought about that situation. . . . They could not make it rain, but they thought they could lower railroad rates.

The difficulty with this argument is its strong policy component. If the voters learn in disasters what they had hitherto not suspected—namely that stronger government intervention in the economy is needed—then droughts ought to push electorates to the ideological left. What they actually do, however, is reduce support for incumbents regardless of their ideological commitments. "Throwing the rascals out" after droughts did lead to left-wing gains in Nebraska in the 1890s; but where left-wing governments have been in power the lack of rain has created surges of right-wing voting, as in the American Dust Bowl in the mid-1930s. Similarly in the case of the sharks, if New Jersey voters in 1916 wanted a better government social safety net enacted, then their swing from Wilson to his Republican opponent was politically quite illogical.

Moreover, whatever the voters learn in natural disasters has a very short half-life. As many scholars have noted, Populism declined rapidly as economic conditions improved in the farming states. Confirming that historical pattern, Table 11.6 suggests that droughts in the first half of a president's term have no consistent influence on the voters. Similarly, by 1920 the Jersey Shore was back to its customary partisanship among New Jersey counties, and the beach areas of Ocean County that had suffered most from the shark attacks were 8 percentage points more favorable to the party of Wilson than the near-beach, just the reverse of their views at the time of the attacks four years earlier. In sum, the voters quickly forget their grievances. Short-term anti-incumbent voting without substantial policy content is the only common pattern in the electorate's response to natural disasters.

An alternative defense of voter rationality is that the electorate punishes incumbents not for the *occurrence* of natural disasters, which are clearly beyond their control, but for insufficient *responses* to those disasters. In this view, voters monitor incumbents' performances in the aftermath of disasters in much the same way, and for much the same reasons, that they monitor other aspects of incumbent performance—imperfectly, based on observed results, in order to *select* competent leaders and provide *incentives* for future performance. This sort of punishment seems wholly consistent with the logic of retrospection we set out in chapter 4.

The problem with this interpretation is that it is manifestly irrational for well-informed voters to punish incumbent politicians for droughts, floods, or other natural disasters *in general*. Any *particular* drought, flood, or other natural disaster may be an occasion for rational punishment of incumbent politicians who fail to take adequate steps to ameliorate its effects. However, a competent electorate must recognize that incumbents' preparations for, and reactions to, the substantial physical and social dislocations resulting from major disasters are, by definition, better than average about half the time.

And while it may be sensible for voters to punish incumbents who perform less well than average in the wake of a disaster, punishing those who perform *better* than average is counterproductive both from the standpoint of selecting competent leaders and from the standpoint of providing proper incentives for future incumbents to do their best under difficult circumstances.

Thus, we should expect to find rational electorates *rewarding* incumbents for better-than-average responses to natural disasters as often as they *punish* incumbents for worse-than-average responses. The evidence strongly contradicts this expectation. Energetic politicians can sometimes successfully claim credit for federal disaster assistance or shift the blame to other levels of government (Abney and Hill 1966; Arceneaux and Stein 2006; Healy and Malhotra 2010; Gasper and Reeves 2011; Brader n.d.). However, the one-sided tendency for voters to punish rather than reward their leaders in times of distress is evident in our statistical results. The estimated drought effects in Table 11.6 represent average effects on incumbent vote shares of all the droughts and floods of the 20th century, including effective responses as well as ineffective ones. If reward and punishment were distributed impartially, the *average* effects of droughts and floods would be zero. Instead, they are preponderantly negative. Voters are much more apt to punish their leaders than to reward them.

In human terms, the voters' behavior is understandable. They see friends and neighbors pitching in to help immediately after the disaster. They do not understand why the government cannot do the same. To citizens, government bureaucracies with their rules to prevent fraud and their accounting regulations may dispense disaster assistance with a heartless attitude and a lethargic spirit. Or, if the money is dispersed more freely, citizens may complain about waste and abuse (Schneider 1995, 70–71). Either way, in the wake of a disaster the government will look inept or uncaring to a devastated and emotionally shaken electorate. Hence, the voters will punish most of the time. But doing so can neither relieve their distress nor produce more competent or caring political leaders.

One final version of the principal-agent argument is more consistent with our evidence. On this view, voters simply punish incumbent leaders any time their own well-being falls below "normal" levels, regardless of whether the incumbents have performed well or badly. Disasters are very likely to cause hardship even when incumbents' responses are vigorous and competent, so this sort of decision rule leads to frequent punishing after disasters, thus matching the evidence. And it is "rational" in the technical sense set forth in chapter 4—if voters are incapable of distinguishing relevant from irrelevant sources of subjective well-being, the best they can do may be to respond identically to both. In that case, voters will respond in much the same way to shark attacks and droughts as they do to poor tax policies and disastrous foreign wars. Incapable of assessing causation, they will mechanically translate pain into electoral punishment. But that is just what we mean by blind retrospection.

The Social Construction of Blame

Thus far we have written of retrospective voting as if hardship itself created electoral backlash. Like many other scholars, we have deemphasized the voters' interpretation of their plight, as if it had little causal importance. In fact, however, we believe that voters' attributions of blame are often crucial in their decisions to punish incumbents. Positive or negative events that voters themselves would recognize as politically irrelevant, such as the outcomes of local college football games, may also influence voting behavior through subconscious effects on voters' moods (Healy, Malhotra, and Mo 2010). But substantial punishment at the polls is likely to be grounded in a belief, however farfetched, that the government is somehow responsible for the voters' pain.

It is easy to overlook the need for social interpretation of hard times, since suggestions about their meaning are typically mass-produced. Political and ideological entrepreneurs have an incentive to construct explanations and solutions, often self-serving, for people's hardships. Amplified by the mass media, these ideas may increase or decrease the likelihood that citizens will attribute responsibility for social problems to the government (Iyengar 1991). In garden-variety economic recessions, the accepted stories about blame are familiar, and the process of generating common understandings occurs so smoothly and easily that its importance may go unnoticed. Natural disasters, by contrast, create deeper and unfamiliar hardships, which lead to uncertainty and even fear. The old complacent assumptions are shown to be mistaken, and a search begins for new explanations that will avoid a repetition of the disaster (Cantril 1958, chap. 1; Birkland 1997). People are ready to listen.

After disasters, the more popular attributions of blame and proposals for reform often come from widely trusted sources and appeal in a clear, simple way to broadly shared values, though not necessarily those that intellectual elites rely on for their political judgments. As Hadley Cantril (1941, 67) put it, "There are short-cut rationalizations which fire the imagination and spread because they somehow express the dissatisfactions from which people have been suffering and at the same time imply a new direction and purpose." If a single nutty or dangerous vision comes to be sufficiently widely shared, demagogues may be able to ride it to power.

Elite culture is usually (though not always) less susceptible to nutty or dangerous visions. It may even play some role in discouraging the most ignorant or vicious attributions of blame. But popular culture is never entirely under the control of the respectable. A variety of unconventional interpretations and nostrums may be available, and under the right circumstances deviant doctrines may attract considerable popular acceptance. Some medieval towns blamed the plague on Jews, prostitutes, beggars, or foreign agents (Herlihy 1997, 65–67). Some New Jersey residents in 1916 thought that German U-boats might have induced the sharks to attack (Fernicola 2001, 166–170). Some Americans in the grip of the Spanish Influenza pandemic two years later feared that "plague germs were inserted into aspirin made by the German drug company Bayer" (Kolata 1999, 3).

Different sectors of the population, immersed in distinct subcultures, may find different explanations appealing. Ideological commitments may color the plausibility of alternative explanations, as with the Federalists' and Republicans' competing accounts of the yellow fever epidemic of 1793. Physicians "divided bitterly over the cause of the epidemic," with Republicans generally attributing it to poor sanitation, climatic conditions, and the unhealthy location of Philadelphia, while Federalists blamed disembarking refugees from Haiti; in fact, "both sides were right" (Pernick 1972, 562–563). If available interpretations are sufficiently contested, and if incumbents can exploit competing explanations to exonerate themselves and blame others, they may sometimes escape blame altogether (McGraw 1991; Arceneaux and Stein 2006).

In other cases, blame may fail not because there are too many available interpretations of disaster but because there are too few. In 1874, for example, locust swarms devastated large swaths of western Nebraska and adjacent states. By fall, many farmers literally faced starvation. The Army had clothing and food supplies stored in the area, but refused to distribute the clothes until several weeks after the fall election, and did not give out food until the following February (Lockwood 2004, 80–84). Nonetheless, the incumbent Republicans sailed to victory in Nebraska in 1874, and repeated plagues of locusts throughout the mid-1870s did not notably dent their popularity in either gubernatorial or presidential elections (Nebraska Legislative Reference Bureau 1918, 436–506). The voters did not punish. The simplest explanation is probably that in the thinly populated farming areas of Nebraska at that time, communication was poor and no shared interpretation of the disaster emerged. A strong ethic of self-reliance also militated against expecting assistance from the government (Lockwood 2004, 38–39). And, perhaps most important, the Populists were not well organized until a decade later and did not mount a serious campaign for governor until 1890. At that point, farmers suddenly had a credible explanation for their troubles and a target for their frustrations—and punishment began.

If our interpretation of the cultural element in natural disasters is correct, then it should be possible to point to a major disaster for which a government was plausibly responsible, yet for which it escaped electoral blame because the case for responsibility was never constructed by political opponents. The Spanish Influenza pandemic of 1918 represents a remarkable case of just that sort. The magnitude of the disaster was epic; most estimates of the world-wide death toll range from 20 million to 40 million, with some as high as 100 million. In the United States alone, the flu killed approximately half a million people—more than the total number of American battle deaths in World War I, World War II, Korea, and Vietnam combined (Crosby 1989; Kolata 1999, 285, ix–x). This was no mere blown college football game. If voters punished the incumbent government whenever they felt significant unhappiness, the millions of people who lost friends or family members to influenza in 1918 would have produced the greatest anti-incumbent land-slide in American electoral history. But electoral retribution requires voters to imagine, however plausibly or implausibly, that incumbent leaders could have prevented or ameliorated their pain. In the case of the flu pandemic, that crucial attribution of political responsibility was lacking. As a result, as best we can tell, the electorate utterly failed to respond to the greatest public health catastrophe in U.S. history.

The 1918 midterm election occurred just as the pandemic was at its peak in many parts of the country, with flu deaths numbering more than one thousand per week in some major cities. Using detailed data on influenza mortality rates from 16 states and 29 major cities (Crosby 1989; Pyle 1986, 46–47), we examined voting patterns in the 1918 midterm election, looking for evidence of electoral retribution aimed either at Democratic gubernatorial candidates or at incumbent governors regardless of party.[29] We also examined the 1920 presidential vote. In no case did we find reliable statistical evidence that voters in the worst-hit states and cities punished anyone at the polls.[30]

One important race was almost certainly affected by the pandemic—the Senate contest in New Mexico, in which President Wilson clumsily attacked Republican Albert B. Fall at the same time Fall was grieving over the deaths from influenza of two of his children. Fall was elected by fewer than 2,000 votes, and Alfred Crosby (1989, 175) quite plausibly argued that "sympathy for the bereaved Fall caused Wilson's attack to backfire." In this isolated case, the horrific effect of the pandemic became a potent political issue; but in the country as a whole, remarkably, it did not.

It is impossible to know, even in retrospect, how much could have been done to minimize the loss of life in what was, after all, a vast and virtually unprecedented tidal wave of human misery. Nevertheless, it seems clear that a rational electorate could reasonably have held its leaders accountable, in part, for the devastating consequences of this natural disaster. Even with due allowance for the less developed public health technology of 1918, there is little reason to doubt that tens of thousands of flu victims could have been saved by more effective government action. Efforts to stem the contagion, or even to track its spread, were slow and disorganized (Crosby 1989, chaps. 1, 2, esp. 49–51; Kolata 1999, 10, 19, 22–23).

So why no electoral retribution? For one thing, blaming the government was not easy: the country was at war, making criticism seem unpatriotic. Both the government and the press downplayed flu risks (Barry 2004, chap. 29). Indeed, the pandemic seems to have received remarkably little national attention. As one historian put it, "When you talk to people who lived through it, they think it was just their block or just their neighborhood" (Crosby, quoted by Kolata 1999, 8). Victims were widely scattered around the country; and since people died of influenza every year, no one could be certain that their own spouse or parent or child was one of the "excess deaths" from the epidemic, much less a death that the government might have prevented.

Most important, no thread of elite rhetoric or popular discourse seems to have suggested any attribution of responsibility to President Wilson or other public officials. As long as no one supplied a convincing argument that the government did control or should have controlled the spread of the pandemic or its horrific consequences, the pain of millions failed to have any electoral impact. President Wilson was berated for the insufficiency of his efforts to stem the tide of shark attacks in New Jersey in 1916 and taunted with editorial cartoons featuring shark fins; but there is no evidence of a comparable outcry over his handling of the flu pandemic, except in an isolated instance in which he insensitively attacked a political opponent whose children had been among the victims.

The striking absence of a broad-based electoral response to the flu pandemic dramatically illustrates the importance of voters' cultural understandings of causation and responsibility. In the language of Deborah Stone's (1989, 283) typology of causal frameworks, voters thought of the pandemic as part of the natural world ("the realm of fate and accident") rather than as part of the social world ("the realm of control and intent"). Obviously, such cultural understandings are subject to change.[31] But at the time, while hundreds of thousands of people died, no one thought to blame the pharaoh.

Conclusion

In most recent scholarly accounts, retrospective voting is a natural and rational feature of democratic politics. In our view it is natural, but not so obviously rational. Indeed, blind retrospection of the sort we have documented in this chapter seems to us to provide a significant challenge to the conventional understanding of political accountability in modern democracies.

We have shown that voters sometimes punish incumbent political leaders for misfortunes that are clearly beyond the leaders' control. Moreover, we have shown that they do so with considerable regularity. The fact that American voters throughout the 20th century punished incumbent presidents at the polls for droughts and floods seems to us to rule out the possibility that they were reacting to subpar *handling* of misfortunes rather than to the misfortunes themselves. After all, it is hard to see how incumbent presidents' handling of droughts and floods could have been substantially worse than average over the course of an entire century.

Of course, voters may themselves contribute to poor disaster preparedness by insisting on low taxes and less intrusive government. In that case, government performance in response to disasters will nearly always seem poor in some absolute sense, and incumbents will be punished accordingly. But this sort of retrospective punishment is self-defeating in exactly the way we have suggested, since the randomness of the punishment from the standpoint of incumbents makes it pointless (in an electoral sense) for any incumbent to invest *ex ante* in adequate preparations for disasters (Healy and Malhotra 2009).

What, if anything, is wrong with blind retrospection? In a world of great uncertainty and costly attentiveness, perhaps this is exactly what voters should do to hold their leaders accountable—"only calculate the changes in their own welfare," as Fiorina (1981, 5) put it, and vote accordingly. Maybe there was something Woodrow Wilson could have done for the Jersey Shore, even if no informed person at the time could think of what that might be. And if a few pharaohs perish needlessly as a result of fanciful causal chains in the voters' minds, is that such a high price to pay for a system in which every incumbent has a strong incentive to do whatever she can to maximize her citizens' welfare? In short, aren't voters behaving rationally when they reward or punish incumbents for good or bad times?

In one sense, this view of retrospective voting is quite right. When voters are utterly ignorant about whether and how their leaders' actions affect their own welfare, blind retrospection may be "rational" in a narrow, technical sense. However, that does not imply that it will be sensible or prudent. Crazy beliefs can make crazy behavior "rational." But as the models presented in chapter 4 demonstrate, ignorance about reality can be quite costly in the realm of democratic politics, just as it is in other aspects of life.

Our account strikes directly at the heart of the common normative justification for the retrospective theory of political accountability. In that view, while voters may know very little, they can at least recognize good or bad government performance when they see it. Thus, they can retrospectively reward or punish leaders in a sensible way. We agree that voters operating on the basis of a valid, detailed understanding of cause and effect in the realm of public policy could reward good performance while ridding themselves of leaders who are malevolent or incompetent. But real voters often have only a vague understanding of the connections (if any) between incumbent politicians' actions and their own well-being. Even professional observers of politics often struggle to understand the consequences of government policies. Politics and policy are complex. As a result, retrospective voting is likely to produce consistently misguided patterns of electoral reward and punishment.

To sensibly translate an assessment of economic or social *conditions* into an assessment of political *performance*, citizens must find—and accept—a valid cultural understanding of the causal relationships linking the actions of public officials to changes in the public's welfare. When is one such understanding accepted rather than another? A healthy democratic culture among political elites can, no doubt, help significantly to constrain the scapegoating impulses of democratic electorates. Yet just as much or more seems to depend on the political folk culture among ordinary citizens, or on different folk sub-cultures for different groups.

Tracing how a specific political attribution of blame attains plausibility among inattentive citizens suddenly in want of an explanation for their troubles is a daunting task. The young and old, the rich and poor, the educated and uneducated are all swept along by the ideas popular in their groups, and sometimes all are swept along together. Certain looks, certain sounds, and certain arguments meet widespread needs in a particular culture at a particular time, nearly always for complex reasons unforeseeable in advance. The only certainty is that there is nothing very rational about the process.

Our analysis suggests that "blind" retrospection on the basis of overall well-being, with no consideration of the impact of government policies on that well-being, is very unlikely to provide much in the way of effective accountability, notwithstanding the fact that it may be "rational" in a narrow sense. Voters ignorant about evidence and causation, but supplied with a tale of incumbent responsibility, will punish incumbents whenever their subjective well-being falls below some fixed standard, regardless of whether or not their pain is in fact traceable to the incumbents' policies.

The "rough justice" (Fiorina 1981, 4) embodied in the electoral verdicts rendered by such voters is likely to be very rough indeed. And the rougher it is, the less incentive reelection-minded incumbents will have to exert themselves on the voters' behalf. As a result, voters who cannot distinguish the effects of shark attacks and droughts from the effects of tax policies and foreign wars are likely to experience more than their share of misguided tax policies and disastrous foreign wars. This sort of voting is hard to square with rosy interpretations of retrospective accountability, and even harder to square with the folk theory of democracy, in which ordinary citizens assess their public life critically, weigh the qualifications of competing candidates for public office, and then choose between the candidates in accordance with their own values.

Democracies take their electoral direction from human beings with limited capacities for self-government. Human passions remain powerful, and human understanding remains weak. Under sufficient pressure, voters sometimes lash out blindly. Such events are not quaint historical footnotes rendered irrelevant by modern education and hygiene. Indeed, in just the past century many citizens—and many prominent intellectuals—have been enthusiastic supporters of Nazis, Bolsheviks, Mao's Communist guerillas, and a host of other brutal demagogues whose policies seemed to offer attractive solutions to fundamental social problems that the previous incumbent rulers had failed to master.

Blind retrospection afflicts us all. It is the inevitable consequence of bewildering social complexity and human cognitive limitations—limitations that the rise of democratic government has not altered. The conventional account of retrospective voting, minimalist as it is, fundamentally underestimates the limitations of democratic citizens and, as a result, the limitations of democratic accountability.

End Notes

1. Unless otherwise noted, our historical account follows that of Fernicola (2001); we also draw upon Capuzzo (2001).
2. Indeed, two scientists who were later called in to investigate the attacks, Dr. John T. Nicols, an ichthyologist and director of the Fishes Wing of the American Museum of Natural History, and Dr. Frederick Lucas, director of the museum, had recently coauthored with a third scientist an article arguing that unprovoked sharks never attack human beings.
3. Parallels to the film *Jaws* and its sequels are no accident. Peter Benchley, the author of the novel on which the film was based, was a New Jersey resident, and the film version, though set on Long Island, New York, included a reference to the 1916 New Jersey attacks.
4. New Jersey electoral data are from the official reports published in the *Legislative Manual of the State of New Jersey*, various years.
5. Throughout the Northeast, the Roosevelt vote from 1912 returned almost entirely to Charles Evans Hughes, the Republican candidate, in 1916. (Socialist and other minor candidates, including Prohibition advocates, were also running in both years, but of course only Roosevelt was a serious third-party contender for the presidency.) Wilson gained less than a percentage point statewide in New Jersey in 1916 from his 1912 totals, and similar results held in other northeastern states. Wilson's 1912 vote is an excellent predictor of his 1916 vote across New Jersey counties, and even at the township level.

6. Adding the Roosevelt proportion of the vote from 1912 generated a small positive, statistically insignificant coefficient. Keeping the Roosevelt variable made no difference in subsequent analyses, and so it was dropped.

7. For this reason, Wilson's vote for governor in 1910 is poorly correlated with his showing in both presidential elections and was not used as a statistical control in our analysis of his 1916 vote.

8. "Foreign" here means that the citizen was foreign-born or had at least one foreign-born parent (the so-called hyphens in the vernacular of the time).

9. None of the residuals from this regression analysis falls more than two standard deviations from zero, and only one of them (Salem's) is near that level, about what would be expected by chance. By contrast, the excluded Essex County observation has a residual 4.6 standard deviations from zero in this analysis, amply justifying its exclusion from the sample.

10. If the machine counties were counted as beach counties, they would fit nicely on the regression line. They are themselves on the water or adjacent to the Hudson River. Capuzzo (2001, 270–273) noted that fear extended well beyond the Jersey Shore counties, up through the machine counties and onto New York State beaches, where the economy was also harmed. One shark was killed with a revolver near a yacht club in machine-controlled Hudson County (Fernicola 2001, 27). Thus it is possible that some of the negative "machine county" effect is, in fact, due to the sharks.

11. Two days after the election (November 9), the *New York Times* headlined "Both Candidates Got Hyphen Vote." For subsequent treatments reaching the same conclusion, see Link (1954, 232–251) on the Germans and Leary (1967) and Cuddy (1969) on the Irish.

12. Another possibility we considered was that Roosevelt might have run worse in the beach counties than in the rest of the state, leaving Wilson fewer voters there to pick up from Progressive Republicans in 1916. This would have created an artificial drop in Wilson's 1916 vote in the beach counties. To the contrary, however, Roosevelt ran *better* along the shore than in the rest of the state, so that the shark attack effect is, if anything, slightly underestimated in Table 11.5.

13. Matawan Township and Matawan Borough, where the final two shark deaths occurred in a river, were excluded from this analysis since they are not beach resort communities and thus suffered no widespread economic loss from their shark attacks or anyone else's. In any case, the rapid growth in the number of voters in both places between 1912 and 1916 makes reliable comparison impossible; more than a quarter of the 1916 voters in Matawan Township had not been there in 1912.

14. Beach Haven cast 112 votes for president in 1912 and 119 in 1916. The corresponding numbers for Spring Lake are 271 and 265.

15. The western border of the near-beach area was set to the current Garden State Parkway, which runs within a few miles of the shore in Ocean County.

16. One beach township, Sea Side Park, apparently split into two between 1912 and 1916 and jointly nearly doubled in size; we dropped it from the analysis.

17. The simplest approach is a differences-in-differences regression model weighted by the 1916 total vote (to take account of the wide range of electorate sizes in these boroughs). Thus, with the change in the Democratic vote percentage from 1912 to 1916 as the dependent variable and beach township as the explanatory variable, we obtain a coefficient of −12.8 percentage points, with a standard error of 4.4 (and a *t*-statistic of 2.9). Alternately, a weighted regression with the Democratic vote in 1916 as the dependent variable, and with beach township and the 1912 Democratic vote as explanatory variables, yields a beach effect of −11.1 percentage points with a standard error of 3.2 (and a *t*-statistic of 3.5). Unweighted regressions, though arguably substantively inappropriate, yield even larger beach coefficients. Finally, if we eliminate two townships with fewer than 50 voters in 1916, the differenced regression produces a beach coefficient of

−8.4 percentage points, while the second regression version yields −8.8, both with t-statistics exceeding 2.7. In short, alternate versions of the beach versus non-beach comparison lead to precisely the same substantive conclusion, which we summarize as a loss of about 10 percentage points in the areas most directly affected by the shark attacks.

18. On one occasion, sharks apparently had a more direct and unfortunate impact on an incumbent political leader. On December 17, 1967, Australian Prime Minister Harold Holt disappeared while swimming in shark-infested waters at Cheviot Beach near Portsea, Victoria. His body was never found.

19. The data were generated by the U.S. government and are publicly available from the National Climatic Data Center (NCDC), a unit of the National Oceanic and Atmospheric Administration in the U.S. Department of Commerce. See http://lwf.ncdc.noaa.gov/oa/climate/onlineprod/ drought/readme.html; also http://ingrid.ldeo.columbia.edu/SOURCES/.NOAA/.NCDC/.CIRS/. ClimateDivision/.dataset_documentation.html.

20. We believe that the Palmer Hydrological Drought Index provides a better measure of the damage associated with droughts and floods than the Palmer Drought Severity Index, which measures the severity of dry or wet spells of weather rather than long-term moisture supplies.

21. PHDI values between 2 and 3 represent "moderate" droughts, values between 3 and 4 represent "severe" droughts, and values less than 4 represent "extreme" droughts, and similarly for positive values indicating wet spells. The distribution of PHDI values is approximately normal, with no asymmetry apparent between the severity of wet spells and dry spells.

22. This calculation assumes that equally severe droughts and wet spells are equally painful to voters. We investigated that assumption by repeating our statistical analyses using separate measures of droughts and wet spells. The estimated effects were generally similar. For example, in the simplest regression model presented in the first column of Table 11.6, distinguishing between droughts and wet spells produced estimated effects of .067 (with a standard error of .047) and .066 (with a standard error of .050), respectively.

23. Most states are composed of between seven and nine climate divisions; eight states have one, two, or three divisions. The climate division boundaries sometimes reflect geographical features such as coastal areas or mountain ranges, but more often follow county lines.

24. All our statistical analyses weight each state in each year by the number of votes cast in the presidential election; thus, populous states and those with heavy turnout get more weight than those with fewer voters, and more recent elections get more weight than those earlier in the century covered by our analysis.

25. The observations in the regression analyses reported in Table 11.6 are clustered by election year, which allows the unmeasured factors affecting incumbent party support in each year to be correlated across states. The result of clustering is to increase the estimated standard errors (and reduce the associated t-statistics) by about 35%.

26. The resulting weights attached to drought index values in the four years leading up to each election are .06667, .13333, .26667, and .53333. Deriving geometrically declining weights from the separate estimates reported in the second (or fifth) column of Table 11.6 would produce roughly similar weights.

27. In addition to the variety of regression analyses reported in Table 11.6 we examined models with separate effects for droughts and wet spells, models with nonlinear variants of our drought indices, models allowing for secular trends in the magnitude of drought effects, models allowing drought effects to vary with prior partisanship, and models employing interactions between local climatic conditions and national climatic conditions. All of these models produced clear evidence of drought effects, but none added significantly—in terms of statistical fit or substantive insight—to the simpler analyses reported in Table 11.6.

28. Drought conditions were most severe in Arizona and Alabama, which had drought index values in excess of 20; Louisiana, Montana, Georgia, Mississippi, Texas, Utah, Wyoming, New Mexico, and Nevada also had drought values in excess of 15. At the opposite extreme, the Dakotas, Vermont, and New York had absolute PHDI values ranging from 15.8 to 20.3.

29. As it happens, 13 of the 16 "registration states" for which detailed mortality data are available had Republican governors in 1918. Thus, voting patterns would look very different depending on whether voters chose to punish incumbent governors or the party of the Democratic president.

30. In most cases, we examined the impact of influenza mortality rates in the final four months of 1918; for some cities we also had more detailed data that allowed us to examine the impact of flu deaths in the weeks immediately preceding the election. Not surprisingly, given the limitations of the available data, all of our statistical results were fairly imprecise and, in some cases, quite sensitive to changes in the sample or variable definitions. On the whole, however, it seems clear that the flu pandemic had little or no political effect. Some of the estimates suggest, quite implausibly, that incumbent governors actually *gained* votes in the major cities with the highest death rates. Only the estimate for Democratic votes at the state level had the "correct" (negative) sign, and even that estimate was of very modest magnitude.

31. Modern governments have certainly believed that the political cost of a major flu epidemic might be considerable, as witnessed by the Ford administration's aggressive—as it turned out, overly aggressive—response to the swine flu scare in the 1970s (Neustadt and Fineberg 1983).

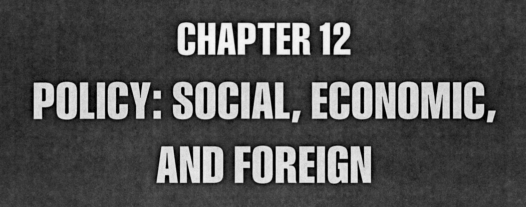

CHAPTER 12
POLICY: SOCIAL, ECONOMIC, AND FOREIGN

WHEN CONGRESS CHECKS OUT[1]

NORMAN J. ORNSTEIN AND THOMAS E. MANN[2]

Failing Oversight

THE MAKING of sound U.S. foreign policy depends on a vigorous, deliberative, and often combative process that involves both the executive and the legislative branches. The country's Founding Fathers gave each branch both exclusive and overlapping powers in the realm of foreign policy, according to each one's comparative advantage-inviting them, as the constitutional scholar Edwin Corwin has put it, "to struggle for the privilege of directing American foreign policy."

One of Congress' key roles is oversight: making sure that the laws it writes are faithfully executed and vetting the military and diplomatic activities of the executive. Congressional oversight is meant to keep mistakes from happening or from spiraling out of control; it helps draw out lessons from catastrophes in order to prevent them, or others like them, from recurring. Good oversight cuts waste, punishes fraud or scandal, and keeps policymakers on their toes. The task is not easy. Examining a department or agency, its personnel, and its implementation policies is time-consuming. Investigating possible scandals can easily lapse into a partisan exercise that ignores broad policy issues for the sake of cheap publicity.

[. . .]

Off Kilter

IN OCTOBER 2005, Representative John Dingell (D-Mich.) reached the 50-year mark for service in the House. Through seven presidents, much of the time as the chair of the Energy and Commerce Committee, often as the chair of its vaunted Oversight and Investigations Subcommittee, Dingell oversaw the executive branch to make sure it acted without bias or malfeasance. He did not shrink from making presidents, Democrat and Republican alike, uncomfortable. At times, even colleagues winced when he grilled bureaucrats. But the result was better execution of policy. [. . .] Perhaps the most noteworthy effort was the Special Committee to Investigate the National Defense Program, which was created during the buildup to World War II to investigate alleged overspending in the construction of a camp for draftees in south-central Missouri. After visiting the site and talking to the president, in February 1941 then Senator Harry Truman proposed the creation of a special committee. Within a few months, the body had begun a long series of hearings. [. . .] Vigorous oversight was the norm until the end of the twentieth century. During the Korean War, a special committee chaired by then Senator Lyndon Johnson strongly criticized the Truman administration. According to the historian Bruce Schulman, it also "reduced waste, improved the efficiency of wartime agencies and reaffirmed the patriotism of administration officials-no trivial matter when [Senator Joseph] McCarthy and his allies saw every small mishap as evidence of disloyalty and subversion." [. . .]

But since George W. Bush has become president, oversight has all but disappeared. From homeland security to the conduct of the Iraq war, from allegations of torture at Abu Ghraib to the surveillance of domestic telephone calls by the National Security Agency (NSA), Congress has mostly ignored its responsibilities. The same is true of less publicized issues involving the United States and the rest of the world, including U.S. relations with trading partners and rivals, allies and adversaries. The year-and-a-half hiatus in the Republicans' control. of the Senate, which came after 9/11 and during a nationwide surge in patriotism, did not noticeably reverse that pattern.

The numbers are striking. Examining reports of the House Government Reform Committee, the journalist Susan Milligan found just 37 hearings described as' "oversight" in 2003–4, during the 108th Congress, down from 135 in 1993–94, during the last Congress dominated by Democrats. [. . .]

Anybody Home?

FOREIGN POLICY has dominated the attention of Americans since 9/U, and especially since the Iraq war began. Major issues have included the formulation and execution of terrorism policy, the invasion Afghanistan, prewar intelligence, the invasion [etc. and yet] Congress has failed to ask how policies in these areas have been carried out, how faithfully laws have been executed [and other related questions]. [. . .]

The Department of Homeland Security (DHs) has been beset by a series of management problems, a lack of consistent focus, and a failure to sort out its numerous responsibilities-all problems that were utterly predictable. From its inception, the department has been a near revolving door when it comes to its top management team, has had major problems integrating agencies, and has had a less-than-stellar record creating an integrated information-management system for the department, not to mention coordinating its computers with those at the FBI. What are the causes of these problems? Poor planning and faulty execution. [. . .]

After vehemently resisting the creation of such a body for almost nine months, in 2002 President Bush made a dramatic turnaround virtually overnight and unveiled a far more sweeping plan, which had been secretly hatched by several key administration aides. There was no deliberative process to question the extent of the reorganization and its breakneck pace. Absent, too, was any talk of starting with a new department of border security and moving incrementally to something grander. When the DHS bill came to Congress, it sparked only one serious controversy: Would civil service protections for the DHS' 170,000 employees be eliminated? That question became a major campaign issue in the 2002 elections, while important questions about what the DHS should be and do were ignored. [. . .] Congress' failure to oversee the DHS has been crushing. [. . .]

For three years after the creation of the department, Congress did nothing to ensure that the preexisting functions of its 22 components were well maintained while new ones were added. The House only reluctantly and belatedly created the Select Committee on Homeland Security and gave it no legislative jurisdiction or control over the DHS' budget or activities. Knowing the committee's relative powerlessness, top officials at the DHS have treated it with indifference or contempt. More generally, there has been no serious oversight of the DHS in either house. Perversely, the problem has been compounded by the incessant demands of the 88 congressional committees and subcommittees that, eager for political cachet and cover, have sought to grab a piece of homeland security jurisdiction by demanding that top DHS officials testify before them. The agency's top managers have spent a lot of time at Congress but almost none seriously examining the DHS' functions and performance. One result was the abject failure of the DHS and FEMA to handle the aftermath of Hurricane Katrina.

A Killer Blind Spot

[. . .] Oversight failures in regard to the Iraq war go back to before the beginning of the war. On June 15 of this year, the House of Representatives convened a debate over the war-which Democrats called a sham-to consider a nonbinding resolution about whether to stay the course or cut and run. It was the first formal discussion of the U.S. military role in Iraq since Congress voted to authorize the use of force in October 2002. And that was not much to brag about. As Thomas Ricks writes in Fiasco: The American Military Adventure in Iraq, "When the House debate began there was just one reporter in the press gallery. At their most intense points, the debates in both the House and Senate attracted fewer than lo percent of each body's members." Unlike during the lead-up to the Persian Gulf War in 9ggo-91, there was little sustained discussion before the Iraq war. As Ricks puts it, "There were many failures in the American system that led to the war, but the failures in Congress were at once perhaps the most important and the least noticed." He adds, "There was little follow-up investigation or oversight. There were, for example, no hearings with returning division commanders." Congress has also done little about the Bush administration's lack of any plan for the post-Saddam Hussein regime, its quashing of the State Department's planning, and its stunning failure to provide adequate armor to all U.S. troops. [. . .]

whatever intermittent oversight there has been so far has come from the media. On July30, 2006, a front-page story in The New York Times reported that the U.S. Agency for International Development had engaged in "an accounting shell game" to hide huge cost overruns in the $1.4 billion reconstruction program in Iraq while "knowingly with[holding] information on schedule delays from Congress." The same day, The Washington Post showcased a major story, headlined "Report on Prewar Intelligence Lagging," about a long-promised oversight report from the Senate Intelligence Committee on the Bush administration's use of intelligence in the lead-up to the war. Nine months earlier, responding to charges by committee Democrats that the report had been sidetracked for political reasons, the committee's chair, Pat Roberts (R-Kans.), had asserted it was near completion. The Washington Post story made clear Roberts' intention to delay its release until after the elections in November. (Pressure from Democrats and two Republican senators resulted in a partial release in September.)

These two articles underscored some of the reasons for the lack of oversight: the executive branch's willfull denial of accurate and meaning fil information to Congress, the growing partisan divide in Congress, and the reluctance of congressional Republicans to criticize the administration (especially Speaker of the House Dennis Hastert, of Illinois; Senate Majority Leader Bill Frist, of Tennessee; and House Armed Services Committee Chair Duncan Hunter, of California). But these accounts barely scratch the surface. Even more worrisome are the broader dynamic that has led to the sharp decline in Congress' influence over foreign policy and the policy failures that have occurred as a result.

Contempt of Congress

[. . .] The Bush administration has aggressively asserted its executive power and displayed a strong aversion to sharing information with Congress and the public. In early 2001, the president issued an executive order granting former presidents, vice presidents, or their representatives the right to block the release of documents "reflecting military, diplomatic, or national security secrets, Presidential communications, legal advice, legal work, or the deliberative processes of the President and the President's advisors." (The order also directed the Justice Department to litigate on behalf of any such blocks.) The Bush administration has also refused to respond to requests for information under the Freedom of Information Act. In an October 2001 directive (planned well before 9/u), Attorney General John Ashcroft announced a departure from the Clinton administration's standard. Eschewing the "foreseeable harm" standard-which required agencies to release records under the Freedom of Information Act as long as there was no foreseeable harm in doing so-Ashcroft adopted a "sound legal basis" standard that allows agencies to withhold information if they have any legal basis to do so. In addition to resisting congressional and public access to information, the Bush administration has substantially increased the number of documents it classifies and decreased the number it declassifies, blocked the release of documents and briefs requested as part of congressional investigations of the terrorist attacks, refused a House committee request for the numbers that were adjusted to reflect the undercounting in the 2000 census [and so on]. [. . .]

President Bush has arguably been stonewalling in the hope of leaving a stronger executive behind. But that ambition cannot explain the behavior of Congress, which has been strikingly supine. Minority Democrats often demanded information with gusto. But without support from the majority, they had little chance of prevailing in battles with the executive or in getting media attention. Some Republican senators, such as McCain, Maine's Susan Collins, South Carolina's Lindsey Graham, and Iowa's Chuck Grassley, and Republican representatives, such as Indiana's Dan Burton and Connecticut's Christopher Shays, fought for the release of critical information, but they seldom had the support of their party's leadership or their colleagues. Even their exceptional efforts have had limited success.

An Ailing Body

Why has Congress abandoned oversight when it is most needed? The most logical explanation, which has been confirmed by comments we have heard from many members of Congress, is that the body now lacks a strong institutional identity. Members of the majority party, including congressional leaders, act as field lieutenants in the president's army rather than as members of an independent branch of government. Serious oversight almost inevitably means criticism of performance, and this Republican Congress has shied away from criticizing its own White House. The weakening of Congress' institutional identity probably began in the 1980s, when the insurgent Republican Newt Gingrich, of Georgia, campaigned to nationalize congressional politics, turning elections from individual referendums on incumbents into national referendums on what he claimed was a corrupt Congress long misled by Democrats. Candidates for congressional seats who picked up on that rhetoric and won in the November 1994 Republican sweep of the midterm elections settled into Congress with little regard for it as an institution. (This was not so, ironically, of Gingrich who, as Speaker of the House, was a staunch congressionalist.) Instead of arriving in Washington excited at the chance of belonging to the storied institution, the new lawmakers saw public service as a dirty job that someone had to do. Since 1994, most new members of Congress have left their families at home in the districts, and many have declared limits on their own terms.

[. . .]

Although fixing the oversight problem is an urgent goal in and of itself, it is also part of a larger challenge: to mend the broken legislative branch and restore a healthy balance to U.S. democracy. At a minimum, oversight demands an aroused public willing to hold its elected representatives accountable and even to toss majority parties out of power when they underperform. That, in turn, means having enough competitive seats to permit more frequent changes of party control on Capitol Hill. Reforming campaign finance and redistricting would be a good place to start. Congress' composition should also be changed; having fewer ideological zealots and partisan warriors and more institutionalists would go a long way toward toughening congressional oversight of the executive. As the Washington Post columnist David Broder has put it, "We need an infusion of men and women committed to Congress as an institution-to engaging with each other seriously enough to search out and find areas of agreement and to join hands with each other to insist on the rights and prerogatives of the nation's legislature, not make it simply an echo chamber of presidential politics." Institutionalists need to be encouraged and rewarded, by the public and the press.

More specifically, better oversight will require a commitment by Congress to do more sustained legislative work. Changing the congressional schedule is a necessary step. Congress has radically cut back on the time devoted to a panoply of traditional legislative activities, including by reducing the number of days spent in session and the number of overall committee meetings and hearings held. The current 109th Congress is slated to have the smallest number of days in session in our lifetimes, with fewer than loo in 2006. In the 1960s and 1970s, Congress held an average of 5,372 committee and subcommittee meetings every two years; in the 1980s and 1990S, the average was 4,793; and in 2003–4, it was 2,135.

The best reform would be to require Congress to hold sessions five days a week for a minimum of 26 weeks a year, with members spending two weeks on, in Washington, and two weeks off, in their home districts. Members of Congress should not be distracted by permanent campaigning; accordingly, fundraising in the capital should be banned when the legislature is in session.

Congress also needs to overhaul its appropriations and authorization processes. In the past, much of the best oversight came from the House and Senate Appropriations Committees. But their activities have deteriorated, as the drive to earmark funds for particular projects in states or districts has replaced the desire to see that taxpayer dollars are spent wisely. Earmark reform would be a step toward revitalizing those committees. The authorization process, in which agencies and programs have to be reapproved every few years, has virtually collapsed in recent years. Leaders of the majority party should commit to reinstating annual or biannual authorizations for major programs. Exacting standards should be expected of the House and Senate majorities that are elected in November. Congressional leaders of both parties should be pushed to pledge that changes will be implemented when the new Congress is organized in January 2007. Meanwhile, Congress has plenty of urgent issues to oversee: whether the administration's plans for an eventual withdrawal from Iraq are appropriate, how to handle a possible confrontation with Iran over its nuclear weapons capacity, and how to deal with the global threat of radical Islamism. If Congress falters again, the chances of policy lapses, mismanagement, corruption, and mistakes borne of arrogance or stubbornness happening will be even higher-and too high for Americans to tolerate.

End Notes

1. *Foreign Affairs*, Vol. 85, No. 6 (Nov. – Dec., 2006), pp. 67–82
2. NORMAN J. ORNSTEIN is a Resident Scholar at the American Enterprise Institute. THOMAS E. MANN holds the W. Averell Harriman Chair and is a Senior Fellow in Governance Studies at the Brookings Institution. They are the authors of The Broken Branch: How Congress Is Failing America and How to Get It Back on Track

IMMIGRANTS AND THE ECONOMY

MICHELINE MAYNARD

Do they help spur growth?

President Trump's vows to protect American jobs and improve national security by tightening U.S. borders are intensifying the debate over immigration's impact on the economy. Many politicians and workers argue that immigrants—legal and illegal—undercut wages and take jobs from native-born workers. They also contend undocumented immigrants burden society with welfare, medical and education costs. Immigration advocates respond that newcomers bring badly needed skills to the American economy, especially in the technology sector, where half the leaders of billion-dollar Silicon Valley companies are immigrants. Advocates also say immigrants often fill low-wage jobs short on workers, from home building to landscaping and dishwashing. Many experts fear the heated debate over immigration may cause the world's most talented young people to avoid studying at American universities or moving to the United States. Meanwhile, "Dreamers"—children brought to the United States illegally—are nervously waiting to learn whether the administration will allow them to stay in this country.

The Issues

After emigrating from Syria to the United States in 1906, Ed Hyder's grandfather got his start peddling shirt collars and dry goods to men maintaining the Erie Canal and railroads in New York state. Hyder's father and uncles eventually took over the business, opening shops that sold meat and groceries.

The first two generations of Hyders would have been dazzled to see what the third and fourth generations of the family have done with the business. In a converted firehouse in Worcester, Mass., Hyder and his son Gregory run a popular Mediterranean market with a staff of 15 workers, drawing an avid foodie audience with far more up-scale tastes than the working-class customers who gave the early Hyders their start. The shelves are filled with big containers of flour and racks of exotic spices, and refrigerator cases contain homemade Middle Eastern specialties and soups.

For Hyder, the heated debate over the Trump administration's hard-nosed immigration plans hits home. Friendly immigration policies allowed his ancestors to immigrate to the United States, he says; restrictive ones would have kept them out. "Limiting immigration limits the possibilities of what we can achieve as Americans," Hyder says. "I don't want to indiscriminately let in people who hate America. But it's a hard call, who's good and who's bad."

Since taking office, President Trump has moved on several fronts to tighten immigration policy. On Jan. 25, he signed an executive order to build a wall on the U.S.-Mexico border to keep migrants from Mexico and Central America from crossing into the United States. He then signed a second order on Jan. 27 temporarily blocking immigration from seven predominantly Muslim Middle East countries. And on Feb. 21, the Department of Homeland Security detailed a more aggressive approach to arresting and deporting undocumented immigrants—even those who have committed minor offenses—including enlisting local police as enforcers, building new detention facilities and speeding up deportations.[1]

Reaction was swift on all sides. Supporters of the tough new policies believe they will protect the country's security and provide more jobs to American citizens. But other Americans and businesses that rely on immigrants to spur innovation and keep operations flowing voiced deep reservations.

The furor underscored how deeply conflicted Americans are over the impact of immigration on jobs and the overall U.S. economy. Opponents focus mainly on illegal immigration and say it takes jobs from Americans and costs the treasury billions of dollars. Supporters discount these concerns and say immigration—especially legal immigration of highly educated foreigners—is a boon to the economy.

After a federal judge issued a stay on implementing parts of Trump's executive order on refugees and travel—which the Trump administration appealed—more than 100 chief executives from technology and other companies filed a brief with the Ninth U.S. Circuit Court of Appeals, arguing the President's so-called "Muslim ban" violated the U.S. Constitution and would badly hurt their businesses.

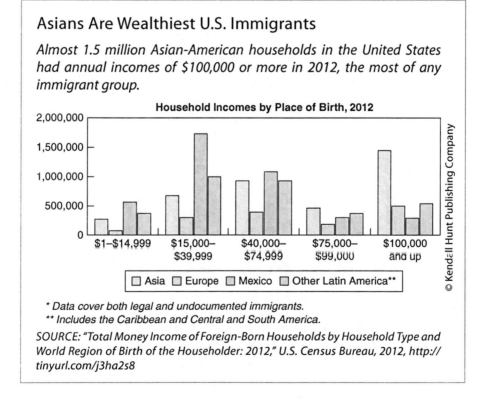

Asians Are Wealthiest U.S. Immigrants

Almost 1.5 million Asian-American households in the United States had annual incomes of $100,000 or more in 2012, the most of any immigrant group.

Household Incomes by Place of Birth, 2012

☐ Asia ☐ Europe ☐ Mexico ☐ Other Latin America**

© Kendall Hunt Publishing Company

* Data cover both legal and undocumented immigrants.
** Includes the Caribbean and Central and South America.

SOURCE: "Total Money Income of Foreign-Born Households by Household Type and World Region of Birth of the Householder: 2012," U.S. Census Bureau, 2012, http://tinyurl.com/j3ha2s8

"The backbone of our engineering team is from overseas," said Randy Wootton, CEO of the advertising-technology firm Rocket Fuel, which signed the brief. "Imagine not having access to that talent—it's a real disservice to American business."[2] (*See sidebar, p. 182.*)

In addition, a coalition of nearly 600 colleges and universities sent a letter to Homeland Security Secretary John Kelly saying the country could maintain its "global scientific and economic leadership position" only if it encouraged talented people to come to the United States.[3]

A number of experts and others dispute these arguments, saying undocumented workers take jobs from Americans and cost state, local and federal governments billions of dollars in educational, health and welfare benefits. Some also oppose legal immigration. Trump's chief strategist, Stephen Bannon, who is pushing an "America First" agenda, said last March that Asian immigrants have been filling American graduate schools and keeping American students from finding work in Silicon Valley and elsewhere. "Twenty percent of this country is immigrants. Is that not the beating heart of this [unemployment] problem?" he asked.[4]

Boston College political science professor Peter Skerry, who has written extensively on immigration issues, says anti-immigration arguments resonate with Americans who believe globalization and the free movement of workers across borders have hurt them. "If you're some white American in a disadvantaged situation, you wouldn't have to be a mean-spirited bigot to say, 'Gee, do we really want more of these guys?'" he says.

The stakes in the debate over the impact of immigration on the U.S. economy are high. The 35 million people who identify as Hispanic are a significant economic force in the United States, representing a consumer market of $1.3 trillion.[5]

Close behind in economic importance are the nation's 12.7 million people who identify as being of Asian descent.[6] (*See graphic, above.*) If current population trends continue, Asian immigrants will outnumber Hispanic immigrants by 2055, according to the Pew Research Center, relying on census data.[7]

The nation's 42 million immigrants are more likely to start businesses than native-born Americans.[8] As a result, immigrants represent 18 percent of all small-business owners but only about 13 percent of the population.[9]

Regarding the impact of legal immigrants on the U.S. economy, experts mostly debate how many additional skilled foreign workers should be encouraged to come to the United States through visas and other means. Richard Florida, a University of Toronto professor of management who coined the phrase "the creative class," warned that Trump's effort to restrict immigration threatens "the very core of America's innovative edge—the ability to attract global talent."[10]

But at the other end of the economic scale, says Skerry, "if you haven't got a high school diploma, you're bound to be competing with immigrants."

Much of the president's focus has been on the nation's 11 million undocumented immigrants, who critics say are more of a drain than a boon to the economy.

The 8 million undocumented immigrants who are working pay about $13 billion a year in state, local and federal taxes, says the Federation for American Immigration Reform (FAIR), a conservative group that wants to restrict immigration. But in a widely quoted 2013 study, the group contended that undocumented immigrants cost the economy $113 billion a year, largely in state and local services—a figure that immigrant advocates dispute.[11]

"Right or wrong, opponents are concerned about the risks of market competition" from immigrant workers who often are willing to work for less, said Cass R. Sunstein, who directs the Program on Behavioral Economics and Public Policy at Harvard Law School. Among the factors he thinks are driving immigrant opponents, he says, "they want native-born Americans to keep their jobs, and they don't want them to face wage cuts."[12]

Because the number of undocumented immigrants equals about 5 percent of the working population, some critics say the nation's unemployment rate could be reduced to zero if authorities expelled as many as 3 million of these people. Others argue they should be allowed to stay legally, which would enable them to earn higher incomes and pay more in taxes.

AnnaLee Saxenian, dean of the University of California, Berkeley School of Information and an expert on Silicon Valley and technology, says much of this discussion misses the point. "The debate over immigration is deteriorating into a conversation over, 'Are they stealing jobs?'" she says.

Undocumented immigrants hold large numbers of jobs in construction, health care and restaurants, especially in Texas, which has the second-largest number of undocumented immigrants behind California. Evicting them, Saxenian says, might mean immediate hardships for the companies that employ them, because of a worker shortage in a tight job market.

Such concerns did not stop Arizona from enacting a series of tough laws between 2000 and 2010 aimed at stemming the flow of illegal immigration.

The state's undocumented immigrant population peaked at about 500,000 in 2007 and has dropped 40 percent since then, in part because the 2008 recession caused construction jobs to dry up. Nationwide, the number of undocumented immigrants has been basically unchanged since 2008, partly because economic opportunities have increased in Mexico due to new investments there, according to the Pew Research Center, a Washington, D.C., polling and research organization.[13]

Saxenian says that although technology and other business sectors highly value immigrants, foreign-born workers look at the controversies over immigration as evidence of an unwelcome American climate. This, she says, could lead some foreign entrepreneurs to establish their companies elsewhere.

"In the 1970s and '80s, everybody felt they were welcome in the U.S.," she says. "And since 9/11, they've encountered a pretty hostile immigration system. Making them feel welcome is important. These are people who would like to stay."

As the immigration debate continues among economists, politicians and the public, here are some of the questions they are asking:

U.S. Immigrant Count on the Rise

The nation's foreign-born population has doubled in the past quarter-century, with more than 40 million legal and undocumented immigrants making up almost 13 percent of the total U.S. population in 2013, the latest tally. The immigrant count dipped in the 1960s and '70s, hitting a low of 4.7 percent of the total, before beginning a sharp increase.

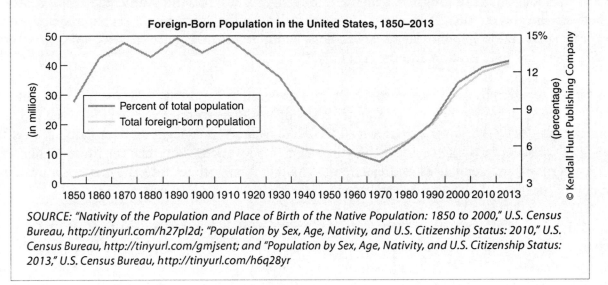

Foreign-Born Population in the United States, 1850–2013

SOURCE: "Nativity of the Population and Place of Birth of the Native Population: 1850 to 2000," U.S. Census Bureau, http://tinyurl.com/h27pl2d; "Population by Sex, Age, Nativity, and U.S. Citizenship Status: 2010," U.S. Census Bureau, http://tinyurl.com/gmjsent; and "Population by Sex, Age, Nativity, and U.S. Citizenship Status: 2013," U.S. Census Bureau, http://tinyurl.com/h6q28yr

Are undocumented immigrants good for the U.S. economy?

As a candidate and now as president, Trump has cited a widely quoted figure from the Federation for American Immigration Reform: Illegal immigration costs U.S. taxpayers about $113 billion a year at the federal, state and local level.[14]

Other conservative think tanks and countless opinion pieces also cite the $113 billion figure as they seek to ban undocumented immigrants or expel them from the country. "Illegal immigration increases income inequality and corrupts our democracy," wrote University of Maryland economics professor Peter Morici in *The Washington Times*.[15]

He added, "When the nation is flooded with immigrants in skill categories without genuine short-ages," such as jobs in which employers would have to pay higher wages in order to find qualified applicants, "illegal immigration drives down wages and increases unemployment, especially for America's lowest-paid workers."

That $113 billion figure, according to FAIR, includes federal expenses for education, medical treatment and law enforcement, as well as other expenditures covering undocumented immigrants, who have been blocked from receiving federal welfare since passage of the 1996 welfare reform law.[16] The bulk of the expense, however, is paid by state and local governments, estimated by FAIR at $84 billion.

The American Immigration Council, a pro-immigrant think tank in Washington, said FAIR's report relied "upon flawed and empirically baseless assumptions to inflate its estimate of the costs." It added: "Much of what FAIR counts as the cost of unauthorized immigration is actually the cost of education and health care for U.S. citizen children." PolitiFact, a Pulitzer Prize-winning fact-checking website, said the cost of undocumented immigrants to the country was as low as $1.9 billion, but noted that the estimates vary widely.

"It's uncertain how much immigrants in the United States illegally cost tax-payers," said PolitiFact.[17]

The Center for American Progress, a liberal think tank, argues that undocumented immigrants contribute significantly to the U.S. economy—and that the country is missing an economic opportunity by creating an atmosphere hostile to newcomers. "Immigrants in fact are makers, not takers," wrote three experts on immigration and the economy.[18]

They cited research by Raúl Hinojosa-Ojeda, an immigration expert at the University of California, Los Angeles, concluding that undocumented residents could contribute $1.5 trillion to the U.S. gross domestic product (GDP) over a decade if all 11 million were granted legal resident status. His reasoning: Legal workers earn higher wages than undocumented workers, and they use those higher wages to buy homes, cars, appliances and electronics. As this money flows into the economy, businesses expand to meet demand, and jobs are added.

James H. Johnson Jr., a professor of strategy and entrepreneurship at the University of North Carolina's Kenan-Flagler Business School, says immigrants have an economic ripple effect that is not widely recognized. "People are not fully accounting for the way that immigrants add value to the economy," Johnson says. "They create additional jobs that would not be there." For instance, undocumented immigrants need attorneys to help them navigate U.S. laws. Or they may need translators or help filing their tax returns.

In addition, some industries might have trouble functioning without undocumented workers. For instance, undocumented immigrants constitute about 50 percent of hired farmworkers, down about 5 percentage points from the peak in 1999–2001, according to a 2016 report by the U.S. Department of Agriculture. About 69 percent of agricultural employees are from Mexico. The same is true in the construction industry; experts say immigrants are helping to fill labor shortages, and they constitute more than 25 percent of the housing construction workforce.[19]

Even as the number of undocumented workers has fallen in recent years in many places, Texas has continued to see its immigrant population rise. In construction, for example, about 25 percent of jobs go to undocumented workers, according to an in-depth series in *The Texas Tribune*. "There are almost always jobs waiting for them," it said, because of a building boom in the state's biggest cities.[20]

But using undocumented workers carries both benefits and costs, according to a study on immigrants' impact on the Texas economy by two researchers for the Texas Public Policy Foundation, a conservative think tank in Austin. "The peripatetic ways of immigrants, both legal and illegal, serve as an economic lubricant," they said. But on the negative side, the authors continued, 65 percent of the state's illegal immigrants are in or near poverty, and a majority are forced to use a "major [Texas] welfare program."[21]

Restaurant owners are among those concerned about a crackdown on undocumented workers. "If every one of [the undocumented immigrants] working in a restaurant was gone tomorrow, you'd have to close down the entire industry," says Mike Monahan, owner of Monahan's Seafood in Ann Arbor, Mich.

The true cost of undocumented workers to American society may be debatable, but Maria Minniti, a professor of entrepreneurship at the Whitman School of Management at Syracuse University, sees advantages, both to the country and the workers themselves.

Many would not be employable in parts of the job market that require higher skill levels, she says. But working in restaurants or in similar jobs lets the newcomers get their bearings while they learn English and the ways of American society, Minniti says. "It's one of the great diversifying features of the country, the importance of freedom, the stress on the market, the commitment to work that gets you where you are," she says.

Do local economies benefit from the arrival of legal immigrants?

In Durham, N.C., City Council member Steve Schewel says his community's economy needs immigrants to prosper.

"Durham is [experiencing] a construction boom and a cultural renaissance," Schewel says. "None of that would be possible without our immigrant population, both documented and undocumented."

Durham is best known as the home of Duke University and Research Triangle Park, one of the nation's leading centers of biotechnology and life sciences research, with more than 200 companies. The city's restaurant scene is flourishing, and Durham has attracted new residents from around the world.[22]

Durham's population has grown from 149,000 in 1990, when only 4 percent were foreign born, to more than 295,000 in 2016, with 14 percent foreign born, primarily from Latin America and Asia, according to the Census Bureau.[23]

The newcomers help fill both lower-paying jobs and positions at startups, Schewel says. "There is almost nothing that we're doing that doesn't depend on immigrant brain power," he says. "We're very much a foodie town, and immigrants are vital to that. We have a massive cluster of startup companies, and immigrants are vital to that."

Immigration opponents see things differently. Trump adviser Bannon has argued that legal immigration hurts American communities and the fabric of American life. "A country's more than an economy. We're a civic society," Bannon said in 2015. Bannon advocates an economic nationalism that puts native-born Americans first.[24]

Ohio real estate agent Mary Theis backs Trump's proposals to limit immigration and renegotiate trade deals that she said favored other countries. Citing the president's business skills as a deal-maker, Theis said that "with Donald Trump negotiating on trade, maybe we'll get some of these [lost] jobs back."[25]

Schewel says he can understand such frustrations, especially among older, white Americans who have been displaced by economic change. "I think that's real. I acknowledge and affirm that experience," he says. "But keeping immigrants out won't help them. It will hurt them [because limiting immigration will limit economic growth]. We need the kind of economy that can grow and be prosperous."

A number of economists argue that legal immigrants boost local economies in several ways. One is their impact on small businesses—the lifeblood of small towns. According to a 2012 report,

18 percent of small-business owners in the United States are immigrants, employing an estimated 4.7 million people and generating revenue of more than $776 billion annually. They are especially well represented in retail, including restaurants, groceries and dry cleaning.[26]

California and New Jersey benefit the most from immigrant-owned businesses in terms of jobs created, said a 2017 study by the personal finance website WalletHub.[27]

Another benefit of immigration is its ability to help revive struggling rural communities, according to the American Immigration Council.[28]

One example the council cited is Ottumwa, a town of 25,000 in south-eastern Iowa. Its Hispanic population rose from 1 percent in 2000 to 11.3 percent in the latest U.S. census, with mostly legal Hispanic workers being drawn by the lure of jobs at a Cargill pork processing plant. As the Hispanic population rose, Latino-owned groceries and restaurants followed. The influx helped spark a downtown revival, city officials said, with new businesses opening, including a home-improvement store and a Kohl's department store. "Hispanics," said loan officer Nicole Banner of U.S Bank, "are pulling this town out of a long recession."[29]

Ottumwa was not alone. The Hispanic population in the Midwest jumped 49 percent between 2000 and 2010, according to the census.[30]

In Michigan, Republican Gov. Rick Snyder said he supports legal immigration because of its potential to boost the state economy. The state's population fell seven years in a row, from 2005 to 2011, reflecting an economy battered by the 2008 recession and job cuts resulting from the auto industry's struggles.

In 2014, Snyder created the Michigan Office for New Americans in an effort to attract foreign entrepreneurs and encourage foreign students to stay in Michigan to get advanced degrees. "We want the world to know Michigan is a welcoming state," Snyder said.[31]

Michigan's efforts to attract more immigrants are paying off in small ways so far. Between 2000 and 2014, Detroit lost 36,000 native-born residents but gained 4,400 immigrants, hardly enough to offset the loss, but at least a sign the city was appealing to newcomers. Statewide, Michigan has gained 50,000 immigrants in the past six years, Snyder said in his most recent state-of-the-state address.[32]

Citing the impact of foreigners in Silicon Valley, the University of California's Saxenian says immigrants bring energy to communities, creating a flow of ideas between their new and old homes—what she calls "brain circulation."

She says she discovered this phenomenon in the 1990s, when she began studying Silicon Valley's venture capitalists.

These company founders set up satellite offices in their home countries, such as India and Taiwan. The practice has encouraged companies in those countries to invest in the United States, too, Saxenian says. More than 600 Taiwanese companies have operations in the United States, while 100 Indian firms have collectively invested more than $15 billion in American operations.[33]

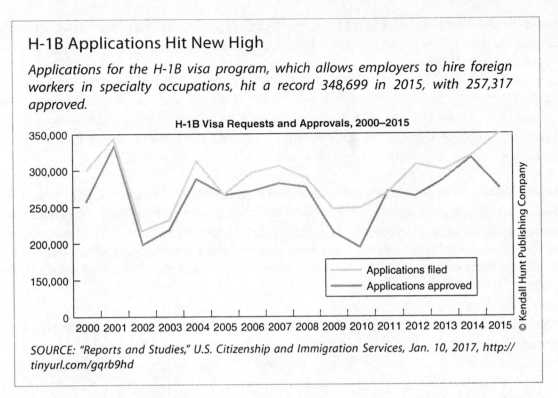

H-1B Applications Hit New High

Applications for the H-1B visa program, which allows employers to hire foreign workers in specialty occupations, hit a record 348,699 in 2015, with 257,317 approved.

H-1B Visa Requests and Approvals, 2000–2015

Applications filed
Applications approved

SOURCE: "Reports and Studies," U.S. Citizenship and Immigration Services, Jan. 10, 2017, http://tinyurl.com/gqrb9hd

Says Saxenian: "This circulation has been mutually beneficial. It's clear there's so much opportunity elsewhere in the world. People can move quickly, and communication is much cheaper."

Should more H-1B visa holders be allowed to remain in the United States?

Every April, foreigners from around the world take part in the H-1B lottery to get one of the coveted, special visas that allow a limited number of highly skilled foreigners into the country each year. The winning applicants are allowed to work in the United States for three years, with the possibility of applying for additional time when their visas expire. Competition is stiff: In 2015, a record 348,699 people applied and 257,317 slots were approved.[34]

Each applicant must have a corporate sponsor, who must show that the applicant is earning as much as native-born employees, that the company has unsuccessfully tried to recruit Americans with similar skills and that the applicant's work is essential to the company's operations.

Applicants generally are scientists, engineers or computer programmers working in highly skilled "specialty occupations." A 2014 estimate said 65 percent of H-1B visas went to tech workers, mostly from India. H-1B visas also are available for those with other graduate degrees, such as MBAs.[35]

Critics say companies use the visas to import cheaper labor to suppress wages across the country. They say universities and hospitals also use the visas to hire low-wage teaching assistants and nurses.

Then-Sen. Jeff Sessions, R-Ala., now the U.S. attorney general, said in 2016 Congress should consider eliminating the program.

"We shouldn't be bringing in people where we've got workers," Sessions said in Indianola, Iowa. "There are a number of ways to fix it. I don't think the republic would collapse if it was totally eliminated."[36]

Trump senior policy adviser Stephen Miller has proposed scrapping the lottery system used to award the visas and potentially replacing it with a program that would seek to prevent foreign workers from undercutting domestic salaries.[37]

Yet, Labor Department records showed that Trump's golf club and model management companies had received two dozen H-1B visas for employees in the past five years, and he later said the United States needed to ensure that companies could retain employees brought to the U.S. under the H-1B program.[38]

The month before Trump took office, he convened a group of tech company CEOs, whose top priorities include expanding the H-1B program in order, they say, to recruit the most talented workers.[39] For years, many executives have been urging the White House and Congress to allow more immigration. In 2013, Facebook CEO Mark Zuckerberg co-founded FWD.us, an effort backed by Silicon Valley companies that is pushing for "commonsense" reform solutions that will satisfy both sides in the debate.

However, some startups and other small firms see the H-1B visa program as favoring bigger tech companies. If employees cannot obtain H-1B visas, they must apply for legal residence, which can take years. "Small companies can't afford to put them through the green-card process," says Syracuse University's Minniti, referring to a permit that allows a foreigner to live and work permanently in the United States.

Infosys, an Indian company whose U.S. operations are based in Plano, Texas, is the country's top applicant for H-1B visas, according to MyVisaJobs.com, a website that track companies' applications. Between 2014 and 2016, Infosys filed 82,506 applications for H-1B visas on behalf of its employees. Of that figure, just 57 were denied or withdrawn, said MyVisaJobs.com. Infosys was sued for visa fraud to circumvent the H-1B system.[40]

In addition to Infosys, Tata Consultancy Services and Wipro, a global technology and consulting firm, both based in India, have made heavy use of H-1B visas to staff their U.S. operations.[41]

The government can bar companies from receiving H-1B visas if they're found to be "willful violators" by displacing U.S. workers with foreign-born ones by failing to recruit Americans for the jobs. Sixteen companies are on the Labor Department's banned list, including technology and fashion firms and even a dairy.[42]

Jiangtao Liu, the business development manager for autonomous driving at Intel, who went to the University of Michigan, is among those working in the United States on an H-1B visa, which he obtained in 2015. Says Liu: "The whole U.S. immigration system is a mess."

But Liu says the H-1B lottery is a crapshoot. "There is no guarantee you will win," says Liu, who was sponsored by Intel. At least 10 of his foreign-born Michigan classmates failed to get H-1B visas and had to leave the country—some to the United Kingdom, others to Australia. In a few cases, their companies reassigned them to subsidiaries abroad.

Liu says he received a three-year H-1B visa that will expire in 2019 and is eligible to apply for a three-year extension. But he also is thinking about applying for permanent residency. "It's a painful process," says Liu. ▪

Background

Immigrants Spur Economy

In the 13 colonies that became the United States, immigration and economic growth went hand in hand.

At Jamestown, Va., the first permanent English colony in North America, the settlers struggled to survive in the early years until they developed a marketable crop—tobacco. But planters needed a labor force, and they first tried indentured servants, an arrangement in which they paid for an English worker's passage to the colonies in return for several years of servitude—usually seven. When the system did not meet the needs of a growing economy, planters increasingly turned to using slaves, who were first brought to Jamestown from Africa in 1619.[43]

Outside of Virginia, immigration surged, with the Scotch-Irish and Germans making up the two largest groups. Between 1683 and 1775, more than 200,000 Scotch-Irish arrived, followed by some 111,000 Germans. By 1750, the colonial population had reached 1.1 million—a sixfold increase from 1700. The polyglot colonies were peopled by immigrants from across Europe; Pennsylvania alone was believed to be one-third German. The new arrivals built an agriculture-based economy, since most colonists were farmers or planters. The rest were artisans, shopkeepers, merchants or lawyers.[44]

Upon the outbreak of the Revolutionary War in 1775, immigration for the most part ceased and did not resume until after the fighting ended in 1781. In 1789 the U.S. Constitution took effect, and Article 1, Section 8, Clause 4 gave Congress the authority "to establish an uniform Rule of Naturalization." Congress then undertook a long line of legislative efforts to define and regulate immigration in the United States.

The Naturalization Act of 1790 declared that any alien who was a "free white person" was eligible to become a citizen after living in the United States for two years. At the time, about 4,000 white people a year were immigrating to the United States.[45] But that figure was about to swell.

In the 19th century the Irish and Germans were the dominant immigrant groups, along with many Chinese. Then Italian immigration surged with more than 4 million coming between 1880 and 1914, while Caribbean natives and more Chinese arrived later in the 20th century.[46]

One of the most notable British immigrants was William Colgate, who left Kent, England, with his family as a boy in 1795. Colgate settled in New York City in 1803 and soon decided that what New Yorkers needed was soap.

In those days, wrote historian Tyler Anbinder, "manufactured soap was considered a luxury item only the wealthy could afford." Most people either used no soap at all, leading to the term "the unwashed masses," or made a crude version by boiling fat drippings from their food with potash. This homemade soap, according to Anbinder, was "greasy, foul smelling and extremely abrasive."[47]

Colgate discovered that if he could significantly cut the price of soap, New Yorkers would be willing to buy it. By 1817, after much experimentation, Colgate was the leading soap in the New York market. By the 1840s, after he had added scent to his soap, Colgate's Manhattan factory was producing 20 tons of soap a day to keep up with demand.

Colgate later expanded well beyond soap to toothpaste, toothbrushes and mouthwash. Today, Colgate is one of the nation's best-known brands.

Great Famine

Ireland's Great Famine, a period of mass starvation and disease caused by catastrophic failures of the potato crop, killed 1 million people and led to the emigration of possibly 2 million more between 1845 and 1849. Most went to the United States, especially Boston and New York.[48]

Some of the earliest Irish arrivals joined New York City's ranks of prosperous businessmen, becoming known as "lace curtain Irish" because they took on an air of respectability. Other, less-educated Irish immigrants, known as "shanty Irish," worked on ships and raised pigs in the city's teeming neighborhoods.

Irish immigrants who settled near City Hall in lower Manhattan received an especially hostile reception. A nativist political party that opposed both immigrants and Catholics—the Native American Democratic Association—condemned the appointment of Irish-Americans to political office. In 1836, the party ran Samuel F.B. Morse, inventor of the single-wire telegraph system, as its candidate for mayor. However, Morse received only 6 percent of the vote, and the party soon faded.[49]

By 1860, the Irish had become New York's largest ethnic group—and they achieved a milestone of sorts in gender history that year: 35 percent of Irish-born women worked at jobs outside their homes, compared with 18 percent of other immigrant women.[50]

The leading jobs were in garment factories, domestic service and needle trades such as sewing; 4 percent of Irish women were listed as business owners, twice as many as other immigrant women.[51]

German immigrants were outnumbered by their Irish counterparts in New York, but they were numerous enough that a swath of the city was called Kleindeutschland—Little Germany. "What multitudes from Germany are in our midst," *The New York Times* wrote in 1855.[52] German influence spread far beyond New York to Chicago, Milwaukee, Cincinnati and smaller cities such as Ann Arbor, Mich.

Many German immigrants prospered, including artisans such as cabinetmakers and gilders, shoemakers, bakers, locksmiths, brewers and cigar makers. Germans owned half the grocery stores in New York, even in Irish neighborhoods.

German Levi Strauss arrived in New York just as men and women from all over the country were streaming to California and points west for the 1849 Gold Rush. He followed them to San Francisco in 1853 and by 1860 was selling tents, clothing and other dry goods to stores from Nevada to Hawaii.

After the Civil War, a tailor came to him with an idea for a more rugged pair of overalls with pockets reinforced with metal rivets. Blue jeans were born in 1873.[53]

But by far, German influence was felt most significantly in big business. John Jacob Astor, the country's first multimillionaire, was of German descent. So was Harvey Firestone, the founder of Firestone Tire and Rubber Co. Others included Henry Heinz, the ketchup company founder; Otto Kahn, the investment banker; Conrad Hilton, founder of the hotel chain; and Isaac Singer of the sewing machine company.

Nevertheless, German immigrants endured two waves of anti-German sentiment, one before and during World War I, the other during World War II.

"World War I had a devastating effect on German-Americans and their cultural heritage," wrote Katja Wüstenbecker, a historian of migration at the University of Jena, Germany.[54]

Until the war's outbreak in 1914, she said, German-Americans were viewed mostly as well-integrated and esteemed. "All this changed with the outbreak of the war. At once, German ancestry was a liability." In 1910, German-Americans made up about 10 percent of the U.S. population, and their presence in virtually every major U.S. city made them instant targets.

"The battle against all things German" ran from business to entertainment, Wüstenbecker said. Music halls closed. Teachers had to sign loyalty oaths. By March 1918, the teaching of German in schools had been restricted or ended in 38 of the 48 states, Wüstenbecker wrote.

In 1918, President Woodrow Wilson declared German-Americans to be "alien enemies." About 2,000 people were confined to internment camps in Utah, Georgia and North Carolina. To protect themselves, some German-Americans anglicized their family and business names. (In Britain, the royal family did so as well, changing its name from the House of Saxe-Coburg and Gotha to the House of Windsor.)

German-Americans were barred from living near military facilities and airports, and business owners had to turn over their books to an "alien property custodian."

After the war ended, Congress passed the Quota Act of 1921, which restricted immigration, and the Johnson-Reed Act of 1924, which banned immigration by anyone from Asian countries. The latter act also set quotas on immigrants from other places.

For instance, 34,000 visas were allotted to Great Britain, but just 6,000 to Poland and 100 to Greece. In all, quotas cut immigration to 164,000 annually in the late 1920s. The figures were not revised until after World War II.[55]

German immigrants faced a new round of trouble when the world went to war in 1939 and the United States entered it in December 1941. Some 11,000 German-Americans were interned during World War II. Ten times that many Japanese-Americans were sent to camps in the United States.[56]

Chinese Contributions

In the nation's early years prejudice stalked another important immigrant group: the Chinese. Migration from China to the United States came in two waves: the 1850s to the 1880s, when Congress halted Chinese migration, and from the 1970s to the present, after U.S.-China relations were normalized in 1972. As a result, Chinese immigrants are now the third-largest ethnic group in the United States, behind natives of Mexico and India.[57]

Chronology

1600s–1800s
Immigration fuels economy.

1607
Virginia Company founds the first permanent English settlement in North America at Jamestown.

1619
First slaves arrive in Virginia.

1775
Revolutionary War causes a near halt to immigration.

1790
Naturalization Act declares that "any alien, being a free white person, may be admitted to become a citizen."

1820
German immigration expands, peaking with about 1.4 million arriving between 1880–1890.

1845
Ireland's Great Famine prompts migration to the U.S. As many as 4.5 million Irish arrive between 1820 and 1930.

1849
Chinese immigration accelerates.

1882
After riots, Congress passes the Chinese Exclusion Act, virtually halting Chinese immigration.

1900s–1950s
Immigration backlash grows.

1907
Peak year for immigration as 1.3 million enter U.S.

1917
Anti-German sentiment builds with U.S. entry into World War I.

1924
Johnson-Reed Act curtails immigration; Asian immigrants are barred entry.

1930s
During the Depression, hundreds of thousands of Mexican immigrants are deported.

1941
U.S. enters World War II. Tens of thousands of Americans, most of Japanese descent, are declared "enemy aliens."

1942
Bracero Program allows Mexican workers to enter the U.S., easing a wartime labor shortage.

1952
McCarren-Walter Act ends Asian exclusion.

1960s–1990s
Illegal immigrations grows.

1965
Hart-Celler Act removes immigration quotas based on nationality.

1972
President Richard Nixon visits China and begins normalization of relations. The move opens the door to increased Chinese immigration.

1975
Vietnam War ends with fall of Saigon to communist forces; emigration from Vietnam, Thailand and Cambodia picks up.

1986
Immigration Reform and Control Act sets fines for employers who knowingly hire undocumented immigrants and amnesty for some 3.2 million undocumented immigrants.

1990
Congress creates the H-1B visa program for skilled foreign workers, allowing them to work in the U.S. for three years.

1996
Undocumented immigrant population reaches 5 million.

2000s–Present
Presidents Bush, Obama and Trump seek to change immigration policy.

2000
H-1B cap is raised to 195,000; in 2004, Congress lowers it to 65,000.

2006
Number of undocumented immigrants reaches 11.6 million.

2007
Congress rejects George W. Bush administration's attempt to create pathway to citizenship for long-time undocumented immigrants.

2012

President Barack Obama signs an executive order protecting undocumented children, known as "Dreamers." An appeals court blocks his actions; the Supreme Court upheld the ruling in 2016.

2014

Immigration reform efforts fail in Congress.

2017

President Trump tightens immigration policy, signing an executive order blocking refugee immigration and temporarily banning entry by nationals from seven Muslim-majority countries. An appeals court upholds a lower court's stay of the order.

A 'Dreamer' Fears for Her Family

Children who were undocumented when they arrived could face deportation.

Surf through the videos Maria Garcia posts on YouTube and you'll get a joyous picture of a young woman who loves the camera. She posts videos about eye makeup, nail polish, the Halloween costumes she makes and last-minute Christmas shopping.[1]

But one of her videos tells a far less upbeat story. Garcia, 20, of Los Angeles is a "Dreamer"—the child of parents who brought her to the United States as an undocumented immigrant. The name comes from a 2012 executive order, signed by then-President Barack Obama, called the Deferred Action for Childhood Arrivals program (DACA).

Under it, more than 725,000 young people provided personal information such as their passport numbers, school records and travel histories in order to obtain work permits, access to driver's licenses and the ability to get college educations. They received a renewable two-year moratorium on deportation.[2]

But DACA has been hotly debated, with opponents saying it encourages illegal immigration. Throughout his campaign for the White House, Republican candidate Donald Trump vowed to quickly repeal the act as part of his broader plan to expel undocumented immigrants. He has not moved to repeal DACA during his first weeks as president, during which he issued a temporary ban on entry to the United States of all refugees as well as immigrants from seven predominantly Muslim countries. (The ban has been stayed by a federal court.) Asked at a Feb. 16 news conference whether he will repeal DACA, Trump did not indicate what he will do, saying this "is a very, very difficult subject for me, I will tell you, . . . because you know, I love these kids."[3]

Garcia says she is watching the immigration debate with dread. "I'm scared for everyone in this undocumented situation," she says. "I can already see the number of families who are going to be affected by Trump's actions. I'm put in a situation where I would be very concerned over my family's safety and unity."

In 2014, House Republicans voted to defund DACA, saying it amounted to a temporary legalization program that ran counter to U.S. immigration law. (The vote had no impact on the program, because defunding failed in the Senate.)[4]

Mark Krikorian, executive director of the conservative Center for Immigration Studies, which wants to reduce immigration, derided the Dreamers act as "green-card lite"—a way for children of undocumented immigrants to permanently stay in the United States.[5]

Garcia, a junior at California State University who is majoring in communications, defends DACA. Her goal, she says, is to become an American citizen. She says her parents emigrated from Jalisco, Mexico, when she was a child and that her younger brother and sister—both born after her parents moved to California—are citizens. But she and her parents are undocumented. She says her father is working, but she declines to be more specific. Her mother is a homemaker.

Garcia says her parents "didn't see much of a bright future in our native country due to the lack of resources and poverty. This caused them to take the risk and migrate to the U.S. That decision has turned into a greater opportunity in education and well-being for myself and my siblings."

Garcia says she faces obstacles that American-born students do not. Obtaining financial aid in the form of student loans is one difficulty. Undocumented students are not eligible for federal assistance and must turn to private aid.[6]

Although she's been able to get small grants, "it is not enough," she says. "I've paid my taxes since I started working when I was 17. I have had to work a bit harder" than native-born students "for the chance to continue to pursue higher education," Garcia says.

It is also difficult for Garcia to travel outside the United States. Many of her fellow students have spent semesters abroad or have vacationed in other countries. For Dreamers, however, "the opportunity is very rare. You have to go through a lot of paperwork and investigation just to be allowed to go."

Says Garcia, "I yearn to learn and experience other cultures. I've heard from my professors that it is an experience that can open your mind and help you grow."

Garcia says her video about her Dreamer status generated personal stories and messages of support from her YouTube followers, but a number of people posted negative comments expressing opposition to the Dreamers act. "You are an illegal student, draining our resources," wrote one, who called himself Julio Iglesias, the same name as the Spanish singer.

"Dreamer = illegal immigrant. I think it's better you cut the bull and get to the point. You want something. For nothing," wrote another, called Onaturalia.[7]

Garcia calls the comments "very upsetting." But she says she will continue posting YouTube videos and, after graduation, will try to become an entrepreneur and create a scholarship fund for undocumented and low-income students.

Beyond that, she wants to create financial security for her family. That would be "part of achieving the American dream," she says.

—*Micheline Maynard*

[1] Maria Garcia's YouTube videos can be found at http://tinyurl.com/h9uvshj.

[2] Griselda Nevarez, "4 Years Later, Lives Built By DACA at Risk in 2016 Election," NBC News, June 15, 2016, http://tinyurl.com/hxzggkw.

[3] "Full Transcript: President Donald Trump's News Conference," CNN, Feb. 17, 2017, http://tinyurl.com/h2ceucw.

[4] Miriam Jordan, "Immigrants Benefit From White House Initiative," *The Wall Street Journal*, Sept. 5, 2014, http://tinyurl.com/hqa6oy3.

[5] *Ibid.*

[6] Federal Student Aid, U.S. Department of Education, http://tinyurl.com/ho9b48e.

[7] The comments were posted on YouTube at http://tinyurl.com/h73zucx.

In the early years, Chinese immigrants took mostly low-skilled and temporary jobs, working in mining, construction (especially helping build the nation's expanding railroads), manufacturing and service industries such as laundries and restaurants. Immigration records show that as many as 300,000 Chinese entered the United States in the first wave, although many returned to China, especially after Congress passed the Chinese Exclusion Act in 1882. That law barred Chinese immigrants from becoming U.S. citizens, a restriction that was not lifted until 1943.

In the 1950s, Chinese immigrants began to return to the United States. Some were escaping the oppressive policies of Communist leader Mao Zedong, while many came from the then British colony of Hong Kong, some arriving illegally.

However, Chinese immigration did not truly accelerate until President Richard M. Nixon and Mao normalized relations between the two countries in 1972. In 1980, Chinese immigrants in the United States numbered 385,000; by 2013, the figure topped 2 million, according to the U.S. Census Bureau.[58]

Unlike the first wave of Chinese migration, the second, still underway, tends to include immigrants who are well-educated and highly skilled. Most Chinese settle in California and New York; Chicago and Boston also are popular.

Nearly half of Chinese immigrants ages 25 or over hold a bachelor's degree or higher, compared with 28 percent of the total immigrant population and 30 percent of the native-born population. Their professions include management, business, science and the arts.[59]

Mexico's Ups, Downs

Today, Mexican immigrants are greeted warily in some parts of the country. The story was different during World War II.

In 1942, the United States and Mexico agreed on what became known as the Bracero Program, which allowed Mexican "guest workers" to fill agricultural jobs left vacant when American servicemen went to war. The Mexicans signed contracts allowing them to work in the United States, with some people coming back multiple times. In all, 4.6 million contracts were signed under the Mexican Farm Labor Program.[60]

Employers were supposed to hire *braceros* (manual laborers) only for jobs certified to have a domestic labor shortage. They also were barred from using the workers as strike breakers. In practice, employers took full advantage of this cheap labor, paying workers 30 cents an hour, according to government statistics. That was slightly higher than the rate for Texas agricultural workers in 1940 but well below the 81 cents an hour that agricultural workers were earning by the end of the war in 1945.[61]

Despite the low wages, workers routinely overstayed their contracts, prompting the Immigration and Naturalization Service in 1954 to undertake Operation Wetback, a pejoratively named policy in which more than 1 million Mexicans and their children were deported. But some major farmers protested and persuaded Congress to extend the Bracero Program.[62]

In 1980, 2.1 million Mexican immigrants were in the United States, according to the Census Bureau. By 2010, the total number of Mexican immigrants had mushroomed to 11.7 million.

Historians say a search for economic opportunity, political instability in Mexico and fears about crime spurred Mexican immigration to the United States.[63] Also, says Boston College's Skerry, many older Mexican immigrants did not intend to stay; their plan was to earn money and then return home.

Once in the United States, Mexican immigrants tend to achieve less than other immigrants and native-born Americans, according to the Migration Policy Institute, a Washington think tank that

Immigrants Help Tech Engine Run

"I don't know if we can close our borders and be self-sustaining."

Lesli Ann Mie Agcaoili, an engineer at Tesla Motors in Fremont, Calif., has a front-row seat to the role that immigrants play in the technology sector—and to their fears of the Trump administration's restrictive plans on immigration.

Throughout the day, she says, she interacts with co-workers from Mexico, Canada, Germany and Australia. She socializes with people from India, who shop in their own section of Fremont called Little India.

Agcaoili says it's normal to hear conversations in different languages. Lately, much of the talk has been about President Trump's executive order—which several federal courts have blocked—temporarily barring entry to nationals from seven Muslim-majority countries.

"It has crossed peoples' minds: 'What if I have to go back?'" Agcaoili says. "People who are here legally ought to be fine, but I think there is some fear and apprehension about the [Trump] administration."

Founded by Elon Musk, who was born in South Africa, Tesla sits among a sea of companies started by people from outside the United States. More than half of 87 technology companies individually worth $1 billion or more have at least one foreign-born founder, according to the National Foundation for American Policy, an immigration research group in Arlington, Va.[1]

About two-thirds of people working in computing and mathematics jobs in San Mateo and Santa Clara counties, which comprise Silicon Valley, were born outside the United States, said the Silicon Valley Institute for Regional Studies, the research arm of Joint Venture Silicon Valley, an organization studying the region's economy. Immigrants make up 60 percent of those working in engineering and architectural jobs.

Critics say Silicon Valley recruits cheap labor from overseas. The tech industry, they say, is especially misusing the H-1B program—special visas that allow a limited number of highly skilled foreigners into the country each year. Sixty-five percent of H-1B petitions approved in the 2014 fiscal year went to tech workers, most of whom were from India, according to the U.S. Citizenship and Immigration Services.[2]

Trump senior adviser Stephen Bannon has denounced "progressive plutocrats in Silicon Valley" who want the freedom to bring overseas workers into the United States. American graduates, as a result, can't find work in the tech field, Bannon complained in March 2016.[3]

However, Trump told technology executives in a recent meeting that his immigration order was intended to stop "bad people" from entering the United States, but said he was open to amending the H-1B program so talented workers can come.[4]

To Agcaoili, the thought of a technology sector minus immigrants makes no sense. "Just in terms of labor, they're vital to the companies and helping make them run," she says. "I just don't think it's going to be good for the economy" if the administration imposes immigration limits. "I don't know if we can close our borders and be self-sustaining."

For Agcaoili, a 45-year-old Asian-American, the issue is personal. Her father is Filipino and her mother's roots are in Japan. Born in Los Angeles, Agcaoili spent her childhood traveling between there and Hawaii, where her ancestors emigrated to work on plantations. Some of her mother's relatives were placed in internment camps during World War II.

Agcaoili, who has also worked for Ford Motor Co. in Dearborn, Mich., and the parent company of BlackBerry in Waterloo, Ontario, says immigration scares have happened before. In the early 2000s, when jobs were scarce, she says foreign-born classmates in business school were worried about whether they would be able to stay in the United States after they earned their degrees.

Continued

"It was a huge, huge deal," she says. "'Will you sponsor a visa?' That was the first thing anyone would talk about before figuring out if a job was a good fit."

Agcaoili says the multiculturalism of Silicon Valley is key to its companies' success. Tech CEOs argue much the same. The problem, they say, is not just a shortage of workers but the need to find the best talent possible. Restricting immigration "will make it far more difficult and expensive for U.S. companies to hire some of the world's best talent—and impede them from competing in the global marketplace," the CEOs of 100 tech companies said in a legal filing opposing Trump's executive order.[5]

Executives say this need extends far beyond Silicon Valley. Manufacturers in Columbus, Ind.—the hometown of Vice President Mike Pence—are heavily dependent on skilled immigrants. Dave Glass, CEO of LHP Engineering Solutions, said his company makes hiring American engineers a priority, but he can't find enough of them to fill openings. "In the last few years, we've had, like, three [Americans] apply," he said. So relying solely on domestic labor is "not an option" for his company, he said.[6]

—Micheline Maynard

[1] Shira Ovide, "Trump Win Is Silicon Valley's Loss on Immigration," Bloomberg News, Nov. 9, 2016, http://tinyurl.com/hx33jzr.

[2] Mica Rosenberg, Stephen Nellis and Emily Stephenson, "Trump, tech tycoons talk overhaul of H1B visas," Reuters, Jan. 12, 2017, http://tinyurl.com/grtljcr.

[3] Frances Stead Sellers and David A. Fahrenthold, "'Why even let 'em in?' Understanding Bannon's worldview and the policies that follow," *The Washington Post*, Jan. 31, 2017, http://tinyurl.com/htcvuhf.

[4] Rosenberg, Nellis and Stephenson, *op. cit.*

[5] Elizabeth Dwoskin and Craig Timberg, "How Canada is trying to capitalize on Trump's executive order," *The Washington Post*, Feb. 10, 2017, http://tinyurl.com/hw2cogg.

[6] Annie Ropeik, "Immigration Executive Order Causes Anxiety In VP Mike Pence's Hometown," NPR, Feb. 16, 2017, http://tinyurl.com/hxsa5l6.

researches immigration. Only 6 percent have college degrees, compared with 28 percent of all immigrants.[64]

Mexican immigrants, both legal and undocumented, are more likely to be employed in service occupations, construction and maintenance jobs than other immigrants or the native-born population, the institute said. Their wages are significantly lower than other immigrants', with their average household income in 2014 at $37,390, compared with $49,487 for all immigrants and $54,565 for native-born residents.[65]

But Mexican immigrants' income in the United States is three times the average household income in Mexico, according to the Organisation for Economic Co-operation and Development (OECD), a Paris-based economic research organization, made up of 34 developed nations, that promotes market-based economic policies. About 28 percent of workers in Mexico work more than 10 hours a day, compared with 13 percent of workers in other OECD member countries.[66]

The higher income helps explain why so many Mexicans risk crossing the border illegally, experts say.

The federal government in recent years has attempted to reform immigration policy, with much of the debate focusing on the economic implications of legal and illegal immigration.

In 1986 the Republican-controlled Senate and Democratic-controlled House passed, and Republican President Ronald Reagan signed, the Immigration Reform and Control Act, which among other things required employers to verify that their workers were in the country legally and created fines for businesses that knowingly hired undocumented immigrants. It also awarded "amnesty" to undocumented immigrants who had entered the United States before Jan. 1, 1982 But experts say the act did little to reduce illegal immigration.[67]

Since then, immigration-reform measures have repeatedly failed to pass, regardless of which party controlled the White House or the chambers of Congress. In 2007, Republican President George W. Bush pushed a comprehensive reform that sought to satisfy supporters and foes of immigration by providing legal status to undocumented migrants and giving them a pathway to citizenship while tightening border security.

He also proposed a controversial temporary worker program that he said would help meet the demands of a growing economy. "This program would create a legal way to match willing foreign workers with willing American employers to fill jobs that Americans will not do," Bush said. "Workers would be able to register for legal status for a fixed period of time, and then be required to go home." But critics opposed the temporary worker program, saying it would harm American workers, and they denounced the granting of citizenship to undocumented immigrants as "amnesty" for lawbreakers. The bill passed the House but died in the Senate. (Democrats controlled both chambers.)[68]

Democratic President Obama's administration tried again in 2013, proposing a reform package that went beyond Bush's. Besides giving undocumented workers a chance at citizenship and tightening border security, it included a new visa program for lesser-skilled workers and provisions designed to attract immigrants with needed work skills, such as in technology. Despite having bipartisan support and being passed by the Democratic-controlled Senate, the measure died after House Republicans opposed the citizenship provision as amnesty.[69]

The Obama administration, meanwhile, was aggressively expelling undocumented immigrants. In all, it deported about 3 million people during Obama's eight years in office, earning him the title of "Deporter-in-Chief" from some immigration groups critical of his policies.[70]   ▪

Current Situation

Immigration in Crosshairs

President Trump is moving aggressively against illegal immigration by cracking down on "sanctuary cities" (places that provide haven to undocumented immigrants) and loosening the rules on who can be deported. Businesses and immigrant advocates are warning in response that limiting immigration will hurt the U.S. economy.

To dramatize the importance of immigrants to the economy, advocates staged a "Day Without Immigrants" on Feb. 16 in which shops and restaurants nationwide closed for the day. Their goal was to show what would happen if the United States were to lose large numbers of foreign-born residents in a crackdown on illegal immigration.

"From doctors to dishwashers, immigrants are integral to daily life in the U.S.," said Janet Marguía, president and CEO of the National Council of La Raza, a Latino advocacy group.[71]

The protest was spurred by Trump's executive order on immigration, his proposal to build a wall on the Mexican border and his crackdown on sanctuary cities, as well as recent federal raids on workplaces.

Homeland Security Secretary John Kelly has signed sweeping guidelines that empower federal authorities to more aggressively detain and deport undocumented immigrants. The department also plans to hire thousands of additional enforcement agents and enlist local law enforcement to help make arrests.[72]

During the week of Feb. 5, U.S. Immigration and Customs Enforcement (ICE) agents arrested hundreds of undocumented immigrants in raids in Atlanta, Chicago, Los Angeles, New York and other cities. The raids and roundups created great fear among undocumented immigrants and their defenders. ICE, however, said the raids were not unusual and the alarms raised are greatly exaggerated. "We do not have the personnel, time or resources to go into communities and round up people and do all kinds of mass throwing folks on buses. That's entirely a figment of folks' imagination," a Department of Homeland Security official told reporters on a conference call. "This is not intended to produce mass roundups, mass deportations."[73]

In Durham, N.C., City Council member Schewel says he hopes authorities do not deport undocumented immigrants or restrict legal immigration. "I think this is one world, and to shut off the immigration spigot is to shut off the way this country was built and made great."

Immigration Restrictions

Tech companies, meanwhile, are campaigning against Trump's plans to tighten immigration controls. Immigration is the lifeblood of the technology sector, they say, with immigrants bringing much innovation to the economy. Half of the technology companies in the United States worth $1 billion or more are headed by chief executives with roots elsewhere, according to a letter signed by more than 200 industry leaders and investors. The roster includes Microsoft and Google, while firms such as Apple have sizable numbers of non-U.S. natives in their management and staff ranks.[74]

"In my conversations with officials here in Washington this week, I've made it clear that Apple believes deeply in the importance of immigration—both to our company and to our nation's future," Apple CEO Tim Cook said in a memo to staff in late January after Trump's immigration order was

At Issue:

Will limiting illegal immigration protect U.S. economic interests?

STEVEN CAMAROTA
RESEARCH DIRECTOR, CENTER FOR IMMIGRATION STUDIES

WRITTEN FOR *CQ RESEARCHER*, FEBRUARY 2017

The notion that enforcing our immigration laws will harm the economy is not supported by the facts. First, illegal immigration is a trivial share of the United States' $18 trillion economy, accounting for 2 or 3 percent of gross domestic product (GDP), according to Harvard's George Borjas, the nation's top immigration economist. This tiny addition to GDP almost entirely goes to the illegal immigrants themselves as wages and benefits.

Yes, the aggregate size of the U.S. economy would fall a little if these immigrants went home—fewer people means a slightly smaller economy.

But what matters is the per capita GDP—the nation's total output, divided by the number of people in the United States—and not aggregate GDP. And there is no indication that reducing illegal immigration would reduce the per capita GDP of natives or legal immigrants.

The best way to think about enforcement is that it creates winners and losers. If more immigrants here illegally went home, low-skilled Americans who compete with them would benefit. Borjas has estimated that by increasing the supply of workers, illegal immigrants may reduce wages by $99 billion to $118 billion a year. Their departure would mean higher wages at the bottom of the labor market. It also would mean that some of the 23 million working-age Americans with no education beyond high school who are not employed might find work.

The other winners from enforcement would be taxpayers. On average, adult illegal immigrants have only about a 10th-grade education. As a result, they tend to earn low wages, and this allows them—or more often their U.S.-born children—to qualify for welfare programs.

My own research indicates that 62 percent of such households use one or more major welfare programs. Consistent with all prior research, a 2016 report by the National Academies of Sciences, Engineering and Medicine found that immigrants with no education beyond high school create significantly more costs for government than they pay in taxes. As a result, the departure of those immigrants in the United States illegally would save taxpayers billions.

It is true that some low-wage employers and the illegal immigrants themselves would lose if we enforced our immigration laws. But the poorest and least-educated Americans would benefit, as would taxpayers. Furthermore, enforcing immigration laws could help reduce crime, enhance national security and restore the rule of law.

EDIBERTO ROMÁN
LAW PROFESSOR; DIRECTOR OF CITIZENSHIP AND NATIONALITY INITIATIVES, FLORIDA INTERNATIONAL UNIVERSITY

WRITTEN FOR *CQ RESEARCHER*, FEBRUARY 2017

Limiting immigration and undertaking mass deportations are not the solutions to the purported immigration crisis. In fact, the leading studies on the subject conclude mass deportation will harm the economy and is an irresponsible policy that will fail, especially if businesses' demands for undocumented labor continue.

The Immigration Policy Center, for instance, said mass deportation would reduce U.S. GDP by 1.46 percent a year. Over 10 years, the cumulative GDP loss would be $2.6 trillion, not including the actual cost of deportation. This approach would lower wages for higher-skilled natives and lead to widespread job loss.

Similarly, the Center for American Progress concluded the "costs of a massive deportation policy would not only be substantial, but in many ways, financially reckless."

A number of prominent Republicans agree. Tom Ridge, former secretary of Homeland Security, for instance, stated: "Attempting to deport everybody is neither feasible nor wise." Sen. John McCain, R-Ariz., said: "I have listened to and understand the concerns of those who simply advocate . . . rounding up and deporting undocumented workers. . . . But that's easier said than done. . . . I have yet to hear a single proponent of this point of view offer one realistic proposal for locating, apprehending and returning to their countries of origin over 11 million people."

Besides the economic costs, mass deportation is simply inhumane. The advocacy group Families for Freedom observed: "Every year, nearly 200,000 non-citizens—many with kids who are U.S. citizens—are deported and torn away from their families . . . resulting in more single-parent households and psychological and financial hardship, or forcing their U.S. citizen children into deportation with them."

It continued: "These American children may have to start over in a country with a new language, fewer resources and an uncertain future. America's immigration laws force American children to lose their parent or their country. Mandatory deportation is a life sentence of exile. Such a severe 'one size fits all' punishment cannot be the basis of our immigration system."

It is thus time to end to baseless assertions that immigration restrictions are a viable option to the immigration debate. We must turn to data, not demagoguery; we must demand facts and not merely accept economically baseless as well as inhumane rhetoric.

announced. "Apple would not exist without immigration, let alone thrive and innovate the way we do."[75]

"The reality is that high-skilled immigrants can choose where to go," said the University of Toronto's Florida. "Countries like Canada and Australia have come to understand the economic advantages of attracting immigrants, and have upped their efforts to attract the top talent from around the globe."[76]

On Feb. 9, Trump suffered another legal setback in his effort to temporarily ban immigrants from seven Middle East countries and halt the flow of refugees for 120 days. The San Francisco-based Ninth U.S. Circuit Court of Appeals refused to lift a lower-court suspension of his executive order, the result of a lawsuit filed by the state of Washington. Trump reacted harshly, saying the judges' motivations were political, the decision was "disgraceful" and the country's security was in peril.[77]

Trump's executive order had caught airports, airlines and immigration officials off guard. *The Washington Post* reported that administration officials were divided over the breadth of the order, especially when it came to holders of green cards, who also were temporarily barred entry back into the United States.[78]

In challenging the order, Washington state's attorney general argued that Trump's actions represented executive overreach and would hurt those who "have, overnight, lost the right to travel, lost the right to visit their families, lost the right to go perform research, lost the right to go speak at conferences around the world."[79]

Throughout the legal wrangling, Trump insisted that the Constitution gives the president wide latitude to set immigration policy, and government lawyers told the appeals court that the president has "unreviewable authority to suspend the admission of any class of aliens"—an assertion the three-judge panel rejected. The Justice Department told the appeals court on Feb. 16 that the administration will rescind the executive order and replace it with a new one.[80]

Sanctuary Cities

Businesses also are worried about the economic impact of Trump's crackdown on sanctuary cities, in which he is threatening to cut off federal funding to any municipality that offers safe haven to undocumented immigrants.

Currently, five states and at least 633 counties have adopted practices meant to shield undocumented residents and refugees from deportation, according to the Immigrant Legal Resource Center in San Francisco. Methods range from declining federal requests to hold arrestees in jail because of their immigration status to limiting police cooperation with federal agents.[81]

Twenty-eight universities also have declared themselves sanctuaries, including Columbia, Wesleyan and all 23 campuses of the California State University system.[82]

University of Michigan President Mark Schlissel said his school would continue to welcome applications from undocumented students and would not disclose information about the immigration status of its international students beyond what was required by law.[83]

But foes of illegal immigration, and some who want legal immigration reduced, say the United States needs to regain control of its borders so it can both keep potential terrorists out and protect American jobs. "Decades of record immigration have produced lower wages and higher unemployment for our citizens, especially for African-American and Latino workers," Trump said in his July acceptance speech at the Republican National Convention.[84]

No matter the outcome of the immigration debate and the court battle over Trump's executive order, Boston College's Skerry says the country is likely to remain divided.

Many Americans, he says, passionately believe immigrants should be allowed to enter the country and undocumented workers should be able to stay, because their own family members had made similar journeys in search of prosperity.

Several advertisements broadcast during this year's Super Bowl made pleas for inclusion and tolerance. An ad by Airbnb, for example, showed a series of people from different races, including a man with a turban. The subtitles read, "We believe no matter who you are, where you're from, who you love, or who you worship, we all belong. The world is more beautiful the more you accept." And in the most-talked about ad, Anheuser-Busch depicted German-born founder Adolphus Busch arriving in America, where he's greeted by people shouting, "Go back home!"[85]

Others, however, feel just as passionately that both legal and illegal immigration harms the economy because foreigners create more competition for jobs that Americans need and are often willing to work for less so they suppress wages.

When the supply of workers goes up, the price that firms have to pay to hire workers goes down" said George J. Borjas, an economics professor at Harvard University. "Wage trends over the past half-century suggest that a 10 percent increase in the number of workers with a particular set of skills probably lowers the wage of that group by at least 3 percent."[86]

Skerry thinks attitudes on both sides of the debate "are pretty dug in right now. The people who are going to feel sympathetic will feel sympathetic, and those who are angry will be angry, and they're going to feed off each other." ▪

Outlook

Searching for Solutions

President Trump remains determined to suspend immigration from seven Muslim-majority countries, and legal experts believe the Supreme Court ultimately may tackle the issue.[87]

In the meantime, Saxenian at Berkeley says immigrant executives and venture capitalists in Silicon Valley are watching closely to gauge whether to invest in the United States or in their overseas operations. She hopes the debate does not scare them—or their potential employees—away.

"To the extent that these ecosystems develop outside the United States, we want to make sure the U.S. remains attractive," Saxenian says. "We're in a space where anxieties over globalization are so strong that we could see a slowing down" of investment.

Minniti at Syracuse University says attracting younger immigrants is critical to keeping the U.S. economy competitive. "There is a strong correlation between age and starting a business," Minniti says, noting many businesses are started by people between the ages of 24 and 35 years old.

"You don't immigrate when you're 70," she says. "You immigrate when you're young." That's equally true for lesser-skilled immigrants, who continue to come to the United States in search of advancement.

"When you come, you want to work," Minniti says. "That is something that's innately entrepreneurial. They don't have the skills that others do in the workforce. But they are able and willing to do a lot of work, usually work that is physically demanding. These are usually the people who are accused of stealing American labor, but it is not true."

Boston College's Skerry says a compromise on immigration is possible. One solution conservatives could embrace, he says, is to establish a nationwide, government-sponsored effort to teach immigrants to become fluent in English. "It needs the oomph of a national campaign to encourage immigrants to learn English," he says, similar to the way Scottish-American industrialist Andrew Carnegie jumpstarted the library system by building libraries across the United States.

Such a campaign could "placate people who supported Trump who understandably have been concerned about the cultural changes that have been taking place," he says. "You tell all those people, 'English is really important. It's our language, and we want people to learn it.' I've never met many immigrants who don't want to learn English."

In the end, Minniti says immigrants everywhere are an easy target for changes caused by technology and changing consumer tastes. "It's not immigrants' fault. It's not the Chinese's fault. Unfortunately, the marketplace changes and requires readjustment. Who pays the price? People with lower skills."

Trump adviser Bannon would agree that Americans with fewer skills are the ones paying the price for globalization. But more immigration is not the answer, he said. The solution, he argued, is to gain control of national borders and construct an economic nationalism that focuses on the needs of the American economy over internationalism.

"Strong countries and strong nationalist movements in countries make strong neighbors," he said. "And that is really the building blocks that built Western Europe and the United States, and I think it's what can see us forward."[88] ■

End Notes

1. "Full Executive Order Text: Trump's Action Limiting Refugees Into the U.S.," *The New York Times*, Jan. 27, 2017, http://tinyurl.com/huz723.; Michael D. Shear and Ron Nixon, "New Trump Deportation Rules Allow Far More Deportations," *The New York Times*, Feb. 21, 2017, http://tinyurl.com/jtr2qmq.
2. Greg Bensinger and Rachael King, "Tech CEOs Take a Stand Against Donald Trump's Immigration Order," *The Wall Street Journal*, Feb. 6, 2017, http://tinyurl.com/hh893na.
3. Letter from the American Council On Education to Homeland Security Secretary John Kelly, Feb. 3, 2017, http://tinyurl.com/zptvsum.
4. Frances Stead Sellers and David A. Fahrenthold, "'Why even let 'em in?' Understanding Bannon's worldview and the policies that follow," *The Washington Post*, Jan. 31, 2017, http://tinyurl.com/htcvuhf.

5. Renee Stepler and Anna Brown, "Statistical Portrait of Hispanics in the United States," Pew Research Center, April 19, 2016, http://tinyurl.com/z7axefn. The definition of "Hispanic" varies by study, and the U.S. census permits people to self-identify as Hispanic or "Latino." See "Hispanic Origin Main," U.S. Census Bureau, http://tinyurl.com/hqbmd2s.

6. Jie Zong and Jeanne Batalova, "Asian Immigrants in the United States," Migration Policy Institute, Jan. 6, 2016, http://tinyurl.com/gqtyet4; "Asian-Americans Are Expanding Their Footprint in the U.S. and Making an Impact," Nielsen Company, May 19, 2016, http://tinyurl. com/hrq882b.

7. "Modern Immigration Wave Brings 59 Million to U.S., Driving Population Growth and Change Through 2065," Pew Research Center, Sept. 28, 2015, http://tinyurl.com/qhfo8js.

8. Jason Furman and Danielle Gray, "10 Ways Immigrants Help Build And Strengthen Our Economy," Obama White House Archives, July 12, 2012, http://tinyurl.com/hto2rum.

9. "Foreign Born Population," U.S. Census Bureau, 2017, http://tinyurl.com/jsbzqc5.

10. Richard Florida, "How Trump Threatens America's Talent Edge," *CityLab*, Jan. 31, 2017, http://tinyurl.com/jros2wj.

11. Alexia Fernández Campbell, "The Truth About Undocumented Immigrants and Taxes," *The Atlantic*, Sept. 12, 2016, http://tinyurl.com/zs9ud27; "The Fiscal Burden of Illegal Immigration on the United States Taxpayer," Federation for American Immigration Reform, 2013, http://tinyurl.com/od66dx3.

12. Cass R. Sunstein, "The Real Reason So Many Americans Oppose Immigration," *Real Clear Politics*, Sept. 28, 2016, http://tinyurl.com/gs9fa27.

13. Jeffrey S. Passel and D'Vera Cohn, "Size of U.S. Unauthorized Immigrant Workforce Stable After the Great Recession," Pew Research Center, Nov. 3, 2016, http://tinyurl.com/hvyqz7j; Anthony Cave, "Has Arizona's Economy Improved Because of Its Immigration Laws?" Politifact Arizona, March 3, 2016, http://tinyurl.com/z99ar2c.

14. "The Fiscal Burden of Illegal Immigration on United States Taxpayers," *op. cit.*

15. Peter Morici, "The real cost of illegal immigration," *The Washington Times*, Sept. 6, 2016, http://tinyurl.com/hd59gwf.

16. For background, see Sarah Glazer, "Welfare Reform," *CQ Researcher*, Aug. 3, 2001, pp. 601–632.

17. "Statistical Hot Air: FAIR's USA Report Lacks Credibility," American Immigration Council, March 29, 2011, http://tinyurl.com/hkdu5gz; Miriam Valverde, "Donald Trump Says Illegal Immigration Costs $113 Billion," PolitiFact, Sept. 1, 2016, http://tinyurl.com/hnuzdsa.

18. Marshall Fitz, Philip E. Wolgin and Patrick Oakford, "Immigrants Are Makers, Not Takers," Center for American Progress, Feb. 8, 2013, http://tinyurl.com/zlzc585.

19. Farm Labor Background Report, Economic Research Service, U.S. Department of Agriculture, 2017, pp. 3, 7, http://tinyurl.com/glrf3ar; Kenneth Megan, "Labor Shortages Make the Case for Immigration," Bipartisan Policy Center, Oct. 23, 2015, http://tinyurl.com/zht7oox.

20. Travis Putnam Hill, "In Texas, Undocumented Immigrants Have No Shortage of Work," *The Texas Tribune*, Dec. 16, 2016, http://tinyurl.com/hhdxy34.

21. Ike Brannon and Logan Albright, "Immigrations' Impact on the Texas Economy," Texas Public Policy Foundation, March 2016, http://tinyurl.com/jzcffbt.

22. Economic Profile, Greater Durham Chamber of Commerce, 2017, http://tinyurl.com/gu5t3bp.

23. Demographics, City of Durham, N.C., 2017, http://tinyurl.com/hdjx4oa; "Durham's Immigrant Communities: Looking to the Future," Latino Migrant Project, 2016, http://tinyurl.com/ztcwpzh.

24. Benjamin Wallace-Wells, "The Trump Administration's Dark View Of Immigrants," *The New Yorker*, Feb. 2, 2017, http://tinyurl.com/hpuk999.

25. Farei Chideya, "Trump's Blue Collar Base Wants More Jobs and an America Like the Past," *Five Thirty Eight*, Sept. 13, 2016, http://tinyurl.com/jrsvsas.

26. "Immigrant Small Business Owners: A Significant and Growing Part of the Economy," Immigration Research Initiative, Fiscal Policy Institute, June 2012, http://tinyurl.com/6vt5fae.

27. "Economic Impact of Immigration by State," WalletHub, Feb. 14, 2017, http://tinyurl.com/hvpc4yt.

28. "How States and Local Economies Benefit From Immigrants," American Immigration Council, http://tinyurl.com/goj2sge.

29. Miriam Jordan, "Heartland Draws Hispanics to Help Revive Small Towns," *The Wall Street Journal*, Nov. 8, 2012, http://tinyurl.com/z2vvqet.

30. *Ibid.*

31. Michigan Population Trends, Michigan Department of Health And Human Services, 2017, http://tinyurl.com/jdjdsk7; "Snyder Creates Office for New Americans," press release, Office of Governor Rick Snyder, Jan. 31, 2014, http://tinyurl.com/gu7e5d2.

32. "How Immigrants Are Helping Detroit's Recovery," *The Economist*, Feb. 16, 2017, http://tiny url.com/zqjqvbk.

33. "Taiwanese Companies in the U.S.," U.S.-Taiwan Connect, 2017, http://tinyurl.com/z3l28el; "Indian Companies Invest Billions in the U.S.," *The Wall Street Journal*, July 15, 2015, http://tinyurl.com/z5wsusa.

34. Sara Ashley O'Brien, "High-Skilled Visa Applications Hit Record High—Again," CNN Money, April 12, 2016, http://tinyurl.com/zs473gb.

35. Mica Rosenberg, Stephen Nellis and Emily Stephenson, "Trump, tech tycoons talk overhaul of H1B visas," Reuters, Jan. 12, 2017, http://tinyurl.com/grtljcr.

36. Paige Godden, "Jeff Sessions Considers Eliminating H-1B Program," *Des Moines Register*, Oct. 25, 2016, http://tinyurl.com/zrksa79.

37. Rosenberg, Nellis and Stephenson, *op. cit.*

38. *Ibid.*

39. *Ibid.*

40. Profile of Infosys, My Visa Jobs, 2017, http://tinyurl.com/jdqut2w, http://tinyurl.com/z7tdykv.

41. "Fearing Tighter U.S. Visa Regime, Indian IT Firms like Infosys, TCS Rush To Hire, Acquire," Reuters, Nov. 29, 2016, http://tinyurl.com/hoyw9h3.

42. "H-1B Debarred/Disqualified List of Employers," U.S. Labor Department, 2017, http://tinyurl.com/zhgkvmr.

43. Edmund S. Morgan, *American Slavery, American Freedom* (reprinted 2003).

44. Richard Hofstadter, *America at 1750: A Social Portrait* (1971), p. 19; Marianne S. Wokeck, *Trade in Strangers: The Beginnings of Mass Migration to North America* (1999), p. 46.

45. Naturalization Acts of 1790 And 1795, George Washington's Mount Vernon, http://tiny url.com/zhc729m.

46. Tyler Anbinder, *City Of Dreams, The 400-Year Epic History of Immigrant New York* (2016), p. xxv.

47. *Ibid.*, p. 110.

48. "Great Famine," *Encyclopedia Britannica*, Jan. 28, 2016, http://tinyurl.com/z7ntujp.

49. *Ibid.*, p. 124.

50. *Ibid.*

51. *Ibid.*, p. 188.

52. "New-York City: Germans in America," *The New York Times*, June 27, 1855. (URL not available.)

53. Our History, Levi Strauss & Company, http://tinyurl.com/zujk3n4.

54. Katja Wüstenbecker, "German-Americans In World War I," *Immigrant Entreprenuership*, Sept. 19, 2014, http://tinyurl.com/jpcxm8y.

55. "Who Was Shut Out?" *History Matters*, George Mason University, http://tinyurl.com/hzjoutz.

56. Tetsuden Kashima, *Judgment Without Trial: Japanese American Imprisonment During World War II* (2003), p. 124.

57. Kate Hooper and Jeanne Batalova, "Chinese Immigrants in the United States," Migration Policy Institute, Jan. 28, 2015, http://tinyurl.com/jqovnxs.

58. *Ibid.*

59. *Ibid.*

60. Bracero History Archive, 2017, http://tiny url.com/82huf75.

61. Marilyn Sworzin, "Wartime Wages, Income and Wage Regulation in Agriculture," *Bulletin of the U.S. Bureau of Labor Statistics*, 1946, Federal Reserve, http://tinyurl.com/gvutub4.

62. *Ibid.*

63. "Most Mexicans See a Better Life in the U.S.; One-In-Three Would Migrate," Pew Research Center, Sept. 23, 2009, http://tinyurl.com/nos7k7c.

64. Jie Zong and Jeanne Batalova, "Mexican Immigrants in the United States," Migration Policy Institute, March 17, 2016, http://tiny url.com/ln449qb.

65. *Ibid.*

66. Mexico, OECD Better Life Index, Organisation for Economic Co-operation and Development, 2017, http://tinyurl.com/3h6oasu.

67. Caroline Mimbs Nyce and Chris Bodenner, "Looking Back at Amnesty Under Reagan," *The Atlantic*, May 23, 2016, http://tinyurl.com/jn60627.

68. Mark Knoller, "The last president who couldn't get Congress to act on immigration," CBS News, Nov. 21, 2014, http://tinyurl.com/hc4qpy2.

69. Seung Min Kim, "Senate Passes Immigration Bill," *Politico*, June 28, 2013, http://tinyurl.com/hth3g3m.

70. Serena Marshall, "Obama Has Deported More People Than Any Other President," ABC News, Aug. 29, 2016, http://tinyurl.com/j7y6wy9. For more see, Reed Karaim, "Immigration Detention," *CQ Researcher*, Oct. 23, 2015, pp. 889–912.

71. Doug Stanglin, "Businesses across U.S. close, students skip school on 'Day Without Immigrants,'" *USA Today*, Feb. 16, 2017, http://tinyurl.com/jptxfhe.

72. David Nakamura, "Memos signed by DHS secretary describe sweeping new guidelines for deporting illegal immigrants," *The Washington Post*, Feb. 18, 2017, http://tinyurl.com/zdg6mln.

73. Nicholas Kulish, Caitlin Dickerson and Liz Robbins, "Reports of Raids Have Immigrants Bracing for Enforcement Surge," *The New York Times*, Feb. 10, 2017, http://tinyurl.com/hwgbj5j; and Lisa Rein, Abigail Hauslohner and Sandhya Somashekhar, "Federal agents conduct immigration enforcement raids in at least six states," *The Washington Post*, Feb. 11, 2017, http://tinyurl.com/jg2wcgm; David Nakamura, "Trump administration issues new immigration enforcement policies, says goal is not 'mass deportations,'" *The Washington Post*, Feb. 21, 2017, http://tinyurl.com/jh7xlk3.

74. April Glaser, "What Silicon Valley Can Expect Under Trump," *Recode*, Jan. 23, 2017, http://tinyurl.com/j5jchlq.

75. Jonathan Shieber, "Apple CEO Tim Cook Sent a Memo to Employees About the Immigration Ban," *Tech Crunch*, Jan. 28, 2017, http://tinyurl.com/jdrndk4.

76. Florida, *op. cit.*

77. Matt Zapotosky, "Federal appeals court rules 3 to 0 against Trump on travel ban," *The Washington Post*, Feb. 9, 2017, http://tinyurl.com/hxc6vd8.

78. Josh Rogin, "Inside the White House-Cabinet battle over Trump's immigration order," *The Washington Post*, Feb. 4, 2017, http://tinyurl.com/gpyx832.

79. Adam Liptak, "The President Has Much Power Over Immigration, but How Much?" *The New York Times*, Feb. 5, 2017, http://tinyurl.com/zu6rm79.

80. "The Ninth Circuit makes the right call on Trump's travel ban," *The Washington Post*, Feb. 10, 2017, http://tinyurl.com/j92wj6x; Julie Hirschfeld Davis, "Supreme Court Nominee Calls Trump's Attacks on Judiciary 'Demoralizing,'" *The New York Times*, Feb. 8, 2017, http://tinyurl.com/

gs6b8tl; and Brent Kendall and Laura Meckler, "Trump Administration Plans New Executive Order Next Week, Ends Legal Push in Appeals Court," *The Wall Street Journal*, Feb. 16, 2017, http://tinyurl.com/z4gfjvg.

81. Jasmine C. Lee, Rudy Omri and Julia Preston, "What Are Sanctuary Cities?" *The New York Times*, Feb. 6, 2017, http://tinyurl.com/hyrw4qc.

82. Yara Simon, "28 Universities That Vow to Offer Sanctuary to their Undocumented Students," *Remezcla*, November 2017, http://tiny url.com/gqx4mor.

83. Mark Schlissel, "Protecting the Interests of Our International Community of Scholars," University of Michigan, Jan. 28, 2017, http://tinyurl.com/z8pgh8r.

84. "Full Text: Donald Trump 2016 RNC draft speech transcript," *Politico*, July 21, 2016, http://tinyurl.com/gt4clje.

85. Michelle Castillo, "AirBnb cofounders personally edited the company's controversial Super Bowl Ad," CNBC, Feb. 6, 2017, http://tinyurl.com/hxkethm; Claire Atkinson, "Anheuser-Busch's Super Bowl ad tackles immigration," *New York Post*, Jan. 31, 2017, http://tinyurl.com/z3y6asl.

86. George J. Borjas, "Yes, Immigration Hurts American Workers," *Politico Magazine*, September/October 2016, http://tinyurl.com/hol5pmp.

87. Jeff John Roberts, "Trump's Travel Ban: The Supreme Court and What Happens Next," *Fortune*, Feb. 6, 2017, http://tinyurl.com/z9rgmah.

88. Sellers and Fahrenthold, *op. cit.*

FOR MORE INFORMATION

American Civil Liberties Union, 125 Broad St., 18th Floor, New York, NY 10004; 212-549-2500; www.aclu.org. Civil rights group that defends immigrants' legal rights.

American Immigrants Lawyers Association, 331 G St., N.W., Suite 300, Washington, DC 20005; 202-507-7600; www.aila.org. Association for immigration lawyers.

Arab-American Institute, 1600 K St., N.W., Suite 601, Washington, DC 20006; 202-429-9210; www.aaiusa.org. Represents Arab-American causes, including discrimination matters and immigration.

Center for Immigration Studies, 1629 K St., N.W., Suite 600, Washington, DC 20006; 202-466-8185; http://cis.org/. Conservative research group whose goal is to restrict illegal and legal immigration.

Federation for American Immigration Reform, 25 Massachusetts Ave., N.W., Suite 330, Washington, DC 20001; 202-328-7004; www.fairus.org. Advocacy group seeking limits on immigration that produced a widely quoted study on undocumented immigration.

Hispanic Federation, 555 Exchange Place, New York, NY 10005; 212-233-8955; http://hispanicfederation.org/. Network of 100 grassroots Hispanic organizations that provides education and job training resources to immigrants and their families.

National Council of Agricultural Employers, 525 9th St., N.W., Suite 800, Washington, DC 20004; 202-629-9320; www.ncaeonline.org. Lobbies on immigration issues and provides guidance to its members on immigration matters.

NumbersUSA, 400 Crystal Drive, Suite 240, Arlington, VA 22202; 703-816-8820; www.numbersusa.com. Advocacy group that wants to reduce legal immigration.

U.S. Border Control, PO Box 97115, Washington, DC 20090; 703-740-8668; www.usbc.org. Federal agency responsible for securing U.S. borders.

Bibliography

Selected Sources

Books

Anbinder, Tyler, *City of Dreams: The 400-Year Epic History of Immigrant New York,* **Houghton Mifflin Harcourt, 2016.**
   A George Washington University history professor tells the stories of immigrants and the role they played in defining a polyglot New York City.

Hsu, Madeline T., *The Good Immigrants: How the Yellow Peril Became the Model Minority,* **Princeton University Press, 2015.**
   An associate professor of history at the University of Texas, Austin tells the history of Chinese immigrants and their path from a loathed ethnic group to an educated and admired migrant group.

Peralta, Dan-el Padilla, *Undocumented: A Dominican Boy's Odyssey From a Homeless Shelter to the Ivy League,* **Penguin Press, 2015.**
   The author, whose family migrated from the Dominican Republic and became homeless, describes his impoverished childhood—and his rise to salutatorian at Princeton University.

Urrea, Luis Alberto, *The Devil's Highway: A True Story,* **Back Bay Books, 2005.**
   A writer tells the story of a group of 26 Mexican immigrants who got lost in the Arizona desert, of whom just 12 survived.

Articles

Borjas, George J., "Yes, Immigration Hurts American Workers," *Politico Magazine,* **September/October 2016, http://tinyurl.com/hol5pmp.**
   An economics professor at Harvard's Kennedy School of Government argues that during the 2016 presidential campaign, neither Republican Donald Trump nor Democrat Hillary Clinton gave a complete picture of immigration's impact on the United States.

Campbell, Alexia Fernández, "The Truth About Undocumented Immigrants and Taxes," *The Atlantic,* **Sept. 12, 2016, http://tinyurl.com/zs9ud27.**
   A journalist explains how many undocumented immigrants collectively pay millions of dollars annually in Social Security taxes, even though they are ineligible to collect retirement benefits.

Davis, Bob, "The Thorny Economics of Illegal Immigration," *The Wall Street Journal,* **Feb. 9, 2016, http://tinyurl.com/jo3pfbm.**
   A journalist explores the steps Arizona took to limit undocumented immigration and how it affected the state's economy, in both negative and positive ways.

Fitz, Marshall, Philip E. Wolgin and Patrick Oakford, "Immigrants Are Makers, Not Takers," **Center for American Progress, Feb. 8, 2013, http://tinyurl.com/zlzc585.**
   Analysts at a liberal public policy think tank look at ways undocumented immigrants contribute to the American economy and their potential for providing more value.

Glaser, April, "What Silicon Valley can expect under Trump," *Recode*, Jan. 23, 2017, http://tinyurl. com/j5jchlq.

Technology industry CEOs discuss their priorities, including immigration reform, during the Trump presidency.

Goodman, H.A., "Illegal immigrants benefit the U.S. economy," *The Hill*, April 23, 2014, http:// tinyurl.com/kefo83e.

The author looks at various data about undocumented immigrants, arguing that they make a positive contribution to the U.S. economy.

Koch, Edward, "Why Americans Oppose Amnesty for Illegal Immigrants," *Real Clear Politics*, June 2, 2010, http://tinyurl.com/255ulm3.

The late New York City mayor argued the United States should expand quotas for legal immigrants rather than allow those here illegally to stay.

Reports and Studies

Brannon, Ike, and Logan Albright, "Immigration's Impact on the Texas Economy," Texas Public Policy Foundation, March 2016, http://tinyurl.com/jzcffbt.

Researchers from a conservative think tank look at the impact of legal and undocumented immigration on the economy of Texas, which has the nation's second-largest number of undocumented immigrants.

Cadman, Dan, "President Trump's Immigration-Related Executive Orders," Center for Immigration Studies, February 2017, http://tinyurl.com/z442bxg.

A fellow at the Center for Immigration Studies, which favors limiting legal immigration, analyzes President Trump's actions on immigration.

Dimock, Michael, "How America Changed During Barack Obama's Presidency," Pew Research Center, Jan. 10, 2017, http://tinyurl.com/hwb8kbk.

A political scientist discusses the changes that took place during the Obama years, including the administration's policy moves on immigration.

Krogstad, Jens Manuel, Jeffrey S. Passel and D'Vera Cohn, "Five facts about illegal immigration in the U.S.," Pew Research Center, Nov. 3, 2016, http://tinyurl.com/gtmhrft.

The authors look at the demographics of the undocumented immigrant population and the immigrants' impact on the broader U.S. population.

The Next Step:

Additional Articles from Current Periodicals

H-1B Visas

Bloomfield, Doni, John Lauerman and Matthew Campbell, "Trump's H-1B Visa Crackdown Threatens Cutting-Edge U.S. Medicine," Bloomberg, Feb. 7, 2017, http://tinyurl. com/jo66u2w.

President Trump's travel restrictions could slow research and deplete the number of skilled immigrants at U.S. biotech firms, industry experts say.

Bukhari, Jeff, "Why H-1B Visas Aren't So Great for Silicon Valley Workers," *Fortune*, Feb. 15, 2017, http://tinyurl.com/zgoyyz9.
Although hiring foreign-born IT workers raised wages nationwide and lowered costs for computer products, domestic employment could have been 10 percent higher in the computer sector without immigrant labor, the author says.

Iyengar, Rishi, "H-1B debate: Trump is making India's tech industry nervous," CNN, Feb. 15, 2017, http://tinyurl.com/hy8lchb.
India's IT outsourcing industry, which generates about 10 percent of the country's gross domestic product, could suffer if President Trump restricts the available number of H-1B visas.

Immigrant-Owned Businesses

Chou, Elizabeth, "Immigrants fueled LA economy to tune of $232.9 billion in 2014," *Los Angeles Daily News*, Feb. 8, 2017, http://tinyurl.com/gptykm6.
Immigrants in Los Angeles County contributed about 35.7 percent of the region's economic output.

Delikat, Stacey, "Immigrant-owned restaurants host 'food diplomacy' meals," Fox 5 NY, Feb. 6, 2017, http://tiny url.com/j2rvybs.
New York-based "food tour guides" are looking to create a cultural bridge and foster community by highlighting restaurants with owners who are from countries affected by President Trump's travel restrictions.

Flynn, Kerry, "What the tech industry would look like without immigrants," *Mashable*, Jan. 31, 2017, http://tinyurl.com/jlpfsdu.
Immigrants and first-generation Americans played central roles in creating some of the United States' biggest tech companies, including Sergey Brin of Google and Jerry Yang of Yahoo.

New Legislation

Burnett, John, "Republican Lawmakers Propose New Law To Reduce Legal Immigration," NPR, Feb. 7, 2017, http://tinyurl.com/gnzxr2y.
A bill offered by two Republican senators would limit the number of green cards given to foreign nationals, slash the number of refugees admitted and remove the diversity lottery that gives visas to countries with low rates of immigration.

Carney, Jordain, "Senate Dems move to nix Trump's deportation order," *The Hill*, Feb. 16, 2017, http://tinyurl.com/jymr2fy.
A group of Senate Democrats introduced legislation to roll back President Trump's executive order on deportation.

Turque, Bill, "In era of Trump, CASA pushing for new laws in Maryland suburbs," *The Washington Post*, Feb. 9, 2017, http://tinyurl.com/jx79ue8.
CASA de Maryland, one of Maryland's biggest immigrant advocacy groups, plans to push for legislation in two of the state's counties that would codify longtime unstated protections for undocumented immigrants.

Political Unrest

Knefel, John, "Inside the Huge JFK Airport Protest Over Trump's Muslim Ban," *Rolling Stone*, **Jan. 29, 2017, http://tinyurl.com/j5j8ogs.**

In response to President Trump's executive order restricting travel from seven majority Muslim countries, thousands of protesters converged on JFK International Airport, setting off a wave of protests around the country, including in Silicon Valley.

Perez-Peña, Richard, and Katie Rogers, "Day Without Immigrants to Hit Washington in the Stomach," *The New York Times*, **Feb. 15, 2017, http://tinyurl.com/h68mmwc.**

Immigrant restaurant owners in Washington, D.C., including big names such as Zaytinya and Oyamel proprietor José Andrés and Busboys and Poets owner Andy Shallal, participated in the "Day Without Immigrants" campaign.

WEALTH AND INEQUALITY

SARAH GLAZER

Does the gap between rich and poor threaten democracy?

The very richest now claim a share of the world's wealth not seen since the Gilded Age of the late 1800s and early 1900s. The world's top 1 percent owns about half of global wealth and the bottom half less than 5 percent, according to French economist Thomas Piketty. President Obama is calling for a variety of steps to help struggling middle-class and poor Americans climb the income ladder and to provide more government revenue for programs benefiting the poor. Among his proposals are a hike in the minimum wage and an end to tax loopholes favoring the wealthiest Americans. Likewise, New York City Mayor Bill de Blasio swept to victory with a proposal to help pay for preschool programs for poor children by taxing the rich. But conservative economists say such measures would punish entrepreneurialism and stifle economic growth, arguing that wealth at the top translates into investment that creates jobs at the bottom.

The Issues

The excavation machines are busy these days in London's most fashionable neighborhoods, digging several stories under historic mansions to create the swimming pools, wine cellars and bowling alleys demanded by their wealthy owners.[1]

Yet many of these houses will remain empty most of the year, as their owners divide their time among other homes in Europe, Asia or the Middle East, according to real estate agents. London's prime homes are becoming a "global reserve currency" where the world's richest people can park their money, London journalist Michael Goldfarb recently wrote. He mourned the loss of neighbors joining the exodus of middle-class families no longer able to afford the city.[2]

In Miami, an apartment in a new luxury building designed by world-renowned architect Zaha Hadid gets the buyer a roof-top helipad and a private vault for storing precious jewelry and artwork. Prices start at $5 million and go up to $45 million for the duplex six-bedroom pent-house, whose 15,207 square feet include an indoor pool, media room, library, gym, staff quarters and more than 1,000 square feet of terrace.

These are just some of the more ostentatious signals that the very rich in the United States and around the world have been doing very well since the recession, even though many middle-class households still struggle. The astounding rise in wealth of the very few continues to make international headlines, such as the recent report by the anti-poverty charity Oxfam that the wealth of the world's 85 richest billionaires now equals that of the poorest half of the world's population.[3]

Once the backwater of economics and the concern of a few public-interest groups, the issue of income inequality—the term used for the growing disparity between the incomes of society's poorest and wealthiest sectors—is getting new attention on the national and international scene. The World Economic Forum, which sponsors the annual Davos gathering of the world's economic glitterati, recently declared the worsening wealth gap the problem most likely to pose a risk on a global scale, based on its survey of 700 experts.[4] The concern raised at Davos that increasing inequality threatens the political and financial stability of nations has also become a new focus of the 188-nation International Monetary Fund, which lends money to countries in trouble.[5]

"The reason we worry about inequality is [that] it's not a good thing to be a plutocracy," says liberal University of Texas-Austin economist James K. Galbraith.

Scott Winship, a senior fellow at the conservative Manhattan Institute think tank, suggests the current preoccupation with equality is related to economic anxiety during and following the recession. "I do believe if the economy picks up and unemployment goes back down to 5 percent, the interest in income inequality will go away again," he says.

In a widely discussed new book, Thomas Piketty, a professor at the Paris School of Economics, warns that rising inequality could threaten the very fabric of democracy and proposes confiscatory taxes on the rich. But those and other tax-increase proposals are strongly opposed by conservatives, who say high taxes stifle growth. Those critics argue that rising wealth at the top doesn't hurt those at the bottom, because as long as the economy is growing overall, all will benefit.

Liberal economist Paul Krugman, a *New York Times* columnist and Nobel Prize winner, is among those referring to the current era as a new Gilded Age, harking back to the 19th century, when so-called "robber barons" such as J. P. Morgan and John D. Rockefeller were accused of accumulating enormous wealth at the expense of the new industrial working class.[6]

Wealthiest Americans Control Record Share of U.S. Income

The wealthiest 10 percent of Americans controlled half of the nation's income in 2012, the largest share since just before the Great Depression.

Income Share of Top 10 Percent of Americans, 1917–2012

SOURCE: Emmanuel Saez, "Striking it Richer: The Evolution of Top Incomes in the United States (Updated with 2012 preliminary estimates)," University of California-Berkeley, Sept. 3, 2013, http://elsa.berkeley.edu/~saez/saez-UStopincomes-2012.pdf; data from http://elsa.berkeley.edu/~saez/TabFig2012prel.xls

In the United States, research shows growing inequality, with the richest 10 percent of families now capturing half of all personal income, a level not seen since 1917 and even greater than the Roaring '20s, according to University of California-Berkeley economist Emmanuel Saez.[7]

Even starker is how far the richest households in America have pulled ahead of everyone else since the 2007–2009 recession. The top 1 percent—those with annual incomes of more than $394,000—saw their incomes grow by 31 percent in the three years following the end of the recession, compared with a less than 1 percent gain for the other 99 percent. As a result, that upper stratum captured 95 percent of the nation's income gains during the recovery, Saez calculates.[8]

The United States reflects a global trend toward concentration of wealth, according to *Capital in the Twenty-First Century*, Piketty's new book. Worldwide, inequality now appears comparable to stratified Europe in 1900–1910, with the top 1 percent holding about half of global wealth, and the rest of the population owning less than 5 percent, according to Piketty.[9]

President Obama has contrasted today's stagnating middle class incomes with the post-World War II years, when wages rose along with the nation's economy. "[F]or some, that meant following in your old man's footsteps at the local plant, and you knew that a blue-collar job would let you buy a home, and a car, maybe a vacation once in a while, health care, a reliable pension," Obama said.[10]

Conservative economists and some liberals say that rosy period of middle-income growth in the 1950s-1970s was unique—before American manufacturing faced global competition and before a high-tech economy required more than a high school education to support a family.

Those factors drove down wages for the less educated: "This is part of globalization and all these changing things about society you can't put back in the bottle," says Salim Furth, senior policy analyst in macroeconomics at the Heritage Foundation, a conservative think tank in Washington. "If [employers] are going to compete, they have to pay global wages," Furth says.

Writing in the op-ed pages of *The Wall Street Journal*, commentator Mickey Kaus, author of *The End of Equality*, suggested Americans are more concerned about social inequality than income inequality. "Do we remember the 1950s as a halcyon egalitarian era because the rich weren't rich—or because rich and poor had served together in World War II?" he asked. He questioned the growing preoccupation with income differences: "If the poor and middle class were getting steadily richer, would it matter that the rich are getting richer much faster?"[11]

Like Kaus, others on the more conservative end of the spectrum who have studied recent trends, tend to agree that income inequality has increased, though some experts say it has increased less drastically than Piketty claims.

Winship of the Manhattan Institute says Piketty has "overstated" the differences between growth in wealth among the richest and poorest because he failed to include safety net programs such as food stamps for the poor. Winship points to a calculation by the Congressional Budget Office that finds—after taxes and employer fringe benefits are accounted for—that the top 1 percent increased their share of national income between 1979 and 2007 from 7 to 17 percent, less than Piketty's 10 to 24 percent.[12]

Even when conservatives accept the general direction of Piketty's findings, they tend to disagree with the implication—that a growing share at the top means less wealth for those below. In testimony before the congressional Joint Economic Committee in January, Winship said living standards have improved for the middle class even as income inequality has grown. "Inequality was high and rising during the late 1990s," he noted, "but because the growing economy was largely benefiting everyone, few people were worried about income concentration at the top."[13]

Liberals such as Yale political science professor Jacob S. Hacker argue that middle-class incomes have stalled mainly because of government policies supported by the rich: "Government rewrote the rules," in three areas, leading to weakening of unions, weakening of oversight of financial markets and looking the other way on exploding executive pay, he says.

However, Winship points out that economic growth has slowed not only in the United States but also in Japan and Europe. "We are talking about global economic trends that are not specific to the U.S.," he says, citing global competition and a freer labor market. "It's not that we crushed unions and that's the whole story," he says, or that pro-union European countries have done a lot better.

"We are the 99 percent," the 2011 slogan of the protest movement Occupy Wall Street, called attention to the advantages of the wealthiest 1 percent, and recently some politicians have taken up the cry. New York City Mayor Bill de Blasio, elected after promising to reduce the gap between rich and poor,

U.S. Has Highest Share of Millionaires

Of the world's millionaires, 42 percent are from the United States, by far the largest share. Canada, France, Germany, Italy, Japan and the U.K. account for a combined 33 percent share of the global total.

Share of Millionaires by Country of Residence

- Japan
- France
- Germany
- United Kingdom
- Italy
- China
- Australia
- Canada
- Switzerland
- Sweden
- Spain
- Taiwan
- United States

NOTE: Percentages do not add to 100 because of rounding.

SOURCE: "Global Wealth Report 2013," Credit Suisse, p. 23, https://publications.creditsuisse.com/tasks/render/file/?fileID=BCDB1364-A105-0560-1332EC9100FF5C83

advocated increased taxes on the wealthy to fund universal pre-kindergarten. On the federal level, Obama has also proposed increasing taxes on the wealthiest Americans.

Yet conservatives warn that raising taxes on the rich will hurt the entire economy because the wealthy will have less money to invest in job-producing activities that benefit the rest of the population. "There is a large literature that high tax rates clearly hurt growth," says the Heritage Foundation's Furth.

Experts and the public remain deeply divided about growing wealth at the top and its implications for everyone else. Here are some of the questions being debated in the press, academia and the political arena:

Does income inequality hamper economic growth?

Middle-class stores like Sears and JCPenney are closing down in malls and downtowns across America, and mid-priced restaurants like Olive Garden and Red Lobster are struggling.[14] Meanwhile upscale dining chains like Capital Grille are thriving as the rich account for a bigger slice of U.S. consumption, *The New York Times* recently reported.[15]

Some economists say the shrinking of middle-class consumption could seriously hurt economic growth—and that a sluggish recovery may already reflect reduced consumer demand.

The top 5 percent of U.S. earners were responsible for 38 percent of domestic consumption in 2012, up from 28 percent in 1995, according to a recent study by two economists from the Weidenbaum Center at Washington University in St. Louis.[16] Since 2009, spending by those top earners rose 17 percent, compared with 1 percent among the bottom 95 percent.[17]

Some economists and activists blame this phenomenon on stagnating middle-class wages since 1980. A middle-income family would have had $18,897 more to spend in 2007, the year before the recession, if there "had been no growth in income disparities since 1979," according to the Economic Policy Institute, a liberal think tank in Washington that focuses on working Americans.[18] More spending from those families would have helped stimulate the economy, argues Princeton economist Alan Krueger, who was a top economic adviser to Obama from 2009 to 2013.

If the shift in income to top earners in recent years had been more evenly distributed, Krueger calculates that annual consumption would be $400 billion to $500 billion higher today, equal to 3.5 percent of gross domestic product (GDP).[19]

Conservatives counter that investment is just as important as consumption to a growing economy and that more wealth at the top means more investment, with benefits trickling down in the form of new jobs. "The combination of more investment, innovation and risk taking at the top that's been facilitated by rising income" has contributed to continued economic growth, says the Manhattan Institute's Winship.

Winship estimates that the increase in the top 1 percent's share of national income between 1979 and 2007 raised GDP during that period and therefore increased household income for the middle class.[20]

"If the top 1 percent continues to get a bigger share of a pie that grows fast enough, then the middle class and poor may receive pretty big gains themselves," he says. The rising share of national income going to the wealthiest—the statistic cited by Piketty that has attracted so much recent attention—"may be the wrong indicator to focus on," Winship says.

One reason the United States may have more inequality than other rich countries is that "we honor entrepreneurs more," says Heritage's Furth. When a young unknown like Bill Gates suddenly becomes a millionaire, he pulls far ahead of everyone else.

"I don't think there's any evidence that inequality hurts growth," says Furth. "The United States has remained at the top of GDP per capita charts for large countries for 60 to 80 years," he says, pointing out that the median household in the United States earns more than its counterparts in countries including Great Britain, France, Italy and Spain.

But others say the pie is being divided unfairly even amid growth. "As long as productivity is growing, someone's getting the money; it just ain't America's middle class," says Heather Boushey, executive director of the Washington Center for Equitable Progress, a project studying inequality at the Center for American Progress, a liberal think tank in Washington.

Economists generally agree that some amount of inequality is inevitable once a country shifts from a mainly agrarian economy, where most people are living at a more or less equal subsistence level, to an industrialized economy.[21]

That theory was first advanced by the influential American economist Simon Kuznets in the 1950s and 1960s. As Piketty explains, Kuznets theorized that as countries shifted to industrialized economies the disparities between those living off the land and those in factory jobs would increase inequality "because only a minority of people would be prepared to benefit from the new wealth." In later stages of a country's development, Kuznets believed, inequality would automatically decrease as a larger and larger fraction of the population shared in economic growth.[22]

"For any kind of functioning economy, you wouldn't want inequality to be zero," says UT-Austin's Galbraith. However, he adds, "It's like blood pressure. . ... When inequality is going up rapidly, it's a sign you have trouble."

A recent international comparison by the International Monetary Fund (IMF) finds countries that have lower inequality, after taking into account taxes and welfare benefits, tend to have "faster and more durable growth."[23]

An earlier study from the IMF, one of the most frequently cited in this debate, found slower recovery from down-turns in countries with high inequality. But "its boosters generally fail to note that only developing nations are examined," says Winship.[24]

"To generalize from that to industrialized countries and the U.S. is egregious," Winship says. Instead, he cites another study supporting his view that "economic growth has benefited from rising inequality" by leaving poor and middle-class households "with a smaller share of a bigger economic pie and no worse off for it."[25]

With so many studies on both sides of the debate, and with conclusions that vary depending on which countries and periods of time they examine, there probably isn't a one-for-one relationship between inequality and growth, concludes Hacker, the Yale political scientist. "The more relevant question is, 'Does income inequality hamper middle-class income growth?'" he says. "In the U.S. you had a big increase in average incomes, but most of that's driven by the rise at the very top."

Increasingly, experts on both right and left have been pointing to America's highly unequal educational system, in which affluent suburbs provide far better public schools than struggling inner cities, as a root cause of inequality. However, they disagree on the solutions—school choice for Republicans, universal pre-kindergarten for Democrats.

That educational gap between rich and poor hurts the economy because the nation doesn't make the most of all its talented citizens, most experts agree. A recent report shows that the gap between low-income and upper-income children in obtaining a college education is large and widening.[26]

In a recent *New York Times* column, liberal economist Krugman said the educational divide "represents a huge and growing waste of human potential—a waste that surely acts as a powerful if invisible drag on economic growth."[27]

Are parental background and inheritance becoming more important for success?

In his book, economist Piketty finds a trend echoing the aristocratic class system described in the 19th-century novels of British writer Jane Austen and French writer Honore de Balzac: Inherited wealth in some European countries is becoming as important for individual financial success as it was in the 19th century, he writes. Inherited wealth accounts for nearly half of the total amount of the largest fortunes worldwide, he estimates.[28]

Even in the United States, where inheritance has historically been less important than in Europe, wealth is providing an ever-more cumulative advantage, Piketty argues, because wealth begets more wealth once invested.

According to *Forbes*' global billionaires list, the top wealth holders have seen their wealth rise at 6 to 7 percent per year from 1987–2013, a rate more than three times faster than the growth in income and output at the global level.[29] That means rich people can accumulate wealth at far higher rates than the majority of workers, whose wages grow no faster than the economy or their own productivity, Piketty argues.

In an interview, Piketty explained, "If wealth is rising three times as fast as the economy and this goes on for several decades, it means the middle class is vanishing and a rising fraction of national wealth will be taken by a small fraction" of people at the very top.

"It's not sustainable unless you are able to accept an oligarchic concentration of wealth, which is not fully compatible with the democratic idea," says Piketty, whose solution is a global tax on wealth combined with higher income taxes on the richest in the United States.

"Growing income and wealth inequality is skewing our democracy: We're supposed to have a system where every vote counts but where increasingly money counts," says Lawrence Mishel, president of the Economic Policy Institute, a liberal think tank in Washington.

In his January State of the Union speech, Obama declared that "upward mobility has stalled" and stressed the need to build "ladders of opportunity into the middle class."[30] Conservative Republicans Rep. Paul Ryan of Wisconsin and Florida Sen. Marco Rubio have given speeches in recent months bewailing social immobility and saying there should be more reward for people who work hard.[31]

But a recent study finds upward mobility in the United States is at a level similar to a generation ago.[32] Yet, many don't see that as good news because it still means most families at the bottom never make it to the top. According to a study led by Harvard economist Raj Chetty, the probability that a child born in 1971 in the bottom fifth of incomes would make it to the top fifth was 8 percent, compared with 9 percent for children born in 1986.[33]

And mobility in the U.S. is about half that in some Scandinavian countries. In Denmark, a poor child has twice the chance of making it to the top fifth as in America.[34]

A new study by University of California-Davis economist Gregory Clark finds the elite status of aristocratic families is amazingly resilient over generations even in a country like Sweden, famous for its income equality.[35] His finding runs counter to most previous studies, which find more upward mobility in Europe and Scandinavia than in the United States.

The American dream of upward mobility for all "is clearly a myth," he recently told a London audience, based on his study of the persistence of elite families in professions like medicine and law.

Clark uses an unconventional method—tracking elite surnames over centuries—and comes to an unconventional conclusion: "We can't find any society that is achieving high rates of social mobility," he says, concluding, "It's not going to be worthwhile making massive social investments in trying to improve social mobility." But he does favor Scandinavian-style welfare to produce more income equality.

There's no question that Sweden's system of welfare benefits evens out differences in income, making that nation one of the most equal of rich countries. Sweden starts out similar to the United States in inequality if just incomes paid by employers before taxes and welfare benefits are counted. In the United States, "The really big story is [that] we redistribute much less," says Janet Gornick director of the Luxembourg Income Study Center, of Luxembourg and New York.

Many policymakers maintain there are ways to boost social mobility in America without recreating a Swedish welfare state. Ron Haskins helped design 1996 welfare reform legislation as a Republican congressional staffer, later serving as a White House adviser to Republican President George W. Bush, and currently serving as a senior fellow in economic studies at the centrist Brookings Institution think tank. He says that with a college diploma, young people born into low-income families can quadruple their chance of making it to the top of the income ladder—from 5 percent to 20 percent.

However, Haskins stresses the role of personal responsibility. In 2009, he analyzed census data to see how adult Americans were doing if they followed three norms of modern society: finish high school, get a full-time job, and wait until age 21 to get married before having children. Young adults who followed all three had only a 2 percent chance of winding up in poverty and a 74 percent chance of reaching the middle class, he found.[36]

"Liberals are very reluctant to talk about personal responsibility because it's blaming the victim," Haskins says.

In the United States, unlike in 19th-century Europe or even in the early 20th-century England portrayed on the PBS series "Downton Abbey," the very wealthy tend to be the "working rich," and there hasn't been a big increase in inherited wealth since the 1980s. In fact, wealth transfers as a proportion of net worth have fallen from 29 percent to 19 percent between 1989 and 2007.[37]

That's a big contrast to Europe, where French economist Piketty finds inheritance is reaching levels not seen since the 19th century as a share of national income.[38]

However, when Piketty looks more broadly at accumulated wealth globally, not just inheritance, he finds it comparable to the levels in Europe in 1900–1910, during France's so-called Belle Époque, when industrialists were accumulating wealth and there was a large underclass. Today the top 1 percent owns about half of all global wealth and the bottom half less than 5 percent.[39]

Wealth, inherited or not, is a huge advantage in becoming even wealthier, Piketty says, because the wealthy have financial advisers and can afford high-risk, high-return investments, compared with the small saver, who can't afford to risk any part of a nest egg.

Yet Americans still believe in the rags-to-riches American dream, polls by the Pew Charitable Trusts find.[40] That may be because most families (84 percent) are making more than their parents, notes Erin Currier, director of economic mobility research for Pew. But the glass is only half-full. "For families at the bottom, yes, they have more money than their parents, but often the increase is so small that it's not enough to move them out of the bottom," she says. Seventy percent of children born into families in the bottom 20 percent never even make it to the middle class as working adults, according to Pew.[41]

Should the wealthy be taxed more?

Increasing taxes on the rich has received new attention as Obama and New York Mayor de Blasio have called on the wealthy to share more of the burden.

A controversial proposal by French economist Piketty to impose a global tax on "wealth"—including all assets such as trusts, partnerships and stocks—has also stimulated debate. To keep the rich from evading the tax by moving their money abroad, such a tax should be global, Piketty argues. While conceding that it is probably utopian to think all governments would agree to that measure, he suggests it would "realistic" for Europe.

For Piketty, his brash proposal is a way to draw attention to his central concern: Accumulating capital is conferring unfair advantages on the rich in a cycle that could eventually see the disappearance of the middle class. "The point is not just to raise taxation—it's to help the diffusion of wealth and make sure the wealth of the middle class expands rather than continues to shrink," he says.

And he thinks this is a more effective way to tax the rich than solely through income tax. "If some people are taxed on the basis of declared incomes that are only 1 percent of actual incomes, then nothing is accomplished by raising income tax rates to 50 or even 98 percent," he writes.[42]

Heritage Foundation conservative Furth objects that taxing capital is like penalizing the modest Swedish millionaire who invests to create jobs and drives a beat-up Saab while favoring the decadent consumption of a "Wolf of Wall Street"-style millionaire.[43] "Investment helps everyone else, consumption only helps you. If you want to help labor, tax capital at zero," he says.

In a recent critique of Piketty's book published in *The Wall Street Journal*, Christopher DeMuth, Republican President Ronald Reagan's deregulation czar in the 1980s and now a distinguished fellow at the conservative Hudson Institute, argued that in practice income redistributed by government often ends up in the hands of the powerful rather than the needy. The pro-government "intellectual imagines redistributing capital profits while leaving owners with the losses, but the opposite—profits for owners and managers, losses for taxpayers—has been frequently observed in the wild," he wrote.[44]

Some concerned about inequality in the United States have proposed raising income tax rates on the rich—now at 39.6 percent on the highest income bracket. Political scientist Hacker says that rate kicks in well below the richest of the rich. He has proposed raising the top rate on the truly rich—to 45 percent for those with annual incomes between $1 million and $10 million and to 49 percent for those with income of $1 billion or more.[45]

Hacker argues that the prospect of such high taxation would stem extremely high corporate pay packages—which have skyrocketed in recent years—because so much would get taxed away. He predicts "companies would pay slightly smaller packages and plow some of that into firm investment or

Americans Divided on Action to Curb Inequality

A majority of Americans belonging to both political parties agree that economic inequality has worsened over the past decade, according to a recent survey. However, 90 percent of Democrats interviewed say the government should take "a lot" or "some" action to reduce the gap, compared with 69 percent of independents and 45 percent of Republicans.

Percent who say the gap between the rich and everyone else has increased (by political party)

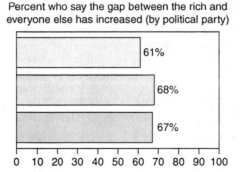

Percent who say government should take a lot or some action to reduce the gap (by political party)

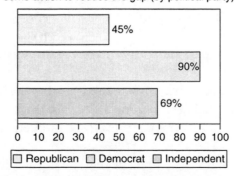

☐ Republican ☐ Democrat ☐ Independent

SOURCE: "Most See Inequality Growing, but Partisans Differ over Solutions," *Pew Research Center*, Jan. 23, 2014, www.people-press.org/2014/01/23/most-see-inequality-growing-but-partisans-differ-over-solutions/

salaries for the rank and file. But the main reason to do it is to raise money and assure the tax code is progressive all the way up the income distribution." (A progressive income tax is one in which the tax rate increases as the payer's income increases.)

Arguments for taxing the rich often stem from "a misguided belief that the economy is a zero-sum game and that reducing the position of the top 1 percent automatically improves everyone else's," Sendhil Mullainathan, a professor of economics at Harvard, cautioned in *The New York Times*.[46]

In a recent public debate, conservative supply-side economist Arthur Laffer argued that the rich already pay enough—more of the nation's income tax than anyone else. He also argued, "You aren't going to get the money from these guys. They can hire lawyers, they can hire accountants. . . . they can hire congressmen, . . . senators."[47]

Former Labor Secretary Robert Reich, who served in the administration of Democratic President Bill Clinton, countered that the country's budget deficits require tax increases and that those ought to come mostly from people at the top because "people at the top have never had it so good."[48]

Conservatives like Furth cite findings that high taxes on the rich remove incentives to continue working and thus ultimately hurt growth. "I'd argue incentive effects matter. Even if the rich have a Learjet, they want more money and are willing to work for it and create more businesses," he says.

That was the argument of Reagan, under whose administration top rates were lowered, as recommended by Laffer. But, says the University of Texas' Galbraith, "We taxed the rich a lot less 34 years ago and got no more investment."

Rather than a high income tax, Galbraith favors a high estate tax to "actively discourage dynasty building." Piketty does not: "Life is very long these days," he says. "If you wait until people die to regulate the consumption of wealth it will be too long; you need a lifetime wealth tax."

Ultimately, the argument comes back to whether the income of the wealthy should be redistributed through the tax system to counter inequality. Haskins of Brookings argues that on that score the "government is already fighting inequality dramatically." Households at the bottom of the ladder earning $8,100 a year received almost $23,000 in government benefits in 2010, including Social Security and Medicare, according to the Congressional Budget Office.[49]

However, those transfers still leave the United States far behind Scandinavia and some European countries on equality measures, because those countries have far more generous welfare benefits.

Yet a self-described budget hawk like Haskins questions how much more the government can afford to do. "After all, we're spending $1 trillion between the federal government and the states on benefit programs, and our tax system is hugely progressive: The upper 20 percent pay over 90 percent of federal income taxes," he says.[50] "You want the rich to pay 96 percent of federal income taxes?"

Even some liberal activists who are calling attention to growing inequality say they're more interested in seeing changes that create more opportunity—like a higher minimum wage, more jobs and more bargaining power for workers. "I think we need to have more taxes on the best-off, but I think what matters for me is what happens in the marketplace," says the Economic Policy Institute's Mishel.

Pointing to trends such as the growing competitiveness of foreign workers and the education gap between rich and poor, Urban Institute tax expert Eugene Steuerle, who served in four White House administrations, both Republican and Democratic, cautions, "The forces in society that are leading to inequality are much larger" than the solutions currently proposed such as "nipping at the taxes the rich pay or bumping up the transfers that low-income people receive." ▪

Background

'Fatal Ailment'

Ancient philosophers and their Enlightenment heirs believed that democracy required not a utopian form of equality but rather laws that would limit the excesses of the wealthy. "An imbalance between rich and poor is the oldest and most fatal ailment of all republics," the Greek philosopher Plutarch (A.D. 45–120) declared.[51]

Chronology

1870s–1900s
Gilded Age sees rising inequality; progressives call for taxes on the rich.

1913
States ratify 16th Amendment to U.S. Constitution, allowing Congress to institute income tax.

1916
U.S. Congress incorporates estate tax into tax code.

1920s–1930s
FDR's Depression-era New Deal creates social programs; increases taxes on the rich.

1929–1933
Great Depression; U.S. unemployment nears 25 percent.

1933
Under President Franklin D. Roosevelt, top U.S. tax rate increases to 63 percent.

1940s–1970s
World War II brings highest U.S. tax rates on the rich.

1941
U.S. enters World War II.

1942
Congress raises top tax rate to 88 percent to pay for war effort. . . . Nation's wealthiest 10 percent see their share of U.S. income drop from about 45 percent to 33 percent, where it stays into the 1970s.

1944
Congress raises top rate again to 94 percent on income over $200,000—$27 million in current dollars.

1954
Union membership peaks at more than one in three workers.

1974
Union membership drops to less than one in four workers—plummeting to 11 percent in 2013.

Late 1970s–1990s
Conservatives support tax cuts as key to growth; middle-class income growth falls behind productivity growth.

1979–1980
Supply-side economics advocates Margaret Thatcher and Ronald Reagan elected to top positions in Britain and the United States.

1981
Economic Recovery Tax Act reduces top U.S. tax rates.

1986
Tax Reform Act of 1986 reduces top income tax rate from 50 percent to 28 percent.

1992–2000
Average income grows 32 percent as economy expands, income of bottom 99 percent grows 20 percent, income of wealthiest 1 percent grows 99 percent.

1992
After 1990–91 recession, President Bill Clinton elected.

2000
Unemployment drops to 20-year low of 4 percent from peak of 7.5 percent in 1992.

2000s
Financial collapse leads to new financial regulation; average family income drops during Great Recession (2007–2009).

2001
Under President George W. Bush, tax cuts adopted despite budget deficit; taxes cut again in 2003.

2008
Global financial crisis follows subprime mortgage collapse.

2010
Dodd-Frank Wall Street reform law increases financial regulation as well as reporting of executive pay.

2012
Top 10 percent capture more than 50 percent of U.S. income—highest share since 1917, according to Berkeley economists.

2013

Berkeley researchers say top 1 percent of earners captured 95 percent of income gains since 2009 recovery. . . . Bill de Blasio elected New York City mayor promising to tax rich to pay for pre-kindergarten. . . . Bush tax cut expires; top tax rates raised from 35 percent to 39.6 percent.

2014

Senate hearings find thousands of U.S. taxpayers hiding money in offshore havens (February). . . . President Obama sends budget to Congress urging taxes on rich, expanded preschool (March).

Tax Havens Shelter Trillions

"The current estimates of inequality are massively understated."

An estimated $21 trillion to $31 trillion is squirreled away in offshore bank accounts, largely untaxed, by the world's 10 million richest people, estimates the British advocacy group Tax Justice Network.[1]

"The current estimates of inequality are massively understated because they exclude offshore wealth," says John Christensen, executive director of the network. Most people with assets of more than $4 million "hold much if not the majority of their wealth offshore—and therefore outside the national statistics."

Offshore tax havens are loosely defined as places that permit individuals and companies to escape their home jurisdiction's laws and regulations—especially those involving taxes—"using secrecy as a prime tool," according to the Tax Justice Network.

The U.S. Foreign Account Tax Compliance Act (FATCA), passed in 2010 and scheduled to be phased in during 2014 and 2015, requires all foreign banks to inform the U.S. Treasury Department about bank accounts held abroad by U.S. taxpayers. The penalty for noncompliant banks is a 30 percent surtax on the banks' U.S. income, which Christensen describes as the "big American stick."

The law is far stricter than a 2003 European Union directive that called for information exchange to ensure proper taxation of interest-bearing accounts, which French economist Thomas Piketty calls "timid . . . meaningless . . . not enforced." (A directive is a legal action that tells European member nations what goal they must achieve, but does not dictate the means.)[2] But even FATCA is not sufficient in his view. It's not comprehensive enough to cover all taxpayers, such as certain trust funds and foundations, he writes, and the penalties against banks may not be enough of a deterrent.[3]

Last year, the leaders of eight of the world's major industrialized economies, known as the G8, called for tax authorities around the world, including those in smaller countries, to share information automatically to crack down on tax evasion.[4]Following that action, and catalyzed by America's new law, famed tax havens such as the Cayman Islands, Luxembourg and Jersey were among more than 40 jurisdictions that agreed in February to pioneer a system of automatic information exchange for offshore bank accounts. Tax Justice Network hailed the move as "the first big step in putting together the nuts and bolts of real change."[5]

Forty-four countries have set a deadline of September 2017 to report investors' tax details to their home governments under plans announced by the Paris-based Organisation for Economic Co-operation and Development (OECD).[6]

"If we were able to put into place effective information-exchange cooperation among countries, the ability to evade taxes would be massively diminished," says Christensen.

Sen. Carl Levin, D-Mich., chairman of the Senate Permanent Subcommittee on Investigations, along with ranking minority member Sen. John McCain, R-Ariz., released a report at a Feb. 26 hearing accusing Swiss banks and the Swiss government of helping to hide billions of U.S. taxpayer dollars in offshore accounts. Zurich-based Credit Suisse is one of 14 Swiss banks under investigation by the U.S. government for helping Americans evade taxes.[7]

The subcommittee reported that Credit Suisse had more than 22,000 U.S. customers with accounts containing the equivalent of $10 billion to $12 billion at the height of its efforts to recruit foreign clients. The committee described how bank employees traveled to the United States to recruit wealthy customers and engaged in secret-agent style transactions—even handing over a customer's bank statements hidden in a *Sports Illustrated* magazine.[8]

But Levin said the effort to collect the taxes and bring the bankers to justice appeared "stalled." Although seven Credit Suisse bankers were indicted by U.S. prosecutors in 2011, none has stood trial. "Less than a handful" of U.S. taxpayers with Credit Suisse accounts have been indicted, he said. "The reason for this near total failure to date is continued Swiss insistence on bank secrecy, and the United States letting them get away with it," Levin said.

In early April, Credit Suisse set aside the equivalent of $477 million to deal with the possible costs of the U.S. Department of Justice probe, leading to speculation that the case was close to a final settlement.[9]

Right now it's so easy for kleptocrats from Eastern Europe or Asia to shift billions out of their home countries, says Christensen, that "this has created a criminogenic global financial market, where it is more profitable for lawyers, bankers and accountants to engage in criminal activity on behalf of clients than to do their job properly."

—Sarah Glazer

[1] "Inequality and Tax Havens," Tax Justice Network, no date, http://tinyurl.com/n49w879.

[2] European Commission, "What are EU directives?," no date, http://tinyurl.com/m4wlc9o.

[3] Thomas Piketty, *Capital in the Twenty-First Century* (2014), p. 522.

[4] George Parker and Vanessa Houlder, "G8 Seeks Rewrite of Global Tax Rules," *Financial Times*, June 18, 2013, http://tinyurl.com/lk3xblg.

[5] Vanessa Houlder, "Global Tax Standard Attracts 42 Countries," *Financial Times*, Feb. 13, 2014, http://tinyurl.com/k6y2etk.

[6] Vanessa Houlder, "Havens Set Deadlines for Reporting Investors' Tax Details," *Financial Times*, March 20, 2014, http://tinyurl.com/mtj3l4q.

[7] Gina Chon, Kara Scannell and James Shotter, "Credit Suisse 'Helped U.S. Tax Evaders,'" *Financial Times*, Feb. 25, 2014, http://tinyurl.com/jvnpzx8.

[8] "Opening Statement of Sen. Carl Levin," Senate Permanent Subcommittee on Investigations Hearing: Offshore Tax Evasion, Feb. 26, 2014, http://tinyurl.com/lnn782o.

[9] James Shotter, "Credit Suisse takes $477m Charge for Tax Inquiry," *Financial Times*, April 3, 2014, http://tinyurl.com/lnvwtg4.

The French Enlightenment philosopher Montesquieu (1689–1755) identified "real equality" as the soul of democracy, but acknowledged that in practice republics could only "fix the differences to a certain point."[52]

Similarly, the architects of American democracy shared a concern that political factions arising from deep class divisions and "unequal distribution of property," in the words of Founding Father James Madison, could undermine democracy. Madison stressed that the new American republic would derive its powers from the people, not from aristocratic or hereditary privileges as in England.[53]

Fear of coming to resemble old Europe was part of American interest in imposing progressive taxes. Throughout the 19th century the United States had no income tax. But the industrial revolution, which created a small class of American plutocrats, changed that.

During that era, some of the rich flaunted their wealth: At an 1897 costume ball in New York, the mother of millionaire John Jacob Astor came as Marie Antoinette in a dress adorned with $250,000 in jewels.[54]

Between 1870 and 1914, an era known as the Gilded Age, the increasing concentration of wealth at the top created extreme inequality. As late as 1919, Irving Fisher, president of the American Economic Association, expressed alarm that the top 2 percent owned more than 50 percent of the wealth while two-thirds of the population "owns almost nothing."[55]

Politicians calling themselves "Progressives," including Republican Theodore Roosevelt, railed against monopolies for stifling competition and for treating workers badly. "The absence of effective state . . . restraint upon unfair money-getting has tended to create a small class of enormously wealthy and economically powerful men, whose chief object is to hold and increase their power," charged Roosevelt in 1910.[56]

Roosevelt, president from 1901 to 1909, championed an estate tax in 1910 to prevent extreme accumulation of wealth, which, along with a graduated income tax, became a key plank of the Republican Party.

In 1913, the states ratified the 16th Amendment to the Constitution, giving Congress the power to collect income taxes; in October of that year, Congress passed a law creating the first permanent U.S. income tax.[57] In 1916, seven years after Roosevelt left office, Congress incorporated an estate tax into the federal code.[58]

Between World War I and World War II, the United States was the first country to try very high tax rates—70 percent on the top tier of income in 1919–22 and 70 percent on estates in 1937. The purpose was to put an end to such large incomes and estates—not to raise revenue, writes Piketty.[59]

After World War I, many countries adopted a progressive income tax, including Britain (1909), France (1914), India (1922) and Argentina (1932).

During the Roaring '20s, an era of rising fortunes, the top income tax rate was cut to 25 percent and again to 24 percent in 1929.

Coming to power during the Great Depression, President Franklin D. Roosevelt immediately moved to raise the top tax rate—and succeeded in raising rates on the wealthiest, first to 63 percent in 1933, then to 79 percent in 1937, surpassing the 1919 record.

As FDR expressed it in 1936, "For too many of us the political equality we once had was meaningless in the face of economic inequality. A small group had concentrated . . . an almost complete control over other people's property, money . . . labor . . . lives."[60]

As part of FDR's program to make sure the excesses that led to the Depression were not repeated, banks were regulated and deposits insured. The securities industry was placed under new tight restrictions; higher taxes were levied on the rich.[61]

Roosevelt's economic officials also supported measures that gave labor unions greater power to organize. Old-age and unemployment insurance provided workers economic protection.

Top U.S. income tax rates reached their highest points during World War II: The 1942 Victory Tax Act raised the top rate to 88 percent; in 1944, Congress raised the rate again to 94 percent on annual income over $200,000—$27 million in current dollars.[62]

Postwar Prosperity

Following World War II, all developed countries including the United States enjoyed high economic-growth rates. Americans' income grew at roughly the same rate no matter how much money they made.

The traditional economic view promoted by American economist Kuznets in the 1950s held that the post-WWII period represented an inevitable trend toward increasing equality and greater upward mobility, which would continue indefinitely.[63]

Luxury Homes Are Hot in London—and Controversial

The world's wealthy spend millions, while locals are priced out.

What do you get for $45 million in London's fashionable Mayfair neighborhood? That was the asking price in March for a narrow four-story house tucked into a mews, one of many cobblestone alleys that once served as the rear quarters for the servants and horses of grand townhouses, but are now enjoying a revival for their charm and proximity to luxury shopping.

Newly built to mimic the 18th-century style of the original house that stood on the 1,500-square-foot lot, this home packs six bedrooms plus a servant's room into 6,500 square feet. And it comes with all the amenities one might expect from the price tag: gym, screening room, separate his-and-hers bathrooms and dressing rooms and walk-in closets for each of the main guest rooms.

But increasingly the foreign buyers who dominate London's high-end market also are looking for Versailles-quality workmanship and prepackaged British taste right down to the candlesticks, according to a real estate agent and developer specializing in the luxury market who led this reporter on a recent walk-through.

Included in the price tag are the bespoke furniture and the carefully displayed *objets*, from the signed Picasso ceramics to an antique volume of the *Encyclopedia Britannica*. A chandelier specially designed for the soaring stairwell required two weeks of assembly by a team of eight working with 800 crystal pieces.

For most prospective buyers, this is their third or fourth home, so they're not interested in furnishing and decorating yet another house, explains Sanjay Sharma, a former investment banker. He cofounded luxury developer Fenton Whelan in 2010 with another London banker to build and renovate luxury homes and to provide investors with "record prices and exceptional returns on capital," according to the company's website.

The antiques and old-fashioned ceiling moldings like those that Fenton Whelan supplies fulfill the "zeitgeist of the moment—the desire to feel they're buying something British rather than generic," says Richard Cutt, an agent specializing in the city's luxury market for London-based international real estate firm Knight Frank.

Growth in the number of super-rich individuals around the world, particularly in emerging markets such as China, is driving London's hot luxury housing market, where prices have soared 65 percent since March 2009, according to Knight Frank.[1] Globally, the number of individuals with net assets of at least $30 million ballooned by 59 percent from 2003 to 2013; in aggregate, their assets total $20 trillion, according to the firm.

Skyrocketing housing prices for low- and middle-income Londoners and a supply shortage have intensified hostility toward new luxury homes. In April, Prince Charles said climbing prices would drive young people away from the city, noting the average London house price is now 10 times an elementary school teacher's salary. His Foundation for Building Community released a report

Continued

criticizing the tendency for the majority of new housing to serve those in the highest income bracket. The report urged more building of affordable five- to eight-story apartment buildings rather than luxury residential towers.[2]

Several recent newspaper investigations finding mansions left empty by wealthy overseas owners have intensified criticism. Central London "is fast becoming a ghost-town where absentee investors park their wealth" while creative types are pushed to the periphery, London club owner Alex Proud recently wrote in *The Telegraph*. "Tax empty houses? Why no. We wouldn't want to upset some ex-KGB thug who looted the Kazakh treasury in the mid-1990s."[3]

An investigation by the *Evening Standard* found more than 700 expensive homes standing empty throughout London. Many of the owners were offshore investors parking their wealth in mansions and hiding behind anonymous overseas post office boxes, the newspaper reported. Expressing shock, London Mayor Boris Johnson called on local city councils, which govern London's neighborhoods and have authority over local taxes, to impose punitive levies on owners of homes standing empty more than two years.[4]

On "Billionaires' Row," the latest moniker of The Bishops Avenue near fashionable Hampstead Heath, once known as Millionaires' Row, mansions owned by Saudi royals and oil magnates are valued at up to 65 million British pounds ($109 million). In a separate investigation, *The Guardian* found one-third standing derelict and empty.[5]

The Guardian expressed indignation at the avenue's 120 vacant bedrooms at a time when more than 6,000 Londoners are homeless and more than 300,000 families are on waiting lists for public housing. The cost of rising house prices is "borne by those lower down on the chain," wrote *Guardian* columnist Aditya Chakrabortty.[6]

In response, liberals have called for a "mansion" tax.[7] In its latest budget, the British government, which is a liberal-conservative coalition, compromised by expanding taxes on luxury homes bought through a corporate structure, citing concerns that rich individuals were using this avenue to avoid taxes.[8]

But some real estate agents say such moves are a xenophobic reaction to the fact that the city is becoming more cosmopolitan. "An Italian banker who is living here five years renting and then buys a house—is he a foreign buyer?" asks Liam Bailey, global head of residential research at Knight Frank.

And, indeed many of the elegant 19th-century houses that made the Belgravia and Mayfair neighborhoods posh were originally built as second homes for English aristocrats who spent much of the year at country estates, Bailey points out. "It's not exactly a new phenomenon."

—Sarah Glazer

[1] Knight Frank, "The Wealth Report," March 2014, http://tinyurl.com/ntseto9.

[2] Prince's Foundation for Building Community, "Housing London: A Mid-Rise Solution," March 2014, http://tinyurl.com/p3zokr7. Also see, *op. cit.*, "Prince Charles: We Need More Homes for Londoners."

[3] Alex Proud, "'Cool London' is Dead, and the Rich Kids are to Blame," *The Telegraph*, April 7, 2014, http://tinyurl.com/nlqneiu.

[4] Jonathan Prynn, *et al.*, "London's £3 bn Ghost Mansions," *Evening Standard*, Feb. 14, 2014, http://tinyurl.com/q5e2eal.

[5] Robert Booth, "Inside 'Billionaires' Row,'" *The Guardian*, Jan. 31, 2014, http://tinyurl.com/qhugbjl.

[6] Aditya Chakrabortty, "How to Handle the Hoarding of Houses on 'Billionaires' Row,'" *The Guardian*, Feb. 3, 2014, http://tinyurl.com/pl4u82z.

[7] James Kirkup, "Liberal Democrats would Tax the Rich to Clear Deficits, says Nick Clegg," *The Telegraph*, Feb. 10, 2014, http://tinyurl.com/paz2hwk.

[8] "Budget 2014: Upmarket Property Ripe for Raiding," *Financial Times*, March 19, 2014, http://tinyurl.com/pw2vq8w.

More recently, conservatives have argued that there's no returning to a time when an unskilled worker with only a high school education could support a family. In 1992, economists John Bound and George Johnson pointed to "skill-based technological change" and globalization as the main reasons wages stopped growing at the same rate after the 1970s.[64]

That argument has been debated by liberal economists such as Hacker, Galbraith and Mishel, who say government policies after 1978 were more important in retarding wage growth. They point to the declining power of U.S. unions—from a peak of one in three workers after World War II, union membership has declined to one in nine—a decline they say was abetted by anti-union government policies.[65]

By breaking the air-traffic-controllers strike in 1981 and appointing a National Labor Relations Board heavily in favor of management, Yale political science professor Hacker charges, Reagan contributed to the increasingly aggressive posture of business against unions and helped create a political vacuum that unions once filled by arguing for middle-class concerns.[66]

The Great Switch

Much of the increase in the very highest incomes in the United States and the United Kingdom came after 1980, following the elections of conservatives Reagan and British Prime Minister Thatcher.

In the United States, the highest tax brackets had averaged 83 percent from 1932–80, according to Piketty, in contrast with continental Europe. In France and Germany, for instance, the top rate in those years never exceeded 30 to 40 percent. Rates in the United Kingdom were closer to those in the United States. In the 1980s, both the United States and United Kingdom cut rates sharply—U.S. top rates fell to 28 percent after the Reagan tax reform in 1986.[67]

According to Piketty, the "spectacular decrease" in the progressivity of income tax rates during those years probably explains much of the increasing fortunes at the top that followed.

However, in his book *Winner-Take-All Politics*, Hacker chooses 1978, when Democrat Jimmy Carter was still president, as "the great switch point."

In 1978, Congress passed a bill with deep cuts in the capital gains tax, mainly benefiting the wealthy, which was signed by Democratic President Jimmy Carter. Congress also sharply raised payroll taxes, a levy that hits workers' pockets hardest, marking the beginning of a pronounced reversal in federal tax policy, Hacker argues.[68]

By 1981, under the Reagan administration, the tax debate had degenerated into a "frenzied bidding war" between Republicans and Democrats to shower benefits on business, writes Hacker.[69] As Reagan budget director Dave Stockman recalled, "the hogs were really feeding."[70]

Under the 1981 Economic Recovery Tax Act, top income tax rates came down sharply, and the tax on multimillion-dollar estates was cut from 70 percent to 50 percent.[71] Hacker's book argues that in the ensuing years, the wealthy have had an outsized influence on government policies and politicians of both parties, noting that in the 1980s and '90s senators voted with the interests of the wealthiest upper third of their constituents.[72]

Continuing into the presidency of Bill Clinton, politicians from both parties increasingly accepted the view that excessive regulation impedes economic growth. During the 1990s, financial deregulation swept across national borders, and by 2001, Piketty writes, the owners of capital were prospering as they hadn't since 1913.

Under President George W. Bush in 2001, a huge tax cut bill was supported by Republicans advocating tax cuts even in the face of big deficits in order to stimulate the economy; more cuts followed in 2003, bringing down top tax rates further.[73]

In March 2008, the investment bank Bear Stearns collapsed, the start of a worldwide financial crisis and recession. While volumes have been written on the causes of the crisis, liberal economists like Boushey and Hacker blame income inequality for driving excessive borrowing by those who couldn't afford it, abetted by lax oversight of the financial industry.

The tax legislation passed at the start of 2013, under Obama, permanently extended the Bush-era tax cuts for most people, but also added a top marginal tax rate of 39.6 percent for those at higher incomes— $400,000 for single filers, $450,000 for married couples filing jointly and $425,000 for heads of household. For tax years 2012 and earlier the highest tax bracket was 35 percent.[74]

However, some critics say the very rich rarely pay that 39.6 percent because of numerous loopholes, including a provision that lets hedge fund and equity fund managers count some income as capital gains, which is taxed at a lower rate. According to analysts, the Bush tax cuts mainly benefited the wealthy and increased inequality but also cut taxes for the middle class.[75]   ▪

Current Situation

Proposed Fixes

The budget that Obama sent to Congress March 4 echoes many of the solutions to inequality proposed by liberals—from more taxes on the rich to funding pre-school for the less advantaged.

"As a country, we've got to make a decision if we're going to protect tax breaks for the wealthiest Americans, or if we're going to make smart investments necessary to create jobs and grow our economy, and expand opportunity for every American," the president said that day.[76]

At Issue:

Do the rich pay enough in taxes?

CURTIS DUBAY
RESEARCH FELLOW, TAX AND ECONOMIC POLICY, HERITAGE FOUNDATION

WRITTEN FOR CQ RESEARCHER, APRIL 2014

When it comes to the rich paying taxes, how much is enough? Because everyone defines "enough" differently, for the debate to move forward, we need to ask better questions.

One "better" question: Do taxes overall need to rise at all? According to the Congressional Budget Office (CBO), tax receipts, as a share of the economy, will hover around 18 percent for the next 10 years—the historical average. Because tax revenues are running at the standard, operational level, it's difficult to argue that there's a crying need to extract more money from current taxpayers, be they rich or otherwise.

The next logical question is: Do the rich pay their fair share of the current tax burden? This, of course, is a more subjective question, but looking at the data can provide some guidance. Again, according to the most recent analysis by CBO, the top 1 percent of households earned just under 15 percent of all income in 2010. Yet they paid 39 percent of all federal income taxes—and more than 24 percent of all federal taxes that year.

These taxpayers paid an average tax rate of 29.4 percent. In other words, President Obama's Buffett Rule, which calls for a minimum tax rate of 30 percent on those who make more than $1 million a year, is essentially already in effect.

What if we broaden the definition of "rich" to the top 10 percent of U.S. households? They paid more than three-quarters of all federal income taxes—or more than half of all federal taxes in 2010.

Any way you slice it, the rich pay the lion's share of the taxes. Still, some may want to gouge the rich more, simply to satisfy their unique sense of fairness. So what would happen if we jacked up taxes on the rich, just to be "fair"? The rich would pay more, certainly. But the non-rich would feel the pain. High-earners also happen to be business owners, investors and entrepreneurs—the people who take risks that create opportunities for the rest of us. Raising their taxes reduces the resources they have to invest and their incentive to do so. Restricted capital means fewer jobs and lower wages.

Do the rich pay enough in taxes? If you think there is too much economic opportunity in America, the answer is "no." Otherwise, you'd have to agree that they already pay more than enough.

PETER DIAMOND
PROFESSOR OF ECONOMICS, EMERITUS, MASSACHUSETTS INSTITUTE OF TECHNOLOGY

WRITTEN FOR CQ RESEARCHER, APRIL 2014

Whatever level of federal government spending comes from the political process, that spending must be covered by taxes. In paying for that spending, the more tax revenue that comes from those with the highest incomes, the less needs to come from everyone else.

In choosing how much to collect from the richest, we need to consider the impact on the economy and the differences in abilities to pay between those at the top and those with less, often much less. While views differ on what makes a tax fair, there should be a greater willingness for higher taxes on the highest incomes since income distribution has become dramatically more unequal over recent decades.

To consider the impact on the economy, we need to recognize that throughout the income distribution, taxes affect behavior—through changes in work and saving, changes in (legal) tax avoidance, and changes in (illegal) tax evasion. These responses affect the efficiency of the economy and affect the level of revenue collected with a given tax structure. Tax avoidance and tax evasion can be reduced by changes in tax rules and changes in tax enforcement, enhancing the ability to collect taxes more fairly and efficiently. And this approach permits more of tax collection to come from those with the greatest ability to pay.

We cannot run controlled experiments on the economy to estimate the additional revenues from tax changes, but we do have many studies of the effects from past tax changes.

While studies differ in their findings, overall, they shed considerable light on the revenue and efficiency implications of tax changes. The evidence supports the view that we can considerably increase the revenues currently being collected by taxes on the highest incomes, while having limited impacts on the functioning of the economy.

In light of this empirical evidence, I favor a federal tax rate on the highest incomes within the historical range from 50 percent (the 1982–86 level under President Reagan) to 70 percent (the level from 1965 to 1981, under Presidents Johnson, Nixon, Ford and Carter).

Collecting these extra revenues can help finance more public investments to enhance our country's future and can help limit the need for higher taxes on those with lower incomes as we deal with our sizable public debt.

But noting the increasing emphasis on raising taxes and redistributing wealth coming from Obama and international organizations such as the International Monetary Fund (IMF), Dan Henninger, deputy editorial page director of *The Wall Street Journal*, wrote, "What's unacceptable about the income-inequality agenda of the Obama Democrats, the United Nations and the IMF is that all assume that the U.S.'s historic century of strong, capital-driven growth is over, and that it must reorder its priorities to admit the reality of reduced long-term economic performance. In short, it's time to slow down and divide up what pie we've got." That's what Europe and Russia did, he added. "That's what the United States would be nuts to do."[77]

Even supporters of Obama's proposals to expand pre-kindergarten and tax credits for low-income workers predicted that Republicans would resist "every dollar" of the $651 billion the president asked for over the next decade, said a *New York Times* editorial, which labeled the administration's budget the "What Might Have Been" budget.[78]

Indeed, the conservative Heritage Foundation instantly pronounced the budget "dead on arrival."[79] It called a cap on deductions for high earners "troubling" because it would apply to retirement savings, health insurance and municipal bond income.

And it singled out Obama's proposal to implement the so-called "Buffet rule" originally put forward by billionaire businessman Warren Buffet—to insure that wealthy millionaires pay no less than 30 percent of their income in taxes after charitable contributions.[80] Heritage said most top earners already meet that bar.[81]

Nevertheless, Obama's proposal shares a bit of common ground with a tax proposal made a week earlier by Rep. Dave Camp, R-Mich., the House Ways and Means chairman, to simplify the tax code. Both proposals would raise taxes on hedge fund managers and both would cap the value of tax deductions for high-income families, according to the Tax Policy Center, a joint project of the Urban Institute and Brookings Institution.[82]

However, the chances for congressional action on Camp's proposal looked slim as the Republican leadership in Congress quickly distanced itself from the document. The House GOP budget unveiled earlier this month did not endorse Camp's tax reform plan.[83]

Steuerle, the Urban Institute fellow who coordinated the tax study in Reagan's Treasury that led to the 1986 Tax Reform Act, holds out hope for eventual action: "The more good things you can put in the hopper, especially if they get bipartisan support, the greater chance that down the road they could become part of something bigger," he predicts.

Obama's proposed budget got lower marks for its efforts to help low-income citizens move up the ladder, according to Steuerle, who conducted a study for the Pew Charitable Trusts of how government spending affects mobility. While expanding preschool education and the tax credit for low-income workers, the amount of help would be small, he stressed.

Haskins of Brookings cautions that most preschool programs aren't good enough to get the sterling results touted by advocates citing studies of high-quality early education. "If we really think preschool is going to bring these kids to the starting line of public schools roughly equal to their more advantaged peers, we need much better teachers, which means we have to pay a lot more money," he says.

Obama's proposal to double the earned income tax credit for low-income workers to $1,000 and expand it to childless adults won praise from liberals as well as from conservative Haskins, who said the credit, while not large enough, addresses what may be the country's No. 1 problem: the low labor force participation rate—66 percent—among young black men ages 20–24.[84]

Obama has proposed an increase in the minimum wage—from $7.25 to $10.10 an hour—but even strong supporters of that measure don't expect it to get past Washington's political gridlock. "I don't think anything is going to pass Congress this year," says Mishel of the Economic Policy Institute, whose wish list also includes to "create lots of jobs, firm up the safety net and retirement, and restore the ability for workers to have collective bargaining."

In recognition of that political reality, Obama has addressed some equality issues by executive order—directing the Labor Department on March 13 to expand overtime to millions of workers, including fast food managers, previously classified as "executive or professional" to avoid paying overtime.

New York's de Blasio swept into office on a platform that vowed to fix the gap between the city's haves and have-nots. He proposed to tax the rich to fund universal pre-K education, which he dubbed a crucial weapon against inequality.

De Blasio's proposed tax became a lightning rod for conservative criticism and a stand-in for the larger debate about whether the rich should be taxed further to cure inequality.

At the end of March, Democratic New York Gov. Andrew Cuomo announced a budget agreement that rejected the mayor's proposed tax on high earners but provided most of the money de Blasio said he needed to create pre-kindergarten for every child in the city.[85]

While conservatives tend to agree with liberals that unequal education is a root cause of inequality, their solutions differ: Conservatives such as Furth back approaches that give parents more choice in picking schools, like vouchers and charter schools.

Executive Pay

Wall Street's 2008 financial melt-down and the accompanying recession focused new scrutiny on executive salaries. The pay for top executives has grown to 300 times that of the rank and file worker in recent years.[86]

As part of the 2010 Dodd-Frank Wall Street reform law that grew out of the crisis, regulators at the Securities and Exchange Commission (SEC) are considering a rule that would require public companies to disclose the ratio of an executive's earnings to a rank-and-file worker's pay.[87] The SEC rule, originally proposed last September, ran into opposition from businesses, which objected that it imposed a heavy logistical burden on companies with employees around the globe. Since then, the commission has been accused of foot-dragging. "Timing is uncertain" for issuance of the final rule, according to an SEC spokesperson.

Another measure, the so-called "say on pay" rule already issued by the SEC, allows shareholders a nonbinding vote on executive pay packages: Since the passage of Dodd Frank, say-on-pay may have given some investors new fortitude to question executive pay: Citigroup shareholders rejected a $15 million pay package in 2012 for the bank's chief executive, Vikram Pandit.[88]

Limiting executive pay could allow more of a firm's profits to go to its workers or be plowed back into the company, advocates hope. Yet some, like Yale's Hacker, are skeptical that the current rules go far enough, calling the say-on-pay rule's nonbinding vote a "weak" weapon.

"I wouldn't put too much faith in the information alone, but if you get some organized actors to shame companies to adopt more rational pay packages, I think that would be helpful," he says. So far, however, the rule is having a minimal effect, he says. "It seems executive pay has been sky-rocketing back." ▪

Outlook

'Oligarchic Evolution'

While some advocates and politicians continue pushing for policies they say would help middle-class incomes grow again as they did pre-1980, others say rapid growth is unlikely to reappear in developed economies as population growth slows.

For French economist Piketty, who predicts a slow-growth future, that presents a potentially apocalyptic scenario if the richest continue claiming a growing share of income. "This risk of oligarchic evolution is something of concern—not just in Russia and China, but also in America and Europe. There is no natural economic mechanism that prevents such an extreme thing from happening," he says.

Conservatives tend to be more optimistic that the economy will pick up again and that workers will share in the benefits. James Sherk, a senior labor policy analyst at the Heritage Foundation, says worker pay has tracked productivity growth closely and will start to grow robustly once the economy picks up again. Policymakers, he says, "should look for ways to make less-skilled workers more productive, such as reducing the cost of higher education. Market forces will then force employers to increase compensation."[89]

Until recently, higher population growth in the United States reduced the relative importance of inherited wealth compared with a more static Europe. But that could soon change. The aging of baby boomers should bring a sudden boom in inheritances and potentially a "flood of princelings," as an article in *The New York Times* put it, peaking in 2031. Economists such as Piketty are predicting that this trend will contribute even further to growing wealth inequality in the United States.[89]

"We have more income inequality, and that means that down the road, we are bound to have more wealth inequality and more inequality of inherited wealth," predicted Piketty.[91]

Since the 1980s, the value of inheritance has drifted upward only slightly, and wealth transfers in the United States as a share of net worth have fallen. But experts say that trend could reverse drastically as baby boomers hand on their wealth to the next generation.

A lot of multimillionaires are men of age 60 or 70, said David Friedman of Wealth-X, an international research firm that studies habits of the wealthy. "They're sensing their mortality now. And there's a growing wave of liquidity that's going to fuel luxury and fuel philanthropy in a way that the market's never seen."[92] ▪

End Notes

1. Eoghan Macguire, "Swimming Pools and Golf Ranges in London's Insane Luxury Basements," CNN, Jan. 24, 2014, http://tinyurl.com/kqx4m7d.
2. Michael Goldfarb, "London's Great Exodus," *International New York Times*, Oct. 12, 2013, http://tinyurl.com/l33hjbq.
3. "Working for the Few," Oxfam, Jan. 20, 2014, http://tinyurl.com/omp8zml.
4. "Worsening Wealth Gap Seen Biggest Risk Facing the World," press release, World Economic Forum, 2014, http://tinyurl.com/n8mpa8c.
5. Eduardo Porter, "In New Tack, I.M.F. Aims at Income Inequality," *The New York Times*, April 8, 2014, http://tinyurl.com/mqdjpjx.
6. Paul Krugman, "Liberty, Equality, Efficiency," *The New York Times*, March 9, 2014, http://tinyurl.com/q8y2grc.
7. Emmanuel Saez, "Striking it Richer: The Evolution of Top Incomes in the United States," University of California, Berkeley, Sept. 3, 2013, p. 3, http://tinyurl.com/o7zo3mm.
8. *Ibid.*, p. 3.
9. Thomas Piketty, *Capital in the Twenty-First Century* (2014), p. 438.
10. "Remarks by the President on Economic Mobility," White House, Dec. 4, 2013, http://tinyurl.com/mk4qe7n.
11. Mickey Kaus, "The Other Kind of Inequality," *The Wall Street Journal*, Jan. 26, 2014, http://tinyurl.com/ms2op6h.
12. Scott Winship, "Inequality Testimony before the Joint Economic Committee," E21: Economic Policies for the 21st Century, Manhattan Institute, Jan. 15, 2014, http://tinyurl.com/lwy9kjm.
13. *Ibid.*
14. Sears has closed about 300 stores since 2010; it closed its flagship store in Chicago in February. JC Penney announced in February it would close 33 stores, http://tinyurl.com/mpzlxgm.
15. Nelson D. Schwartz, "The Middle Class is Steadily Eroding," *The New York Times*, Feb. 2, 2014, http://tinyurl.com/l7fwj86.
16. Barry Z. Cynamon and Steven M. Fazzari, "Inequality, the Great Recession, and Slow Recovery," Washington University, Jan. 23, 2014, http://tinyurl.com/k4zvcup.
17. Schwartz, *op. cit.*
18. "The State of Working America, 12th Edition," Economic Policy Institute, March 17, 2014, http://tinyurl.com/4vb2ct.
19. Nelson D. Schwartz, "How Eroding the Middle Class Hits Economic Growth," *Economix* blog, *The New York Times*, Feb. 5, 2014, http://tinyurl.com/mlo6hnb.
20. Winship, *op. cit.*
21. See for example, Andrew G. Berg and Jonathan D. Ostry, "Inequality and Unsustainable Growth: Two Sides of the Same Coin?" International Monetary Fund, April 8, 2011, http://tinyurl.com/445a8t6.
22. Piketty, *op. cit.*, p. 13.
23. Jonathan D. Ostry, *et al.*, "Redistribution, Inequality and Growth," February 2014, International Monetary Fund, http://tinyurl.com/q5qz6l6.
24. Berg and Ostry, *op. cit.* Also see Winship, *op. cit.*
25. Winship, *op. cit.*
26. College completion rates increased only 4 percentage points from the generation of low-income children born in the early 1960s to those born in the 1980s. For high-income children the increase was 18 percentage points. "Gains and Gaps: Changing Inequality in U.S. College Entry and

Completion, NBER Working Paper No. 17633, National Bureau of Economic Research, March 10, 2014, http://tinyurl.com/kp 49o9y.

27. Krugman, *op. cit.*

28. Piketty, *op. cit.*, pp. 438–440.

29. Eduardo Porter, "Economix: Q&A on the Wealth Divide: Thomas Piketty," *The New York Times*, March 11, 2014, http://tinyurl.com/myxvxkz.

30. "President Barack Obama's State of the Union Address," White House, Jan. 28, 2014, http://tinyurl.com/kemgt7x.

31. Sean McElwee, "Republicans Suddenly Can't Stop Talking about 'Mobility,'" *The New Republic*, Feb. 19, 2014, http://tinyurl.com/lfwxxg8.

32. "Class in America: Mobility Measured," *The Economist*, Feb. 1, 2014, http://tinyurl.com/n9t3ar7.

33. Raj Chetty, *et al.*, "Is the United States still a Land of Opportunity?" National Bureau of Economic Research, January 2014, http://tinyurl.com/lphlkz2.

34. "Class in America," *op. cit.*

35. Gregory Clark, *The Son Also Rises: Surnames and the History of Social Mobility* (2014).

36. Cited in Ron Haskins, "Mobility Is a Problem: Now What?" Dec. 23, 2011, http://tinyurl.com/mnuuezj. The data was published in a book written by Haskins and Isabel Sawhill, *Creating an Opportunity Society* (2009).

37. Annie Lowrey, "What Comes after Rich Baby Boomers?" *New York Times Magazine*, March 11, 2014, http://tinyurl.com/l2xa7lv.

38. Inheritance as a share of national income in France was 20 percent from 1840 to 1914, declined to a low of 5 percent in the 1950s and rose to 15 percent in 2010. See Piketty, *op. cit.*, pp. 380–381.

39. Piketty, *op. cit.*, p. 438.

40. Pew Charitable Trusts, "Economic Mobility and the American Dream," May 2011, http://tinyurl.com/l5l4rc2.

41. "Pursuing the American Dream: Economic Mobility Across Generations," Pew Charitable Trusts, July 9, 2012, http://tinyurl.com/872oy5z.

42. Piketty, *op. cit.*, p. 525.

43. The Oscar-nominated film "Wolf of Wall Street" is based on the story of Jordan Belfort, who served 22 months in prison for security fraud between 2004 and 2006. See, "Real-life Wolf of Wall Street says his life of debauchery 'even worse' than in film," *The Guardian*, Feb. 28, 2014, http://tinyurl.com/o6oo3vs.

44. Christopher DeMuth, "Capital for the Masses," *The Wall Street Journal*, April 7, 2014, http://tinyurl.com/keenuwn.

45. Jacob S. Hacker and Nate Loewenthal, *Prosperity Economics* (2012), p. 48.

46. Sendhil Mullainathan, "A Top-Heavy Focus on Income Inequality," *The New York Times*, March 8, 2014, http://tinyurl.com/qdqkddd.

47. "The Rich are Taxed Enough," Intelligence Squared U.S., Oct. 24, 2012, p. 16, http://tinyurl.com/lb9q58c.

48. *Ibid.*

49. "The Distribution of Household Income and Federal Taxes," Congressional Budget Office, December 2013, p. 7, http://tinyurl.com/pxzutsz.

50. Households in the highest quintile paid 93 percent of federal income taxes in 2010. *Ibid.*, p. 13.

51. Jacob C. Hacker and Paul Pierson, *Winner-Take-All Politics* (2010), p. 75.

52. *Ibid.*

53. *Ibid.*, p. 76.

54. Chrystia Freeland, *Plutocrats: The Rise of the New Global Rich and the Fall of Everyone Else* (2012), p. 6.

55. Piketty, *op. cit.*, p. 506.

56. President Teddy Roosevelt's New Nationalism Speech, www.whitehouse.gov/blog/2011/12/06/archives-president-teddy-roosevelts-new-nationalism-speech.

57. "History of Income Tax in the U.S.," about. com, http://tinyurl.com/n2wep8k.

58. Tim Rutten, "And the Rich Get Richer," *Los Angeles Times*, Dec. 18, 2010, http://tinyurl.com/37ku7aq.

59. Piketty, *op. cit.*, p. 507.

60. Hacker, *op. cit.*, p. 87.

61. *Ibid.*, p. 88.

62. "History of Federal Individual Income Bottom and Top Bracket Rates," National Taxpayers Union, undated, http://tinyurl.com/2f3c277. Calculation of current dollars: http://tinyurl.com/lcywoao.

63. Eduardo Porter, "Free Market is no Remedy for Disparity," *International New York Times*, March 13, 2014, p. 15.

64. *American Economic Review*, cited in James K. Galbraith, *Inequality and Instability* (2012), p. 125.

65. Hacker, *op. cit.*, pp. 56–57.

66. *Ibid.* Also see Andrew Glass, "Reagan fires 11,000 striking air traffic controllers August 5, 1981," *Politico*, Aug. 5, 2008, http://tinyurl.com/yg8c9gq.

67. Piketty, *op. cit.*, pp. 507–509.

68. Hacker, *op. cit.*, pp. 99–100 and pp. 133–134. The capital gains tax, which taxes profits such as those from the sale of stock or business assets, was cut from 48 percent to 28 percent.

69. *Ibid.*, p. 134.

70. William Greider, "The Education of David Stockman," *The Atlantic*, December 1981, http://tinyurl.com/d43yal3.

71. "General Explanation of the Economic Recovery Tax Act of 1981," Joint Committee on Taxation, Dec. 29, 1981, p. 229, http://tinyurl.com/lf9w9pd.

72. Hacker, *op. cit.*, p. 111. The research cited is by political scientist Larry Bartels.

73. Hacker, *op. cit.*, p. 217.

74. "Federal Income Tax Table," http://tinyurl.com/cnrhnns. Also see, "New 39.6 Percent Tax Bracket," *Politico*, Jan. 22, 2014, http://tinyurl.com/kb3nwob.

75. "The Legacy of the Bush Tax Cuts in four Charts," *The Washington Post*, Jan. 2, 2013, http://tinyurl.com/b9l5vca.

76. "Remarks by the President Announcing the FY 2015 Budget," White House, March 4, 2014, http://tinyurl.com/kapxcj6.

77. Dan Henninger, "The Income Inequality Love Train," *The Wall Street Journal*, April 2, 2014, http://tinyurl.com/l4xgwmt.

78. Editorial, "The What Might Have Been Budget," *The New York Times*, March 4, 2014, http://tinyurl.com/ktgyugc.

79. Stephen Moore, "Why Obama's Budget Should Be Dead on Arrival," The Foundry, Heritage Foundation, March 4, 2014, http://tinyurl.com/mfa2grw.

80. "FY 2015 Budget," White House, http://tinyurl.com/oo6gsdd.

81. Heritage Foundation on Obama Budget: "Live Analysis," Heritage Foundation, March 4, 2014, http://tinyurl.com/n3poqup.

82. Howard Gleckman, "A Tale of Three Agendas," Tax Vox, March 4, 2014, http://tinyurl.com/k6nyta3.

83. John D. McKinnon, "New House Budget Doesn't Back Rep Camp's Tax Reform Plan," *The Wall Street Journal*, April 1, 2014, http://tinyurl.com/mg8fb2z.

84. "Barack Obama says Fewer Black, Latino Young Men Participate in the Labor Force than Young White Men," *Tampa Bay Times, Politifact.com*, Feb. 28, 2014, www.politifact.com/truth-o-meter/ statements/2014/feb/28/barack-obama/barack-obama-says-fewer-black-latino-young-men- par/. The labor force participation rate includes those employed and searching for work.

85. Thomas Kaplan and Javier C. Hernandez, "State Budget Deal Reached," *The New York Times*, March 29, 2014, http://tinyurl.com/mofuy4s.

86. "Exposing the Pay Gap," *The New York Times*, Sept. 25, 2013, http://tinyurl.com/kdfovsp.

87. Dave Michaels, "CEO-to-Worker Pay-Ratio Disclosure Proposed by Divided SEC," Bloomberg, Sept. 18, 2013, http://tinyurl.com/kjma4z7.

88. Editorial, "The Boss and Everyone Else," *The New York Times*, May 2, 2012, http://tinyurl. com/74dxau6.

89. James Sherk, "Productivity and Compensation; Growing Together," Heritage Foundation, July 17, 2013, http://tinyurl.com/mv2rh9g.

90. Lowrey, *op. cit.*, http://tinyurl.com/ku9fkhd.

91. *Ibid.*

92. *Ibid.*

FOR MORE INFORMATION

Brookings Institution, 1775 Massachusetts Ave., N.W., Washington, DC 20036; 202-797-6000; www. brookings.edu. Think tank that covers a wide range of topics, with scholars who are generally moderate to liberal.

Economic Mobility Project, Pew Charitable Trusts, 901 E St., N.w., Washington, DC 20004; 202-552-2000; www.pewtrusts.org/our_work_detail.aspx?id=596. Research project investigating U.S. economic mobility.

Economic Policy Institute, 1333 H St., N.W., Suite 300, East Tower, Washington, DC 20005; 202-775-8810; www.epi.org. Think tank that studies low- and middle-income workers.

Heritage Foundation, 214 Massachusetts Ave., N.E., Washington, DC 20002; 202-546-4400; www. heritage.org. Think tank that promotes conservative policies based on free enterprise.

Oxfam, 226 Causeway St., Boston, MA 02114; 800-776-9326; www.oxfamamerica.org. Antipoverty charity that recently released a report on the global rich.

Tax Policy Center, Urban Institute, 2100 M St., N.W., Washington, DC 20037; 202-833-7200; www. taxpolicycenter.org. Joint project with the Brookings Institution that provides nonpartisan analyses of tax legislation.

Urban Institute, 2100 M St. N.W., Washington, DC 20037, 202-833-7200; www.urban.org. Think tank that focuses on U.S. social and economic issues.

Washington Center on Equitable Growth, 1333 H St., N.W., Washington, DC 20005; 202-682-1611; http://equitablegrowth.org. Project housed at the liberal Center for American Progress that investigates the effect of inequality on economic growth.

Bibliography

Selected Sources

Books

Clark, Gregory, *The Son Also Rises: Surnames and the History of Social Mobility,* **Princeton University Press, 2014.**
   A University of California-Davis economist finds movement up the social ladder has changed little over eight centuries, even in highly equal countries such as Sweden.

Freeland, Chrystia, *Plutocrats: The Rise of the New Global Rich and the Fall of Everyone Else,* **Penguin Books, 2012.**
   While a Reuters economics reporter, Freeland, now a member of the Canadian Parliament, wrote this book describing the world of today's global super-rich and their historic rise.

Galbraith, James K., *Inequality and Instability: A Study of the World Economy Just Before the Great Crisis,* **Oxford University Press, 2012.**
   A University of Texas-Austin economist argues that the rise of inequality mirrors the rise of finance and free-market policies.

Hacker, Jacob S., and Paul Pierson, *Winner-Take-All Politics: How Washington Made the Rich Richer—and Turned its Back on the Middle Class,* **Simon and Schuster, 2010.**
   A Yale political scientist (Hacker) and a University of California-Berkeley political scientist argue that the American political system has been hijacked by the very rich, leading to government policies favoring the wealthy.

Piketty, Thomas, *Capital in the Twenty-First Century,* **Belknap Press, 2014.**
   In this much-discussed study of 20 countries over 300 years, a professor at the Paris School of Economics argues that wealth is becoming too concentrated at the top and advocates a global wealth tax.

Articles

DeMuth, Christopher, "Capital for the Masses," *The Wall Street Journal,* **April 7, 2014, http://tinyurl.com/keenuwn.**
   A conservative critique of Thomas Piketty's *Capital in the Twenty-First Century* says the book bolsters arguments for privatizing retirement systems such as Social Security.

Krugman, Paul, "Liberty, Equality, Efficiency," *The New York Times,* **March 9, 2014, http://tinyurl.com/q8y2grc.**
   A liberal economist asks whether redistribution of economic wealth hurts growth—and answers in the negative.

Lowrey, Annie, "What Comes after Rich Baby Boomers?" *The New York Times Magazine,* **March 11, 2014, http://tinyurl.com/l2xa7lv.**
   An economics reporter forecasts a new wave of well-to-do "princelings" will inherit wealth from the aging baby boomers.

Mullainathan, Sendhil, "A Top-Heavy Focus on Income Inequality," *The New York Times*, March 8, 2014, http://tinyurl.com/qdqkddd.

A Harvard economist argues that reducing income for the wealthy through higher taxes does not necessarily mean more for everyone else.

Saez, Emmanuel, "Striking it Richer: The Evolution of Top Incomes in the United States," Sept. 3, 2013, p. 3, http://tinyurl.com/o7zo3mm.

This unpublished paper by a University of California-Berkeley economist has been widely cited for its chart showing that the upper 10 percent now command an even greater share of national income than in the 1920s.

Reports and Studies

"Moving on Up," Pew Charitable Trusts, November 2013, http://tinyurl.com/jvw2egz.

The research group examines why some Americans move up the social ladder and others do not, finding that college education greatly increases one's chances.

"Offshore Tax Evasion: The Effort to Collect Unpaid Taxes on Billions in Hidden Offshore Accounts," U.S. Senate Permanent Subcommittee on Investigations, Feb. 26, 2014, http://tinyurl.com/lnn782o.

The Senate subcommittee, which found thousands of U.S. taxpayers hiding billions of dollars in offshore tax accounts, criticizes the Swiss government and Credit Suisse for secrecy, and says the U.S. Justice Department acts too slowly against possible wrongdoers.

"The Distribution of Household Income and Federal Taxes," Congressional Budget Office, December 2013, http://tinyurl.com/pxzutsz.

The nonpartisan agency looks at the incomes of a range groups in the United States both before and after taxes.

"The State of Working America, 12th Edition," Economic Policy Institute, March 17, 2014, http://tinyurl.com/4vb2ct.

A book-length report analyzes data on income, mobility, wages, jobs, wealth and poverty.

"The Wealth Report," Knight Frank, March 2014, http://tinyurl.com/ntseto9.

In its annual report, a London-based real estate firm examines recent trends of the global rich—where they live, where they're buying property and how they're consuming.

"Working for the Few," Oxfam, Jan. 20, 2014, http://tinyurl.com/omp8zml.

An anti-poverty charity finds the world's 85 richest billionaires have combined fortunes equal to those of the world's poorest half.

The Next Step:

Additional Articles from Current Periodicals

Executive Pay

Baer, Justin, "Morgan Stanley CEO's Pay Increases 85% in 2013—Update," *The Wall Street Journal*, March 28, 2014, http://tinyurl.com/kvwga3c.

Morgan Stanley gave CEO James Gorman an 85 percent raise, from $9.75 million in 2012 to $18 million in 2013.

Strauss, Gary, Barbara Hansen and Matt Krantz, "Millions by millions, CEO pay goes up," *USA Today*, April 4, 2014, http://tinyurl.com/lekzasd.

With 15 CEOs and others at publicly held companies breaking into the $100 million-plus compensation club, 2013 could be a record breaker for executive pay.

Symonds, Matt, "Big Company CEOs Just Aren't Worth What We Pay Them," *Forbes*, March 6, 2014, http://tinyurl.com/mxkly6m.

Two business school professors say very large financial incentives can actually worsen CEO performance and that recruiting processes for top positions are limited or ineffective in identifying proper candidates.

Income Gap

Heavey, Susan, Bill Trott and Gunna Dickson, "U.S. divided over how to tackle income gap, poverty: poll," Reuters, Jan. 23, 2014, http://tinyurl.com/nz9zmgz.

Americans are strongly divided along party lines over how to close the growing income gap, according to a Pew Research Center poll.

Krugman, Paul, "Why We're in a New Gilded Age," *The New York Review of Books*, May 8, 2014, http://tinyurl.com/nbxrlcu.

A liberal U.S. economist's review discusses how French economist Thomas Piketty's book *Capital in the Twenty-First Century* has brought on a "revolution in our understanding of long-term trends in inequality."

Schuman, Michael, "There's a Class War Going On and the Poor Are Getting Their Butts Kicked," *Time*, April 1, 2014, http://tinyurl.com/mt2eqfg.

A China-based business and economics correspondent says economic policy in the United States and around the world is biased against the poor, which hurts everyone and the global economy.

Inherited Wealth

"Forbes Releases 28th Annual World's Billionaires Issue," *Forbes*, March 3, 2014, http://tinyurl.com/n3m65ej.

Roughly two-thirds of those on *Forbes*' annual billionaire list were self-made, with 207 inheriting their wealth and 352 inheriting at least a portion, out of the total 1,645 billionaires on this year's tally.

Weisman, Aly, "Anderson Cooper Won't Inherit A Dime From Mom Gloria Vanderbilt's $200 Million Fortune," *Business Insider*, **April 1, 2014, http://tinyurl.com/ml7s5jm.**

CNN anchor Anderson Cooper says he is OK with not inheriting his mother's fortune, calling inheritance a curse and an "initiative sucker."

Offshore Havens

Chokshi, Niraj, "How Maine hopes to recover $10 million a year from tax havens," *The Washington Post*, **April 3, 2014, http://tinyurl.com/mp2ytkp.**

Proposed legislation in Maine would recover an estimated $10 million annually, part of which would be taxed by the state, by requiring corporations to report income from 38 known offshore tax havens.

McKinnon, John D., "More Countries Agree to Help U.S. Crack Down on Tax Dodgers," *The Wall Street Journal*, **April 2, 2014, http://tinyurl.com/ktyxslp.**

The U.S. Treasury Department has added 19 nations to the list of countries that have agreements with the United States to prevent American citizens from evading taxes using offshore havens.

Skiba, Katherine, "Caterpillar digs in at hearing on taxes: 'We pay everything we owe,'" *Chicago Tribune*, **April 1, 2014, http://tinyurl.com/lesnpev.**

Sen. Carl Levin, D-Mich., said at a Senate hearing that Caterpillar Inc.'s affiliate in Switzerland allows the company to save $300 million a year in taxes.

APPENDICES

THE CONSTITUTION OF THE UNITED STATES

WE THE PEOPLE OF THE UNITED STATES, in order to form a more perfect Union, establish Justice, insure domestic Tranquility, provide for the common defence, promote the general Welfare, and secure the Blessings of Liberty to ourselves and our Posterity, do ordain and establish this Constitution for the United States of America.

Article I

Section 1   All legislative Powers herein granted shall be vested in a Congress of the United States, which shall consist of a Senate and House of Representatives.

Section 2   The House of Representatives shall be composed of Members chosen every second Year by the People of the several States, and the Electors in each State shall have the Qualifications requisite for Electors of the most numerous Branch of the State Legislature.

No Person shall be a Representative who shall not have attained to the Age of twenty five Years, and been seven Years a Citizen of the United States, and who shall not, when elected, be an Inhabitant of that State in which he shall be chosen.

Representatives and direct Taxes shall be apportioned among the several States which may be included within this Union, according to their respective Numbers, which shall be determined by adding to the whole Number of free Persons, including those bound to Service for a Term of Years, and excluding Indians not taxed, three fifths of all other Persons. The actual Enumeration shall be made within three Years after the first Meeting of the Congress of the United States, and within every subsequent Term of ten Years, in such Manner as they shall by Law direct. The Number of Representatives shall not exceed one for every thirty Thousand, but each State shall have at Least one Representative; and until such enumeration shall be made, the State of New Hampshire shall be entitled to chuse three, Massachusetts eight, Rhode-Island and Providence Plantations one, Connecticut five, New-York six, New Jersey four, Pennsylvania eight, Delaware one, Maryland six, Virginia ten, North Carolina five, South Carolina five, and Georgia three.

When vacancies happen in the Representation from any state, the Executive Authority thereof shall issue Writs of Election to fill such Vacancies.

The House of Representatives shall chuse their Speaker and other Officers; and shall have the sole Power of Impeachment.

SOURCE: The Constitution of the United States, 1787

Section 3   The Senate of the United States shall be composed of two Senators from each State, chosen by the legislature thereof, for six Years; and each Senator shall have one Vote.

Immediately after they shall be assembled in Consequence of the first Election, they shall be divided as equally as may be into three Classes. The Seats of the Senators of the first Class shall be vacated at the Expiration of the second Year, of the second Class at the Expiration of the fourth Year, and of the third Class at the Expiration of the sixth Year, so that one third maybe chosen every second Year; and if Vacancies happen by Resignation, or other wise, during the Recess of the Legislature of any State, the Executive thereof may make temporary Appointments until the next Meeting of the Legislature, which shall then fill such Vacancies.

No Person shall be a Senator who shall not have attained to the Age of thirty Years, and been nine Years a Citizen of the United States, and who shall not, when elected, be an Inhabitant of that State for which he shall be chosen.

The Vice President of the United States shall be President of the Senate, but shall have no Vote, unless they be equally divided.

The Senate shall have the sole Power to try all Impeachments. When sitting for that Purpose, they shall be on Oath or Affirmation. When the President of the United States is tried, the Chief Justice shall preside: And no Person shall be convicted without the Concurrence of two thirds of the Members present.

Judgment in Cases of Impeachment shall not extend further than to removal from Office, and disqualification to hold and enjoy any Office of honor, Trust or Profit under the United States; but the Party convicted shall never theless be liable and subject to Indictment, Trial, Judgment and Punishment, according to Law.

Section 4   The Times, Places and Manner of holding Elections for Senators and Representatives, shall be prescribed in each State by the Legislature thereof, but the Congress may at any time by Law make or alter such Regulations, except as to the Places of chusing Senators.

The Congress shall assemble at least once in every Year, and such Meeting shall be on the first Monday in December, unless they shall by Law appoint a different Day.

Section 5   Each House shall be the Judge of the Elections, Returns and Qualifications of its own Members, and a Majority of each shall constitute a Quorum to do Business; but a smaller Number may adjourn from day to day, and may be authorized to compel the Attendance of absent Members, in such Manner, and under such Penalties as each House may provide.

Each House may determine the Rules of its Proceedings, punish its Members for disorderly Behaviour, and, with the Concurrence of two thirds, expel a Member.

Each House shall keep a Journal of its Proceedings, and from time to time publish the same, expecting such Parts as may in their Judgment require Secrecy; and the Yeas and Nays of the Members of either House on any question shall, at the Desire of one fifth of those Present, be entered on the journal.

Neither House, during the Session of Congress, shall, without the Consent of the other, adjourn for more than three days, nor to any other Place than that in which the two Houses shall be sitting.

Section 6   The Senators and Representatives shall receive a Compensation for their Services, to be ascertained by Law, and paid out of the Treasury of the United States. They shall in all Cases, except Treason, Felony and Breach of the Peace, be privileged from Arrest during their Attendance at the Session of their respective Houses, and in going to and returning from the same; and for any Speech or Debate in either House, they shall not be questioned in any other Place.

No Senator or Representative shall, during the Time for which he was elected, be appointed to any civil Office under the Authority of the United States, which shall have been created, or the Emoluments whereof shall have been encreased during such time; and no Person holding any Office under the United States, shall be a Member of either House during his Continuance in Office.

Section 7   All Bills for raising Revenue shall originate in the House of Representatives; but the Senate may propose or concur with Amendments as on other Bills.

Every Bill which shall have passed the House of Representatives and the Senate shall, before it become a Law, be presented to the President of the United States; If he approve he shall sign it, but if not he shall return it, with his Objections to that House in which it shall have originated, who shall enter the Objections at large on their Journal, and proceed to reconsider it. If after such Reconsideration two thirds of that House shall agree to pass the Bill, it shall be sent, together with the Objections, to the other House, by which it shall likewise be reconsidered, and if approved by two thirds of that House, it shall become a Law. But in all such Cases the Votes of both Houses shall be determined by yeas and Nays, and the Names of the Persons voting for and against the Bill shall be entered on the Journal of each House respectively. If any Bill shall not be returned by the President within ten Days (Sundays excepted) after it shall have been presented to him, the Same shall be a law, in like Manner as if he had signed it, unless the Congress by their Adjournment prevent its Return, in which Case it shall not be a Law.

Every Order, Resolution, or Vote to which the Concurrence of the Senate and House of Representatives may be necessary (except on a question of Adjournment) shall be presented to the President of the United States; and before the Same shall take Effect, shall be approved by him, or being disapproved by him, shall be repassed by two thirds of the Senate and House of Representatives, according to the Rules and Limitations prescribed in the Case of a Bill.

Section 8   The congress shall have Power To lay and collect Taxes, Duties, Imposts and Excises, to pay the Debts and provide for the common Defence and general Welfare of the United States; but all Duties, Imposts and xcises shall be uniform throughout the United States.

To borrow Money on the credit of the United States;

To regulate Commerce with foreign Nations, and among the several States, and with the Indian Tribes;

To establish an uniform Rule of Naturalization, and uniform Laws on the subject of Bankruptcies throughout the United States;

To coin Money, regulate the Value thereof, and of foreign Coin, and fix the Standard of Weights and Measures;

To provide for the Punishment of counterfeiting the Securities and current Coin of the United States;

To establish Post Offices and Post Roads;

To promote the Progress of Science and useful Arts, by securing for limited Times to Authors and Inventors the exclusive Right to their respective Writings and Discoveries;

To constitute Tribunals inferior to the supreme Court;

To define and punish Piracies and Felonies committed on the high Seas, and Offences against the Law of Nations;

To declare War, grant Letters of Marque and Reprisal, and make Rules concerning Captures on land and Water;

To raise and support Armies, but no Appropriation of Money to that Use shall be for a longer Term than two Years;

To provide and maintain a Navy;

To make Rules for the Government and Regulation of the land and naval Forces; To provide for calling forth the Militia to execute the Laws of the Union,

suppress Insurrections and repel Invasions;

To provide for organizing, arming, and disciplining, the Militia, and for governing such Part of them as may be employed in the Service of the United States, reserving to the States respectively, the Appointment of the Officers, and the Authority of training the Militia according to the discipline prescribed by Congress;

To exercise exclusive Legislation in all Cases whatsoever, over such District (not exceeding ten Miles square) as may, by Cession of particular States, and the Acceptance of Congress, become the Seat of the Government of the United States, and to exercise like Authority over all Places purchased by the Consent of the Legislature of the State in which the Same shall be, for the Erection of Forts, Magazines, Arsenals, dock-Yards, and other needful Buildings;—And

To make all Laws which shall be necessary and proper for carrying into Execution the foregoing Powers, and all other Powers vested by this Constitution in the Government of the United States, or in any Department or Officer thereof.

Section 9   The Migration or Importation of such Persons as any of the States now existing shall think proper to admit, shall not be prohibited by the Congress prior to the Year one thousand eight hundred and eight, but a Tax or duty may be imposed on such Importation, not exceeding ten dollars for each Person.

The Privilege of the Writ or Habeas Corpus shall not be suspended, unless when in Cases of Rebellion or Invasion the public Safety may require it.

No Bill of Attainer or ex post facto Law shall be passed.

No Capitation, or other direct, Tax shall be laid, unless in Proportion to the Census or Enumeration herein before directed to be taken.

No Tax or Duty shall be laid on Articles exported from any State.

No Preference shall be given by any Regulation of Commerce or Revenue to the Ports of one State over those of another : nor shall Vessels bound to, or from, one State, be obliged to enter, clear, or pay Duties in another.

No Money shall be drawn from the Treasury, but in Consequence of Appropriations made by Law, and a regular Statement and Account of Receipts and Expenditures of all public Money shall be published from time to time.

No Title of Nobility shall be granted by the United States: And no Person holding any Office of Profit or trust under them, shall, without the Consent of the Congress, accept of any present, Emolument, Office, or Title, of any kind whatever, from any King, prince, or foreign State.

Section 10   No State shall enter into any Treaty, Alliance, or Confederation; grant Letters of Marque and Reprisal; coin Money; emit Bills of Credit; make any Thing but gold and silver Coin a Tender in Payment of Debts; pass any Bill of Attainer, ex post facto Law, or Law impairing the Obligation of Contracts, or grant any Title of Nobility.

No State shall, without the Consent of the Congress, lay any Imports or Duties on Imports or Exports, except what may be absolutely necessary for executing it's inspection laws: and the net Produce of all Duties and Imposts, laid by any State on Imports or Exports, shall be for the Use of the Treasury of the United States; and all such Laws shall be subject to the Revision and Controul of the Congress.

No State shall, without the Consent of Congress, lay any Duty of Tonnage, keep Troops, or Ships of War in time of Peace, enter into any Agreement or Compact with another State, or with a foreign Power, or engage in War, unless actually invaded, or in such imminent Danger as will not admit of delay.

Article II

Section 1   The executive Power shall be vested in a President of the United States of America. He shall hold his Office during the term of four Years, and, together with the Vice President, chosen for the same Term, be elected as follows.

Each State shall appoint, in such Manner as the Legislature thereof may direct, a Number of Electors, equal to the whole Number of Senators and Representatives to which the State may be entitled in the Congress: but no Senator or Representative, or Person holding an Office of Trust or Profit under the United States, shall be appointed an Elector.

The Electors shall meet in their respective States, and vote by Ballot for two Persons, of whom at least shall not be an Inhabitant of the same State with themselves. And they shall make a List of all the Persons voted for, and of the Number of Votes for each; which List they shall sign and certify, and transmit sealed to the Seat of the Government of the United States, directed to the President of the Senate. The President of the Senate shall, in the Presence of the Senate and House of Representatives, open all the Certificates, and the Votes shall then be counted. The Person having the greatest Number of Votes shall be the President, if such Number be a Majority of the whole Number of Electors appointed; and if there be more than one who have such Majority, and have an equal Number of Votes, then the House of Representatives shall immediately chuse by Ballot one of them for President; and if no Person have a Majority, then from the five highest on the List the said House shall in like Manner chuse the President. But in chusing the President, the Votes shall be taken by States, the Representation from each State having one Vote; A quorum for this Purpose shall consist of a Member or Members from two thirds of the States, and a Majority of all the States shall be necessary to a Choice. In every Case, after the Choice of the President, the Person having the greatest Number of Votes of the Electors shall be the Vice President. But if there should remain two or more who have equal Votes, the Senate shall chuse from them by Ballot the Vice President.

The Congress may determine the Time of chusing the Electors, and the Day on which they shall give their Votes; which Day shall be the same throughout the United States.

No Person except a natural born Citizen, or a Citizen of the United States, at the time of the Adoption of this Constitution, shall be eligible to the Office of President, neither shall any Person be eligible to that Office who shall not have attained to the Age of thirty five Years, and been fourteen Years a Resident within the United States.

In Case of the Removal of the President from office, or of his Death, Resignation, or Inability to discharge the Powers and Duties of the said Office, the Same shall devolve on the Vice President, and the Congress may be Law provide for the Case of Removal, Death, Resignation or Inability, both of the President and Vice President, declaring what Officer shall then act as President, and such Officer shall act accordingly, until the Disability be removed, or a President shall be elected.

The President shall, at stated Times, receive for his Services, a Compensation, which shall neither be encreased or diminished during the Period for which he shall have been elected, and he shall not receive within that Period any other Emolument from the United States, or any of them.

Before he enters on the Execution of his Office, he shall take the following Oath or Affirmation:—"I do solemnly swear (or affirm) that I will faithfully execute the Office of President of the United States, and will to the best of my Ability, preserve, protect and defend the Constitution of the United States."

Section 2   The President shall be Commander in Chief of the Army and Navy of the United States, and of the Militia of the several States, when called into the actual Service of the United States; he may require the Opinion, in writing, of the principal officer in each of the executive Departments, upon any Subject relating to the Duties of their respective Offices, and he shall have Power to grant Reprieves and Pardons for Offenses against the United States, except in Cases of Impeachment.

He shall have Power, by and with the Advice and Consent of the Senate, to make Treaties, provided two thirds of the Senators present concur; and he shall nominate, and by and with the Advice and

Consent of the Senate, shall appoint Ambassadors, other public Ministers and Consuls, Judges of the supreme Court, and all other Officers of the United States, whose Appointments are not herein otherwise provided for, and which shall be established by Law; but the Congress may by Law vest the Appointment of such inferior Officers, as they think proper, in the President alone, in the Courts of Law, or in the Heads of Departments.

The President shall have Power to fill up all Vacancies that may happen during the Recess of the Senate, by granting Commissions which shall expire at the End of their next Session.

Section 3 He shall from time to time give to the Congress Information of the State of the Union, and recommend to their Consideration such Measures as he shall judge necessary and expedient; he may, on extraordinary Occasions, convene both Houses, or either of them, and in Case of Disagreement between them, with Respect to the Time of Adjournment, he may adjourn them to such Time as he shall think proper; he shall receive Ambassadors and other public Ministers; he shall take Care that the Laws be faithfully executed, and shall Commission all the Officers of the United States.

Section 4 The President, Vice President and all civil Officers of the United States, shall be removed from Office on Impeachment for, and Conviction of, Treason, Bribery, or other high Crimes and Misdemeanors.

Article III

Section 1 The judicial Power of the United States, shall be vested in one supreme Court, and in such inferior Courts as the Congress may from time to time ordain and establish. The Judges, both of the supreme and inferior Courts, shall hold their Offices during good Behavior, and shall, as stated Times, receive for their Services, a Compensation, which shall not be diminished during their Continuance in Office.

Section 2 The judicial Power shall extend to all Cases, in Law and Equity, arising under this Constitution, the Laws of the United States, and Treaties made, or which shall be made, under their Authority;—to all Cases affecting Ambassadors, other public Ministers and Consuls;—to all Cases of Admiralty and maritime Jurisdiction;—to Controversies to which the United States shall be a Party;—to Controversies between two or more States;—between a State or Citizens of another State;—between Citizens of different States;—between Citizens of the same State claiming Lands under Grants of different States, and between a State, or the Citizens thereof, and foreign States, Citizens or Subjects.

In all cases affecting Ambassadors, other public Ministers and Consuls, and those in which a State shall be held in the State where the said Crimes shall have been committed; but when not committed within any State, the Trial shall be at such Place or Places as the Congress may by Law have directed.

Section 3 Treason against the United States, shall consist only in levying War against them, or in adhering to their Enemies, giving them Aid and Comfort. No person shall be convicted of Treason unless on the Testimony of two Witnesses to the same overt Act, or on Confession in open Court.

The Congress shall have Power to declare the Punishment of Treason, but no Attainder of Treason shall work Corruption of Blood, or Forfeiture except during the Life of the Person attained.

Article IV

Section 1 Full Faith and Credit shall be given in each State to the public Acts, Records, and judicial Proceedings of every other State. And the Congress may by general Laws prescribe the Manner in which such Acts, Records and Proceedings shall be proved, and the Effect thereof.

Section 2 The Citizens of each State shall be entitled to all Privileges and Immunities of Citizens in the several States.

A Person charged in any State with Treason, Felony, or other Crime, who shall flee from Justice, and be found in another State, shall on Demand of the executive Authority of the State from which he fled, be delivered up, to be removed to the State having Jurisdiction of the Crime.

No Person held to Service or Labour in one State, under the Laws thereof, escaping into another, shall, in Consequence of any Law or Regulation therein, be discharged from such Service or Labour, but shall be delivered up on Claim of the Party to whom such Service or Labour may be due.

Section 3 New States may be admitted by the Congress into this Union; but no new State shall be formed or erected within the Jurisdiction of any other State; nor any State be formed by the Junction of two or more States, or Parts of States, without the consent of the Legislatures of the States concerned as well as of the Congress.

The Congress shall have Power to dispose of and make all needful Rules and Regulations respecting the Territory or other Property belonging to the United States; and nothing in this Constitution shall be so construed as to Prejudice any Claims of the United States, or of any particular States.

Section 4 The United States shall guarantee to every State in this Union a Republican Form of Government, and shall protect each of them against Invasion; and on Application of the Legislature, or of the Executive (when the Legislature cannot be convened) against domestic Violence.

Article V

The Congress, whenever two thirds of both Houses shall deem it necessary, shall propose Amendments to this Constitution, or, on the Application of the Legislatures of two thirds of the several States shall call a Convention for proposing Amendments, which, in either Case, shall be valid to all Intents and Purposes, as Part of this Constitution, when ratified by the Legislatures of three fourths of the several States, or by Conventions in three fourths thereof, as the one or the other mode of Ratification may be proposed by the Congress; Provided that no Amendment which may be made prior to the Year One thousand eight hundred and eight shall in any Manner affect the first and fourth Clauses in the Ninth Section of the first Article; and that no State, without its Consent, shall be deprived of its equal Suffrage in the Senate.

Article VI

All Debts contracted and Engagements entered into, before the Adoption of this Constitution, shall be as valid against the United States under this Constitution, as under the Confederation.

This Constitution, and the Laws of the United States, which shall be made in Pursuance thereof; and all Treaties made, or which shall be made, under the Authority of the United States, shall be the supreme Law of the Land; and the Judges in every State shall be bound thereby, any Thing in the Constitution or Laws of any State to the Contrary notwithstanding.

The Senators and Representatives before mentioned, and the Members of the several State Legislatures, and all executive and judicial Officers, both of the United States and of the several States, shall be bound by Oath or Affirmation, to support this Constitution; but no religious Test shall ever be required as a Qualification to any Office or public Trust under the United States.

Article VII

The Ratification of the Conventions of nine States, shall be sufficient for the Establishment of this constitution between the States so ratifying the Same.

Done in Convention by the Unanimous Consent of the States present the Seventeenth Day of September in the Year of our Lord one thousand seven hundred and Eighty seven and of the Independence of the United States of America the Twelfth. In witness thereof We have hereunto sub-scribed our Names,

Go: WASHINGTON—Presid. and deputy from Virginia

New Hampshire

John Langdon Nicholas Gilman

Massachusetts

Nathaniel Gorham Rufus King

Connecticut

Wm. Saml. Johnson Roger herman

New York

Alexander Hamilton

New Jersey

Wil: Livingston David Brearley Wm. Paterson Jona: Dayton

Pennsylvania

B. Franklin Thomas Mifflin Robt Morris Geo. Clymer Thos FitzSimons Jared Ingersoll James Wilson Gouv Morris

Delaware

Geo: Read Gunnin Bedford jun John Dickinson Richard Bassett Jaco: Broom

Maryland

James McHenry Dan of St Thos. Jenifer Danl Carroll

Virginia

John Blair—James Madison Jr.

North Carolina

Wm. Blount Rich'd Dobbs Spaight Hu Williamson

South Carolina

J. Rutledge Charles Cotesworth Pinckney Charles Pinckney Pierce Butler

Georgia

William Few Abr Baldwin

Attest:

William Jackson. Secretary

AMENDMENTS TO THE CONSTITUTION

ARTICLES IN ADDITION TO, and Amendment of the Constitution of the United States of America, proposed by Congress, and ratified by the Legislatures of the several States, pursuant to the fifth Article of the original Constitution.

Amendment I

Congress shall make no law respecting an establishment of religion, or prohibiting the free exercise thereof; or abridging the freedom of speech, or of the press; or the right of the people peaceably to assemble, and to petition the Government for a redress of grievances.

Amendment II

A well regulated Militia, being necessary to the security of a free State, the right of the people to keep and bear Ar ms, shall not be infringed.

Amendment III

No Soldier shall, in time of peace be quartered in any house, without the consent of the Owner, nor in time of war, but in a manner to be prescribed by law.

Amendment IV

The right of the people to be secure in their persons, houses, papers, and effects, against unreasonable searches and seizures, shall not be violated, and no Warrants shall issue, but upon probable cause, supported by Oath or affirmation, and particularly describing the place to be searched, and the persons or things to be seized.

Amendment V

No person shall be held to answer for a capital, or other wise infamous crime, unless on a presentment or indictment of a Grand Jury, except in cases arising in the land or naval forces, or in the Militia, when in actual service in time of War or public danger; nor shall any person be subject for the same offence to be twice put in jeopardy of life or limb; nor shall be compelled in any criminal case to be a witness against himself, nor be deprived of life, liberty, or property, without due process of law; nor shall private property be taken for public use, without just compensation.

Amendment VI

In all criminal prosecutions, the accused shall enjoy the right to a speedy and public trial, by an impartial jury of the State and district wherein the crime shall have been committed, which district shall have been previously ascertained by law, and to be informed of the nature and cause of the accusation; to be confronted with the witnesses against him; to have compulsory process for obtaining witnesses in his favor, and to have the Assistance of Counsel for his defence.

Amendment VII

In Suits at common law, where the value in controversy shall exceed twenty dollars, the right of trial by jury shall be preserved, and no fact tried by a jury, shall be other wise reexamined in any Court of the United States, than according to the rules of the common law.

Amendment VIII

Excessive bail shall not be required, or excessive fines imposed, nor cruel and unusual punishments inflicted.

Amendment IX

The Enumeration in the Constitution, of certain rights, shall not be construed to deny or disparage others retained by the people.

Amendment X

The powers not delegated to the United States by the Constitution, nor prohibited by it to the States, are reserved to the States respectively, or to the people. [The first ten amendments went into effect December 15, 1791.]

Amendment XI

The Judicial power of the United States shall not be construed to extend to any suit in law or equity, commenced or prosecuted against one of the United States by Citizens of another State, or by Citizens or Subjects of any Foreign State. [January 8, 1798.]

Amendment XII

The Electors shall meet in their respective states, and vote by ballot for President and Vice-President, one of whom, at least, shall not be an inhabitant of the same state with themselves, they shall name in their ballots the person voted for as President, and in distinct ballots the person voted for as Vice-President, and they shall make distinct lists of all persons voted for as President, and of all persons voted for as Vice-President, and of the number of votes for each, which lists they shall sign and certify, and transmit sealed to the seat of the government of the United States, directed to the President of the Senate;—The President of the Senate shall, in the presence of the Senate and House of

Representatives, open all the certificates and the votes shall then be counted;—The person having the greatest number of votes for President, shall be the President, if such number be a majority of the whole number of Electors appointed; and if no person have such majority, then from the persons having the highest numbers not exceeding three on the list of those voted for as President, the House of Representatives shall choose immediately, by ballot, the President. But in choosing the President, the votes shall be taken by states, the representation from each state having one vote; a quorum for this purpose shall consist of a member or members from two-thirds of the states, and a majority of all the states shall be necessary to a choice. And if the House of Representatives shall not choose a President whenever the right of choice shall devolve upon them, before the fourth day of March next following, then the Vice-President shall act as President.—The person having the greatest number of votes as Vice-President, shall be the Vice-President, if such number be a majority of the whole number of Electors appointed, and if no person have a majority, then from the two highest numbers on the list, the Senate shall choose the Vice-President; a quorum for the purpose shall consist of two-thirds of the whole number of Senators, and a majority of the whole number shall be necessary to a choice. But no person constitutionally ineligible to the office of President shall be eligible to that of Vice-President of the United States. [September 25, 1804.]

Amendment XIII

Section 1   Neither slavery nor involuntary servitude, except as a punishment for crime whereof the party shall have been duly convicted, shall exist within the United States, or any place subject to their jurisdiction.

Section 2   Congress shall have power to enforce this article by appropriate legislation. [December 18, 1865.]

Amendment XIV

Section 1   All persons born or naturalized in the United States, and subject to the jurisdiction thereof, are citizens of the United States and of the State wherein they reside. No State shall make or enforce any law which shall abridge the privileges or immunities of citizens of the United States; nor shall any State deprive any person of life, liberty, or property, without due process of law; nor deny to any person within its jurisdiction the equal protection of the laws.

Section 2   Representatives shall be apportioned among the several States according to their respective numbers, counting the whole number of persons in each State, excluding Indians not taxed. But when the right to vote at any election for the choice of electors for President and Vice President of the United States, Representatives in Congress, the Executive and Judicial officers of a State, or the members of the Legislature thereof, is denied to any of the male inhabitants of such State, being twenty-one years of age, and citizens of the United States, or in any way abridged, except for participation in rebellion, or other crime, the basis of representation therein shall be reduced in the proportion which the number of such male citizens shall bear to the whole number of male citizens twenty-one years of age in such State.

Section 3   No person shall be a Senator or Representative in Congress, or elector of President and Vice President, or hold any office, civil or military, under the United States, or under any State, who, having previously taken an oath, as a member of Congress, or as an officer of the United States, or as a member of any State legislature, or as an executive or judicial officer of any State, to support the Constitution of the United States, shall have engaged in insurrection or rebellion against the same, or given aid or comfort to the enemies thereof. But Congress may by a vote of two-thirds of each House, remove such disability.

Section 4 The validity of the public debt of the United States, authorized by law, including debts incurred for payment of pensions and bounties for services in suppressing insurrection or rebellion, shall not be questioned. But neither the United States nor any State shall assume or pay any debt or obligation incurred in aid of insurrection or rebellion against the United States, or any claim for the loss or emancipation of any slave; but all such debts, obligations and claims shall be held illegal and void.

Section 5 The Congress hall have power to enforce, by appropriate legislation, the provisions of this article. [July 28, 1868.]

Amendment XV

Section 1 The right of citizens of the United States to vote shall not be denied or abridged by the United States or by any State on account of race, color, or previous condition of servitude—

Section 2 The Congress shall have power to enforce this article by appropriate legislation.—[March 30, 1870.]

Amendment XVI

The Congress shall have power to lay and collect taxes on incomes, from whatever source derived, without apportionment among the several States, and without regard to any census or enumeration. [February 25, 1913.]

Amendment XVII

The Senate of the United States shall be composed of two senators from each State, elected by the people thereof, for six years; and each Senator shall have one vote. The electors in each State shall have the qualifications requisite for electors of the most numerous branch of the State legislature.

When vacancies happen in the representation of any State in the Senate, the executive authority of such State shall issue writs of election to fill such vacancies: *Provided*, that the legislature of any State may empower the executive thereof to make temporary appointments until the people fill the vacancies by election as the legislature may direct.

This amendment shall not be so construed as to affect the election or term of any senator chosen before it becomes valid as part of the Constitution. [May 31, 1913.]

Amendment XVIII

After one year from the ratification of this article, the manufacture, sale, or transportation of intoxicating liquors within, the importation thereof into, or the exportation thereof from the United States and all territory subject to the jurisdiction thereof for beverage purposes is hereby prohibited.

The Congress and the several States shall have concurrent power to enforce this article by appropriate legislation.

This article shall be inoperative unless it shall have been ratified as an amendment to the Constitution by the legislatures of the several States, as provided in the Constitution, within seven years from the date of the submission thereof to the States by Congress. [January 29, 1919.]

Amendment XIX

The right of citizens of the United States to vote shall not be denied or abridged by the United States or by any State on account of sex.

The Congress shall have power by appropriate legislation to enforce the provisions of this article. [August 26, 1920.]

Amendment XX

Section 1 The terms of the President and Vice-President shall end at noon on the twentieth day of January, and the terms of Senators and Representatives at noon on the third day of January, of the years in which such terms would have ended if this article had not been ratified; and the terms of their successors shall then begin.

Section 2 The Congress shall assemble at least once in every year, and such meeting shall begin at noon on the third day of January, unless they shall by law appoint a different day.

Section 3 If, at the time fixed for the beginning of the term of the President, the President-elect shall have died, the Vice-President elect shall become President. If a President shall not have been chosen before the time fixed for the beginning of his term, or if the President-elect shall have failed to qualify, then the Vice-President elect shall act as President until a President shall have qualified; and the Congress may by law provide for the case wherein neither a President-elect nor a Vice-President-elect shall have qualified, declaring who shall then act as President, or the manner in which one who is to act shall be selected, and such person shall act accordingly until a President or Vice-President shall have qualified.

Section 4 The Congress may by law provide for the case of the death of any of the persons from whom the House of Representatives may choose a President whenever the right of choice shall have devolved upon them, and for the case of the death of any of the persons from whom the Senate may choose a Vice-President whenever the right of choice shall have devolved upon them.

Section 5 Sections 1 and 2 shall take effect on the 15th day of October following the ratification of this article.

Section 6 This article shall be inoperative unless it shall have been ratified as an amendment to the Constitution by the legislatures of three-fourths of the several States within seven years from the date of its submission. [February 6, 1933.]

Amendment XXI

Section 1   The eighteenth article of amendment to the Constitution of the United States is hereby repealed.

Section 2   The transportation or importation into any State, Territory or possession of the United States for delivery or use therein of intoxicating liquors, in violation of the laws thereof, is hereby prohibited.

Section 3   This article shall be inoperative unless it shall have been ratified as an amendment to the Constitution by convention in the several States, as provided in the Constitution within seven years from the date of the submission thereof to the States by the Congress. [December 5, 1933.]

Amendment XXII

Section 1   No person shall be elected to the office of the President more than twice, and no person who has held the office of President, or acted as President, for more than two years of a term to which some other person was elected President shall be elected to the office of the President more than once. But this Article shall not apply to any person holding the office of President when this Article was proposed by the Congress, and shall not prevent any person who may be holding the office of President, or acting as President, during the term within which this Article becomes operative from holding the office of President or acting as President during the remainder of such term.

Section 2   This article shall be inoperative unless it shall have been ratified as an amendment to the Constitution by the legislatures of three-fourths of the several states within the seven years from the date of its submission to the States by the Congress. [February 27, 1951.]

Amendment XXIII

Section 1   The District constituting the seat of government of the United States shall appoint in such manner as the Congress may direct:

A number of electors of President and Vice-President equal to the whole number of Senators and Representatives in Congress to which the District would be entitled if it were a State, but in no event more than the least populous State; they shall be in addition to those appointed by the States, but they shall be considered, for the purposes of the election of President and Vice-President, to be electors appointed by a State; and they shall meet in the District and perform such duties as provided by the twelfth article of amendment.

Section 2   The Congress shall have the power to enforce this article by appropriate legislation. [March 29, 1961.]

Amendment XXIV

Section 1   The right of citizens of the United States to vote in any primary or other election for President or Vice President, for electors for President or Vice President, or for Senator or Representative in Congress, shall not be denied or abridged by the United States or any State by reason of failure to pay any poll tax or other tax.

Section 2   The Congress shall have power to enforce this article by appropriate legislation. [January 23, 1964.]

Amendment XXV

Section 1   In case of the removal of the President from office or of his death or resignation, the Vice President shall become President.

Section 2   Whenever there is a vacancy in the office of Vice President, the President shall nominate a Vice President who shall take office upon confirmation by a majority vote of both Houses of Congress.

Section 3   Whenever the President transmits to the President protempore of the Senate and the Speaker of the House of Representatives his written declaration that he is unable to discharge the powers and duties of his office, and until he transmits to them a written declaration to the contrary, such powers and duties shall be discharged by the Vice President as Acting President.

Section 4   Whenever the Vice President and a majority of either the principal officers of the executive departments or of such other body as Congress may by law provide, transmit to the President protempore of the Senate and the Speaker of the House of Representatives their written declaration that the President shall immediately assume the powers and duties of the office as Acting President.

Thereafter, when the President transmits to the President protempore of the Senate and the Speaker of the House of Representatives has written declaration that no inability exists, he shall resume the powers and duties of his office unless the Vice President and a majority of either the principal officers of the executive departments or of such other body as Congress may by law provide, transmit within four days to the President protempore of the Senate and the Speaker of the House of Representatives their written declaration that the President is unable to discharge the powers and duties of his office. There upon Congress shall decide the issue, assembling within forty-eight hours for that purpose if not in session. If the Congress, within twenty-one days after receipt of the latter written declaration, or, if Congress is not in session, within twenty-one days after Congress is required to assemble, determines by two-thirds vote of both Houses that the President is unable to discharge the powers and duties of his office, the Vice President shall continue to discharge the same as Acting President; otherwise, the President shall resume the powers and duties of his office. [February 10, 1967.]

Amendment XXVI

Section 1   The right of citizens of the United States, who are eighteen years of age or older, to vote shall not be denied or abridged by the United States or by any State on account of age.

Section 2   The Congress shall have power to enforce this article by appropriate legislation. [June 30, 1971.]

US Government Record

THE DECLARATION OF INDEPENDENCE

SECOND CONTINENTAL CONGRESS

When in the course of human events, it becomes necessary for one people to dissolve the political bands which have connected them with another, and to assume among the powers of the earth, the separate and equal station to which the laws of nature and of nature's God entitle them, a decent respect to the opinions of mankind requires that they should declare the causes which impel them to the separation.

We Hold These Truths to be Self-Evident

That all men are created equal; that they are endowed by their Creator with certain unalienable rights; that among these are life, liberty, and the pursuit of happiness; that, to secure these rights, governments are instituted among men, deriving their just powers from the consent of the governed; that whenever any form of government becomes destructive of these ends, it is the right of the people to alter or to abolish it, and to institute new government, laying its foundation on such principles, and organizing its powers in such form, as to them shall seem most likely to effect their safety and happiness. Prudence, indeed, will dictate that governments long established should not be changed for light and transient causes; and accordingly all experience hath shown that mankind are more disposed to suffer, while evils are sufferable than to right themselves by abolishing the forms to which they are accustomed. But when a long train of abuses and usurpations, pursuing invariably the same object, evinces a design to reduce them under absolute despotism, it is their right, it is their duty, to throw off such government, and to provide new guards for their future security. Such has been the patient sufferance of these colonies; and such is now the necessity which constrains them to alter their former systems of government. The history of the present King of Great Britain is a history of repeated injuries and usurpations, all having in direct object the establishment of an absolute tyranny over these states. To prove this, let facts be submitted to a candid world.

He has refused his assent to laws, the most wholesome and necessary for the public good.

He has forbidden his governors to pass laws of immediate and pressing importance, unless suspended in their operation till his assent should be obtained; and, when so suspended, he has utterly neglected to attend to them.

He has refused to pass other laws for the accommodation of large districts of people, unless those people would relinquish the right of representation in the legislature, a right inestimable to them, and formidable to tyrants only.

SOURCE: The Declaration of Independence, 1776

He has called together legislative bodies at places unusual uncomfortable, and distant from the depository of their public records, for the sole purpose of fatiguing them into compliance with his measures.

He has dissolved representative houses repeatedly, for opposing, with manly firmness, his invasions on the rights of the people.

He has refused for a long time, after such dissolutions, to cause others to be elected; whereby the legislative powers, incapable of annihilation, have returned to the people at large for their exercise; the state remaining, in the mean time, exposed to all the dangers of invasions from without and convulsions within.

He has endeavored to prevent the population of these states; for that purpose obstructing the laws for naturalization of foreigners; refusing to pass others to encourage their migration hither, and raising the conditions of new appropriations of lands.

He has obstructed the administration of justice, by refusing his assent to laws for establishing judiciary powers.

He has made judges dependent on his will alone, for the tenure of their offices, and the amount and payment of their salaries.

He has erected a multitude of new offices, and sent hither swarms of officers to harass our people and eat out their substance.

He has kept among us, in times of peace, standing armies, without the consent of our legislatures.

He has affected to render the military independent of, and superior to, the civil power.

He has combined with others to subject us to a jurisdiction foreign to our Constitution and unacknowledged by our laws, giving his assent to their acts of pretended legislation:

For quartering large bodies of armed troops among us;

For protecting them, by a mock trial, from punishment for any murders which they should commit on the inhabitants of these states;

For cutting off our trade with all parts of the world; For imposing taxes on us without our consent;

For depriving us, in many cases, of the benefits of trial by jury;

For transporting us beyond seas, to be tried for pretended offenses;

For abolishing the free system of English laws in a neighboring province, establishing therein an arbitrary government, and enlarging its boundaries, so as to render it at once an example and fit instrument for introducing the same absolute rule into these colonies;

For taking away our charters, abolishing our most valuable laws, and altering fundamentally the forms of our governments;

For suspending our own legislatures, and declaring themselves invested with power to legislate for us in all cases whatsoever.

He has abdicated government here, by declaring us out of his protection and waging war against us.

He has plundered our seas, ravaged our coasts, burned our towns, and destroyed the lives of our people.

He is at this time transporting large armies of foreign mercenaries to complete the works of death, desolation, and tyranny already begun with circumstances of cruelty and perfidy scarcely paralleled in the most barbarous ages, and totally unworthy the head of a civilized nation.

He has constrained our fellow-citizens, taken captive on the high seas, to bear arms against their country, to become the executioners of their friends and brethren, or to fall themselves by their hands.

He has excited domestic insurrection among us, and has endeavored to bring on the inhabitants of our frontiers the merciless Indian savages, whose known rule of warfare is an undistinguished destruction of all ages, sexes, and conditions.

In every stage of these oppressions we have petitioned for redress in the most humble terms; our repeated petitions have been answered only by repeated injury. A prince, whose character is thus marked by every act which may define a tyrant, is unfit to be the ruler of free people.

Nor have we been wanting in our attentions to our British brethren. We have warned them, from time to time, of attempts by their legislature to extend an unwarrantable jurisdiction over us. We have reminded them of the circumstances of our emigration and settlement here. We have appealed to their native justice and magnanimity; and we have conjured them, by the ties of our common kindred, to disavow these usurpations which would inevitably interrupt our connections and correspondence. They too, have been deaf to the voice of justice and of consanguinity. We must, therefore, acquiesce in the necessity which denounces our separation, and hold them as we hold the rest of mankind, enemies in war, in peace friends.

We, therefore, the representatives of the United States of America, in General Congress assembled, appealing to the Supreme Judge of the world for the rectitude of our intentions, do, in the name and by the authority of the good people of these colonies solemnly publish and declare, That these United Colonies are, and of right ought to be, *FREE AND INDEPENDENT STATES;* that they are absolved from all allegiance to the British crown and that all political connection between them and the state of Great Britain is, and ought to be, totally dissolved; and that, as free and independent states, they have full power to levy war, conclude peace, contract alliances, establish commerce, and do all other acts and things which independent states may of right do. And for the support of this declaration, with a firm reliance on the protection of Divine Providence, we mutually pledge to each other our lives, our fortunes, and our sacred honor.

CPSIA information can be obtained
at www.ICGtesting.com
Printed in the USA
FFOW02n0846221117
43681407-42517FF